MY SOUL IS A WITNESS

NEW DIRECTIONS IN NARRATIVE HISTORY
John Demos and Aaron Sachs, Series Editors

The New Directions in Narrative History series includes original works of creative nonfiction across the many fields of history and related disciplines. Based on new research, the books in this series offer significant scholarly contributions while also embracing stylistic innovation as well as the classic techniques of storytelling. The works of the New Directions in Narrative History series, intended for the broadest general readership, speak to deeply human concerns about the past, present, and future of our world and its people.

MY SOUL IS A WITNESS

The Traumatic Afterlife of Lynching

MARI N. CRABTREE

Yale

UNIVERSITY PRESS

New Haven and London

Published with assistance from the foundation established in memory of Philip Hamilton McMillan of the Class of 1894, Yale College.

Yale University Press books may be purchased in quantity for educational, business, or promotional use. For information, please e-mail sales.press@yale.edu (U.S. office) or sales@yaleup.co.uk (U.K. office).

Printed in the United States of America.

Library of Congress Control Number: 2022932122

ISBN 978-0-300-25041-1 (hardcover : alk. paper)

A catalogue record for this book is available from the British Library.

This paper meets the requirements of ANSI/NISO Z39.48-1992 (Permanence of Paper).

10 9 8 7 6 5 4 3 2 1

For the victims and survivors

Contents

Acknowledgments

SOME MEMORIES YELLOW AND fade with the passage of time. Others linger and wait, stalking around the subconscious, repressed but lurking, unbeckoned but waiting to break through into consciousness. Traumatic memories of lynching are a leaden weight that Black southerners carried for decades and still carry today—a weight that binds horror and anger to pain as thick as their love for those lost to a mob's bloodlust. Survivors of lynching bore the heaviest burdens of memory. Those who knew and loved the victims and those who witnessed their deaths often had the greatest difficulty talking about traumatic memories, for the trauma remained too raw, the memories too laced with pain, the deaths too viscerally real. For a scholar, their stories are some of the most difficult to recover, buried, as they are, deep inside to make room enough to breathe and be and keep living.

Whispers of their memories survive among the living, however. In ways both direct and indirect, survivors occasionally passed fragments of lynching memories on to their children and grandchildren, just as they left them other inheritances steeped in love and care. Even for the children and grandchildren who had not lived through a lynching, however, the weight of the past could be crushing. For this reason, I am especially grateful to the victims and survivors of lynching who entrusted me, a stranger, with their stories and the stories of their families. My deepest gratitude goes to them: Lester Gibson, who heard the legend about God sending a devastating tornado to destroy Waco, Texas, as an act of divine vengeance for the 1915 lynching of Jesse Washington and whose own family tried to fend off a lynch mob in 1922; Audrey Grant, the great-granddaughter of Mary and Hayes Turner, who were lynched in Georgia

ix

in 1918; Robert Hall, who had childhood memories of a white man who had lynched Mary Turner walking along the road into town and who had witnessed the grim aftermath of another lynching on his way to a fishing hole; Willie Head Jr., whose great-uncle Will Head was lynched just days before the Turners; Clarence Hunter, whose parents instructed him to read the *Washington Afro-American* and the *Pittsburgh Courier* cover to cover every week to learn of the perils of lynching; Jesse Pennington, who narrowly escaped a Mississippi lynch mob in 1954, just one year before Emmett Till faced down his lynchers but didn't survive; James Reed, whose great-aunt told him stories in the 1950s about the ghost of a lynched man who haunted an Alabama courthouse; Monroe Saffold Jr., whose grandfather refused to bring him on trips back to Mississippi because Till's lynching was the latest in a string of lynchings that reminded him that he could do little to protect his grandchild from the destructiveness of white southern rage.

They shared their stories with me, not so they could see their names in print, but to honor and mourn the dead and to cherish the living whose survival was far from promised, both during and after Jim Crow. These interviews about lynching memories so often testified to bonds within Black communities that were always stronger than what white people did to degrade and destroy Black people and their communities. Audrey Grant, whose great-grandmother and great-grandfather were lynched, made sure to tell me not just about the deep sadness her grandmother, Leaster Grant, felt decades after the lynchings, but also about how she tended roses, canned vegetables from her garden, sang spirituals off key while she tidied up her home, and would make her older brother's favorite dishes when he visited. Willie Head invited me into his home, and, when our conversation turned to his parents and grandparents, he walked to the other side of his living room to bring me a photograph of them that had been quietly watching over us on a nearby ledge. Lester Gibson told me matter-of-factly that his people "would bite you back" if anyone came for any member of the family, and Jesse Pennington channeled his harrowing escape from a lynch mob into a career of providing the kind of legal assistance that was out of his grasp when he needed it most. Living with this project for the past decade has often meant living with the specter of lynching as a second shadow. Yet what kept me from drifting too deeply into despair over the future of this country were these people and their stories of living through and beyond lynching. For as much as this book is about horror and devastation, it is suffused with the tragicomic hope of the blues.

This book would not have been possible without the generous financial support I received from several institutions. Princeton University's Department of African American Studies deserves special thanks for awarding me a yearlong fellowship that supported the book's completion with a book manuscript workshop, book subvention, research funds, and the truly invaluable mentoring of Eddie Glaude, Tera Hunter, and Imani Perry. The School of Languages, Cultures, and World Affairs and the African American Studies Program at the College of Charleston funded research trips and an interdisciplinary research group, and covered publication costs. At Cornell University, I received funding from the Sage Fellowship, the Society for the Humanities Graduate Travel Research Grant, the Society for the Humanities Dissertation Writing Group Grant, the Walter and Sandra LaFeber Research Assistance Fund, the George B. Kirsch Scholarship, the Joel and Rosemary Silbey Fellowship, the American Studies Graduate Research Grant, the Graduate School Research Travel Grant, and the Daughters of the American Revolution Fellowship. I received additional financial support from the John Hope Franklin Research Center for African and African American History and Culture at Duke University, the Burney Parker Research Fellowship at Baylor University, and the Forris Jewett Moore Fellowship at Amherst College.

Archives and libraries are the lifeblood of my scholarship, and along the way, archivists and reference librarians provided me guidance and research leads at dozens of institutions from New York to Texas. I am especially grateful for the encyclopedic knowledge of Randall Burkett of Emory University, from whom I learned so much about the memory of lynching in archival collecting practices, and I am deeply indebted to the correspondence that Joseph F. Jordan, director of the University of North Carolina's Sonja Haynes Stone Center for Black Culture and History, provided me regarding his work as the curator of *Without Sanctuary*. Also, I am thankful to have gained the trust of so many people, from Mark P. George, the coordinator for the Mary Turner Project in Valdosta, Georgia, to Tracey Rosebud with the Emmett Till Historic Intrepid Center (ETHIC), and Clarence Hunter with the Mississippi Department of Archives and History, all of whom graciously vouched for me and introduced me to many of the people whose stories grace these pages.

A short excerpt from chapter 3 appeared in "The Art and Politics of Subterfuge in African American Culture" (Summer 2018) and is reprinted with permission from *Raritan*.

The ideas I grapple with in this book have deep roots in my first intellectual home, the Black Studies Department at Amherst College. The book bears the imprint of David Blight's field-defining research in memory studies, and the brief flights into poetry, fiction, and art grew out of careful instruction on interpretation from Rhonda Cobham-Sander, Andrea Rushing, and Rowland Abiodun. The turn to Baldwin and the blues, and to Ellison and clever elision, reflects the brilliant mind of my advisor and friend, Jeffrey Ferguson. Jeff taught me how to find my voice as a writer, how to make meaning with clarity and grace, how to engage with giants in the field, and how to find so many wells of joy in the life of the mind. Cancer took Jeff in 2018, too soon for us to have the conversations I imagined we would have about this book and others yet unwritten, but I am grateful that he left me with the gift of his laughter, irreverence, skepticism, and incisiveness, and the memory of the hours we spent together working through ideas. His generosity led me to mentors who knew him and took up his mantle, most especially Nicole Guidotti-Hernández, whose careful reading of chapter 4 sharpened my analysis of sexual violence, and whose support and sage advice over the years has carried me through the occasional rough patches in academic life.

My mentors at Cornell University helped me build upon ideas that had been percolating for years and hone them into first a dissertation and then a book. Nick Salvatore struck the perfect balance between guiding the development of the book and giving me the freedom to roam across and between disciplinary boundaries, and he inspired me to record oral histories as I crisscrossed the South. Robert Harris grounded my work in scholarship on the long civil rights movement and introduced me to his brother-in-law, James Reed, whose story of a ghost in an Alabama courthouse haunts the pages of this book. I also wish to thank Kenneth McClane, whose poetic sensibilities and the questions he posed to me about what literature has to offer the historian planted the seed for this project. Deep appreciation goes to Russell Rickford—a consummate thinker, radical visionary, and generous reader—for giving me the language to describe the book's major interventions. I also presented several early drafts of chapters at Cornell University's History Colloquium and countless drafts of the book manuscript to several writing groups. Special thanks go to Ed Baptist, Judith Byfield, Duane Corpis, Ray Craib, Mostafa Minawi, Jon Parmenter, and Margaret Washington for helping me position the project relative to a wide range of fields, as well as to Catherine Biba, Ryan Edwards, Sarah Ensor, Abi Fisher, Melissa Gniadek, Sinja Graf, Kyle Harvey, Kate Horning, Maeve Kane, Amy Kohout, Peter Lavelle, Nicole Maskiell, Daegan Miller, Trais Pearson, Jacqueline Reynoso, Rebecca Tally, and Darla Thompson for fine-tuning my ideas and prose.

At the College of Charleston, my colleagues in the extended constellation of African American Studies—Matthew Cressler, Shannon Eaves, the late Conseula Francis, Anthony Greene, Jon Hale, Kameelah Martin, Jonathan Neufeld, the late Ade Ofunniyin, and Lisa Young—provided valuable support and feedback on chapter drafts. Special thanks go to Casey Smith for patiently navigating the exasperating world of image permissions. The book manuscript workshop organized by Princeton University's Department of African American Studies during my fellowship gave me extensive and valuable suggestions for revising the manuscript. I am especially grateful to Tera Hunter for helping me create a clearer and historically grounded frame for the book's argument about continuity over time. Kali Gross prompted me to more precisely map out the forms of silence I discuss in chapter 2; the narrative choices I make throughout the book when writing about violence were shaped by her keen observation that many Americans are gratified by reading about anti-Black violence, even if they don't admit it in public, because they find comfort in knowing such violence protects them from the horrors Black southerners faced. Finally, Courtney Baker encouraged me to dig deeper into the work of Kevin Quashie and Saidiya Hartman, in particular their scholarship on the distinctions between quiet and silence and the narrative choices we make as scholars.

This is truly a pandemic book. In the final year of revising the book, disease upended the world, plunging us all into an imposed solitude that was necessary to keep one another safe. Amid immense loss and fear and separation, my dear friends and writing partners—Tara Bynum, Shannon Eaves, Amy Kohout, Jacqueline Reynoso, and Lisa Young—sustained me through the long haul. Amy also provided thoughtful feedback on every part of the manuscript, often several times over. I feel lucky to have such a meticulous and incisive reader as a friend; her friendship made the exhausting process of revising a book during a pandemic bearable, as did the friendship and wisdom of Liz Blake, Clifton Granby, Maeve Kane, Ada Kuskowski, and Xine Yao.

This book was well tended to by my editor at Yale University Press, Adina Berk, and the series editors for New Directions in Narrative

History, John Demos and Aaron Sachs. I am honored that the editors included this book in a series that understands that the writing of history can be an art and that good writing is more than a stylistic flourish. In particular, I am grateful for Aaron's unflagging encouragement, the painstaking precision of his line edits, and our conversations about writing that covered the book's arguments and structure as well as how to avoid didacticism, the importance of holding onto the moral core of a story, and how saying less can sometimes do more for your writing. Thank you for being a discerning and generous reader.

Finally, I thank my parents, Benjamin and Eiko Crabtree, and my siblings, Martin and Christina Crabtree. And my love, Molière Thelusca: this book exacted a heavy toll on me and yet there you were, to lighten my load.

The afterlife of traumatic memories hits close to home for me, as I am sure it does for many others. I have witnessed people I love cover in shrouds of silence the traumas they survived, and their experiences inform the ethical decisions I have made about representing lynching on the page. My maternal grandmother, Nagasue Hanako, survived the US military dropping an atomic bomb on Hiroshima in 1945 and took care of the sick and dying at the local hospital in Yoshida-machi, just outside the city. Only when my mother asked her about the bomb's aftermath, close to fifty years later, did she speak of the horrors of this monstrous new technology of death. Molière, my partner, was in Port-au-Prince when the 2010 earthquake destroyed most of the city, killing 300,000 people. The two of us have spoken about the specifics of what he survived only once: the good fortune of an early dismissal from class, the ground shaking and buildings collapsing, bodies piled up along the side of the road as he walked home in a daze, muffled screams coming from beneath the rubble, the stench of death, the terror of aftershocks that made him distrust the ground under his feet, the friends and family members he never saw again. A few summers ago, I was making my way through books by the Haitian novelist Dany Laferrière, and I asked Molière if he wanted to read Laferrière's memoir about surviving the earthquake, *The World Is Moving around Me.* "I don't want to read it. I was there," was his response. I also understood what went unsaid: *and isn't that more than enough to bear?*

For survivors, to tell their stories is to relive them and allow pain that they have contained and carried to drift back into consciousness. Violence stains the pages that follow. At times I resurrect horrific memories that for some were unspeakable, and I remain ambivalent about doing so, unsure whether writing about other people's lives, in particular other people's pain, in service of an argument is unseemly or even exploitative. I can't know how this book will be received by readers, if a study about memories of lynching will be worth the price of dredging up such pain, if the collective introspection necessary to come to terms with the past is actually possible. Yet I hope this book strikes a balance between recovering traumatic memories that so often were obscured and respecting the memory of those lost to lynching.

We are still living in the afterlife of lynching. We are still living with lynching.

MY SOUL IS A WITNESS

Introduction

Reckoning

In our family, we had come to expect that people can disappear into thin air. All traces lost except in the vivid eyes of one's memory.

—EDWIDGE DANTICAT, *Breath, Eyes, Memory*

THE ARTIST HAS MUCH to offer the scholar. Beauty, pleasure, and certainly a dexterity with language and sound and images, but also a gift for reflecting the world back onto us and revealing the nuances and mysteries of the human condition. Art—the good stuff, anyway—compels us to pause and think more deeply. It demands the self-reflection that prompts us to ask who we are and what we can become, and it urges us to abandon stale questions and imagine new ways of seeing the world. Much of my own writing has been refracted through art, especially as I worked through this project on the traumatic legacies of lynching in the US South. A turn of phrase in a Yusef Komunyakaa poem provided a flash of insight into the impulse to trap painful memories inside and the costs of carrying the burden of that pain to the grave. A scene from a Toni Morrison novel prompted me to wonder if a place—a tree, a courthouse, the land itself—can really hold the memories of the dead. A blues lyric and the slow bending of a blue note from a Lightnin' Hopkins song made me feel, just for a moment, the desperation of searching for relief when faced with the limits of otherworldly justice.

Those artists and many others gave shape to this book, but a short story by James Baldwin, "Going to Meet the Man," planted the seed. In a mere twenty-one pages, Baldwin captured the enduring power of lynching memories in the South, how the legacies of lynching infiltrated the everyday lives of southerners.[1] He brought into sharp relief how the past and present can collapse and bleed into one another. He named lynching as a southern, if not American, trauma. He exposed the central place that racial violence occupies in US culture and recognized how memories of lynching seem to cling more tightly to those who attempt to shake them off. Perhaps most important for my work, he caused me to approach the archive with new questions. Rather than asking what happened during a lynching, I sought answers to the question, what happened in the wake of a lynching? I looked beyond the episodic—beyond lynchings as discrete events in time—in search of scabbed-over wounds scattered across time and space, pain that was silenced and pushed deep into the unconscious, people and places haunted by lynching long after bodies were cut down and buried, battle cries of civil rights protesters that echoed the screams of lynching victims, the despair and hope captured by a blues singer's moan.

"Going to Meet the Man" portrays a white deputy sheriff in the Jim Crow South named Jesse who fears that the civil rights protests and Black voter registration drives in the 1960s are chiseling away at the edifice of white supremacy. For comfort and reassurance, he returns to a childhood memory of a grisly lynching. The story opens with Jesse in bed with his wife, wanting sexual release but being unable to become aroused. Earlier that day, he rained blow after blow upon a young Black protest leader, trying to force him to quiet the other protesters in jail singing freedom songs. But violence—his tried and true method for asserting control over and instilling fear in African Americans—failed him for the first time. The protest leader refused to submit, despite being beaten within an inch of his life, leaving Jesse unsteady and bewildered as his grasp on power seemed to slip away. In bed next to his sleeping wife, with the sound of protest songs from the jail still ringing in his ears, he drifts back to a memory of a lynching he witnessed as a child—it was the moment he was initiated into the power and meaning of whiteness and patriarchy in the South. There, perched atop his father's shoulders, he watched his father's friends lower a Black man into flames as his mother gazed at the man's burning, naked body with a placid smile on her face. His fear melted away, as did his empathy for Black suffering. His father's friend grabbed a knife to castrate the Black man, and Jesse "began to feel a joy he had never felt before" and "wished that he had been that man [holding the knife]."[2] The mob then descended upon the nearly dead man, tearing off "souvenir" body parts and drenching what was left in kerosene before engulfing the body in a wall of flames. As the Black man's mangled corpse still smoldered on a pile of ash, Jesse, his parents, and hundreds of his white neighbors walked to the picnic tables to feast and celebrate.

Jesse grew into the image of that man with the knife, the man he had idolized as a child. He arrested Black women so he could rape them. He clubbed and kicked the protest leader then put a cattle prod to the man's genitals, and though he had wavered when the protest leader refused to submit to his will, the memory of the lynching restored his sense of place and order in society and assured him that he was a good man. As his mind drifted back from this memory to that restless night in bed, the sense of power, joy, and belonging that he had felt at the lynching returns. He pulls his sleeping wife close, at first out of a nervous fear for the day to come—another harrowing day of confrontations with Black protesters— but, aroused by the memories of the lynching from his childhood and the beating from earlier in the day, he gets his sexual release at last.

Baldwin articulated how racial violence remained embedded in the subconscious of white southerners like Jesse for decades. Not only did that memory inform his identity as a white southern man, but it could be powerfully wielded to rationalize Jim Crow and oppose racial justice decades after the lynching itself. Several months after reading "Going to Meet the Man," the story still hounded me. The graphic violence it described was seared into my memory, as was the way Baldwin so clearly laid bare the psychological dimensions of white supremacy and the lasting legacies of anti-Black violence. As I sat with Baldwin's short story, and as it sat with me, I wondered whether a scholar could recover the psychological and cultural legacies of lynching that Baldwin revealed to be so persistent, and I wondered, in particular, about the hauntedness of Black survivors.[3] Whereas Baldwin focused on white southerners, I wanted to know how Black survivors of lynching lived with their memories over decades and across generations, how they processed the echoes of howling mobs and the cries of lynching victims, how they lived through its painful aftermath.[4] I also remained curious about how the interplay between African American and white memories brought into sharp relief the discordant resonances between them. For instance, we see the vast gulf between white and Black southerners when the silence a Black father demanded of

his son who had barely escaped a Mississippi lynch mob in 1954 is juxta-
posed with the denial and projection of a white woman from Mississippi
insisting that the lynching of three civil rights workers in 1964 was a
communist hoax. White southern memories of lynching also provided a
critical (though certainly not the only) piece of the backdrop against
which Black southerners remembered the horrors of lynching. Whether
their responses came in the form of denial or prudent silences or lynched
effigies or lynched Black bodies, white southerners, as Baldwin pointed
out, continued to understand their place and power in society via lynching in ways that impacted how Black southerners processed the trauma of
lynching. In the pages that follow, the white southern memories of lynching that I discuss capture what Black southerners were up against in the
social and cultural landscape of the Jim Crow South—but, above all, I
foreground the memories of Black people.[5]

In this book, I have taken what Baldwin unearthed about the cultural
and psychological legacies of lynching and combined his insights with the
theoretical foundations of memory studies.[6] This scholarly literature explores how memories illuminate more than just what happened in the
past. Memories reflect back to us how the past lives deep within us in the
present, shaping what we do and who we imagine ourselves to be, pushing
us to see the world through the lenses of its creation. In an essay, "White
Man's Guilt," Baldwin observed: "History, as nearly no one seems to
know, is not merely something to be read. And it does not refer merely, or
even principally, to the past. On the contrary, the great force of history
comes from the fact that we carry it within us, are unconsciously controlled by it . . . and history is *literally* present in all that we do."[7] Memory
studies confirms Baldwin's insight into the mingling of past and present—
how what lingers from the past bleeds into the present and how what we
remember of the past contains something of the present. The study of
lynching and memory, then, captures how, as survivors of lynching lived
during the era of Jim Crow and beyond, the trauma of anti-Black violence
never left them. Every racist slight, every cry for justice, every family
gathering with someone missing was, in part, filtered through their traumatic memories of lynching. The memory studies framework also wrests
control over the temporal boundaries of lynching from white perpetrators. Rather than thinking about lynchings as episodic—as beginning
when white lynch mobs assembled and ending when they dispersed—
memory studies shows them to be ongoing intergenerational tragedies,
traumas that are continually unfolding.

Baldwin, a fiction writer not tethered to specific historical evidence, could develop nuanced and detailed constructions of Jesse's emotions and thoughts, and the subconscious wanderings of his mind, but actual historical figures were often not fully conscious of their inner thoughts, nor did they consciously or unconsciously leave such evidence in the historical record. I was able to recover some of the interiority of lynching survivors through oral histories, both those I conducted and the ones I listened to in oral history collections across the South, but I still worried that some memories of lynching would be too deeply buried to be recovered or that the silences in oral histories would leave too much unsaid. And I wondered if traumatic memories that survivors had secreted away were best left undisturbed, if opening old wounds was an intrusion or, worse, a violation.[8]

After nearly a decade of researching, writing, and revising this book, that final question still troubles me. At this point, I have agonized over some narrative choices for months and even years—the turn of a phrase, my tone, the vividness of a description of violence, the perspective from which I write—and I have questioned the ethics of telling certain details of stories. The result is a book that wades into the deeper recesses of traumatic memories of lynching, into memories that sank down into and seeped through generations, even into the minds of those who were not yet alive to bear witness to these spectacles of death. But to avoid reducing the people whose stories I tell to victims of white violence, I prioritize the telling of whole stories when possible instead of simply gathering shards and fragments from the very worst moments of their lives—when white supremacist violence was most destructive. Lynching fractured families, so my work as a writer is the work of reconstruction, which includes the recovery of moments of joy and love and pleasure, too. It means surrounding the people I write about with their communities, not just the lynch mobs that took their lives. It means retracing the local lore passed on (and sometimes passed over) that connects generations of lynching survivors to one another. It means reclaiming lives that lynch mobs turned into objects of entertainment and derision. It means recovering Black voices—treating them as living, breathing, feeling, thinking subjects of history—and therefore tempering the impulse to render African Americans as the silent victims of white oppression.

This book also uses cultural studies frameworks to peel back the layers of meaning embedded in traumatic memories of lynching and to uncover a full range of narrative strategies that African American southerners forged to process those memories. These narrative strategies lay the groundwork for theorizing African American responses to trauma and unearthing the nuances and complexities of the traumatic afterlife of lynching, or what Christina Sharpe has called "the wake" in the context of enslavement and its aftermath. What Sharpe calls "the contemporary conditions of Black life, as it is lived near death, as deathliness, in the wake of slavery," reveals the long legacies of enslavement in the present, and that metaphor extends to Black life in the wake of lynching, too.[9] After all, the violence of lynching was an extension of the violence of enslavement. White people deployed and continue to deploy anti-Black violence to enforce and reinforce white supremacy, the system of power underlying both enslavement and Jim Crow. In the face of that violence, both the enslaved and lynching survivors developed strategies to bury, cope with, and confront traumatic memories. Sharpe describes this process of "imagin[ing] new ways to live in the wake of slavery, in slavery's afterlives, to survive (and more) the afterlife of property" as "wake work," which, in the context of lynching, was a matter of making it through and beyond the ritual desecration of Black bodies, of people being turned into strange fruit.[10]

Southern lynching was at its peak between roughly 1880 and 1940, but in the decades that followed, lynching was not merely an abstraction or a fraying and brittle memory to African American southerners.[11] The necessity of wake work was an everyday reality. Survivors often had personal connections to lynching victims and even knew the identities of perpetrators of lynching, and yet these lynchers still walked free on the streets. Survivors regularly encountered these and other physical and rhetorical reminders of lynching. Its specter lingered in the branches of lynching trees and the beams of hanging bridges that carried invisible marks of death. Its memory survived in local lore passed on to children and grandchildren. Its power pulsed through the political rhetoric of segregationists and the slogans of civil rights activists. And sadly the practice itself persisted in some pockets of the South, without the large crowds and souvenir postcards of earlier decades, but with the same intent to terrorize African Americans and celebrate white supremacy. Living amid what Sharpe names constant "deathliness"—that is, the everyday specter of anti-Black violence that she describes as akin to "the weather"—Black southerners imagined pathways to survival and even freedom in the wake of these collective traumas. Conceiving of anti-Blackness as "the weather" strikes me as ceding too much space in Black people's minds to white supremacy, but even when anti-Blackness is decentered, "wake work" still takes place through the process of remembering trauma itself, creating memories and returning to them, and sometimes passing them on.[12]

"Wake work," as Sharpe conceives of it, also implicitly challenges the resistance paradigm within African American studies, which gives primacy to resistance—especially in its most overt forms—and deems resistance the most virtuous reaction to the enduring problem of white supremacy. The resistance paradigm emerged in response to the dominant (read: white, patriarchal, and capitalist) culture and historiography, which denied agency and subjectivity to African Americans for centuries. In an effort to combat the stereotype of the shuffling "Uncle Tom," scholars of the African American experience have often amplified the most vocal and the most provocative freedom fighters at the exclusion of other Black voices. Consequently, vulnerability—or what Kevin Quashie has so eloquently named "quiet"—and that feeling of being very nearly consumed by trauma have become, in the eyes of many scholars, less legitimate and less legible responses to white supremacist violence.[13] "Wake work," however, encompasses more than just the "resistance" of the Harriet Tubmans and Ida B. Wellses in the Black community and recognizes how surviving suffering and pain, which so often were truly debilitating, is also a form of "work."[14]

As I researched this project, I kept my ears attuned to what Ralph Ellison called "the lower frequencies"—those memories of lynching only spoken in whispers or on the sly or in code or not at all—and sought out, gingerly of course, the tender and sometimes raw spots within those memories.[15] African American southerners processed the trauma of lynching in myriad ways, including overt protests, but more often in indirect, private, and covert ways, under the protective armor of silence and through local lore that used the supernatural as an intermediary to grieve the dead and condemn the crimes that took their lives. Sometimes they hid painful parts of the past from family and even from themselves just to survive the everyday "weather" of anti-Blackness. In addition to discovering what memories people passed on, I was equally interested in why some African American survivors chose not to pass on the harm contained within these memories to their children, for I see virtue in that refusal, too. By developing an ear for silences and calculated misdirection, I recovered voices that are more typical and no less extraordinary than those of well-known activists whose stories grace the pages of history books.[16] For obscuring the intensity of pain and sorrow, the depths of bitterness and despair, and the power of hope and love betrays the humanity and flattens the nuance and complexity of a people whose resilience and tenacity carried them through troubled times.

Given the range and nuances of these traumatic memories of lynching, I interpret them through five major themes that give shape to the organization of the book: silence, haunting, violence, protest, and the blues. This thematic approach reveals how culture shapes the emplotment of narratives, and it uncovers the deeper layers of meaning behind memories of lynching—layers that cut across the simplistic binary of resistance or submission. Survivors of lynching were often haunted by traumatic memories that, like ghosts, refused to leave them in peace, but they also sometimes passed on stories about the vengeful ghosts of lynching victims to their families and friends. To express their disgust with members of lynch mobs who evaded legal justice, they spoke of deathbed confessions made by lynchers tormented by their past. By interpreting these forms of haunting as part of a tradition of telling ghost stories for both their entertainment value and political critique, I make the case that, although a ghost or deathbed confession displaces the critiques of racism from the mouth of the person telling the story, the creative act of constructing these stories powerfully illustrates the capacity of African American cultural traditions to help people cope with and process trauma. In other words, as much as I seek to accurately reconstruct the past through these memories, when analyzing memories themselves, my concern is why people remembered what they did and in the way that they did. I ask why the ghosts made their way into these stories, not whether the ghosts were real.

The book unfolds, not chronologically, but along the arc of a steady crescendo, from an unsettled silence to the murmurings of haunting to the shouting of violence and protest and finally to the mournful cries of the blues. For survivors, trauma itself manifested in nonlinear fits and starts, often in shards, often stirred awake after decades of lying dormant, so the book's narrative arc does not track a gradual shift to louder and more direct lynching narratives over time but rather captures the myriad ways that Black southerners gave voice to (or refused to give voice to) their memories of lynching. In broad strokes, Black southerners more vociferously spoke out against lynching and opened up about these painful memories as the civil rights movement chipped away at Jim Crow and the danger of speaking out subsided a bit, but trauma refused to unfurl along a linear timeline. At the same time, white southerners generally grew reticent to publicly defend or celebrate lynching, though even those patterns of shame and prudence shaping white behavior were uneven at best. Some lynching survivors buried painful memories of loss and horror for a lifetime, while others published denunciations of lynchings just days after the fact. With the perpetrators of lynchings still walking the streets decades after committing heinous crimes and with the constant occurrence and evolution of lynching throughout the civil rights era and beyond, these traumas remained ongoing and unresolved, and traumatic memories followed no singular trajectory. Despite the great social upheaval of the civil rights movement that eroded racist practices like segregation and disenfranchisement, many lynching survivors were no less haunted by their memories in 1970 than they were in 1920. At the same time, the continuities between the antilynching crusade of Ida B. Wells and the civil rights protests sparked by the lynching of Emmett Till attested to the fact that Black protest was a steady and consistent response to lynching.

At first glance, the wide variety of narrative strategies adopted by African American southerners to process traumatic memories of lynching might seem wildly disparate, but at their core they share a sensibility rooted in the African American cultural tradition: the sensibility of the blues. Though "the blues" typically brings to mind the musical genre and conjures up images of Bessie Smith and Son House performing in smoke-laced juke joints, it also encapsulates the cultural impulse behind the music to live amid *and despite* one's troubles, not in order to wallow in pain and sadness but to confront that pain and sadness, and put the blues as such—that is, feeling blue—in their place. The blues sensibility informed how African American southerners forged ways to live in the wake of lynching. It was a strategy and a disposition underlying wake work that offered no pat solutions to these traumatic memories, for it recognized that, even when confronted, the blues as such linger, hopefully as nothing more than a dull ache but too often as an angry wound, always raw and throbbing. The novelist and memoirist Kiese Laymon described this ironic bent of the blues as "the perpetual reckoning with what should be agony, but finding ways of making that reckoning pleasurable. The agony and the pleasure exist right up next to one another."[17]

Returning to the blues as such through music, folktales, family lore, art, and even protest, or what Laymon calls "the art of rhythmically manipulating repetition," was not an attempt at selective amnesia or escapism, but remembering: holding the blues up to the light and maybe even crying through them before hurling them into the darkness, to get the relief necessary to continue living.[18] The blues sensibility provided a means to process, manage, and live with trauma, not through a stagnating cycle of repeatedly trudging over the same painful terrain but through a far more creative and transformative reckoning. For the cultural critic and novelist Albert Murray, ingenuity, not retrenchment, was at the core of the blues:

> The blues is for confrontation and improvisation—you see, confrontation of the fact that life is a low-down dirty shame or a dangerous proposition at best. And then you improvise playfully—hopefully playfully. If you can do it playfully, in come options which are going to add up to elegance, which is beauty, and now you're making art.[19]

For Murray, the confrontational and improvisational edges of the blues explained why performing and listening to blues music made people feel better rather than worse—the blues simply refused stagnation. Even if lynchings had no clear resolution—a life cannot be untaken, and punishment, even delayed, does not deliver true justice—the blues carved out space for Black people to live and breathe and *be*.

   This book proposes a theory of African American collective trauma and cultural memory developed through closely reading traumatic memories of lynching as expressions of the blues sensibility. In many ways, the chapters that follow grapple with a question Laymon poses: "how do we [African Americans] most effectively hold ourselves together through the pain, through the suffering, and through the agony?" Much of the trauma studies literature does not speak to the specific historical circumstances of the African American experience, much less the cultural sensibilities that informed African American strategies for working through traumas like lynching. Formative texts in trauma studies ground their analyses in the Holocaust and Europe more generally, emphasizing the long history of antisemitism in Europe and the political will within post–World War II West Germany to memorialize the horrors of Hitler's "final solution" and to prosecute Nazis in widely publicized trials.[20] In contrast, the blues sensibility is a homegrown metaphor for "working through" trauma that reflects the cultural sensibilities of a people who lived beyond enslavement and Jim Crow, and who are living through the current system of carceral control over Black bodies. The blues sensibility itself emerged from within and alongside a nation that, outside the Black community, has continued to be reluctant to acknowledge, much less grapple with, lynching and other white supremacist violence. The explanatory power of the blues sensibility lies not just in its capacity to capture the variety of narrative strategies for working through African American trauma, but also, as Laymon points out, in its ability to express joy, love, and humor in tandem with utter despair and misery.[21]

Although I don't usually reference actual blues music when I speak of the blues as a sensibility in this book, the music itself is steeped in this sensibility in ways that are revealing. When Billie Holiday cries out, "My days have grown so lonely / For you I cry, for you dear only / Why haven't you seen it / I'm all for you body and soul," the lyrics, though devastating, when sung in her delicately weathered voice, have a sensual and painfully beautiful quality that doesn't exactly dull the sharpness of the anguish she expresses, but embraces the pain and tenderness contained in a single breath.[22] Holding pleasure and pain, or the tragic and the comic, in a single breath or a single thought or a single brushstroke lies at the center of the lynching memories recovered in this book. Like Holiday's "Body and Soul," which contains both agony and pleasure, a ghost story about an African American man who haunted the Pickens County courthouse in Alabama revels in the pleasures of revenge and otherworldly justice but is no less tragic in marking the death of an innocent man who was denied this-worldly legal justice.[23] The blues sensibility, like the music itself, also recognizes the limits of language: the ways in which silences can speak volumes, the expressiveness of a sigh or a wry laugh or a melancholy groan, the depths of feeling contained in a blue note. For silence could be a tactic of refusal, and a gentle, consoling touch or a knowing glance could express more than words. Those survivors of lynchings who never again spoke lynching memories into existence were protecting themselves and refusing to give narrative control over their life stories to white perpetrators of violence.

The blues sensibility encompasses the full range of Black southern lynching memories, not only because it can express seemingly contradictory feelings at the same time and at different narrative registers, but also because it refuses the interpretive narrowness imposed upon Black experiences by a singular (or near singular) emphasis on resistance to white supremacy. As much as lynching traumatized survivors, and for all the horrors of white supremacy, African American life simply cannot be reduced to resistance to white supremacy, to the omnipresence of the white gaze, to ceaseless suffering. By imagining Blackness through a more vulnerable frame—a frame that recognizes how suffering can be debilitating but also how it can be eased by love and laughter—the blues sensibility says yes to life. Even when the source of the blues as such is white rapacity, the blues sensibility is a way of being—a posture toward life—that is primarily concerned not with white people, but rather with the process of getting right with oneself, or what Jeffrey B. Ferguson calls the "creative endeavor to re-shape emotion" through "the internal resources of the individual to affirm life, even in the darkest times."[24] Black southern lynching narratives, like blues songs themselves, were inward-facing for the most part. They were shared, if they were shared at all, almost exclusively among other Black people, sheltered far from the white gaze. This book uncovers the myriad ways Black southerners processed the traumatic afterlife of lynching through the blues sensibility, and it argues that the African American cultural tradition gave African Americans not just tools for survival, but also the grace to live through the trauma, to love, and to create beyond it. These silences, these hauntings, these protests, these blues all constituted ways to "hold ourselves together through the agony," as Laymon put it, to keep the blues as such at bay, even if just for a spell.

Writing about lynching, and, in particular, narrating these horrific scenes of Black death, raises questions about the ethical responsibilities that writers have to victims and survivors. Even those writers with the best of intentions—those who want to expose the unvarnished truth of the sheer brutality of lynching—can unintentionally stray into the gratuitous and the salacious, and can reproduce the very violence they intend to condemn. They can reinscribe the dehumanization of Black people onto the page, make voyeurs of their readers, and intrude upon the privacy of victims and their families. These ethical responsibilities to minimize harm and respect privacy sometimes conflict with scholarly commitments to dig deeper, unearth, and reveal. In the chapters that follow, the violence on the page is sometimes unavoidable, so I have tried to manage this tension between writing about trauma and dredging up unwanted traumatic memories (or traumatizing readers) by limiting extended descriptions of graphic violence to instances when those details are necessary to understand the trauma itself and how survivors processed traumatic memories. Though imperfect, this approach aims to neither sanitize the history of lynching nor descend into gratuitous descriptions of violence that resurrect the spectacle of Black death and the desecration of Black bodies.[25]

The first chapter, in particular, includes extended narratives of two lynchings: that of Jesse Washington, lynched in 1916, and that of Mary Turner, lynched in 1918. Both of these cases, along with the lynching of Emmett Till in 1955, anchor the analysis in subsequent chapters, and I weave these three lynchings, alongside many others, throughout the book to capture the web of silence, haunting, violence, protest, and the blues that the trauma of lynching spun. This first chapter unpacks the layers of meaning embedded in the ritual of lynching by describing and then closely analyzing the Washington and Turner lynchings as well as what occurred in their immediate aftermath. This analysis sets up the various ways that traumatic events unfolded over time through the memories of survivors and, to some extent, the memories of perpetrators. The narratives of the Washington and Turner lynchings are graphic and disturbing, and therefore difficult to read, but without discussing what happened in 1916 and 1918 and its significance, subsequent analyses of their traumatic reverberations lose their points of reference, and the continuities between lynchings and their aftermaths are less legible.

In writing this book, I hope that the potential for harm from reviving traumatic memories is outweighed by the value of bringing to light how generations of African Americans lived in the wake of lynching. Their stories and memories have rarely surfaced in public beyond Black communities, and, when they have, they usually have emerged with understandable reluctance and wariness. The question of how to individually and collectively grapple with the long afterlife of lynching has even more rarely entered into the national conversation and, even then, only in fits and starts—recent memorialization efforts and overdue (and belated to the point of being merely a symbolic gesture) antilynching legislation notwithstanding.[26] But despite collective struggles to put into words and confront something as horrifying as lynching, the historical fact of lynching lurks just beyond the consciousness of the nation, waiting to be examined, mulled over, and reckoned with. Even those in the deepest denial often can't help but sense its presence, for lynching haunts every corner of the United States. We hear echoes of lynching in Eric Garner's cry, "I can't breathe!" and see its remnants in nooses left hanging in a UPS facility and a GM plant in Ohio to threaten African American employees, and in a photograph of students at the University of Mississippi posing with guns in front of a defaced sign memorializing the

life and death of Emmett Till.[27] Lynching also stalks contemporary political rhetoric: in a 2017 Facebook post, a Republican lawmaker from
Mississippi threatened to lynch anyone who took down Confederate
monuments; a man at a Donald Trump rally in Minnesota wore a t-shirt
with "Rope. Tree. Journalist." printed on the back; and a Missouri bar recently welcomed its patrons with a "Lynch Kaepernick" doormat. Barack
Obama was regularly lynched in effigy across the United States before
and after he won the presidential election in 2008.[28]

　　These and so many other remnants of lynching leach into the present,
and they haunt all of us, for memory is not just old stories but something
we carry. Such horrors as lynching fester and refuse to loosen their grip,
allowing for no clean escapes for either the descendants of victims and survivors or the descendants of perpetrators. In the ever prescient words of
James Baldwin, "My memory stammers: but my soul is a witness."[29]

CHAPTER ONE

An Anatomy of Lynching

Those ladders to fire—the burning of the witch, the heretic, the Jew, the nigger, the faggot—have always failed to redeem, or even to change in any way whatever, the mob. They merely epiphanize and force their connection on the only plain on which the mob can meet: The charred bones . . . are the sum total of their individual self-hatred, externalized. The burning or lynching or torturing gives them something to talk about. They dare no other subject, certainly not the forbidden subject of the bloodstained self.

—JAMES BALDWIN, "To Crush a Serpent"

JESSE WASHINGTON KNEW HE was going to die. Waiting for the all-white Texas jury to return with what would undoubtedly be a guilty verdict and a death sentence, he looked out at the sea of hostile white faces in the courtroom, his gaze placid, as though the certainty of his impending death might somehow muffle the terror coursing through his body. The jury had left the courtroom just long enough to deliberate his fate—a mere four minutes during which the seventeen-year-old farmhand must have doubted that this sham trial could possibly pacify the growing mob of twenty-five hundred that spilled out of the McLennan County Court-house onto the streets of Waco, Texas. Sitting, waiting for the jury to file back into the courtroom, he knew that if the law didn't hang him, these people would.[1]

In the week between his arrest and the trial, two lynch mobs from Robinson, Texas, had piled into cars and buggies to demand that Sheriff Samuel S. Fleming hand Washington over—once at the Waco jail and again at the Hillsboro jail in the neighboring county. Robinson was a small farming town just a few miles down the road from Waco where, on the previous Monday, Lucy Fryer's dead body had been discovered, her head resting in a pool of her own blood. Both times Sheriff Fleming had had the foresight to spirit Washington away before the mobs could kill him, and for good measure, Fleming struck a bargain with the Robinson mobs: they promised not to lynch Washington if the law promptly convicted and executed him. The sheriff made a similar deal with Washington. In exchange for a confession, the sheriff assured him that he would keep the lynch mob at bay until "justice" was served.[2]

So far, the sheriff had held up his end of the bargain, but with every second that passed, the crowd hovering around Washington grew more impatient. He probably knew better than to hope he would live past May 15, 1916, the date of his trial. Since the opening gavel only an hour earlier, rowdy spectators had repeatedly disrupted the proceedings. As Washington entered the courtroom, flanked by several deputies, a scuffle had broken out. A hotheaded white man brandishing a revolver had shouted, "Might as well get him now!" but after a few chaotic moments, another member of the crowd had tackled and disarmed him. "Let them have their trial," growled the man who had wrested the gun away. "We'll get him before sundown, and you might hurt some innocent man."[3] Judge Richard I. Munroe had to call for order several times to silence some chatty boys sitting in the balcony, who, like their adult counterparts, had been drawn to the thrill of witnessing what a local newspaper described as "the lustful brute" on trial.[4] Another man yelled out, "We don't need any courts!" and, although that outburst had been largely ignored by others in the courtroom, it spoke volumes about the prevailing idea of justice in the white South. What little faith Washington had placed in the law, in the promises of the sheriff, in the grossly outnumbered deputies posted around the courtroom to protect him, had probably vanished.

Long before his personal brushes with mob violence, Washington likely knew the odds were low that he or any other Black man accused of murdering a white woman would escape a lynch mob in Texas. The Waco newspapers published predictions that he would be convicted and executed by day's end, but he didn't need a newspaper to tell him he would soon die, nor could he read one anyhow since he was illiterate, another casualty of the Jim Crow educational system. He was a Black southerner, so his baptism in the ways of Jim Crow most likely came much earlier in life, and his parents, Martha and Henry, almost certainly provided him and his younger brother, William, with an education in surviving the often fickle and dangerous ways of white folks. After all, since the early nineteenth century, central Texas had a deeply entrenched tradition of lynching African Americans and other nonwhites.[5] More recently, in 1905 when Washington was just six years old, a lynch mob of six hundred farmers from around Robinson broke down the steel gates of the Waco jail with sledgehammers and seized Sank Majors, a Black man accused of assaulting a white woman. After a lively debate between two factions of the lynch mob over whether to burn Majors alive or hang him, the men and women in the mob strung him up from the Washington Street Bridge, later slicing off fingers and pieces of rope as souvenirs.[6]

Washington may have been too young to remember the Majors lynching, and his parents may have shielded him from the horrifying details. But he most certainly had heard about the barbaric lynching of Will Stanley the previous summer in nearby Temple, Texas. A mob of between five and ten thousand had tortured Stanley in the town square, slowly burning him alive, until one member of the mob shot him. Perhaps the shooter took pity on Stanley. Perhaps the flurry of excitement generated by the crowd made him trigger happy. Either way, the bullet killed Stanley, but the mob continued to drag his body through the flames until all that remained was a charred corpse with large portions of the legs and arms burned off and turned to ash. His mangled body was then hung from a telephone pole and left dangling at the end of a chain so that white people, including little boys and girls, could pose with his corpse in souvenir photographs.[7] Everyone in Waco knew the violence Texas lynch mobs were capable of unleashing upon Black bodies.

Back in the Waco courtroom, the jury had returned, and the foreman read the verdict: "We, the jury, find the defendant guilty of murder as charged in the indictment and assess his penalty at death." As the judge recorded the decision, the room was momentarily still except for the court reporter and Sheriff Fleming slipping out the door. After this brief pause, someone yelled, "Get the nigger!" which sent the mob surging toward

Washington over chairs, tables, people, and anything else in the way. The next few minutes were a blur. An avalanche of arms descended upon his body, dragging him down the back stairs of the courthouse to the street where four hundred more people waited. The mob paused just long enough for someone to wrap a heavy chain around his neck before pressing onward toward the suspension bridge just one block from where Sank Majors had been hanged eleven years earlier. Hands tore at his plain calico shirt and overalls, and he shrieked in agony as the rowdy mob lunged at him, plunging knives into his flesh and beating him with bricks and shovels. The bewildered teenager must have wondered what drove white people to act with such intense malice, what produced such glee in inflicting pain and suffering.

By the time the suspension bridge was in view, Washington was fading in and out of consciousness. The chain tugging at his neck went slack for a moment while the mob rehashed a debate from eleven years earlier: should they hang him from the bridge as planned or burn him at the stake in front of city hall where a woodpile had already been gathered? The mob changed direction, dragging him toward city hall, a grand structure and the centerpiece of the downtown market square. He staggered forward, blood pouring out of his wounds onto his naked body, until they reached a tree just below the mayor's office window. Washington could barely stand so he leaned up against the tree for support, hoping for mercy, hoping that death would come swiftly. The chain around his neck was thrown up around a tree branch, and by now the crowd had ballooned to upwards of fifteen thousand men, women, and children, some hanging out of windows around the square for a better view of his slow torture and death. Several men grasped the chain and pulled his body up into the air. At the sight of his body, the mob howled with delight as Washington gasped for breath. They lowered him to the ground, and those closest to the tree scrambled to slash at his body, castrating him and cutting off fingers, toes, and ears as souvenirs.[8] A second wave of excitement rippled through the crowd as people pressed forward to light the bonfire that would devour much of his body. Washington's charred, lifeless corpse was raised up into the air again like a trophy, eliciting yet another round of shouts and cheers, before being left on the smoldering coals below.

After his prolonged tortures, he had finally been freed from the pain and suffering of this hell on earth called Waco, Texas. The desecration of his body, however, continued. A man lassoed the corpse—all that was left was the torso, head, and the stumps of the limbs—and dragged it behind his horse as he galloped around city hall and through the streets of downtown Waco. The head snapped off as the horse bounded down a main street, and some little white boys scurried after it. The torso was then stuffed into a bag, dragged several miles behind a car back to Robinson, and hung on a telephone pole outside a blacksmith's shop for public viewing. An officer later retrieved the remains for burial in a potter's field.[9]

Breathe. Let your eyes lose focus. Let them wander from the page. Breathe.

The horrors and tragedies of that week, stacked one upon the next, were a lot to bear then and are a lot to bear witness to now. Among this inventory of incalculable tragedies is the scant record of Jesse Washington's life. The lurid details of his death were strewn across front-page headlines that spread throughout the nation and even crossed oceans, but traces of his life remain faint. The urge to counter the gruesome details of his death with some revelation of his life as it was before the lynching, this teenager as he was among family and friends and even foes, bump up against the archival ephemerality of a Black life taken. The desire to give space to the grief and horror his family felt comes up against the transitory nature of tenant farming, of fleeing for one's life, of fleeing the memories of a loved one's lynching.[10] And yet the impulse to remember what cannot be remembered stubbornly persists. And yet the reverberations of this life and this death ripple across time and space and memory.

Breathe.

The tree, a small oak, stood just a few yards from the banks of the Little River. One of its gnarled limbs stretched across the lonely country road that led to Barney, Georgia, as if straining to reach the tree across the way. The scorching midday sun beat down on the oak, but only a few rays penetrated through the canopy of the forest to the thick underbrush below. That canopy would soon provide a shroud not just to the bramble and vines but to the shallow grave of Mary Turner and her unborn baby.

The mob from in and around Barney arrived shortly after noon and settled on the oak with its outstretched limb as the site of the day's tortures. A few members of the mob hoisted Mary Turner, their most recent victim, up in the tree by her ankles as she struggled and screamed, eliciting laughter and jeers from the men in the crowd when her dress fell around her waist, exposing her body to their leers. Turner was eight months pregnant, and her belly was heavy and swollen with her third child; as a hot breeze rustled through the leaves of the oak, the knotty limb sagged and creaked under her weight. Suspended in the air, blood rushing to her head, her mind might have raced from the baby growing inside her to her two older children, Otha and Leaster (pronounced lee-ES-ter), still in hiding with relatives, or so she hoped. Or maybe she thought of her dead husband, whom she knew she would join in death shortly.

As Turner used her last breaths to let out piercing screams, the mob leapt into action, splashing gasoline and motor oil on her dress, and with a single match, flames enveloped her entire body. The more her anguished cries and shrieks of pain pierced the air and the more she violently writhed as the blistering heat that consumed her clothing burned her skin, the more the mob roared with laughter and delighted in her slow death. Even after every scrap of her clothing had burned, she still clung to life. A man emerged from the crowd carrying a large knife used to butcher hogs, and he plunged the knife into her belly, which was still holding her unborn child, then jerked the knife down, tearing open her womb. Out of that gash her baby tumbled and let out two short whimpers before a man, likely the one wielding the knife, stomped on the baby's head with the heel of his boot. Perhaps death spared Turner the horror of witnessing her baby's death just moments after drawing its first and only breaths of life, but then again, perhaps, in her final conscious moments, she watched as her helpless child, the one she would never hold in her arms, died.

The morbid entertainment continued under the branches of the oak. The jovial mob riddled Turner's corpse with hundreds of bullets, then cut the rope bound around her ankles so she dropped into a crumpled pile on the ground. Someone thought, as a joke, to mark the hastily dug grave of mother and child with an empty whiskey bottle, and in the neck of the bottle, someone stuffed the butt of a cigar that had helped one man's sensitive nostrils stand the stench of gasoline and burning human flesh. The members of the mob dispersed, returning to the nearby towns and farms where they lived, and they left Mary Turner and her baby buried a few yards from the foot of the small oak tree.[11]

The mob inflicted such excessive violence upon Turner and her baby, not as punishment for a heinous crime, but because, according to an

Atlanta newspaper, she had made "unwise remarks."[12] The previous day, a mob of about forty men had seized her husband, Hayes Turner, from the sheriff and had lynched him on the hanging tree where Morven and Barney Roads met near Quitman, Georgia. His hands remained bound behind his back by the sheriff's handcuffs as his corpse swayed in the breeze, and hundreds of spectators passed by to gawk at his body. The authorities left his body hanging for three days before sending some convict laborers to cut it down and bury it just a few feet from the tree. In her fury and anguish, his widow had vowed that, if the identities of the men who lynched her husband came to light, she would pursue legal action against them, and she disputed the charge that her husband was involved in their white employer's death. Her defiance of white supremacy, her demand for justice, and her defense of her husband's innocence enraged the white people of Brooks County, who expected absolute deference from Black people, and, as a newspaper reported, "in their indignant mood [they] took exceptions to her remarks as well as her attitude" and made her and her unborn child pay in no uncertain terms.[13]

The Turners were killed during a six-day lynching rampage sparked by the murder of a prominent white farmer, Hampton Smith, on the evening of May 16, 1918. The young couple worked on one of Smith's farms along with several other farmhands, and they all endured the abuses of their employer, who routinely beat his workers and cheated them out of their wages. Smith did not reserve his blows for the men who worked for him. He had severely beaten Mary Turner on several occasions, and Hayes Turner, out of devotion to his wife and a desire to protect her, had made verbal threats against Smith that landed him on the chain gang for a spell. The Turners insisted on affirming their birthright claims as US citizens and their innate human right to dignity and respect, but their refusal to adhere to their prescribed station in life as subservient and degraded laborers was intolerable to their white neighbors. Their defiance proved deadly.

Smith was so notorious for abusing his farm laborers that he struggled to find people willing to work for him. One of his white neighbors described him as "a mean one, all right . . . [who] never paid his debts to white men or niggers and wasn't liked much around here."[14] Smith often resorted to paying the fines of Black men sitting in jail for petty crimes so he could compel them to work on his farms as repayment. One such man was nineteen-year-old Sidney Johnson, whom the county court in Quitman had fined thirty dollars for gambling. After Smith paid his fine,

Johnson worked for the ill-tempered Smith, but once Johnson worked off his debts and Smith still didn't pay him, the two men got into a heated argument. A few days later, Johnson became ill and did not go to work in the fields, and his boss beat him mercilessly. This beating would be Smith's last. Like Hayes Turner, Johnson made verbal threats to kill Smith, and soon after, another farmhand, named Will Head, allegedly stole Smith's gun while Smith's wife was distracted in the kitchen preparing dinner. That night, Johnson allegedly fired four shots into the Smith home, hitting Smith in the shoulder and chest, and striking Smith's wife in the shoulder. The shooter fled into the swamps under the cover of darkness. Smith's wife survived with minor injuries; Smith died instantly. Despite Smith's reputation, the white community still turned him into a martyr. As one local man remarked to an undercover NAACP investigator, "It's a matter of safety—we gotta show niggers that they mustn't touch a white man, no matter how low-down and ornery he is."[15]

Once the authorities discovered the body, posses scoured the swamps, forests, and homes in the area for Smith's farmhands. By the following Wednesday, Will Head, Will Thompson, Julius Jones, Hayes Turner, Eugene Rice, Chime Riley, Simon Schuman, Mary Turner, the Turners' unborn baby, three unidentified Black men, and finally Sidney Johnson had all died at the hands of local lynch mobs. Johnson eluded capture the longest, but on Wednesday, May 22, he found himself cornered in a Valdosta, Georgia, home by a posse led by the police chief, Calvin Dampier. Refusing to be taken alive, Johnson decided to defend himself. The exchange of fire attracted a mob of several hundred people to the neighborhood, and after the posse no longer heard shots fired from the house where Johnson had been hiding, they cautiously approached and found him dead from gunshot wounds. With the chief of police and his deputies present, members of the mob castrated Johnson's dead body, threw his severed genitals into the street, and dragged the corpse behind an automobile up Patterson Street in Valdosta then another fifteen miles to the Mount Zion Camp Ground Methodist Church near Morven. On the church grounds, the mob, which included many members of the congregation, gathered wood around a large pine stump with Johnson's body lying across it and then doused his body with oil. Having been denied the spectacle of watching Johnson slowly tortured and killed, they burned his body until all that was left was a pile of smoldering ashes.

In the six days between Smith's murder on May 16 and Johnson's lynching on May 22, mobs lynched at least thirteen and possibly as many as eighteen African Americans.[16] The bodies that were left hanging from trees for days and the corpses that surfaced in the Little River and the ashes at the Camp Ground and the grave marked by a whiskey bottle reminded whites and African Americans alike how little Black lives mattered in southern Georgia.[17]

Breathe.

Those two children, orphaned. One winces just imagining the immense pain contained in their little bodies, only ages eight and five when they lost both parents and the baby to lynch mobs. They had each other, brother and sister, to cling to amid the fury. They had their Aunt Ola and Uncle James, who raised them and loved them as their own. They had their cousins and grandparents and friends. They had a Black community that protected them from the stories whispered with a shudder about their parents, especially their mother. As they grew up, they did what they could to protect their insides, to find beauty and joy in this world, to steady themselves, to make a life on their own terms, but there was no antidote to being haunted by the unspeakable. They knew the way the unspeakable could unfurl inside and wrench them back into the past. For the rest of their lives, they knew the burden of memory and felt the weight of these losses.

Breathe.

———————

Lynching tore through the fabric of Black communities, leaving wounds that, over time, hardened into scarred ridges that never fully disappeared. White southerners deployed lynching against Black southerners as a tool of terror, devastation, and social control, and terror certainly struck these communities, as did waves of grief and despair and disgust. However, as with most tools of white supremacy, lynching did not always have the intended effect of galvanizing white power. African American communities also tapped into wells of resistance and love, to confront white power and to console and protect their own.

In the wake of Jesse Washington's lynching, the Black community in and around Waco distanced itself from Washington—his murder conviction made publicly defending him difficult, even if many Black people were skeptical of the courts in Texas. After the recent display of savagery by the white citizens of McLennan County, few African Americans had the audacity and steely nerves to publicly condemn what their white neighbors had done. One notable exception was A. T. Smith, the managing editor of the local Black college's newspaper, *Paul Quinn Weekly*. Smith placed the blame for the lynching squarely on the shoulders of what he called the "thirsty blood crackers of the city."[18] He believed that Washington, like most lynching victims, had not committed the crime he was accused of but was a convenient scapegoat for the sheriff, and instead he accused Lucy Fryer's husband, George Fryer Sr., of murdering her. Quite naturally the widower took exception to Smith's accusation and sued Paul Quinn College for libel. The college paid a symbolic fine of one dollar, and Smith spent a year doing hard labor on the county chain gang as punishment.[19]

With endless examples of fabricated accusations of rape and murder leading to a lynching and sham trials that made a mockery of the justice system and overzealous vigilantes lynching the wrong person, Smith's skepticism was far from baseless.[20] Many local African Americans could still remember other instances of white lawlessness and indiscriminate terror. During the frenzied search for an assault suspect on the run that eventually led to the 1905 lynching of Sank Majors, roving mobs of armed white farmers rounded up dozens of innocent Black men along the banks of the Brazos River and detained them for questioning. Frustrated and perhaps restless since the suspect continued to evade capture, some members of the posse passed the time by hanging a Black man they accused of aiding the fugitive until he nearly suffocated, such was the disposability of Black people's lives.[21]

In the years following Washington's lynching, Smith's sentiments gained more public traction within the Black community, especially after May 1922 when another Waco mob, this time five thousand strong, once again lynched the wrong man. Jesse Thomas had matched the description of a murder suspect in that he was Black and had a gold tooth, which was enough for a recently deputized white man to arrest him and bring him to the home of a witness for identification. The witness was still recovering from her attack when she erroneously identified Thomas as the killer, at which point her father shot Thomas several times. Within an hour, a mob of several hundred stole Thomas's lifeless body from an undertaker and then dragged it behind a truck to city hall where, six years earlier, a mob had burned and mutilated Jesse Washington. Thomas's dead body was also stripped naked and burned before being dragged around the business district a second time. Several months later, another man was arrested and convicted of the crime Thomas died for.[22]

Smith's denunciation of Waco's lynching culture in 1916 had precedent within the local Black community. In 1905, the morning after the lynching of Sank Majors, all of the Black employees of a downtown Waco hotel quit en masse. The following day, another Black Wacoan condemned the lynching of Sank Majors, and for speaking out he received 150 lashes from a white vigilance committee.[23] That the backs of so many formerly enslaved people were crisscrossed with a maze of thick scars was not lost on the members of the vigilance committee. The whipping was a conscious, symbolic nod to enslavement that expressed the white community's intolerance for any challenge to Jim Crow by reestablishing the social "place" of Black people in Waco through the lash. The whipping probably had a chilling effect on those hotel workers who had quit in protest, each stripe left by the lash serving as a warning to them.[24] Whether whipping or hard labor, the consequences for condemning extralegal violence were severe, and yet some African Americans remained undeterred.[25]

Violent reprisals muted most public protests against lynching, but silence did not mean acceptance. Soon after Washington's lynching, the National Association for the Advancement of Colored People (NAACP) sent the white suffragist Elisabeth Freeman to Waco to investigate, and after speaking with several members of the Black community privately, she reported to the national office: "The feeling of the colored people was that while they had one rotten member of their race the whites had 15,000."[26] Silence, too, was clearly relative and reserved for circumstances in which speaking out was too dangerous. Talking to a white woman working for the NAACP under the cover of anonymity offered safety to those who condemned Washington's lynching, and, according to the blues and jazz musician Sam Price, among themselves, Black Wacoans were even more frank regarding their feelings about the white people in Robinson who orchestrated the lynching. They switched out the lyrics to the popular blues song, "Hesitation Blues," singing, "I never have, and I never will / Pick no more cotton in Robinsonville," before belting out the chorus.[27] Private condemnation of "rotten" whites and blues songs about Black refusal to pick cotton in Robinson (often referred to as Robinsonville in the early twentieth century) were limited in that they could not transform the social conditions produced by white supremacy, but, as manifestations of the blues sensibility, they steadied the nerves in the here and now, and built up an armor around Black people's insides as they weathered the storms that raged outside. In the long battle over the collective memory of lynching, the blues sensibility was foundational to forging alternatives to celebratory white lynching narratives—it centered the needs of Black communities and made clear that they had morality on their side.

The extraordinary viciousness of the Waco mob terrorized but did not paralyze the Black community. Given the hostile racial climate, two leading Black ministers, Reverend John W. Strong and Reverend I. Newton Jenkins, publicly offered reassurances to the white community, denouncing the murder of Lucy Fryer without mentioning the sadistic lynching that followed. Strong's and Jenkins's conciliatory, if not obsequious, public remarks were a common refrain among the "respectable" African American leadership who had little choice but to parrot what whites wanted to hear, but they told the NAACP investigator in confidence that they were disappointed by the lukewarm responses of Waco's white clergy after the lynching.[28] Three years later, in June 1919, Strong and Jenkins, along with the outspoken A. T. Smith, applied to become charter members of the Waco Branch of the NAACP.[29] Strong and Jenkins practiced a carefully choreographed deception with deep roots in the African American cultural tradition, including the blues. While their public comments soothed white racial anxieties about Black defiance of white supremacist social codes in the aftermath of Fryer's murder, they turned around and organized in their community to undermine and destroy Jim Crow.

In the months following the unspeakable violence that swept through Brooks County, Georgia, in May 1918, the local Black community also responded to their grief, horror, and anger with defiance. Mary Turner's death weighed most heavily upon the survivors. If their white neighbors could lynch a pregnant woman and her baby with such relish, they themselves could only imagine what devastation might be in store for the rest of the community were they to object openly to the violence. If the parishioners who gathered at Mount Zion Camp Ground Methodist Church could lynch three men within sight of the pews where they worshipped every Sunday, they wondered what distorted version of the Gospel this congregation followed, what depraved moral code led them to commit these acts of violence. If the sheriff could lead lynch mobs and allow Black bodies to be hanged and burned and cut open and dragged down the highway and blasted full of bullets, they knew, as they had long known, that the meaning of justice in Georgia's courts rang hollow.[30]

The lynchings of Turner and her unborn child tested the resolve of local Black people to remain on the land that they and their ancestors had worked for decades as enslaved laborers, as sharecroppers, as tenant farmers, as farmhands, and, for some, as landowners. Despite strong ties to the land and to the community, more than five hundred African Americans picked up and left Brooks County and neighboring Lowndes County in the weeks following the lynching rampage. Most of them decided to uproot their families out of fear and disgust, but also to protest the lynchings. Only one or two generations removed from enslavement, they knew the significance of leaving white landowners without laborers in May. Moving to other parts of the South or even to northern cities meant an uncertain future, but in the face of such unpredictable violence, this decision helped them preserve some semblance of control over their lives.

Those who remained either did not have the means to relocate or stubbornly refused to give in to the terror and give up their claim to land secured over several generations. Judge Head, whose brother, Will Head, had been the first person lynched during the rampage, decided to wait out the storm. He worked as a sharecropper for decades until he saved enough money to purchase a small plot near Pavo, Georgia, also in Brooks County—land that his grandson, Willie Head Jr., still farms. Survivors like Judge Head mourned the deaths of those killed in what locals called "that reign of terror" in May 1918. They mourned, but they also organized. On May 23, 1919, one year and one day after a lynch mob killed Sidney Johnson in Valdosta, Georgia, a group of fifty African Americans met in the small city to apply for a charter to set up a local branch of the NAACP. Despite the dangers involved in establishing an NAACP branch where a lynching rampage had just terrorized the Black community, these courageous citizens, who included barbers, laborers, housewives, and doctors, refused to allow the violent tendencies of their white neighbors to define their place in southern Georgia. And even before that, in the months immediately after the rampage, five Black men in Quitman, Georgia, located in Brooks County, aided the NAACP national office in its investigation of the lynchers. One man even agreed to testify against the lynchers, who included his own employer, until arrangements for his safe passage to the North broke down. In the end, he worried about a prolonged separation from his three children, who had recently lost their mother, and he worried about the safety of the family he would be leaving behind in Quitman. He had already lost so much, and could not risk losing any more.[31]

The records of the national office do not contain any correspondence about the subsequent activities of the Valdosta Branch, but the existence of the branch itself spoke volumes about the Black community's perseverance and strength. In fact, the national office of the NAACP proudly touted the courage of the Valdosta Branch and its commitment to racial justice. When the leadership of the Dallas Branch complained in 1923 that the threat of the Klan prevented the branch from convening meetings, the director of branches, Robert W. Bagnall, wrote:

> Mrs. Addie H. Hunton, our field secretary, is now making an extended tour throughout the South, covering the states of North Carolina, South Carolina, Georgia, Alabama, Florida and Louisiana. She even plans to visit Valdosta, Georgia. Under these circumstances, it is apparent that there is no real reason why our [the NAACP's] work should not be conducted in Dallas.[32]

Bagnall cited the perseverance of the Valdosta Branch to urge the Dallas Branch to hold regular meetings—or perhaps to shame the members into meeting—despite real pressure from the Klan. While the white community in Brooks and Lowndes Counties had earned a reputation for lynching a pregnant woman and a baby, their Black neighbors established a reputation among NAACP officials for their defiance in the wake of lynching.

In the immediate aftermath of the lynching rampage, however, the Black community turned its attention to the Turners' two orphaned children, Otha and Leaster. Mary Turner had brought her children to her parents' home for their safety following the arrest of her husband, and after losing both parents and an unborn brother or sister to lynch mobs in a matter of days, the children passed between their aunts and uncles on their mother's side of the family for several years. The blues sensibility softly drifted among and enveloped the family as they found ways to live after the horror of the lynchings. Amid this grief and loss, the children grew up alongside their cousins, but still, their relatives, afraid that whites might try to harm the Turner children, gave Otha and Leaster assumed names as a precaution.[33] Otha left Brooks County and moved to Florida as soon as he could make a living on his own. His sister, Leaster, remained in Georgia, and she married a farmer who owned a stretch of land just a few miles from the place where her mother and the baby had been killed. For the remainder of her life, her family and friends wouldn't speak of the lynchings in her presence, to protect her from reliving those traumatic memories. That story was hard enough to talk about among themselves, even when spoken of in whispers. They choked back tears and swallowed their own pain so they could offer her solace, or at least a refuge from her grief.

Those closest to the epicenter of lynchings found ways to make it through and beyond the trauma, but often with great difficulty. Their pain as survivors who had lost people they loved was compounded by the disavowal of their pain by a white southern public that largely shrugged off or even relished Black death. Even as more white southerners shed their open defense of lynching across the twentieth century, the traumatic reverberations of lynching experienced by Black survivors in places like Brooks and Lowndes Counties defied linearity and couldn't be mapped neatly onto these shifts in white public opinion or even advances made by the Black freedom struggle. Survivors like the Turners' children never knew when, if ever, to trust that a change of heart among white southerners was genuine. They never knew if they could trust that social changes like desegregation and the removal of racist voting restrictions would stick, or if they would morph into new forms of degradation and injustice as they had in the past. Instead, those most devastated by the trauma of lynching focused on what they could trust—themselves and their closest confidants. In a move imbued by the blues sensibility, they turned inward to their most tender wounds and vulnerable places, and even as some layers of the pain lifted over time, as grief settled into the marrow of life, the protective armor of the blues sensibility often remained. Those further removed from the epicenter more often had the emotional distance necessary to focus their attention outward at white supremacists and to push back against the injustices perpetrated under Jim Crow, but even they heard a faint echo of the blues trailing them on their journey to something closer to liberation.

The story of Mary Turner's lynching traveled, both across generations and throughout the nation, shaping African American memories of racial and sexual violence against Black people. Passing along local lore to younger generations kept these memories alive, as did articles published in Black newspapers and magazines that circulated throughout the region and the nation.[34] As a child growing up in Chester, South Carolina, during the 1940s, J. Charles Jones heard his father, Joseph Jones, teach him the local lore about the Klan going to the house of a Black man who had "said something" to a white woman. As the younger Jones explained to an interviewer from Duke University in 1993, when the Klan discovered the man was not home, the mob "proceeded to take his wife, who was about eight months pregnant, to a tree, strung her up by the legs, slit her stomach, and the baby rolled out. They left them both. And to this day, nothing was ever done about that."[35] Jones appeared to have blended elements of the Mary Turner lynching with the lynching of Bertha Lowman near Aiken, South Carolina, in October 1926. In the Aiken case, Lowman and two relatives were being held in the local jail while appealing their murder convictions, and the sheriff turned them over to a Klan-led lynch mob that shot the three victims multiple times in a nearby field.[36] The disturbing details of Mary Turner's death left such a deep impression on Jones's mind that, even though her lynching happened hundreds of miles from where Jones grew up, he subconsciously made her story local and personal.[37]

The image of Joseph Jones's face, which expressed both fear and indignation as he told his son the lynching story, remained vivid in Charles Jones's memory in 1993 when he recalled that moment. Perhaps his father thought that passing on this grisly account would serve as a warning that his son should avoid talking to white women, but recounting the details of the lynching, especially that no lynchers faced legal action, also instilled in his son a refusal to tolerate injustice. Jones enfolded Mary Turner's story into his local and personal history and carried the memory of her lynching with him for years. As a young man living in North Carolina during the 1960s, J. Charles Jones joined the Student Nonviolent Coordinating Committee (SNCC) to challenge that same Jim Crow system that celebrated the lynchings of Bertha Lowman and Mary Turner.

Many Black families in and around Waco shared Joseph Jones's decision to pass on stories about lynching. In a time when white men in Waco would "laugh about lynching or a killing," African Americans in and around the city rarely talked about Jesse Washington within earshot of white people as a matter of personal safety, but within the privacy of their homes, fraternal lodges, and churches, those stories persisted in the local lore over several generations.[38] In May 1916 when Jesse Washington was lynched, Eliza Jane Owens and her husband, Robert, lived on a farm just north of Robinson with their widowed son and their granddaughters. The Owenses lived among the leaders of the lynch mob, local whites who most likely knew the Fryers personally. Owens had been enslaved in Georgia and, after emancipation, had walked from Georgia to Texas, and though she rarely dwelled on the past—her memories of enslavement, her long journey across the South, the death of her daughter-in-law and several grandchildren—she didn't shy away from telling her granddaughter Alice, who was just eight years old in 1916, what their white neighbors had done to Jesse Washington. Perhaps she made an exception to her usual reticence to warn the child about the hatred in many a white person's heart—to prepare her to survive the unpredictable world of Jim Crow. Alice never understood how even the deepest of hatreds could drive people to drag, torture, and burn another human being, but from a very young age Alice had no illusions about the potentially deadly repercussions for crossing white folks.[39]

In telling stories about Washington's lynching, Owens also imparted a much more uplifting lesson to her granddaughter, one imbued with the blues sensibility's self-assured and practical handling of hardship through an affirmation of cautious hope, one steeped in the power of religious faith that gave her comfort amid so much despair. As an eighty-five-year-old woman still living in Waco, Alice Owens Caulfield recalled that "dragging people and bringing them to the city hall and burning them, those were the kind of stories I could hear my grandmother saying that this will not happen always."[40] Her grandmother, a deeply religious woman, who could not read but could recite scripture from memory, believed that a just God would provide respite for those enduring injustice. Writing about the experiences of freedpeople like Owens in 1935, W. E. B. Du Bois intoned, "To most of the four million black folk emancipated by civil war, God was real. They knew Him. They had met Him personally in many a wild orgy of religious frenzy, or in the black stillness of the night. His plan for them was clear; they were to suffer and be degraded, and then afterwards by Divine edict, raised to manhood and power; and so on January 1, 1863, He made them free."[41] Owens prayed for the Lord to protect her family from lynching and to deliver the nation from the evil of mob violence, and although she was sure she would never see that deliverance in her lifetime, her faith in the righteousness of the Lord provided hope that her granddaughter Alice would.

For many African Americans though, protest, silence, and prayer could not provide the solace or protection needed to cope with the horror of Jesse Washington's death, and in the months that followed, many Black families left their homes in Waco for good, as so many others would leave their homes two years later in southern Georgia.[42] Waco contained too many reminders that Black death was an entertaining spectacle for their white neighbors, and the standing threat to their lives posed too great a risk to stay.

To seek out the prototypical lynching—the one among the many thousands that exemplified all the gruesome rituals and well-rehearsed narratives and regional variations, the one that most palpably revealed the collective significance of the practice for Black and white communities—would be foolhardy.[43] Lynchings took a wide range of forms, from mass public spectacles to small bands of vigilantes killing their victims in the middle of the night. Some victims were hanged, while others were burned or shot. Some were tortured and mutilated, but, for other victims, death came more swiftly. In the US South, lynchings reinforced white patriarchal control and could arise out of myriad circumstances, including labor disputes, clashes over political power, personal jealousy, minor social transgressions, violent crimes, and economic competition. Lynchings in the US West, while usually entangled with white supremacy, often served the colonialist and state-building ends of the United States as well.[44] Lynching encompassed too wide a range of practices for a single example or two to capture their totality, but even so, close readings of the Jesse Washington and Mary Turner cases illuminate the deeper meaning of lynchings: the composition and assemblage of lynch mobs, the specific rituals performed by mobs, and the racial and gender myths they reinforced. The constituent parts of lynchings that gave structure and meaning to the practice—their anatomy, if you will—not only made the practice easily replicable throughout the South and the nation, but also galvanized white identity around highly performative, collective violence against Black people.[45] The Washington and Turner cases, though necessarily unable to represent all lynchings, demonstrate how white southerners beat back anxieties about race, gender, and class through spectacles of Black death. Returning to lynchings when they were at their peak in the South—how and why they unfolded as they did—also reveals how the extraordinary range of southern lynching memories in the decades that followed were tethered to Black and white responses to lynching in their immediate aftermaths: grief and silence, protest and refusal, gleeful celebration and smug pride, shame and denial.

The Mob

Despite perceptions then and now that lynchings were the product of an irrational, frenzied mob mentality, the violence that white southerners unleashed upon Washington's and Turner's bodies was no spontaneous expression of rage but the central element of well-organized, carefully planned affairs that tried to stamp out white racial and sexual anxieties with lethal force. Jim Crow made the physical and psychological brutalization of Black people routine, and, though lynch mobs could be exceptionally sadistic, lynchings were an extension of this routine brutalization. By the early twentieth century, the ritual of lynching had become so deeply ingrained in southern culture that in places like Waco the sheriff could anticipate the lynching and see the need to relocate Washington to another county jail ahead of the trial. Local whites had attempted to lynch Washington twice before they succeeded in doing so, and by the date of his trial, the fact of his lynching, the location of his lynching, and the manner by which he would die were all practically preordained. The enormous crowds that congregated at the courthouse, bridge, and city hall the morning of the trial knew where to go and when to be there.[46] The lynching was so well coordinated that a Waco photographer of some regional prominence, Frank Gildersleeve, received a call on the morning of the lynching to give him ample time to set up his equipment in city hall. He photographed Washington's grisly death, not merely to document the lynching but to profit from selling copies of the photographs as souvenirs.[47] That mobs assembled so quickly and in predictable patterns was less a reflection of outrage over a particular incident and more the product of a violent culture, steeped in memories (local and national) of lynching, that made Black death routine.[48]

The assemblage of lynch mobs performed an important social function within the white community, bolstering white racial solidarity while rooting white southern identity in the desecration and torture of Black bodies.[49] In Waco, which had a white population of fewer than thirty thousand in 1916 when Washington was lynched, the mob of fifteen thousand represented a significant portion of the white community.[50] The size of the mob in Waco was exceptionally large, even in comparison to other mass mobs, but even so, all lynchings, even those with only a handful of lynchers, were community affairs, often overseen by elected officials and civic leaders. Sheriff Fleming and Judge Munroe did nothing to prevent the mob from seizing Washington, and Mayor John R. Dollins and chief of police Guy McNamara watched the entire violent spectacle from the mayor's office in city hall.[51] In an interview with the NAACP investigator, Elisabeth Freeman, the sheriff claimed that his legal duty to protect a prisoner ended once the trial started, and when pressed to explain why his deputies failed to prevent the lynching, he glibly retorted, "Would you want to protect the nigger?"[52] The mayor, who had watched Washington suffer and die from the perch of his city hall office, expressed more concern about potential damage to the tree outside his window than the dying teenager chained to it.[53] In places like

Waco, where one of the candidates for county sheriff was "said to have three dead 'niggers' to his 'credit,' " lynch mobs reinforced white community norms regarding race and hierarchy, and established a sense of belonging around anti-Black violence.[54] Members of the mob were rarely ostracized by their white neighbors, much less reported to the police or indicted by grand juries or prosecuted by the state, thereby giving tacit, and often explicit, approval to their ghastly deeds.[55]

Even more striking than the sheer mass of white people gathered to watch Washington die was the near unanimity with which the mob acted in service of white supremacy. The reporter for the *Waco Times-Herald* dramatized the synchronized, coordinated efforts of the mob:

> Great masses of humanity flew as swiftly as possible through the streets of the city in order to be present at the bridge when the hanging took place, but when it was learned that the negro was being taken to the city hall lawn, crowds of men, women and children turned and hastened to the lawn.
>
> . . . As rapidly as possible the negro was then jerked into the air at which a shout from thousands of throats went up on the morning air, and dry goods boxes, excelsior, wood and every other article that would burn was then in evidence, appearing as if by magic. . . . The negro's body was swaying in the air and all of the time a noise as of thousands was heard and the negro's body was lowered into the box.
>
> No sooner had his body touched the box than people pressed forward, each eager to be the first to light the fire, matches were touched to the inflammable material and as smoke rapidly rose in the air, such a demonstration as of people gone mad was never heard before. Everybody pressed closer to get souvenirs of the affair. . . .
>
> . . .
>
> Women and children who desired to view the scene were allowed to do so, the crowds parting to let them look on the scene.[56]

The language the reporter used suggested swarms of people combining to become a single, monstrous body. In the panoramas of the crowd that Gildersleeve took, individual faces disappeared under an endless sea of hats surrounding Washington's body. The uniform pattern of blurry hats in these photographs captured both the anonymity of the individuals in the mob and the unity of the white community. The mob literally contracted when it feverishly closed in on Washington's body to collect souvenirs, and the singular purpose with which the mob scrambled to gather wood and set Washington's body ablaze reflected how lynching fortified the white community's shared interest in remaining in near absolute control over all aspects of Black life.[57]

The immediate causes of individual lynchings varied, but many functioned as a means to quash Black social and political power, and to bolster white economic domination. The lynching rampage in which Mary Turner died had its origins in a labor dispute between a white farmer and Black farmhands—an argument over repeated instances of physical abuse, overwork, and exploitative contracts. The lynching spree was, in essence, the white community using terror to prevent future labor uprisings and to protect the exploitative economic relationships white farmers had with Black farmhands, tenant farmers, and sharecroppers. In the aftermath of the violence, Black families fled in droves, leaving many whites without their labor force. Flight came at a cost, however. Black families often left behind farms and homes that their white neighbors gladly plundered in their absence, which depleted Black wealth for generations. Fleeing the violence also severed social ties, so while lynchings strengthened bonds among whites, they often fractured Black communities, scattering whole families across the nation.[58]

Lynching culture was, by design, intergenerational. For white children, witnessing these rituals was an initiation during which they were taught that—like their parents, their white neighbors, and their civic and political leaders—they should be invested in maintaining white supremacy. Unlike Black parents who tried to divert their children *away* from mobs and violence, at least one white father in the crowd held up his son so he could get a clearer view. Another little boy sat perched in the upper branches of the tree that Washington was chained to, and he remained there until the flames consuming Washington's body started creeping up its trunk. Several white boys, probably no more than ten or eleven years old, stood within a half dozen yards of Washington's body to watch the tortures unfold. They were skipping school to watch Washington die, but they received an education of another kind, an education about how expendable Black life was in Texas.[59] No wonder African Americans had this saying about white folks: "If you kill a nigger, I'll hire another nigger. . . . If you kill a mule, I'll buy another one."[60]

The Washington lynching was a public display of unity within the white community, but it was also a means to silence dissent among its ranks. One eyewitness to the lynching, Joseph Martin Dawson, recalled, "I was present at City Hall within a few feet of where the Negro was burned, entirely helpless because five thousand monsters participated and who was I, a lone individual, to do anything about it?"[61] Dawson, the pastor at Waco's First Baptist Church, later delivered a Sunday sermon criticizing mob rule, though the impact of his belated tongue-lashing probably failed to stir the consciences of the mob members among his flock. Within weeks of Washington's death, he also introduced to the Waco Pastors' Association a resolution denouncing lynching.[62] Whether moved by his conscience or by the obvious contradictions between the Christian gospel and ritualistic torture and murder, Dawson risked going against prevailing white public opinion, though clearly from a position of safety as a well-respected white southern minister. Other white ministers supported his resolution, but none of them joined him in leading a public campaign against lynching. In fact, fifty-five years later, he lamented, "Such noble people as Dr. Charles T. Caldwell, pastor of First Presbyterian Church for a long period and highly regarded, refused to say a thing about [the lynching], due likely to his intense Southern uprearing."[63] A culture of lynching sustained by whites with an "intense Southern uprearing" ultimately drowned out voices of southern white dissent like Dawson's.

As news of the city's barbarity spread across the country and around the world, Waco faced a flood of condemnation, and the unwelcome notoriety prompted some city boosters and white elites to become more circumspect about the lynching, at least in the presence of outsiders. Over time, many whites hoped that silence—pretending the lynching did not happen, returning to regular routines, displacing culpability for the lynching, not pursuing legal action against the lynchers—would somehow absolve them of guilt and erase this ugly episode from their memories. However, even the belated, tepid protests from the white community that were often grudgingly extracted out of shame rather than from a sense of justice were too little, too late. As far as the editor of the Black newspaper, the *Houston Informer*, was concerned, after roasting Jesse Washington alive in 1916 and burning the corpse of Jesse Thomas in 1922, the white people of the self-anointed "City with a Soul" had earned their city a new nickname, Barbecueville.[64]

Even so, both during and long after these gruesome spectacles, lynch mobs not only represented a collective expression of punishment for particular crimes and transgressions, but also served the collective interests of the white community, which was still preoccupied, if not obsessed, with maintaining control over the South after emancipation and Reconstruction had unsettled the foundations of white supremacy. The mob silenced dissent among its ranks and enforced white solidarity through collective anti-Black terrorism. The mob, quite simply, embodied white power.[65]

The Ritual

The festive atmosphere that surrounded lynchings had an eerie resemblance to more mundane social gatherings like county fairs, weddings, and church revivals, even when lynchings took place in the dead of night. At both kinds of gatherings, people often dressed in their finest clothing with their children in tow, hoping to come away from these memorable occasions with a souvenir. But as deadly public performances of white supremacy, lynchings tended to generate a heightened buzz of excitement, for the "reward" for the white community was a collective release of built-up anxiety, paranoia, anger, and guilt. As a general rule, communal rituals function to make meaning and establish tradition, to create the social pressure necessary to enforce norms by offering both a reprieve from the everyday and the comfort of familiarity. The rituals that developed around lynching were no different. The attempt to compel a confession and bleed out a plea for mercy, the slow torture and disfigurement of Black bodies, the resemblance to a blood sacrifice that assuaged the guilt of the sinful, and the prolonged display of dead corpses and souvenirs cultivated a sense of belonging and unity among white southerners by publicly performing the real meaning of whiteness: power.[66]

For all the prolynching rhetoric about punishment and justice, lynch mobs were far less focused on what the victim had allegedly done to spark the lynching and more concerned with performing the social function of lynching rituals. In many cases, lynching the "right" person was an afterthought because the ritual breaking of Black bodies mattered more than the particular bodies being broken. Black bodies were, in the eyes of the lynch mob, interchangeable—they were reduced to objects of white contempt. Chime Riley, one of the victims of the lynching spree in Brooks County, Georgia, for instance, was not even remotely involved in the death of Hampton Smith. After he died, the mob tied his hands and feet, and weighed his body down with cups used to catch turpentine so that his body would sink to the bottom of the Little River near Barney. Riley's lynching was not unusual. To the mob, his was just another Black death to add to the body count.[67] Just as killing the "right" victim was of little concern to many mobs, the circumstances of the perceived transgression often fell by the wayside as well. Hampton Smith was far from beloved among his white neighbors, but because he was white like them (and like many of them a landowner who employed Black tenant farmers), avenging his death, though he was known to be a cruel and unsavory person, was deemed necessary for upholding the racial and economic order.[68]

Though some historians have drawn distinctions between lynchings that drew large crowds in broad daylight and those covertly conducted under the cover of darkness, the spectacle itself always remained a consistent ritual element. Lynchings where thousands of spectators attended, photographers sold souvenir postcards, or the torture and mutilation of the bodies was particularly sadistic were clearly intended to be a spectacle. The goal was not simply to kill a victim but to inflict and prolong suffering until the mob was satisfied that the ritual breaking of the Black body had provided the desired relief from its fury and anxiety over some real or imagined racial indiscretion. The lynching of Mary Turner was, at every step, a collective performance of dehumanization, a process of transforming a Black woman who protested the unjust lynching of her husband into an object upon which to unload the mob's fury. The lynching was a public demonstration of white power rooted in a faith that Turner's death would somehow protect them, that her screams and her tortured body would save them from the threat they imagined their Black neighbors posed. After burying her body, they went home, reassured that they were, once again, safely in control.[69]

However, even absent those overt demonstrations of violence or prolonged suffering, the public display of dead bodies in the aftermath of lynchings was, itself, a spectacle. The lynched body of Mary Turner's husband, Hayes Turner, for instance, remained hanging from a tree at a major crossroads for several days before being cut down, so that whites who weren't present at the lynching could still witness his death and take in the symbolic meaning of his lifeless body. His hanging corpse also served as a warning to African Americans, both those who dared to venture out during the lynching rampage and those who simply knew that his body was left to rot for days.

Long after the bodies of lynching victims were removed from public view, souvenirs harvested from lynchings—whether preserved in picture frames or in pickling jars—provided material reminders of white su-premacist violence that participants and their descendants, relatives, and friends returned to. These grisly "mementos" ranged from body parts hacked off a mangled body and photographs of a lynching in progress to staged photographs that members of the mob took with lynched bodies and objects taken from the site of the lynching like bits of rope and scraps of a makeshift scaffold or pyre. During Washington's lynching, members of the mob sliced off his fingers, toes, ears, and shreds of cloth-ing, and afterwards some purchased the links in the chain around his neck for twenty-five cents apiece as well as souvenir photographs from Gildersleeve.[70] One man bought Washington's teeth for five dollars each from the little boys who had extracted them from what remained of his severed and badly charred head.[71]

A white Texan named James Kuykendall Evetts recalled the symbolic power of these souvenirs in telling the story of his father who, as the county attorney for Bell County, had tried to protect a Black man from falling into the hands of a lynch mob in 1912. Evetts recounted: "And the Negro was taken and lynched and the man, the next day, that had been a friend of Dad's—never was after that—came up there [to his father's of-fice] and brought a toe bone from the Negro's pyre where they burned him and handed it to Dad. And it made Dad so mad that Dad got up and threw him down the stairway."[72] The bone functioned like a talisman. The literal repossession of a Black body (part) harkened back to slavery, reassuring this former friend that white mastery, even with slavery long since abolished, was secure once again.

The rituals associated with lynching, for all the violent disfigurement and dismemberment, provided a perverse comfort and reassurance to white southern communities, but, as James Baldwin observed, the "flames meant to exorcise the terrors of the mob" were merely a distraction from white self-hatred, a deflection from their inner demons.[73] Those feelings of relief, which were the product of bloodlust, were ill gotten and fleet-ing. Sacrificing lynching victims could never provide members of these mobs the redemption they desperately sought, but African Americans, from Du Bois to Langston Hughes, found amid the horror some re-demptive possibilities for Black people in these rituals. They saw intimate connections between the crucifixion of Christ and the lynching of Black people, or what James Cone called "the cross and the lynching tree," both of which became "symbols that represented both death and the promise of redemption, judgment and the offer of mercy, suffering and the power of hope."[74] The paradox that suffering was redemptive for Black people rhymed with the cautious optimism of the blues sensibility, itself an expression of joy and hope amid terror and pain.[75]

The Myth

Although the lynching of Jesse Washington was grislier than most, those drawn to the spectacle of his death attended the lynching in large part because of an insidious myth that the Black antilynching activist Ida B. Wells described as "the old thread bare lie that Negro men rape white women."[76] The myth of the Black rapist originated in the white fixation upon Black men's genitalia and proslavery rhetoric that described Black men as brutes who needed to be tamed by the rigid controls of enslavement and later lynching. As historian George Fredrickson explained, "The only way [for white southerners] to meet criticisms of the unspeakably revolting practice of lynching was to contend that many Negroes were literally wild beasts, with uncontrollable sexual passions and criminal natures stamped by heredity."[77] In doing so, white southerners projected their guilt about their own brutality and sexual desires onto Black people—brutality that included the largely overlooked crime of white men raping Black women, a crime made visible on the faces of generations of mixed-race children. Fears about miscegenation (at least in cases involving Black men and white women) were wrapped up in white men's sexual anxieties over their own virility and who controlled women's bodies, especially white women's bodies. Emancipation only heightened these sexual anxieties since free Black men stood to compete for economic, social, and political power in the South. Rape discourse became the terrain for managing white men's economic, social, and political anxieties.[78]

In light of the cultural currency that "protecting" white womanhood enjoyed in the South, the prevalence of castration of lynching victims, including Washington, is unsurprising. Castration as a punishment for Black men originated in the colonial period when several American colonies made certain offenses, including rape, striking a white person, and running away, punishable by castration, and in all of the colonies with these laws except Pennsylvania, the punishment applied exclusively to African Americans and Native Americans. "Writing sexual retaliation into law," as Winthrop Jordan put it, only underscored the depths of sexual insecurity among white men and the "fairly widespread and strong feeling on the 'protection' of white women."[79] Emasculating Black men in the colonial period as a legal punishment and during Jim Crow through lynching provided a means for white men to publicly demonstrate their dominance over Black men whom they saw as sexual competition for women, thereby easing their sexual insecurities.[80] Through rhetoric that claimed this violence protected white women, white men maintained racial and patriarchal control while conferring the benefits of whiteness upon white women. White women could spell death for a Black man with a rape accusation or a consensual relationship gone sour or even no indiscretion at all, while Black women were exposed to violence, degradation, and exploitation with few if any protections.[81]

Despite the pervasiveness of the Black rapist myth in the South, in reality, most Black men who were lynched were not accused of rape; in Washington's case, the white community simply assumed Lucy Fryer had been raped from the moment coverage of her murder appeared in newspapers but without any corroborating evidence.[82] Waco newspapers claimed that Fryer had been brutally raped before she was killed, but the trial raised serious doubts about the alleged rape. Washington admitted to murdering Fryer in his initial verbal confession, but only in the written version, which he certainly did not write himself, did he confess to rape and murder. Even with this written confession in hand, the grand jury did not charge Washington with rape, and during the trial, the prosecution neglected to ask the doctor who performed the autopsy on Fryer, Dr. J. H. Maynard, whether she had been raped, even though Washington's full confession was read aloud in court. The prosecution's decision to ignore that line of questioning is particularly curious since, only a week earlier, the *Waco Times-Herald* reported, "Dr. Maynard declared this morning [the morning after the body was discovered] he was positive that Mrs. Fryar [*sic*] had been ravished."[83] The trial may have been a mere formality, but the prosecution's omission of any reference to rape may have reflected a reluctance to further sully the justice system with a fabricated charge that simply fit the most common excuse for lynching.

The sexual violence performed during lynchings was not limited to the castration of Black men. When lynch mobs targeted Black women, they often used sexual violence to enforce racialized and gendered expectations for Black women, in particular the idea that Black women were naturally licentious and sexually available to white men whenever they so desired and that they were beneath consideration as mothers and wives. In 1911, a lynch mob in Okemah, Oklahoma, raped Laura Nelson before hanging her from a bridge next to her son whose body was stripped from the waist down. Lynch mobs often targeted Black women like Nelson for being accomplices to alleged crimes or for simply being related to the perpetrators of alleged crimes and social indiscretions, most especially in cases in which the alleged perpetrators evaded capture.[84] Four years later, the *Chicago Defender* reported that a mob that had stripped and hanged Cordelia Stevenson in Columbus, Mississippi, had also raped her before ending her life.[85] The white men who raped and then lynched Black women, like the white men who castrated and then lynched Black men, enacted a desecration of Black bodies to symbolically destroy Black families. Their deaths alone devastated families and communities for generations, but the rape of women like Nelson and Stevenson added further horror and humiliation, while further emasculating their male family members by implying that they were powerless to protect them. The public sexual violation of Black women also drew an even starker distinction between Black women (particularly Black mothers) and white women, marking Black women as beyond the protection of society *as women* and forcing them outside the boundaries of southern womanhood.[86]

The political implications of lynching Black women were no less meaningful in the Jim Crow South since lynch mobs also policed their engagement in public discourse. Mary Turner became a target of a lynch mob precisely because she decried the lynching of her husband and demanded legal justice.[87] At a time when Black men were functionally disenfranchised and women were legally disenfranchised, her remarks, in effect, made a claim to political and social power reserved for white men, which made her refusal to remain silent all the more threatening to the white patriarchal social order. To punish her transgressions and stanch further protest from the Black community, the mob killed her. In the process, the white community marked her as unfit for the political power she claimed for herself and unworthy of the gendered protections granted to white mothers.[88]

Lynch mobs intended to reinforce the strength and vitality of white patriarchal power by tapping into the fears and anxieties that enveloped the myth of the Black rapist. The ubiquitous acceptance of this myth within the white community, however, certainly did not extend to Black southerners. The antilynching pamphlets of Wells and later the NAACP's campaigns to pass antilynching legislation dispelled the Black rapist myth, but Black communities had easily seen through this "threadbare lie" because, unlike their white neighbors, they didn't need to believe it—they didn't rely on self-deception in the way that white southerners, who needed to comfort themselves with illusions and smokescreens, did. White southerners rationalized white supremacist violence by projecting their own violence, especially their own sexual violence, onto Black men. Having endured the brunt of white supremacy for centuries, Black people knew that the rape of Black women by white men was far more rampant and virtually unprosecuted. They already knew, and they had to know as a matter of safety and survival, that lynching was about securing white power, not rape.

––––––––––––

After the smoke cleared and the mobs dispersed, a semblance of calm settled over Waco and Brooks County, and these communities resumed their old routines. Despite the appearance of normalcy, the traumatic wake of these lynchings had washed over these communities and pooled in the collective memories and the scenes of violence themselves, leaving no one untouched, not even those clinging to their own denials.[89] As violent spectacles, lynchings were supposed to attract witnesses who would remember, and leave survivors who couldn't forget. The sites of lynchings, as well as the souvenir photographs and bones and chains and fingers preserved in pickling jars, were also vessels of memory, perhaps not containing the specific details of a particular lynching but certainly holding the force and meaning of lynching as a means to protect white power. By design, lynchings long outlived their perpetrators and survivors, leaching from one generation of southerners to the next through local lore, and the daily reminders of white supremacy's power continued to shape all manner of social interactions and systems of power.

To track down the afterlife of a lynching, then, is as much a process of recovering narratives themselves as it is a process of understanding narrativity, most especially listening to gaps and pauses for meaning, leaning into slight misdirections and cloaked metaphors for clues about the past. A lifetime after a close brush with Jesse Washington's lynching, Carrie Skipwith Mayfield retold her experience for an oral memoir recorded at the Baylor University Institute for Oral History, but *how* she remembered revealed just as much as *what* she remembered of that day in May 1916. Before she went to school on the morning of the lynching, her father, Vivienne Skipwith, told her not to take her usual route down Sixth Street. Not wanting her to ask too many questions or to defy him, he decided not to explain the diversion. But his headstrong thirteen-year-old let her curiosity get the best of her and weaved through the crowd of white men congregated on the courthouse lawn, waiting, she would later learn, for Jesse Washington. On her way home from school that same afternoon, she and her friends walked by the storefronts of downtown

Waco's white-owned businesses, and they noticed charred chunks of what they eventually would learn was human flesh proudly displayed in store windows. When Mayfield walked through the doorway of her home that afternoon, her father didn't hush up the neighbors who were "up in the air talking about it [the lynching of Jesse Washington]" because by then the truth could not be avoided.[90] Her father's decision to map a different route for her was as much an act of love and protection as an act of resistance, as much a detour away from the path of the lynching as a detour away from the venom of white supremacy. He could try to shield his daughter from becoming a witness to and survivor of the lynching, but in the end he could not protect her from knowing that a mob had burned and sliced souvenirs from a Black man's body, just blocks from home.[91]

Remembering that day more than seven decades later, Mayfield struggled to find the words to capture her father's act of love:

> I said, "Lord have mercy, that's why Papa didn't want me to go that way," because he knew what was happening, but he did not want me to know. That was the most—ooh. And I don't know what to say—I've never—the tree where they hanged his [Washington's] body and brought it up Sixth Street. Brought it right up, dragging it behind a car, right up on Sixth Street. But we got home before all that happened. We didn't get to see any of that. We just heard of it after it happened. I don't know what I would have done if I had have seen it. You know, just to see the actual thing. But it happened. It absolutely happened. It happened in my day.[92]

Though grateful for being spared the terror of watching the slow torture and desecration of Washington's body, as she replayed scenes from that day more than seven decades later, she hesitated—she shuddered—and the memories trickled back. The distance between past and present closed, and the past came back haltingly, in fragments. Long after the mob wandered home from the square around city hall and Washington's body had been dragged away, signs of the Waco horror lingered as Mayfield retraced, through her memories, the path where his body had been dragged. From the souvenir body parts in window displays to the burnt leaves on the tree branches from which his dead body had hung, the mob left physical reminders of the violence on the landscape, the memory of which would become psychological debris that Mayfield carried for the rest of her life. The

wincing pain that dug into her pauses, the hesitation surrounding her refusal to put some memories into words, much less in narrative form, revealed how deeply the trauma had taken root. The unuttered words and
the trauma she couldn't shake, however, mingled with memories of her father's love, which carried her through and beyond the lynching.

In "The Haunted Oak," the poet Paul Laurence Dunbar renders literal the lingering presence of lynching in southern geographies, a nod to
the trauma that lynching survivors like Mayfield experienced over their
lifetimes.[93] The poem imagines an oak tree narrating the tale of an innocent man whose lynching has cursed the limb from which he was hanged:

> Pray why are you so bare, so bare,
>   Oh, bough of the old oak-tree;
> And why, when I go through the shade you throw,
>   Runs a shudder over me.
>
> . . . .
>
> Oh, foolish man, why weep you now?
>   'Tis but a little space,
> And the time will come when these shall dread
>   The mem'ry of your face.
>
> I feel the rope against my bark,
>   And the weight of him in my grain,
> I feel in the throe of his final woe
>   The touch of my own last pain.
>
> And never more shall these leaves come forth
>   On a bough that bears the ban.
> I am burned with dread, I am dried and dead,
>   From the curse of a guiltless man.
>
> And ever the judge rides by, rides by,
>   And goes to hunt the deer,
> And ever another rides his soul
>   In the guise of mortal fear.
>
> And ever the man he rides me hard,
>   And never a night stays he;
> For I feel his curse as a haunted bough,
>   On the trunk of a haunted tree.[94]

The old oak tree bore more than witness to the lynching. It bore "the curse of a guiltless man" and bore the responsibility to pass along the dead man's story, a weight that thousands of southern lynching sites and many hundreds of thousands of southern families carried for generations. Not everyone who paused in the shade of a lynching tree would feel the slight chill of a ghost's presence or see in a blighted branch the curse of an unresolved crime that ate at their consciences, but some southerners shuddered as they passed through these spaces that carried the burden of memory. The judge in the poem, haunted by the lynched man riding his soul, had his very real counterparts among white southerners saddled with guilt. Less remorseful whites would smile as they passed the bough that refused to grow leaves. African Americans, too, felt haunted by memories of the dead, through visions of their corpses that returned from time to time, from the emptiness left by their absences. And for many more, the curse of the haunted bough silently lurked in the darker recesses of their minds, waiting, watching, biding its time.

CHAPTER TWO

Silence

Memory

salted, the wounds healed away,

but here, by the sea, grew raw again.

—ISHION HUTCHINSON, "Terminus"

THE MOMENT JESSE PENNINGTON burst into the house, his mother started screaming—screaming because she knew, though not a word had passed between her and her fifteen-year-old son, that he was in "white folks trouble." As a car sped toward the house, his frantic mother warned, "You can't run. You gotta hide." The teenager ducked out through the back door and crawled under the house into a large hole dug for installing a septic tank. His father had headed north for a job in Chicago a few weeks earlier, so when Pennington hid, he left his mother and sister alone to face the three hotheaded white men who barged into their home. Just above his head, the men barked, "Where is he? Where is he?" as they tore up the house, looking for the impudent Black teenager who dared to knock down a white man, a deputy sheriff at that. To each question hurled at her, his mother insisted, "He is not here! He is not here!" Unable to find Pennington among all the upturned furniture, the men eventually left.[1]

Earlier that afternoon, Pennington had been walking home after a slow day at work in a Greenville, Mississippi, milk bar. It was late June

47

1954, and the Delta had already settled into another hot, sticky summer. Surrounded by rows and rows of cotton, he plodded along Highway 1, which cuts through the Mississippi Delta from north to south. As he made his way home, a car slowed and pulled to the side of the road in front of him. Out stepped a deputy sheriff and two other white men who ambled over to Pennington. One of the men owned a construction company, and somebody had been using his equipment after hours without his permission. He eyed the teenager and said, "I got a report that said you look like the boy who's been doing it." Pennington placated them with the usual signs of deference that whites expected of Black boys—smiles and yes sirs and no sirs—assuring the men he wasn't the one using the equipment, and after several tense minutes of bluster, the owner of the construction company finally let up, convinced that he had interrogated the wrong person after all.[2]

The deputy sheriff wasn't satisfied, though. Perhaps the Supreme Court decision to desegregate public schools just one month earlier had exposed the fragility of his sense of authority and intensified the rawness of his anti-Black resentment, as it had for so many other white southerners.[3] He wanted Pennington to feel the sting of humiliation. The deputy probably suspected Pennington hadn't taken the equipment, but he wanted to degrade and humiliate him anyhow. He wanted to feel secure in his power as a white southern man and as the law. He and the other two men jeered at Pennington, telling him that, like all Black boys, he looked like a monkey. Then, the deputy spotted a pile of cow dung next to Pennington's foot. He looked down at the half-crusted manure, glanced back at the teenager's face, and said, "I wonder what this nigger would look like if I wiped this shit in his face." The deputy sheriff reached down and grabbed a handful of manure, but before he could smear it on Pennington's face, the young man reflexively hit him with a quick left and right, knocking him to the ground. Pennington took off, tearing through fields and woods until he got home to his mother.

An hour after the three men had torn through the Penningtons' belongings, they returned, but with reinforcements: a truck with several men piled in the back, two more carloads of men, and bloodhounds. Pennington's sister told him to hide as the caravan approached, but with bloodhounds to evade, the hole under the house would no longer provide reliable cover. He couldn't be sure that he could outrun all those men and the dogs, and the Delta's perfectly flat cotton fields offered no cover anyhow. His only option was the outhouse in the backyard. Never an especially pleasant place to be, the outhouse was particularly fetid that afternoon. The outhouse hole was practically filled to the brim with sewage that had been stewing under the Mississippi summer sun all day, but, left with no alternatives, he snuck out and climbed into the hole. As he sank down into the warm sewage, the bloodhounds picked up his scent and led the posse to the outhouse. Hearing the dogs howling and barking excitedly just outside the door, the teenager's mind was racing. "Is this it? Am I going to die?" he wondered. The dogs knew he was hiding just below the toilet seat, but when the man holding the dogs' leashes kicked in the door and the stench hit him like a brick wall, he backed away, telling the others, "Naw, he can't be in there." The dogs tugged against their leashes, their noses just inches from his face, but the man jerked them away. Disappointed, the posse piled back into their vehicles, leaving one man behind to keep watch for a few hours more before he, too, gave up and left.

Pennington's mother sprang into action. She got word to her father in nearby Scott, Mississippi, that her son was in trouble, and she directed him to hide in the woods on the other side of the field until a neighbor could drive him up to Scott, where he washed off and got a clean change of clothing. As luck would have it, Pennington's aunt, his father's older sister, had driven down from Chicago that day to visit her other brother in Hollandale, Mississippi, a Delta town south of Greenville. To this day, Pennington does not know how his mother got in touch with his aunt, but once she reached Hollandale around midnight, she turned right around and picked up Pennington at his grandfather's house in Scott. With a lynch mob and sheriff still out looking for him, he crawled into the trunk of his aunt's car and remained stowed away until they reached Kentucky. He was alive. He had escaped Mississippi alive.

Just over one year later, on August 28, 1955, a fourteen-year-old Black boy from Chicago, named Emmett Till, wasn't so lucky. He did not escape Mississippi alive. He died in the Delta, lynched by two white men infuriated by his insistence that he, too, had a right to his dignity. Till reportedly refused to temper his defiance of the Jim Crow social mores that demanded Black deference to his killers, nor did he beg for mercy, and so they beat and tortured and then shot him.[4] Both boys swung back, so to speak, but only Pennington lived to tell his story.[5] Pennington, who was living in Chicago when Till's corpse was brought back from Mississippi for a public viewing, soon came face to face with what might have been his fate. Till's mother, Mamie Till-Mobley, had decided to show the world her son's body to expose the abject barbarity of white Mississippians, and thousands of Chicagoans paid their respects, including Pennington. As he walked toward Till's open casket, hundreds of people were crying, screaming, and fainting all around him. He remembered the viewing as the most intense expression of grief he ever witnessed.

Pennington's brush with lynching remained unsettled and unsettling. He owed his life to the courage and quick thinking of his family—his mother, his sister, his grandfather, his aunt, his uncle—but what began with his mother's screams ended with a long, painful silence. Almost sixty years later, he recalled:

> When I got to Chicago . . . my aunt took me in to see my father. And I ran out to him and said, "Daddy! Daddy! Let me tell you what happened." And he said, "I don't want to talk about it. Stop. I don't want to hear about it." No, that was it. That was it. And that's—people don't understand that Black folk kept [quiet about] violence. They didn't talk about things that happened to people, did not talk about it. They would just—you didn't talk about it. Many things that happened to folks, they didn't talk about it within the family. You just didn't talk about it. You just buried it. You didn't talk about it. And remember I said, from that moment on, it was buried. I mean, it was just in my psyche. It affected me in a certain way. It affected me in that I didn't know that it had affected me.[6]

Pennington buried those memories and all the feelings that accompanied them, but they had not disappeared. Those memories lay dormant in a hidden corner of his subconscious, waiting for him.

Pennington's father imposed this silence upon his son—on the whole family, in fact—but his reaction was more complex than unfeeling coldness or a lack of compassion. During his son's harrowing escape from the lynch mob, he had been too far away—up in Chicago preparing for his family to join him—so he could not intervene when the bloodhounds and mob arrived at his doorstep. Even if he had been in Greenville instead of Chicago, he probably would have been powerless to intervene on behalf of his son. For generations, lynching had given white communities a way to assert control over Black bodies, especially Black men's bodies, but mob rule and Jim Crow more generally also subverted Black parents' roles as providers and protectors of their families. Perhaps his father's terse response to this terrifying experience grew out of his feeling ashamed and frustrated that he had been unable to uphold his paternal responsibility to protect his child. He didn't want to be reminded of his family's vulnerability to the violent whims of white people or of his forced abdication of responsibility, so he enveloped his son's traumatic memories in silence.

Violence moved the Penningtons from Greenville to Chicago, but even before that deputy sheriff tried to smear cow manure on their teenaged son's face, violence had moved the Penningtons. One morning a few years earlier, Pennington's mother had told him, "They found Mary's body in the river. I knew that was going to happen," and soon after that the family picked up and moved to Greenville. Mary was a family friend who had often "gone with" white men, and when the last of these men had ordered her to have sex with all of his friends at a hunting party and she had refused, they killed her and threw her body into the river. White supremacist, patriarchal violence was endemic to the Delta, but to the Penningtons, Jesse wasn't a stranger in a far-off place or even a neighbor like Mary. He was *theirs*. He was their son, brother, nephew, and grandson, and he had hidden in their outhouse and the trunk of their car to evade a posse of white men set on lynching him. Pennington's parents could find the words to discuss with their son what had happened to Mary, but they refused to talk about his near lynching precisely because his emotional proximity to them made those wounds too tender to reopen. He was too close and too precious, and his escape had been too precarious and too lucky. His survival had been so hard fought that, in the aftermath, the life of the strong-willed Black boy who punched a white man in Mississippi seemed too delicate and fragile to dwell upon, even after he had safely made it to Chicago.

The silence that enveloped the Penningtons was not the only silence in the cultural memory of lynching in Greenville, Mississippi. The white community had its share of silences, too. In a collection of interviews with Mississippi writers published in 1982, the editor said to the historian and novelist Shelby Foote, "I have read that a lot of people think that the fact that there wasn't ever a lynching in Washington County [where Greenville is located], and the fact that the Klan never gained a foot in the local politics.... [Foote: Yes.] ... and even the fact that Hodding Carter could come there and write freely this type of [liberal] journalism, was due to the atmosphere that the [socially and politically prominent] Percy family created."[7] Foote, a native of Greenville, noted that the presence of many prominent Jews in Greenville helped to curb the activities of the Klan, and he added:

> The Percy influence was the main current sociological bar to the Klan. They set a style and an adherence to truth and justice that the Klan could have no part in, and people subscribed to that, so they had a high example in the community to go by, to guide them. . . . Senator [LeRoy] Percy was strongly anti-Klan and expressed himself so at every opportunity. Mr. Will [Percy] as a young man did what he could in that direction, too. In *Lanterns on the Levee*, he tells about the election that was held and how the Klan candidates were defeated. There are still some prominent men in Greenville who were members of the Klan, and old citizens know who they are and don't feel too kindly toward them to this day. It was not really as horrendous a thing as it sounds now. The Klan was political, almost social. I don't think that they intended to lynch anybody or put anybody in ovens or anything like that. Most of the members of it were politicians who were looking for bloc votes.[8]

Foote's reminiscences indulged in a nostalgia that, though comforting to him, also conveniently erased racial violence from his hometown. To begin with, Washington County was certainly not a safe haven from lynching. Between 1890 and 1914, at least fifteen people lost their lives to lynching, and several of those lynchings took place in Greenville where, according to Foote, the Percys, a powerful political and literary family, had kept the lawless element at bay.[9] A certain segment of the Greenville elite may have opposed the Klan and preferred the so-called paternalism of the planter class, but, though the Klan and later the Citizens' Council didn't "put anybody in ovens," they certainly served as more than toothless social or political clubs.

Clashes between race-baiters and the more outwardly measured planters were persistent features of the southern political landscape, but the Percys' motives for opposing the Klan were less than altruistic. During Reconstruction, W. A. Percy deemed the violent tactics of the Klan unnecessary to "redeem" the South from African Americans and northern Republicans, but he did not challenge the desirability of Redemption—violently restoring political control to white Democrats—itself. Several decades later, in the 1920s, his son LeRoy Percy expended great political

and social capital to curtail Klan activity, but for the purposes of preserving his own political influence and keeping the Black labor force on his
plantation from leaving the Delta. Father and son opposed the violence
of lynch mobs and the race-baiting demagoguery of politicians like James
K. Vardaman and Theodore Bilbo, but neither man gave a second thought
to exploiting their Black workforce, often in ways that closely resembled
enslavement. In fact, that ill-treatment probably explained why the Penningtons moved off the Percy plantation two months after their son was
born in 1938.[10]

Foote curiously placed blame for lynching squarely on the Klan even
though the Klan was not active between 1890 and 1914, and this displacement of responsibility for racial violence away from the white men
and women in his hometown who organized and joined lynch mobs constructed an imaginary barrier between Greenville and lynching. Foote
preferred to keep lynching at a comfortable distance from himself and
his beloved community because he wanted to believe it was a cultured
literary oasis in the heart of the Mississippi Delta. He imagined himself
as part of a literary lineage that included "progressive" white journalists
like Hodding Carter and celebrated novelists like Will Percy, and he
hoped that that insulated him from the racial violence that enveloped the
Mississippi Delta. If the near-lynching of Jesse Pennington was too close
and painful for the Penningtons to revisit, the history of lynching in
Washington County was too close and shameful for Foote to admit,
much less confront.

Silences litter the collective memories of any historical phenomenon.
What Michel-Rolph Trouillot said about historical narratives—that they
are "a particular bundle of silences"—applies equally to collective memories and to individual memories.[11] The custodians of collective memories,
from professional historians to the keepers of family lore, consciously
and unconsciously exclude or push aside or erase parts of the past, ignore
difficult questions, and dismiss certain voices and details while amplify-
ing others. In the process of constructing and reconstructing these memories, southerners of all races silence parts of the past, especially those
parts they don't want to remember, don't want to hear, don't want to pass
on, or don't want to believe. The reasons for these silences are by no
means uniform. The Pennington family's silence was motivated by protection and care, which was a far cry from the denial among white Americans that James Baldwin described as "so thoroughly unattractive a

delusion."[12] But just because some remnants of the past were ignored or rendered invisible at a given point in time did not mean that they disappeared. These omissions told stories of their own, and many of these hidden memories refused to remain stowed away for good.

The silences surrounding memories of lynching were leaden to African Americans who suppressed them to protect themselves and their families and to whites who suppressed them out of denial, but Black and white southerners certainly did not bear equally the weight they carried. White southerners used silence primarily to reinforce the lie that they were untouched by crimes committed on behalf of the white race. As shifting social mores after World War II, especially during the civil rights movement, rendered lynching increasingly a cause for shame rather than celebration, whites went to great lengths to conceal the history of lynching, distort their collective memories of the past, and preserve the myth of white innocence. These white silences, whether secrets about lynching or deflections away from lynching that morphed into claims of white victimhood, offered protection from public shame and ridicule through their evasion of white culpability. Perhaps more aptly described as white *noise*, many white silences and denials attempted to drown out and speak over obvious truths about southern lynching.[13] This gradual move toward white silence was not absolute, however. Some white southerners continued to brazenly endorse lynching and carry out lynchings, and even those who chose silence often still clung to old memories of lynching for the comfort of knowing that they, unlike Black southerners, were protected by and from that violence. For many, ignoring or erasing lynching simply provided a thin cover for their complicity in white supremacist violence—these silences were ploys crafted by people who publicly denied things that they knew to be true or publicly reviled things they actually relished. Whether a matter of prudence or shame, denial simply served their interests.

Take, for instance, what the manager of the Monroe-Walton County Chamber of Commerce, C. W. Sherlock, told President Harry Truman about some local Black churches and a Black school in the county that had been burned to the ground in 1947. In an attempt to explain away these racially motivated arsons, most likely committed by the Klan, he assured the president, "We are positive that in no place in these United States are our colored friends treated with more respect and deference than in Walton County, Georgia."[14] Sherlock neglected to mention that his hometown of Monroe, which is the county seat of Walton

County, was the site of a gruesome and highly publicized quadruple lynching of two African American couples only one year earlier.[15] White southerners like Sherlock cultivated an image of racial harmony in the South, despite clear evidence to the contrary, because with Congress debating antilynching legislation in the 1940s, openly defending lynching could invite federal intervention in local affairs. He erased the lynchings. He denied the handiwork of the Klan. He silenced local white memories of anti-Black violence, all to maintain Jim Crow.

Rather than ignoring the quadruple lynching, F. P. Bennett from nearby Decatur, Georgia, tried a different tactic: indulging in conspiracy theories that deflected attention from the real and obvious causes of anti-Black violence. He claimed, "Now that the F.B.I. has taken over the investigation of the slaying of the four negroes, I wonder if they will go so far as to ascertain whether this violence was perpetrated by a group of those few people in Georgia who are so hell-bent on setting up racial equality in the State. . . . Personally, I think the same little group would stop at nothing to achieve their aims."[16] The "little group" Bennett accused of lynching four African Americans as part of a grand hoax to force racial equality upon the South was the NAACP. Silence in the form of deflecting attention from white supremacist violence and trading in conspiracy theories was quite loud, public, and performative, but it silenced white involvement in lynchings nonetheless. Like Bennett, other white southerners parroted similarly fantastical conspiracy theories throughout the civil rights era, usually to draw attention away from the protracted history of anti-Black violence, but also to pretend that Black southerners were indifferent to Jim Crow.[17]

Denial and conspiratorial thinking proved to be the overwhelming impetus behind white southern silences about lynching, especially after 1945, but for African Americans like Jesse Pennington, silences in the traumatic aftermath of lynching were usually a matter of psychological self-preservation and physical safety. African Americans had been using strategic silences for generations, including when the Works Progress Administration (WPA) interviewed formerly enslaved people in the 1930s. Many freed people intentionally omitted from their testimony the most brutal aspects of enslavement, in part because many of the interviewers were white southerners whom they distrusted.[18] Talking too loosely about white men raping enslaved women or severe whippings that permanently maimed their victims could get them killed or lead to retaliation against their entire community. At other times, formerly enslaved people would say that their former enslavers were kind and fair, but also tell stories about "other people" who had cruel enslavers, to stand in for their own experiences. Within the African American community, however, the formerly enslaved showed a greater willingness to discuss their experiences, though even then many remained reluctant to fully divulge all the painful stories from their pasts. Sometimes the world of Jim Crow was reminder enough of their degraded position in southern society, and they didn't want their sadness or bitterness or pain to seep into their children's or grandchildren's impressionable minds.

In the wake of lynchings, some silences were nearly absolute, like the silence Pennington's father imposed on his son or the silences that encircled unspeakably traumatic memories, but others were partial and dependent on context.[19] What might go unsaid in public or in front of white people might be openly aired within the Black community or among family. A mother might not discuss lynching in front of her children, but might unburden her fears for her family's safety in the company of friends. Her children, too, might confide in their siblings and cousins about seeing a lynched body or wonder what their parents whispered behind closed doors but not dare to ask what secrets they kept from them. As a small child, Cleo Jeffers and her family had to flee Mississippi in the dead of night, and though her parents never told her what precisely her father was running from, she knew their leaving was a matter of life and death: "My daddy was a strong man, and that's why—And I'll tell you what . . . when we left Mississippi, something come up and I was, I was too young, but we left by night now and that's all I know. We left by night, and my daddy stayed in a boxcar, and he sent my mother and us on the train, but I don't know what was up because I was too small."[20] Silence was often thickest among those closest to the victims and near-victims of lynching—parents, children, partners, close friends— but the further removed a survivor was from the victim, including in time, the more silences tended to ease into a greater willingness to speak.

The "bundle of silences" African American southerners constructed around lynching were usually informed by an ethic of protection— protecting one's children from the horror of lynching, protecting oneself from memories that would lacerate the soul with each return to the past, protecting the community from reprisals. In addition to providing protection, these silences also carved out room at the center of African American identity and collective memory for self-definition beyond the white gaze, beyond the harm of white supremacy, beyond what

James Baldwin called "the white man's fantasies" about Blackness.[21] Silence, then, could be wielded as a weapon against white perceptions of Blackness and white lynching narratives. For if lynching was a violent ritual that whites used to terrorize their Black neighbors in an attempt to strip them of their humanity and dignity, as well as of their rights as citizens, then these silences could also speak to Black *refusal*, a refusal to recognize white degradation of Blackness as legitimate and as a defining factor in their lives.[22] Though silence often gets conflated with absence and powerlessness, southern Black communities deployed silence as a powerful means to mourn the dead, to protect loved ones among the living, and to reject white lynching narratives—both those that scrubbed lynching from the past and those that celebrated Black degradation.

These Black silences—both protective silences and those that decentered anti-Black violence—spoke the language of the blues. Silences that gave shelter to loved ones amid the worst that Jim Crow threw at Black people paired love with pain in ways that could be a salve amid the hardships of everyday life. Silences that foregrounded Black subjectivity, that cherished hard work and goodness and joy, were expressions of Black self-determination in the face of white domination. Some pain, left to fester in silence, tragically corroded the insides of lynching survivors, but the quiet introspection of the blues sensibility, its private turn inward to the self, gave survivors room to process pain away from the white gaze. For at the heart of the blues sensibility was a creative ingenuity that opened up pathways to transcend the unjust conditions of Jim Crow, even as those conditions often felt as ubiquitous as the weather.

The boy's eyelids were heavy with exhaustion, but dread and fear overshadowed his body's desire for sleep. Bobbing between wave after wave of drowsiness, he willed himself awake, careful to avoid disturbing his siblings dozing off around him. Robert Hall's quiet struggle to keep his eyes open betrayed the intensity of the anxiety that gripped him. Every night the same image flashed before him the moment his eyelids shut: a dead Black man hanging near the churchyard by a wire wrapped around his neck.

Ever since Hall had been old enough to play outside on his own, his mother, Eva Hall, had strictly forbidden him from going to the grounds of a church that locals in Morven, Georgia, referred to as the Camp Ground. One Saturday morning in 1959 or 1960 when his mother was out, Hall disregarded his mother's repeated warnings, and he joined his older brother Jimmy and three other neighborhood boys to go fishing at the creek down by the Camp Ground. Hall recalled how he and the other boys had snuck off that morning:

> My brother, you know, he was a lot larger than we were, so he, he would always take the lead. And we crossed the highway, and we went into a little wooded area right alongside Highway 76. That highway leads from Quitman, which is in Brooks County, all the way to Adel, Georgia. And as we were going through the little trail (because quite a few people would go down there to fish), and he stopped right quick. And he said, "Hey, look there!" And there we saw this Black man hanging, you know, in the tree with a piece of wire around his neck. And so when we saw that, we took off and went back home. We never told my mother about it because I knew what she would have done because she told us not to go down there.[23]

Hall was born and raised in that stretch of southern Georgia where, in May 1918, lynch mobs killed between thirteen and eighteen African Americans, including Mary Turner. Hall and his brother had often wondered why the Camp Ground was off limits. Their mother never told them that members of the Camp Ground Methodist Church had lynched several African American men in the clearing on the church grounds when she was just nine or ten years old. That was one secret she refused to burden her children with, and her children didn't dare ask her about it, either. Hall explained, "Well, you know, back in those days you really didn't question your parents. [chuckling] You really didn't question them because if you, if I had said, 'Well, why, mama?' she would have told me I was a bad boy. 'Don't ask me no questions. Just don't go.' "[24] So when Hall saw that dead Black man strung up in a tree, he, too, kept what he had witnessed to himself to avoid punishment for disobeying his mother. His silence kept this traumatic episode unprocessed, kept his experience beyond the grasp of language, kept the line hazy between a mother's admonishment and the punishment that Black man endured. Even so, he had learned from the dead man hanging near the churchyard what had always gone unsaid between mother and son, that she worried he might encounter the very worst of what the white world was capable of doing to Black people, that white people might take his life and leave his limp body hanging from a tree.

The traumatic memory of the dead man's body haunted him for years—the dead man returned, unbeckoned, through horrifying flashes of memory. When his mother would turn down the kerosene lamp before bedtime, Hall and his brother, Jimmy, insisted that she not turn it all the way off so that its dim glow would provide some comfort when that image crept into their dreams. Neither brother dared to reveal the real reason behind their desire for just a little light amid the forbidding darkness. Besides, their mother had reason to believe other dangers caused her sons to fear the dark. Throughout Hall's childhood in the 1950s and into the early 1960s, hooded night riders carrying torches galloped through their neighborhood when a member of the Black community had done something to subvert the racial order. On those nights, Hall's mother would hastily extinguish the lamps, draw the shades, and corral her children under the bed, hushing them up so they wouldn't draw the attention of the night riders who might spray bullets into their home. Huddled under the bed in terror, the children absorbed a lesson simply from seeing the fear on their mother's face: staying silent around white people could be the key to their survival in the Jim Crow South.

Care and love rested at the core of Eva Hall's silent protection of her children, but with her silence came an unmistakable defiance. When her sons stumbled upon the lynched man in the woods near the Camp Ground, Eva Hall was working as a domestic for a white woman named May Lawson. The Monday after that lynching, she returned to work as usual. With a cruel smile on her lips, Lawson sneered, "Eva, there's a colored man hanging up down there at the Camp Ground. Uh, if I gave you some kerosene, would you go down there and burn him?" As Robert Hall told it, his mother calmly replied, "Miss Lawson, I don't know that man down there. That man didn't know me. If you want him burned, you go burn him yourself."[25] She took off her apron, left it neatly folded on the dining room table, and walked out of the Lawsons' house for good. Only when her youngest child, Robert, reached adulthood did she tell him how she had quit her job that day, and only then did her son reveal what he had seen that Saturday morning he had gone fishing by the Camp Ground.

Long before raising ten children with her husband and working for the Lawsons, Eva Hall had been exposed to the cruelty and horror of white violence against African Americans. She had been a young girl during the 1918 lynching rampage, and back then even the children knew the stories. Worse, some children had witnessed the violence firsthand.[26]

She had been spared that horror, but she knew that, during that lynching spree, Mary Turner had been hunted down after publicly airing her intention to press charges against the white mob that lynched her husband, Hayes Turner. She knew about the ghastly way the mob killed her. She knew of the unspeakable way the unborn child Mary Turner had been carrying for nearly nine months was killed. She knew of the scores of other deaths that terrorized her family and community.

As adults, Eva Hall and her friends would speak in whispers about those times, but they never did so in front of their children and certainly not around their friend, Leaster Grant, who was the Turners' daughter. If a child happened to sneak in or wander into one of these conversations, the adults would shoo them away. Even in these hushed tones, Hall and her friends would inevitably reach a point in the telling of the story when language broke down and tears took over. They choked on the words that made real again Mary Turner hanging by her ankles and screaming, her body engulfed in flames, but words gave way to tears the moment they tried to narrate how a white man in the mob had killed the baby. The violence was too shocking and the memories were simply too painful to put into words.[27]

The Black community in Brooks County struggled for generations to narrate and process those lynchings, but that history was even more fraught for Otha Manning and Leaster Grant, the two surviving children of Hayes and Mary Turner. Once he was old enough to support himself, sometime in the 1920s, Otha Manning left Brooks County and moved to Miami. He remained very close to his younger sister, sending her letters and occasionally coming home to visit. But as much as he cherished spending time with his family and eating his sister's home cooking, he kept his visits to Georgia brief. Manning told his family he could never live in southern Georgia where Black people still seemed to live under a form of enslavement, where white people hated them so much. He never talked about how white people had lynched three members of his immediate family when he was just a child, but his resentment toward local whites was hardly a secret. If white neighbors dropped in, he would ignore them and stew in silence on the porch until they left. During his visits, he rarely left his sister's home, but on at least one occasion he went to the general store in Morven and returned fuming. His great-niece, Audrey Grant, never knew what precisely unfolded at the store, but she remembered that when he came home that day, "he was upset, something about what happened at the store. And he said, 'They think they're

the only people that got money, they're the only people that have anything. I've got money. I've got a car. I've got a big house in Florida. . . . I
just couldn't stay around here. They treat you like shit.' "[28]

Despite these moments of anger and bitterness, Audrey Grant described her great-uncle as "full of life" and always joking. In the hours
before he would return to Miami, Manning and his younger sister would
hug and cry, and as he was driving home, sometimes he would turn back
to spend just a few more moments with his sister. Behind this cheerful,
loving exterior, though, was a troubled man who struggled with alcohol-
ism until the day he died. His intense disdain for white people in southern Georgia and his tearful goodbyes when he left his sister behind in
Barney seemed to point to painful memories of lynching that haunted
him and only loosened their grip in death.

Manning's younger sister, Leaster, married a local vegetable grower
in Barney, named A. D. Grant, and settled on a farm in the Cooper's
Quarter neighborhood, just a couple of miles from the site of her mother's lynching. A proud, independent man who was fiercely protective of
his wife, A. D. Grant insisted on doing all the shopping for the household, including purchasing his wife's clothing, even though he was blind.
He tolerated his wife's white acquaintances, including some white neighbors, dropping by the house now and then, but he insisted that she never
work in a white household as a domestic. He told her that she had plenty
of work to do in her own home between cleaning the house, cooking
meals, canning vegetables, and planting and harvesting her garden. His
desire to limit her time outside their home had less to do with exerting
control over his wife and more to do with protecting her from the indignities of Jim Crow she would encounter in white homes, white stores,
and on the sidewalks of Barney and Morven. He also protected her from
other longstanding threats from her childhood. Immediately after the
1918 lynchings, the two orphans, Otha and Leaster, had hidden in the
homes of relatives under assumed names, since their aunts and uncles
worried that the lynch mob would come for the children, too. In a sense,
A. D. Grant simply continued what his wife's intensely private family had
been doing for decades: sheltering her from white people who might
want to kill her. Jim Crow had cost his wife so much already. He was determined to protect her from suffering any more pain and sadness at the
hands of white folks.

Although Leaster Grant spent most of her time at home, family and
friends visited her often. In the 1960s, when her grandchildren were still

in grade school, she would sing spirituals and gospel songs with them, and they would sit around and listen to her tell stories about growing up in Barney. One of her granddaughters, Audrey Grant, recalled that sometimes the grandchildren would ask her to tell them stories about her parents. These questions upset her greatly, and their grandfather would step in, telling them, "Leave your grandmamma alone about that. Stop asking your grandmamma those questions. She don't like to talk about that." Their grandfather's strictly enforced buffer of silence only intensified their curiosity, so they took to asking their grandmother questions about her family on the sly, when their grandfather wasn't around. Even then, Leaster Grant didn't say much about her mother to her grandchildren. Once she mentioned that she remembered her mother was a beautiful woman, but most other times she would hang her head and say, "They killed my mother. They did a lot of very bad things to my mother. I had another brother, and they killed him too." Tears rolled down her cheeks as she revisited those memories in front of her grandchildren, but she could never bring herself to utter the details of her mother's death— those were unspeakable acts, the memories of which she quietly carried but lacked the words to express.[29]

Leaster Grant's granddaughter supposed, "Things that bothered [my grandmother], she kept it away and didn't even talk about it. She kept it inside." Perhaps in quiet moments, when the grandkids were away and she was alone, she would visit with those memories, or maybe she would be visited by them. Those tears her grandchildren saw were the sadness trapped inside spilling out as she struggled to disentangle her mother's beauty from the trauma of her death. Her silence meant that her granddaughter Audrey didn't find out until the early 2000s that her great-grandmother, Mary Turner, had been lynched. A few years later she heard the grisly details of her death for the first time. Only then did she more fully understand the depth and texture of her grandmother's grief and silence.[30]

When Willie Head Jr. declared, "By nature, and by spiritual occupation, I'm a farmer," he made it known not just that the fields he tended sprouted wheat and greens—turnip, mustard, and collard greens, to be precise—but that his connection to the land was a matter of his spirit.[31] Head came from a long line of farmers, and he tilled the same land his grandfather, Judge Head, had owned and farmed for decades. Judge Head purchased that small stretch of uncultivated land in Pavo, and with nothing but a shovel and a mule, he dug up stumps that were upward of

4 feet in diameter for 10 cents apiece until, 3,000 stumps later, he had the $300 down payment for that land. His grandson's connection to the land was as much about his love for coaxing life out of the earth as it was about his love for his family and his appreciation for the many sacrifices that made a small piece of earth his. Not only did owning his family farm signal his independence in a southern agricultural economy in which Black men often sharecropped or worked as farm laborers on white-owned plantations, but also, by identifying farming as part of his very "nature" and as his "spiritual occupation," he centered his sense of self on what suited him and brought him joy, not on what the white world thought of him.

Willie Head Jr. grew up in Pavo, Georgia, just a few towns west of Morven and Barney, where the Halls and the Grants lived. Like Robert Hall, he had heard the stories about the May 1918 lynching spree when he was growing up in the 1960s, and his father had told him about how the old white man who used to walk along Highway 76 toward Barney had cut open Mary Turner and killed her baby. Head also had a deeply personal connection to this reign of terror: his great-uncle, Will Head, had been the first to die at the hands of a lynch mob that week the Turners were killed. His parents told him about his great-uncle's death when he was still a child, but said only that he had been hanged for allegedly stealing a gun from a white man. Not until the 2000s did he learn the context of his great-uncle's death, and, when he did, he heard it from local activists seeking to memorialize the lynching victims, not from his own family. Though they would talk about the Turners with him, his parents reasoned that telling their son about a lynching in the family would only cause him to hate white people and would plant the seed for seeking revenge. Reflecting on his mother's attempts to shield him, he mused, "That was their way of defending us, to keep us from building up a resentment against white people . . . which didn't do a whole lot of good, but, you know, because I've had my experiences [with white supremacy], and those things [the lynchings] came up in my mind when I would have an encounter, a racial encounter with someone."[32] His parents' protection could go only so far: even though they cautiously revealed to him fragments of the local lynching lore, they could not shield him from the daily reminders that white supremacy and Black degradation gave shape to the world outside the Black community.

Head carried these local stories about lynchings with him into adulthood. They were never far from his consciousness, nor *could* they stray too far from his consciousness, since living in southern Georgia provided constant reminders of anti-Blackness. But it was easier for Head, who was further removed from his great-uncle and his death, to decenter the lynching than it was for his grandfather and great-grandfather. Will Head's death devastated his father, Frank Head, who would break down and cry whenever he talked about what had happened to his son. Born enslaved in Georgia, Frank Head must have had his faith in the promise of freedom shaken when, even in freedom, a Black man's life was so worthless. Eventually Frank Head moved away from Brooks County to somewhere in Florida, where that big oak tree and the smug looks on white men's faces would not remind him of his son's terrible death. Even though moving meant leaving many of his children and their families behind, finally he could mourn in peace.[33] Judge Head also mourned the death of his brother; his grandson described him as a sensitive man who would cry at the thought of his brother's lynching. Judge Head, however, refused to leave. He had dreams of farming his own land where he grew up. His insistence on staying was an act of defiance, a refusal to bend to the lynch mob's terrorism. His brother Will had been a farm laborer for an abusive, hot-tempered white man, and not only did Judge Head refuse to leave, but his persistence led him to purchase a farm of his own with no one but himself as his boss.

As an adult, Willie Head Jr. also refused to be moved from the land. He refused the white entitlement to the land that a lynching rampage that had happened decades before his birth had intended to reinforce. He refused to acquiesce to his white neighbors who believed that Black life and Black property were theirs for the taking. In essence, Head silenced white narratives that glorified lynching by the very way in which he lived his life. In an interview, Head recalled that, after any given racist encounter, "That would be the first thing I would think about—remembering what my mom and dad say about how they [whites] did Hayes Turner and Mary Turner. . . . That was one of the things that inspired me to buy this farm."[34] He then pointed to a framed photograph of his grandparents and parents, taken in the 1940s, and trained his eyes on the spot, just a few yards from his home, where his grandparents' home had been—the home where Judge Head had lived and died. More than six decades after Judge Head had purchased the farm, the family still owned and farmed that same land and acres more. Willie Head Jr. absorbed his grandfather's independent spirit as well as the memories of lynching passed on to him from his parents, and they inspired him to remain on the family's land.

Even when many of his relatives moved away to Detroit and Trenton, Head followed in the footsteps of his grandfather. Even when local white farmers tried to drive him away with renewed threats and withheld loans, he stayed on this hard-earned piece of land, for his approach to living was tinged by the blues. The death of his great-uncle remained ever present, as did the untimely deaths of his wife and daughter, but he made it through, keeping his grandfather's defiance of white supremacy, his deep love for his family, and his spiritual connection to the land at the center of his life.

The gradual fading of lynching from white southern memory came in fits and starts in the decades following official US involvement in World War II. Some corners of the white South continued to openly defend lynching, past and present, but those pockets of society eventually began to shrink and became more marginal. As civil rights activists chipped away at Jim Crow and white public opinion grew generally less tolerant of the most brazen white supremacist violence, public denials of lynching and, in turn, the deflection of that violence onto others became dominant strategies for silencing lynching narratives. These silences reflected a profound anxiety over threats to what many white southerners called "the southern way of life" or "the southern tradition." Through these silences, they desperately tried to preserve and defend a white supremacist society that was slipping through their fingers as public schools desegregated, African Americans registered to vote in growing numbers, and old forms of racial deference faded. Faced with this extraordinary social upheaval and a nation less outwardly tolerant of the violence that ensured the survival of their "way of life," many white southerners spoke less openly about lynching as they constructed a more palatable image of Jim Crow.[35]

White southerners had relished spectacles of white power since the gibbeting of Black insurrectionists and public whippings of enslaved people in the colonial period, and their open endorsement of anti-Black spectacle violence continued unabated well into the twentieth century. When Republicans in Congress introduced antilynching bills in the 1920s and 1930s, southern Democrats not only invoked states' rights arguments against federal intervention, but also extolled the virtues of lynching.[36] In 1940 when the Senate took up the last antilynching bill to pass the House in the twentieth century, many white southerners didn't bother to veil their enthusiasm for lynching as they urged their representatives to defeat the bill. In a letter to Senator Tom Connally of Texas, Maud Burnette, a stenographer from Dallas, insisted that lynching, not the law, was the best way to deter and punish Black male rapists:

> This probability or possibility of lynching, is the best thing to hold over the bad niggers of the South, as they fear that more than anything else—for the reason, when a mob goes after them, there is no escape, but if they are convicted by the courts, there is always a big chance they will escape the chair, as some little lawyer trying to make a name, will appeal frist to the State Supreme Court and perhaps get a reversal and then the chance is, he may get life instead of the chair—then a chance to escape the penitentiary or in some way come out free.[37]

White southerners were equally forthcoming with personal anecdotes about lynching. G. D. Meredith of Rice, Texas, wrote a letter to Representative Luther A. Johnson about a lynching in Neshoba County, Mississippi, during the 1880s to explain why antilynching legislation would leave white southerners unable to retaliate against Black suspects. A Black man allegedly had assaulted a white woman whom Meredith had known, before slitting her throat and throwing her body into a well. Her bereaved husband, with the help of some other men, splayed the Black man across a log and chopped off his head to avenge her death.[38] Meredith proudly defended lynching as a way to protect a white man's honor and seemed to get a thrill out of retelling the story. He even asked Johnson to share his letter with Connally.

Southern politicians tended to be better at holding their tongues, in the *Congressional Record* at least. Just before the House passed the Gavagan Anti-Lynching Bill in 1937, the chair of the House Judiciary Committee, Hatton Sumners of Texas, made a forceful speech against the bill grounded in a constitutional argument that federal intervention in state affairs undermined a government by the people. Sumners claimed that the lynching of Roosevelt Townes and Bootjack McDaniels in Duck Hill, Mississippi, two days earlier made him so angry that he "might have joined your mob [that is, supporters of the bill] to lynch the Constitution" had they voted the day before. Then he quickly slipped into a well-worn excuse for voting against the bill: lynching was understandable in cases of white women being raped by Black men.[39] Although he claimed that "every drop of my blood revolts against the lynching of a human being," his sympathies were with the mob. He wondered aloud whether, as the bill stipulated, arresting the father of a rape victim—"tak[ing] that father away from the bedside of that little torn girl"—or imposing a $10,000 fine paid to the family of "this hound of hell that had destroyed that child's life" would prevent lynchings.[40] Sumners asked his fellow members of Congress to sympathize with lynchers and leave the South to handle its own affairs. He upheld the pretense of a principled argument, however dubious, but other members of Congress, like Mississippi's notorious race-baiting senator, Theodore Bilbo, dispensed with such pretense: Bilbo simply excused lynchings as an understandable but unfortunate reaction to the rape of white women.[41]

Between the late 1940s and the Supreme Court's 1954 *Brown v. Board of Education* decision, overt endorsements of lynching gradually moved into the shadows as they were replaced by veiled and more "respectable" rationalizations of white supremacy. Mississippi senator James O. Eastland still received correspondence from constituents who supported lynching, but public disapproval of lynching had grown enough that, in this new political landscape, southern politicians had to appear more circumspect in their public pronouncements regarding lynching in particular and white supremacy in general.[42] Southern Democrats could still block legislation making permanent the wartime antidiscrimination agency, the Fair Employment Practices Commission (FEPC). They could still defeat the 1948 civil rights bill with a drawn-out filibuster, but openly defending lynching came with considerable political risks, including inviting more federal intervention and jeopardizing Jim Crow. With support for civil rights reforms on the rise nationwide, most white southerners—and not just politicians—were put on the defensive.[43] With the "way of life" that lynching enforced and celebrated coming under attack, white defiance of civil rights activism became inextricably entangled in lynching memories they now held closer to the chest.[44]

When Bilbo died in office in 1947, Eastland became the senior senator from Mississippi, and although Eastland became a demagogue in his own right, he operated under the pretense of representing a more genteel, respectable white supremacy that could be embraced by polite society. From time to time, Eastland could unleash hateful barbs reminiscent of Bilbo's unvarnished race-baiting—in a 1945 speech against the FEPC, he derided African American soldiers as inept cowards unworthy of the uniforms they wore—but his strategy to save Jim Crow primarily hinged on denial. In a 1957 interview with journalist Mike Wallace, Eastland disputed that only

4 percent of African Americans in Mississippi could vote and that local registrars discriminated by race, and he unequivocally insisted that his home state had no local chapters of the Klan.[45] Purporting to speak for all Mississippians, the senator defended Jim Crow, explaining, "the way [segregation] is handled is endorsed by ninety-nine percent of the people of both races [in the South] who live in peace and harmony, and we have more peace and harmony than any section of the country . . . and we have less racial prejudice."[46] This combination of denial and outright lies—this silencing of discrimination, the indignities of Jim Crow, grassroots opposition to racial injustice led by Black southerners, and lynching—stood at the core of his four-decade career in the Senate.

Eastland stood on a more prominent soapbox to express his denial than the average citizen, but his views on "racial harmony" reflected popular opinion and resonated with whites across the South. Just twelve days after Medgar Evers, the NAACP field secretary in Mississippi, was gunned down in front of his Jackson home, Kate H. Steele, a white woman from Chattanooga, Tennessee, wrote a letter to all the Democrats in the Senate claiming, "The WHITE people of the South have never mistreated the negro—They have done what no other section of the country has done—They have GIVEN him schools GOOD SCHOOLS—helped him build his churches—have given him jobs—helped him earn a living and above ALL they have given him FRIENDSHIP—There are negroes who appreciate this and are on the side of the White people."[47] Despite widespread coverage of Evers's assassination, Steele painted the South as a place of racial harmony and noblesse oblige. Whether she believed her own paternalistic rhetoric is doubtful.[48]

Eastland's constituents also shrugged off the violence of Jim Crow by sending him anecdotes about African Americans who opposed the civil rights movement. One clipping from Mississippi's *Jackson Daily News* showed three photos of smiling African Americans returning to Jackson from Chicago, suitcases in tow, under the headline, "Coming Back Home to 'Home Sweet Home.' "[49] Another constituent sent a letter to the editor written by a Black porter named James Maxie who seemed to embrace the paternalism Steele endorsed: "I am very happy to be a Mississippi Negro. I have no complaints about the way of life I am used to. . . . I am concerned about the attitude of many of my race who suddenly think that everything ought to be changed in Mississippi."[50] White southerners trotted out Maxie and other "good Negroes" to stave off criticisms of Jim Crow, but they also sought out these exceptions to reassure themselves that Black people also supported a system designed to benefit whites. Hoyt Bass, the wife of a pecan grower in Lumberton, Mississippi, reported to Eastland that, at her son's funeral, "about a hundred [Black mourners] stood on one side of the grave, near enough to hear every word, [and] it was really a wonderful point of contact."[51] In the senator's reply to Bass, he wished "our northern friends" could see "in moments of great sorrow ... the demonstration by southern negroes at [white people's] funerals," and he wondered aloud if those northerners supporting civil rights legislation might just be "jealous of the life that has been evolved in the South of two races living side by side and getting along so well together."[52] So when Black southerners demanded the right to vote, job opportunities, and legal protections from violence, whites insisted that this desire for justice came from without—whether from "a few yellow Northern Negroes ... [who] urge[d] on the humble Negro of the South" or "professional agitators from afar ... [who] invaded the South and have browbeaten and otherwise persuaded negro children to force themselves into the white school."[53]

Behind Eastland's public denials of racial unrest lurked a closely guarded, ugly family secret involving his father, Woods Eastland. On February 3, 1904, about ten months before the future senator was born, a Black man named Luther Holbert had a violent confrontation with Woods's brother, James Eastland, and another man who worked for the Eastlands on their Doddsville, Mississippi, plantation. Holbert allegedly shot and killed the two men and fled for the Yazoo River with his wife, Mary. Upon hearing that his younger brother had been murdered, Woods Eastland swore he would personally avenge his brother's death, so he assembled a posse to hunt down the Holberts. While waiting for bloodhounds to arrive from a nearby town, an impatient Woods shot and killed a Black man who worked on his plantation on the suspicion that he was an accomplice. Three days later, the posse successfully apprehended the Holberts near the Yazoo River, but not before shooting three other African Americans who had no connection to the murders. Although the Holberts were captured on a Saturday, Woods waited until after Sunday church services to mutilate, torture, and burn the couple in front of a Black church near the Holberts' home.

The well-publicized burnings orchestrated by Woods attracted more than one thousand spectators. Members of the lynch mob cut off the victims' fingers and ears, and they beat Luther Holbert, leaving him with a skull fracture and one eye hanging out of its socket. Before burning the couple alive, a white man used a large corkscrew to bore into their arms, legs, and torsos, extracting long ribbons of flesh from their bodies. Woods led the pursuit and burning of the Holberts, but he never stood trial since his lawyer, Senator Anselm J. McLaurin, convinced the judge to dismiss the case. McLaurin argued that the state had insufficient evidence that Woods had lit the pyres, and furthermore, he reasoned that, given the circumstances, Woods had justifiably lynched the Holberts.[54]

Born two months after his father's case was dismissed, James O. Eastland grew up in the shadow of his namesake's death. Even though the family didn't openly discuss how Woods Eastland had lynched two African Americans and murdered another as retribution, the senator probably knew the details of the Holberts' lynchings. These memories resurfaced—in private, among older friends and family—most especially when Jim Crow seemed poised to crumble. When "one of [his] old Rebel friends and neighbors" wrote the senator a letter denouncing the Freedom Rides in May 1961, this family friend assumed Eastland would recognize the reference when he wrote: "I often think of your father Judge Eastland; we had lots of fun together. . . . I would like to hear from the Hon. Jim Eastland from the deep south, raise up on his back legs and let them have both barrels, like the Judge did in the good old days."[55] The leap back in time from the Freedom Rides to the "good old days" of lynching said so much about the continued hold of lynching memories on white southerners. This "old Rebel friend," John S. Boyette, had lived just a couple of miles north of Doddsville until 1945, and since the lynchings had been common knowledge among locals, he didn't need to explicitly name the Holberts or mention the lynching in his letter as he waxed nostalgic about "the good old days" when Freedom Riders wouldn't dare to ride through the South on buses "with the purpose of exciting a riot."[56] What was considered common knowledge (and therefore went unsaid) for the senator's generation was lost to the next generation. The senator's four children remained unaware of the family secret well into adulthood.[57]

Another acquaintance of "Mr. Woods," Ruby Sheppeard Hicks, penned a letter to the senator the night of the October 1962 riot that erupted in Oxford, Mississippi, when James Meredith integrated the University of Mississippi. Alarmed and frightened by the presence of almost twenty-five hundred federal troops in Mississippi, Hicks "wander[ed] tearfully through my long hall of memories" in search of something comforting, and she settled on a memory from 1903. Sunflower County, where she and the senator had grown up, had refused to be "degraded with a Negro postmistress" that President Theodore Roosevelt had reappointed, and rather than withdrawing his support for postmistress Minnie Cox, Roosevelt had closed the post office. That story of white Mississippians rebuking a president who meddled in their racial affairs reassured Hicks, who hoped the current confrontation with President John F. Kennedy would also end in a return to the way things were. To drape in nostalgia an era of white racial control, Hicks had to do some creative reimagining of the past. When she reminisced that "the murder of your uncle Jim was the first real tragedy I remember," she conveniently neglected to mention the lynching and murder of six Black people that immediately followed.[58] As the civil rights movement gained momentum and support, white southerners like Hicks and Eastland were compelled by shifting social norms to paper over local lynchings, creating a distorted, mythic vision of Jim Crow that provided just enough of a veneer of racial harmony to defend white supremacy.

As efforts to dismantle Jim Crow grew, deflection and distraction became common strategies for white southerners to silence the real and obvious causes of lynching and other white supremacist violence, including assassinations.[59] Although the embrace of a version of Martin Luther King Jr. defanged of his radicalism every January might suggest otherwise, a considerable slice of the United States openly reviled him even following his assassination on April 4, 1968. Many white southerners thought President Lyndon Johnson's order to fly US flags at half-staff to mourn his death dishonored the flag. Eastland suggested, "It has been apparent that King was assassinated by a hired assassin and we may never know the source of the money," though only a few lines later he confidently asserted, "I think the theory that there may have been some Communist money involved and a Communist conspiracy in the assassination of King has a lot of validity."[60] Whether the communists behind the assassination were from China or Cuba or Russia, he couldn't be sure, but he was certain that the white South's conscience was clean. Fantastical conspiracy theories like the ones Eastland parroted deflected attention from the actual perpetrators of anti-Black violence, a tactic they hoped would distract the nation from the moral case for Black liberation.

During the summer of 1964, Mississippi revived its taste for lynching. On June 21, three civil rights workers with the Council of Federated Organizations (COFO), James Chaney, Andrew Goodman, and Mickey Schwerner, drove to Philadelphia, Mississippi, from their offices in

Meridian to meet with leaders of Mount Zion Methodist Church, which the Klan had burned to the ground a few days earlier. They never made it back to Meridian. While returning to the COFO offices that afternoon, the three men were pulled over by a deputy sheriff and Klan member, Cecil Ray Price, who took them into custody purportedly for speeding. Price arranged for other Klan members to intercept the civil rights workers as soon as they were released from the Neshoba County Jail, and by the end of the night, the Klan, which included several members of local law enforcement, had killed and buried Chaney, Goodman, and Schwerner. Federal investigators arrived to locate the missing civil rights workers, but their bodies remained undisturbed inside an earthen dam until August 4, when the FBI excavated their badly decayed remains. Goodman and Schwerner, white New Yorkers, each had a bullet lodged in their torso. Chaney, a Black Mississippian, had three bullets in his torso, and his jaw had been shattered, his shoulder and arm mangled. Chaney's skull had been battered so badly that one side of his head had caved in. Goodman and Schwerner appeared to have died in an execution-style murder, but the Klan members had poured their hatred, frustration, and anger onto Chaney's body, trying to beat back with each blow the advance of the Black freedom struggle in Mississippi.[61]

During the forty-four days the men remained missing, speculation ran rampant as to their whereabouts. The governor of Mississippi, Paul B. Johnson, quipped that the civil rights workers could be "up North or in Cuba," but "there are so many possibilities it would be foolish to make a guess."[62] In a speech Eastland gave on the floor of the Senate, he all but called the lynchings a hoax:

> No one wants to charge that a hoax has been perpetrated because there is too little evidence to show what did happen. But as time goes on and the search continues, if some evidence of a crime is not produced, I think the people of America will be justified in considering other alternatives as more valid solutions to the mystery, instead of accepting as true the accusation of the agitators that a heinous crime has been committed.[63]

In a private letter, he confided to a sympathetic constituent, "There are growing indications that the Philadelphia incident may have been manufactured, though no one, in view of present information, could make this assertion, and I certainly would not want to do anything further than to call attention to such a possibility. I hope that it develops this way."[64] Not all white Mississippians shared in these conspiracies. Some took issue with their elected officials' insensitive, if not outrageous, remarks, especially once the bodies were located and the intimate ties between the Klan and law enforcement came to light, but Johnson's and Eastland's unwavering popularity attested to the dominance of their views in white southern society, views that endured long after the bodies were exhumed.[65]

What elected officials like Johnson and Eastland hinted at with veiled rhetoric, many of their constituents made explicit. Unhampered by an obligation to uphold even the veneer of civility, some whites sneered that the mother of one of the missing men didn't appear sufficiently bereaved to have lost her son to the Klan and that her television appearance was just a ploy to engender sympathy for COFO's voter education and voter registration drive.[66] Ann Parker of Jackson, for instance, scoffed at what she considered a publicity stunt to drum up support for Freedom Summer:

> Now look to the three who are missing after being released from jail in Philadelphia on Sunday night. The station wagon plainly set on fire etc. I said at once: "Another Emmett Till case." You remember *five* reputable Drs. examined the body pulled out of the river and stated "It is the body of a mature man & not a boy." Still Mississippi is today called the murderer! The three I am sure *lost* themselves to put another *blot on Miss.*[67]

Having already dismissed Till's lynching as a fabrication, Parker didn't require much prodding to point an accusatory finger at the civil rights workers themselves.[68] She even claimed to have seen Schwerner walking around Lynch Street near the COFO headquarters in Jackson a few days after they went missing. Dozens of other alleged sightings cropped up across the country, which revealed the depths of white determination to erase the "blot" of racial violence from Mississippi and the United States more generally.

In the weeks between the disappearance of the three civil rights workers and the recovery of their bodies, the Chaney, Goodman, and Schwerner families mourned, and Congress passed the 1964 Civil Rights Act, which once again raised the stakes for the white counteroffensive against civil rights. One year later, the Voting Rights Act became the law of the land, further challenging white political control. But at a moment when denying lynchings past and present became most imperative for saving

Jim Crow, militant white supremacists like Klansmen and lone vigilantes responded to advances in voter registration and desegregation with an escalation of bombings, arsons, death threats, and murders, producing even more acts of violence to explain away and cover up and ignore.

The exculpatory power of silence also found an outlet in projection, or the rejection of one's own feelings and desires, and the displacement of those feelings and desires onto others. White southerners could, through projection, shed their guilty consciences by inverting the roles of victim and perpetrator, despite the glaring, and often deeply ironic, contradictions that resulted. They often pointed fingers at the North for enabling supposed Black criminal tendencies by failing to enforce a strict racial code as white southerners did.[69] A white banker from Carthage, Mississippi, J. A. Sasser, boldly claimed in 1957: "Race relations in the South are not nearly as bad as they are in Northern states. Up to now we have had no violence in our State. A majority of our white people believe [in] and practice fair play with the Negro. Most of our people have a greater affection for the negro than the people who were not reared with them."[70] Sasser hailed from the state with the highest number of lynchings—the same state where, just two years earlier, Till had been lynched for allegedly flirting with a white woman and Reverend George Lee and Lamar Smith had been murdered for registering to vote—yet he claimed there was no racial violence in Mississippi.

The most common targets of white southern projection were African Americans. Notwithstanding the long history of white southerners lynching Black southerners, white projection often inverted this history by turning white southerners into the victims of African American "mobs" past and present. In 1957, Judy Barnett, a white woman from Houston, sent Eastland materials she had stumbled upon while doing genealogical research: a short description of a monument dedicated to Confederate veteran Calvin Crozier by the chapter of the United Daughters of the Confederacy in Newberry, South Carolina. She thought the description, which described a vengeful Black "mob" from the 1860s, was pertinent to the ongoing debate in Congress over the civil rights bill. According to the brief account of his death included with this description, Crozier was released from a federal prison after the Confederate Army surrendered, but on his way home to Texas, he had a brief entanglement with a Black Union soldier in Newberry who had allegedly spewed "gross insults" at a young white woman traveling with Crozier. In retaliation, Black soldiers took him into custody:

[Crozier] was hurried in the nighttime to the bivouac of the reg-
iment to which the [African American] soldier belonged, was
kept under guard all night, was not allowed communication with
any citizen, was condemned to die without even the form of a
trial and was shot to death about daylight the following morning
and his body mutilated.[71]

Crozier's death in 1865 had inverted resonances with thousands of
southern lynchings. The protection of white womanhood, the circum-
vention of the law, a victim murdered by members of another race who
didn't face legal consequences, and the physical mutilation all had a familiar ring, but the victim in this case was a white southern man during
Reconstruction, not a Black southern man during Jim Crow. The Crozier monument was dedicated in 1913 at a moment when white supremacy and Jim Crow seemed steadfast and secure, but Barnett's note,
written on the precipice of the Second Reconstruction, came in an age
more closely resembling the era in which Crozier died. This story of
white Confederate victimhood certainly reflected Barnett's anxieties that
federal civil rights legislation might become law for the first time since
Reconstruction, and she projected nearly one hundred years of lynching
African Americans onto Black Union soldiers in an effort to evade the
white South's violent past.[72]
    Going back to the 1890s, when Ida B. Wells forcefully denounced
the "reign of mob rule" that gripped the South, the rhetoric of "mob
rule" and "mob violence" was racialized. Southern newspapers would run
sensationalist headlines like "Buggy Collision Incites Mob to Lynch Ala.
Negro" or "Two Saved from First Mob Are Lynched by Second Mob" or
"Negro Killed by Mob after Slaying Three / Downed by Machine Gun
Fire After 15-Hour Chase" or "Courthouse, Negro Burned / Mob Destroys Three Blocks in Negro Part of Sherman."[73] Lynching tropes were
so deeply ingrained in the popular imagination that the whiteness of
these mobs was implied by the Blackness of their victims. The rhetoric of
mob rule remained salient in the South during the 1950s and 1960s, but
white southerners usually reserved the "mob" label for Black protesters
participating in nonviolent demonstrations, sit-ins, and boycotts, rather
than the white counter-protesters across the South erupting in violence
and vitriol reminiscent of lynch mobs. Just like their ancestors who projected their own barbarity onto African Americans to justify lynching,
these anti–civil rights mobs ignored their own lawlessness, which they

then projected onto Black protesters through an inversion of lynching rhetoric.

Thick plumes of black smoke billowed above the Greyhound bus as a stream of choking, coughing, bleary-eyed people poured out onto the shoulder of the highway near Anniston, Alabama. Its tires slashed, its windows bashed in, its interior consumed by flames, the battered bus fared even worse than its passengers who stumbled down its stairs, gasping for air. Later that day in May 1961 a second bus pulled into the station in Birmingham, only to be greeted by members of the Klan, who had coordinated with local law enforcement to allow them ten minutes to beat the passengers with pipes before the police arrived. A third bus arrived in Montgomery a couple of days later. The sixteen Alabama patrol cars that had accompanied the bus from Birmingham for the passengers' protection disappeared as they entered Montgomery, and again hundreds of angry white Alabamians met them at the bus station with baseball bats, clubs, and chains for bludgeoning the passengers. When that third bus made it to Jackson, Mississippi, the riders were promptly arrested without incident, despite a Jackson banker warning that "much bloodshed will result from Robert Kennedy's inspired freedom riders when they hit Mississippi."[74] Organized by the Congress of Racial Equality (CORE) and the Student Nonviolent Coordinating Committee (SNCC), the Freedom Riders had come to the Deep South to test the enforcement of a Supreme Court decision banning segregation in interstate bus travel. Met by throngs of irate whites, they exposed in blood and cracked bones the violence perpetrated by white southern mobs underlying Jim Crow.[75]

An editorial in the *Washington Post* optimistically reported that these "unhappy incidents" had made white southerners "[realize] the dangers of incendiary public behavior and mob response," but the local coverage carefully avoided using the terms "rioters" or "mob" to describe white Alabamians.[76] Instead, white southerners branded CORE and SNCC activists as rabble-rousers. A state representative from Mississippi, Walter Sillers, wrote that the Freedom Riders "[were] making these invasions with the hope of provoking violence and disorder" as part of a well-organized communist conspiracy.[77] In the spring of 1963, just two years after the Freedom Rides, African Americans in Birmingham launched a campaign to protest segregation and employment discrimination in the city. The mayor, Arthur J. Hanes, told the chairman of the Senate Sub-Committee on Internal Security, "Citizens of Birmingham [are] determined not to tolerate further mob action fomented by anyone and certainly not by the Negro [Martin Luther] King."[78] Hanes also turned the rhetoric of mob violence on its head. When mobs of whites had clubbed the Freedom Riders, white Alabamians blamed civil rights activists for their own beatings. When police dogs and fire hoses scattered a "mob" of activists peacefully protesting in Birmingham, Hanes believed the activists had provoked the police to club them with nightsticks. Through this inverted rhetoric about mob action, many white Alabamians claimed unearned absolution for their violent rage against Black protesters, for looking away from themselves, avoiding the blood on their hands, was how they lived with their desire to dominate.

A few months later, on the steps of the Lincoln Memorial, King spoke about an unpaid promissory note, and SNCC's John Lewis implored, "Wake up America! Wake up!" Hundreds of thousands of Americans gathered on the national mall that sweltering August afternoon for the March on Washington for Jobs and Freedom to demand the passage of civil rights legislation, and they left feeling uplifted and hopeful yet knew their work remained far from finished. In the weeks leading up to the march, many white southerners predicted chaos and violence would erupt in the nation's capital.[79] Mrs. Frank M. Bianca of Natchez, Mississippi, wrote, "This mass civil rights march which is only a 'mob march' controlled and led by many communists is degrading to the American way of life."[80] The Martaks, a couple from Memphis, wrote to Tennessee's congressional delegation, "We feel that the rights of Life, Liberty, and our Happiness has been encroached upon by mob actions, sit-ins, marches, the invasion of private businesses, churches, etc., by these mobs."[81] Many white southerners agreed with Bianca and the Martaks that the nation had descended into a mobocracy—that "mobs" of civil rights activists controlled the president and Congress—even though the activists themselves worried that the coming legislative debate would water down the bill. Claiming oppression for themselves revealed deeper anxieties among white southerners, in particular what it would mean to lose the protection that lynching had afforded them for decades.[82]

Just three weeks after the March on Washington on the morning of September 15, 1963, a powerful explosion tore through the walls of Birmingham's Sixteenth Street Baptist Church just before Sunday services. Most of the parishioners emerged from the church unscathed or with minor injuries, but four little Black girls chatting in the church basement after Sunday school were killed by the blast. Coming on the heels of the March on Washington, the bombing provided a sobering reminder that the fight for racial justice in the South could have deadly consequences, even for Black children, even at church on Sunday. In the tense days that followed, two more Black children were shot and killed. Armed guards had been patrolling homes in a middle-class Black neighborhood nicknamed Dynamite Hill since a wave of bombings orchestrated by the Klan damaged several homes throughout the civil rights era, but the bombing of a church on a Sunday morning and the deaths of Addie Mae Collins, Denise McNair, Carole Robertson, and Cynthia Wesley made people around the world wonder what moral boundaries, if any, those who most fiercely defended Jim Crow would respect.[83]

Many white southerners expressed shock and horror at the deaths of four children attending church, and some local whites even visited the families of the slain girls to offer their condolences. Others reverted to the comforting habit of denial and projection. William M. Spencer, a native of Birmingham, blamed the bombing on outside agitators determined to start a race riot, and he resented accusations that whites from Birmingham were responsible for the deaths of four Black girls.[84] Gene Oliver of Knoxville, Tennessee, thought the NAACP had perpetrated the bombing to generate revenue, explaining that "having lived in Georgia most of my life, and coming in contact with Negroes, I have a reasonably good idea as to their cunning. Therefore, I cannot help but wonder if the various bombings are not—to a great extent anyway—the work of their own hands."[85] Exactly three weeks after the March on Washington, King gave a eulogy at the funeral of three of the girls, in which he reaffirmed his faith in redemptive suffering, expressing his conviction that their deaths might provide a "redemptive force" for justice in the South. In front of eight thousand mourners, including hundreds of white clergy, he held out hope that "this tragic event may cause the white South to come to terms with its conscience."[86] For some, the deaths filled them with shame, but others surrounded their conscience with an impenetrable wall of silence. From the Freedom Rides to the Birmingham campaign to the March on Washington to the bombing of the Sixteenth Street Baptist Church, the inversion of mob rhetoric and even more racist violence left many African Americans wondering whether moral appeals to people who refused introspection would ever produce a more just society.

Over time, lynching survivors like Jesse Pennington and Robert and Eva Hall eventually were moved to break their silence. Time had not necessarily blunted the force of their pain and horror, but the dangers of

breaching these collective silences had subsided and changed as racial violence evolved since their childhoods under Jim Crow. In the aftermath
of the civil rights era, white Americans rearticulated and reimagined
white supremacy—and white supremacist violence, wily as ever, shape-
shifted once again. The night riders on horseback were replaced by police
patrols in Black neighborhoods. The nominally "extra-legal" violence of
lynchings was absorbed into other state-sponsored violence, such as police killings, the death penalty, and mass incarceration.[87] The vitriol of
racist demagogues fell behind a thin veil of colorblind platitudes and the
rhetoric of law and order. And for some, the traumatic memories of
lynching were joined and sometimes displaced by some other, new horror. Robert Hall, for instance, served with the 25th Infantry Division in
the Vietnam War in 1967, and though seeing that lynched man as a child
prepared him for the carnage of war, this imperialist war spawned new
nightmares he would endure for decades.[88]

For Pennington, who had made it safely out of the Mississippi Delta
to Chicago in 1954, faint echoes of his mother's screams still rang in his
ears decades later. Even though he had locked away his memories of the
day he evaded a lynch mob, echoes of her pained cries followed him to
college, to the Vietnam War, to law school, and to his practice as a civil
rights lawyer in Mississippi. In 2004 Pennington went to view a traveling
exhibit of lynching photographs that the self-described "southern picker"
James Allen had collected and purchased from estate sales and flea mar-
kets, and walking the halls of the exhibit, *Without Sanctuary*, he found
that those distant cries of his mother grew to a thunderous crescendo:

> As I walked in, I could hear the music play, and as I got halfway
> down the hallway, I—I can feel it now—just started crying. I
> mean, I just burst. I cried, I cried, I cried. And they had to come
> help to get me because what happened, everything that hap-
> pened to me came back up because from that moment, I had
> suppressed from that moment on, I suppressed everything—all
> the horror, the escape, the getting away. Everything was just sup-
> pressed inside. Now when I saw [the exhibit], I could hear the
> music. I could see the [exhibit's] sign[s]. I could see the lynching,
> hanging, and all this stuff. I mean, I just went crazy. That was the
> first time that it ever came [back]. I had never, never, ever talked
> about it. Never [told] any[one] about it. They didn't even know.
> [I] never talked about it. And that's when it, that's when it came

back. Uh, and that's, that's how, say, that's to say [that's what] black people would do. Family would not talk about it. They'd just leave it [unintelligible]. But it affected you in a certain way. It affected you. . . . It came back.[89]

The images of dead bodies, the stories of each victim printed on little cards, and the sound of spirituals and field hollers playing in the background cracked the wall of silence he had erected around those memories. Piece by piece the barrier crumbled, and the past flooded back. First he remembered the look of terror on his mother's face when he burst into the house; then came the sound of her screaming, "They're going to kill you! They're going to kill you!" He could hear the white men berating his mother, and the howling of the bloodhounds, and then he was back in that outhouse with the bloodhounds straining against their collars to get him. Overwhelmed by guilt and sadness, he cried for the next three days. He cried for endangering his family. He cried for the pent-up fear and panic he felt that day. He cried for all the stories of lynchings and beatings and insults and abuse he had heard growing up. As he shed tears, he also shed some of the burden of keeping his silence for fifty long years.

Without Sanctuary originally appeared at a New York art gallery in 1999, but the crowds that came to see the exhibit became so large that the exhibit was moved to the New-York Historical Society and later traveled to the Andy Warhol Museum in Pittsburgh, the Martin Luther King Jr. Center for Social Change in Atlanta, and elsewhere, before arriving at Jackson State University where Pennington saw the collection.[90] The art historian Anthony Lee notes with distinct discomfort the ways in which the crowds that assembled to view the lynching photographs reproduced the spectacle of violence and the objectification of victims. There were at least fifty thousand visitors—witnesses, voyeurs, and viewers, if you will—at the exhibit in the first four months in New York alone. The crowds of people clamoring to see these images of ritualized violence— some waiting in line more than three hours to get a glimpse of these photographs—often left with a self-congratulatory glow.[91] Pennington, as an African American survivor of lynching, clearly viewed the exhibit as a different kind of witness than the typical visitor. He was not there primarily to learn about the history of lynching but to face a trauma he had stowed away in the far recesses of his memory.

As liberating as it was for Pennington to confront those emotions, and as hard as his family had tried to protect him from the ravages of white supremacist violence, his response to the photograph collection provided a sobering reminder of the burden he and his family had carried for half a century. Unlike Pennington himself, who set up a civil rights law practice in Jackson after graduating from Howard Law School, his mother returned to Mississippi only once after leaving in 1954. A cousin she had been particularly close to had passed away, and she drove down from Chicago for the funeral. During her visit, a white person said something that upset her, and she vowed never to return to Mississippi. Reminiscing about his mother, Pennington mused with a chuckle, "my mother has these things about some of these southern white folks," but in light of his own experience at the exhibit, he also wondered if whatever had transpired between her and that white person triggered waves of bitter memories of Jim Crow she had tried to forget.[92]

Silence had often protected the Penningtons and so many other African Americans from the persistence of traumatic memories. Through silence as a form of refusal, generations of survivors left in the wake of lynchings could drain these white supremacist rituals of their intended purpose to terrorize and degrade Black people. Sapping power from lynching still left room for mourning and memorializing the dead. Refusal did not blunt the pain of lynching for Black families, as Judge Head's tears for his lynched brother attested, but, while carrying the past, in silences and in stories, African Americans could create their present and their future. Unlike literal silence—the absence of sound—these cultural silences were far from empty and weightless. They could exact a heavy, and often hidden, toll over the years, and they could return, unwelcomed, with a vengeance.

CHAPTER THREE

Haunting

People pay for what they do, and, still more, for what they have
allowed themselves to become. And they pay for it, very simply:
by the lives they lead.

—JAMES BALDWIN, *No Name in the Street*

The dead never stop talking and sometimes the living hear.

—MARLON JAMES, *A Brief History of Seven Killings*

OMINOUS GRAY CLOUDS BLANKETED Waco on the morning of May 11,
1953. By mid-afternoon, the rain began to fall, sending the people running errands downtown scurrying to nearby buildings for shelter to wait
out the storm, but this was no ordinary storm. The sky darkened as more
and more clouds converged over downtown. A low rumbling in the distance disturbed the soft pattering of the rain, but then the rumbling grew
louder like dozens of jet engines descending from the sky. According to a
local Huaco legend, this stretch of land along the Brazos River was protected from tornadoes, but for almost thirty-seven years to the day, God
had watched the unrepentant city of Waco ignore and leave unpunished
an unspeakable crime.[1] On this spring afternoon, God had come to this
sad corner of Texas for blood.

As hail and rain battered the city and the skies dimmed to near blackness, the raging winds of the tornado blew out windows and swept up cars and telephone poles. As the hand of God crashed down upon the R. T. Dennis Furniture Store, the hysterical people huddled inside gasped in terror as the five-story building collapsed into a pile of rubble. Then God breathed life into the ALICO Building—the pride of Waco and once the tallest building in Texas—stretching and twisting and bending its steel frame so that the hulking marble building leaned over and smashed an adjacent parking lot with all God's might, killing dozens of people, before being jerked upright again.

Barreling down Franklin and Austin Avenues, the tornado headed straight for the city hall square, the heart of the city and what had been the site of the crime. God reached down from the twister and sent dozens of cars flying around the square, with each car crashing into contorted heaps of metal as He swatted them to the ground. The tornado leapt up across the Brazos River to Bridge Street in East Waco, ripping up block after block of businesses and homes along the way before turning back toward downtown on Garrison Street. With God's wrath satisfied, the twister ascended back up into the sky, leaving much of downtown Waco leveled. The square, where a mob of fifteen thousand had gathered on May 15, 1916, to torture, mutilate, hang, and burn Jesse Washington, had been flattened. The path of destruction left by the tornado marked the path where a white man from the nearby town of Robinson had lassoed Washington's charred corpse from atop his horse and had dragged it through the streets of downtown, whooping and waving his hat in the air as he galloped along. God had not forgotten the city's sins. He emblazoned on the land an unmistakable reminder that the Lord was the ultimate arbiter of justice and righteousness, even in Waco, Texas.[2]

Or so the stories went.

Until recently, this story about the 1953 tornado circulated exclusively among African Americans. In a 1988 interview for Baylor University, Maggie Langham Washington (no relation to Jesse Washington) told her surprised, if not skeptical, white interviewer, "That tornado relived the story of that lynching." Rather than asking follow-up questions about the story, all the confused interviewer could muster in response was a polite "oh really," "that's interesting," and "how interesting."[3] Most white Wacoans had little interest in revisiting an event that had tarnished the reputation of the city. Confronted with white neighbors who preferred to suppress those memories or even chuckle about the lynching among themselves, African Americans, who had little leverage under Jim Crow to begin with, looked to otherworldly forces for justice. Even if they couldn't point an accusatory finger directly at white folks without facing severe repercussions, they took some consolation in knowing that the tornado had punished the city by taking lives and livelihoods, and had left a physical reminder of the racial violence perpetrated there. Telling this story provided a measure of satisfaction to African Americans, and what Maggie Washington told that interviewer not only wrenched the lynching from the shadows of obscurity but marked downtown Waco as the scene of a crime.

When African Americans swapped this story among themselves, they were more concerned with affirming their faith in divine justice and the moral case against racism than with prompting the white community to confront its culpability in the lynching. Vengeance, but in particular divine justice, carried cultural significance in a community that was deeply religious and had witnessed at least three lynchings in downtown Waco alone. When Lester Gibson, who moved to Waco from nearby Freestone County in 1958, retold the story about the ALICO Building, divine justice stood front and center:

> We got one high building [in Waco]. That's the ALICO Building.... That building leaned over in the parking lot and killed oh about forty people in the parking lot and then raised and straightened back up, you understand. So from a spiritual point of view, this was like Moses crossing the water, you understand, when God parted the water, you know. So that was that retribution.... It was payback time.[4]

Gibson's story illustrated in no uncertain terms that, in God's judgment, the city of Waco had incurred His wrath for lynching Jesse Washington and others. The fifteen thousand people in the mob who had attended Washington's lynching had blood on their hands, making this truly a collective sin for the white people of Waco and McLennan County.[5] Texas courts never brought Washington's lynchers to justice, so many members of the Black community believed that the tornado was, in a sense, a supernatural disaster. God intervened, just as He had when Moses led the Israelites to Canaan, when the legal system refused to do so.[6]

These stories not only reminded African Americans of the traumatic aftermath of Washington's violent death and the moral failings of their white neighbors but also resonated with the historical moment in which they lived. Jim Crow was alive and well in 1953. Many of the stores and restaurants in downtown Waco refused to serve African Americans or made them enter through the alley. At the white-owned clothing stores that did serve Black people, they could not try on clothing or hats, and, though African Americans paid the same price as whites for a ticket at the movie theater, they could only sit up in the balcony—what African Americans in Memphis called the "pigeon roost." The buses had a section in the back for Black riders, and, of course, the schools remained segregated until the 1960s. Many African Americans in Waco refused to subject themselves to the indignities of alley doors and pigeon roosts by taking their business elsewhere, and although the tornado demolished many Black businesses on Bridge Street, too, at God's bidding the high winds also swept away the physical reminders of racism in downtown Waco.[7]

Over the years the 1953 tornado—among the deadliest in Texas—became a pivotal moment in Waco's history. The tornado destroyed more than one thousand buildings, caused $51 million in damage, and left 114 people dead and 1,097 others injured. Even after the piles of broken glass, bricks, and twisted metal debris were cleared away, the downtown business district and surrounding neighborhood never fully recovered from the devastation. Businesses relocated to other parts of the city, and the once bustling downtown area languished. The heart of the self-proclaimed "City with a Soul" slowly decayed over time, leaving physical traces of God's fury that helped the cultural traces of miscarried justice endure.[8]

The vengeful 1953 Waco tornado was not an isolated case of a lynching coming back to haunt a community. Throughout the South, African Americans told stories about haunted courthouses, inexplicable afflictions, mysterious deaths, and agonized deathbed confessions that resurrected the ghosts of local lynchings. These stories came out of a folk tradition, born in slavery and with roots in Africa, that used "haints," spirits, and signs not only to entertain but also to give cultural expression to social critiques and to impart lessons about morality and justice. During slavery, enslavers dictated many aspects of African American life and wanted to impose their own distorted racial perceptions onto African Americans to maintain control over them. Far from being quaint superstitions divorced from Black people's material circumstances, folk beliefs provided the enslaved with what Lawrence Levine called "sources of power and knowledge alternative to those existing within the world of the master class."[9] In essence, these folkways empowered Black people to subvert and reject a dominant cultural sensibility that defined them as inferiors who were undeserving of human dignity and human rights.[10]

Among the enslaved, encounters with ghosts occurred regularly. They were, as Jordan Smith put it in his WPA narrative, "as common as pig tracks."[11] Long after the American-born enslaved population outnumbered the African-born enslaved population, elements of Central and West African belief systems persisted in African American culture, including the "good" ghosts of deceased relatives offering protection, guidance, and the path to buried treasure, and the "bad" ghosts of enslavers and overseers who had left thick scars crisscrossing the backs of the enslaved. A self-emancipated man from Kentucky, Lewis Clarke, recalled watching two other enslaved men dig a six- or seven-foot-deep grave for their deceased enslaver, and when Clarke asked them why they dug so far down, they replied that they "wanted to get the old man as near *home* as possible." Clarke and the two men "hauled the largest [stone they] could find, so as to fasten him down as strong as possible."[12] Given the dead man's fondness for the lash and his affinity for devilishness, they didn't want to take any chances in case he came back from the dead to whip them. Having had too much of their cruelty in this life, many of the enslaved people Clarke knew asked to be buried far from their enslavers' and overseers' graves.[13]

With so many ghosts stalking around the South, these spirits slipped into folk stories. In the towns near South Carolina's Congaree Swamp, African Americans passed on a tale of a particularly cruel slave trader, Ole Man Rogan, who took a fiendish pleasure in selling husbands away from their wives and children away from their mothers. Even in the twentieth century, local Black people swore that the sound of clinking chains, the cries of screaming babies, and the wails of inconsolable mothers calling their children's names echoed across the moonlit creek called Boggy Gut, which had been Ole Man Rogan's favorite spot for fishing. Through the darkness, they might catch glimpses of distraught mothers and children, and shackled men slumped over with their hands covering their faces while the ghost of Ole Man Rogan cackled at their misery. According to legend, neither God nor even the devil would take Ole Man Rogan, so his spirit was cursed to wander the swamps without rest.[14]

Sadistic white men like Ole Man Rogan might terrorize the living from beyond the grave, but ghosts of the enslaved also returned from the afterlife, often to avenge the injustices they suffered under slavery. According to Jane Arrington's WPA narrative, an enslaved man in North Carolina named John May haunted the two white men who had beaten him to death. Every night as the terrified men lay in bed, May tormented them with his groans and shrieks, and they fitfully tossed and turned in their sleep, moaning, " 'Go [a]way John, please go away.' "[15] Just like Ole Man Rogan, whose soul would never rest in peace, the two men who killed May suffered for their sins for the rest of their lives. The tales of Ole Man Rogan and John May brought into stark relief the emotional and physical violence of slavery in order to expose the moral depravity of owners, overseers, and slavers, and this impulse to use ghost stories to condemn white supremacy as morally repugnant continued to inform Black folklore.

Ghosts and signs remained ubiquitous in Black folk culture more than a century after emancipation, especially among African Americans in the rural South. When asked by an interviewer in 1995 whether her mother had told her tales about haints and signs, Theresa Pearson retorted, "I've seen them myself!" The incredulous interviewer somewhat more cautiously asked, "Oh, really?" Pearson then launched into a veritable inventory of all of the haints she and her brother, Will Swanigan, had seen. In fact, Will had seen so many ghosts that "most every time he would go down that road, he would see something like a haint. I got tired of trying to keep up with him and them haints."[16]

For people like Theresa Pearson and Will Swanigan, ghosts were real, but over time, skepticism about their existence crept into the Black community. As a little girl growing up in the Arkansas Delta in the 1910s and 1920s, Cleo Jeffers sat around the fire eating peanuts and listening intently to her father telling stories about the haints he had seen. In an interview from 1995, she told several stories about her relatives' personal encounters with ghosts—stories she herself seemed skeptical about— then paused for a moment, musing, "But I don't know where they are now. I don't see no haints now. But now they really believed then."[17] Even though by the mid-twentieth century fewer people believed ghost stories were literally true, African Americans continued to tell these stories, and their cultural meaning remained salient.

Many of these stories passed from one generation to the next for their entertainment value rather than social commentary—thrilling stories about a headless ghost walking down the railroad tracks or a ghost that lapped up whiskey poured on the ground or a family of ghosts that

sat around the dining room table of a house down the street.[18] Other stories, however, translated these haunted landscapes into discursive spaces
for processing and confronting difficult memories—memories like local
lynchings. Under the strictures of Jim Crow, African Americans knew
that merely speaking of lynchings within earshot of whites—much less
overtly demanding that whites reckon with their violent past—could
have deadly consequences. Many Black southerners looked to the supernatural to register their moral condemnation of these unpunished
crimes. Denied legal justice because southern sheriffs and courts refused
to prosecute known lynchers, African Americans found a measure of spiritual justice in ghost stories and tales of divine retribution. Ghosts and
supernatural signs also provided them with multiple layers of plausible
deniability, the same plausible deniability that double entendre embedded into a clever blues lyric, and the same subversive and tragicomic un-
dertones of a blues lament overlaid on a dance beat. They could claim
that these were merely stories, merely entertainment, as an evasive maneuver to placate any whites who might overhear their conversations.
Because these ghosts became a medium for expressing their own moral
disgust, they could also claim that it was the ghost's vengeful wrath and
the ghost's condemnation of lynching, not theirs, that gave shape to the
story. In short, if whites had a bone to pick with these stories, they
should take it up with the ghosts.

Ghosts typically remained suspended between the living and the
dead on account of unfinished business—improper burials, the desecration of their bodies, and unresolved crimes.[19] Many ghost stories that
came out of slavery and those that were inspired by lynchings gave cultural expression to the sentiment that whites who committed violent
transgressions against African Americans did not walk away unscathed.
They might be cursed by a vengeful ghost. They might suffer psychological anguish caused by a guilty conscience. Even the most unrepentant
would have to live with their corroded sense of human decency, what
Baldwin once called "the death of the heart."[20] Punishment could come
from within or without; punishment could come in this life or the next.

Ghost stories laid bare the internal anguish that haunted some white
folks, and when lynchers faced retribution from without—from God or a
ghost or a streak of bad luck—the costs incurred by defending white supremacy became apparent.[21] This folk tradition preserved and affirmed
for generations to come the righteousness of Black moral convictions
and a faith in supernatural justice when the dominant culture refused to

recognize lynching as evidence of white inhumanity.[22] Tales of lynchers haunted by their crimes certainly provided an outlet for righteous indignation, but they also offered a counter-narrative to the overwhelming tendency among white southerners to silence or justify the South's violently anti-Black past. By naming lynchings as crimes to be condemned, these ghost stories fortified a moral code consistent with Black understandings of justice, which was a code they held one another to, and in this way the stories sustained African Americans and empowered them to control the memory of lynching, at least among themselves.[23]

Lynching often left behind physical scars, like the charred branches of a tree or the rope still tied to the beam of a bridge after a body had been cut down, but the sites of lynching themselves seemed to absorb the memories of the crimes perpetrated there. Even when the physical markers of lynching disappeared from the landscape—the tree or telephone pole or courthouse or bridge—injustice lingered as though the air and earth were saturated with memories of violence. The sense that memories can cling to a place is what Toni Morrison captured in a scene from *Beloved* in which a self-emancipated woman, Sethe, warns her daughter, Denver:

> Some things go. Pass on. Some things just stay. I used to think it was my rememory. You know. Some things you forget. Other things you never do. But it's not. Places, places are still there. If a house burns down, it's gone, but the place—the picture of it— stays, and not just in my rememory, but out there, in the world. What I remember is a picture floating around out there outside my head. I mean, even if I don't think it, even if I die, the picture of what I did, or knew, or saw is still out there. Right in the place where it happened.... Where I was before I came here, that place is real. It's never going away. Even if the whole farm— every tree and grass blade of it dies. The picture is still there and what's more, if you go there—you who never was there—if you go there and stand in the place where it was, it will happen again; it will be there for you, waiting for you. So, Denver, you can't never go there. Never. Because even though it's all over—over and done with—it's going to always be there waiting for you.[24]

A decade after emancipation, Sethe believed the horrors of slavery would still be lurking around the Kentucky farm where she had been held in bondage, waiting not just for her but also for Denver and subsequent generations of African Americans. Like many trauma survivors, Sethe had little control over when those memories would come back to haunt her, so, in a way, they existed outside of her even while they were a part of her. These memories existed outside of her in another sense, too: even after Sethe would no longer be alive to remember her suffering, her memories would remain tied to the site of physical and psychological violence during slavery. When she described the farm with its cruelly misleading name, Sweet Home, as "real," she not only referred to the all-too-real vividness of those memories *in her mind* but also to the permanence and timelessness of those memories that stubbornly clung *to that place*.

Morrison's novel memorializes the trauma of enslavement, not lynching, but its insights into trauma, memory, and place have many resonances with the spectral presences haunting lynching sites. Just as Denver could bump into the "rememories" of humiliation, rape, and death at Sweet Home decades after emancipation, for the descendants of lynching survivors, the sites of lynchings remained haunted well after the memories of those who experienced lynching firsthand had vanished. At first glance, the memories embedded in these places might seem too elusive to recover—and some of them are forever lost, locked away in the minds of the dead—but many of these seemingly ephemeral memories took a tangible form through the local lore that passed from one generation to the next. Suspended in the collective memories of African Americans, the ghosts revealed how rememories lie in wait for those who might stumble upon them in the present.

From a second-story window of the small brick courthouse in Pickens County, Alabama, a face, etched onto the windowpane, peers out onto the tiny town of Carrollton. For the locals, that pane of glass has become the stuff of legend or, to be more precise, legends. Most explanations for the apparition in the courthouse involve the lynching of a Black man, but the differences between Black and white memories of the haunting reveal how these disparate memories of the apparition in the window served very different purposes for each community.

Growing up in Hattiesburg, Mississippi, during the 1940s and 1950s, James Reed heard his great-aunt, Maggie Rose Barnett Reed, tell all kinds of stories about living in rural Mississippi at the height of Jim Crow. When the extended family came over to visit, they talked about everything from Klan violence to the daily humiliations of segregation, but one story in particular stuck out, a story about a face that would appear in a courthouse window. Reed remembered it this way:

> Growing up, my great-aunt who raised me used to tell me of a story of a situation that took place back in the, oh I guess, early twenties, of an African American being lynched in some [part] of Alabama, which was actually, it was right across the river. Let's see, Noxubee County is [where] we were, our family was. And it was right across the river, so it had to be the Tombigbee River in Alabama. So whatever is close to Noxubee County in Alabama is where this took place. The story goes, there was this African American that was allegedly dating a white woman, and he was arrested and killed. And he said that he was not guilty of anything. He hadn't raped—it was a rape situation—that he had not raped this woman. But they took him out and killed him anyway. The story goes is that he said, "You will see my face in the courthouse window once a month," or something to that effect. And according to [the] way it was told to me, they tried changing out the window and everything, and regardless of the number of times they tried to change the window out, his face would appear as he predicted.[25]

By the 1920s, the legend had not only crossed the Tombigbee River and reached Noxubee County, but it had piqued the interest of Reed's great-aunt and her brother, Bud, enough that they drove to Carrollton to see the face in the window for themselves. With all the cousins and grandkids and aunts and uncles gathered around, Maggie Reed told her rapt audience how she had seen that ghostly face in the uppermost window of the Pickens County courthouse. That innocent man had kept his promise to remind anyone who walked by the courthouse that this edifice of the justice system was the scene of a horribly unjust crime.

For African Americans like Maggie Reed, the folklore about what was most likely the 1893 lynching of James Williams was emblematic of the violence and racism African Americans endured under Jim Crow. In other words, the injustice of lynching stood front and center in her telling of the story. The Reeds passed this story on to the younger generation during the 1940s and 1950s precisely because racial violence remained alive and well, as the 1955 lynching of Emmett Till, the 1959 lynching of Mack Charles Parker, and several other post–World War II

lynchings in Mississippi attested. Her depiction of Williams helped to restore his dignity and reputation. To begin with, she described him as unwavering in his defiance. He was no coward; he was no criminal. She also
maintained that the victim was erroneously accused of raping a white
woman, a crime that white southerners repeatedly deployed to justify
lynching despite the relative paucity of actual cases involving rape.[26]
Since Williams's threat to haunt the town was contingent upon his innocence, to Black locals, the face in the window not only confirmed his innocence but also betrayed the stereotype of the Black brute and the
association between lynching and rape. This ghost story, though in a
muted way, levied the same critiques against lynching and its defenders
that outspoken activists like Ida B. Wells and the NAACP's Walter White
had been making for decades, but, unlike those activists who directly
condemned lynching, the Reeds used the ghost as an intermediary to
mark the courthouse as the scene of an unpunished crime. By telling the
story among family members into the 1950s, the Reeds made certain that
this counter-memory of lynching survived in their community.

Among whites in Pickens County, the story was no less widespread,
but the differences between white and Black historical memories are
striking. A brief sketch of the story titled "The Face in the Window" appeared in *Records of Pickens County, Alabama*, a collection of documents
about white settlement in Pickens County compiled by Mrs. C. P. Mc-
Guire Sr. and the Birmingham Genealogical Society in 1959. According
to McGuire, the face in the window was the likeness of a Black man
named Henry Wells who allegedly torched the newly rebuilt county
courthouse on November 16, 1876. After two years without any leads or
a suspect, the sheriff arrested Wells, who was also accused of committing
a few other petty crimes. A mob of angry whites began to gather in town,
so the sheriff hid him in the garret of the new courthouse, which had
been rebuilt soon after the 1876 fire. A storm was brewing, and, as Wells
looked out the garret window, lightning struck, stamping the image of
his face on the pane. The mob apparently dispersed, and Wells died in
jail from wounds inflicted when he tried to escape sometime later. This
version of the story entirely erased the lynching from the town's past.[27]

Journalist Kathryn Tucker Windham and folklorist Margaret Gillis
Figh spun a slightly different tale about Wells in their collection of ghost
stories, *13 Alabama Ghosts and Jeffrey*, published ten years later, in 1969.
In their version, after many months without any leads or suspects in the
arson case, the sheriff began to feel pressure from his constituents to

make an arrest. He eventually took Wells into custody, based on scant circumstantial evidence. Legend has it that Wells looked down from the window of the garret at the mob struggling to break into the courthouse and defiantly shouted, "I am innocent. If you kill me, I am going to haunt you for the rest of your lives!"[28] At that moment, lightning struck, forever searing the image of Wells's face on the pane of the garret window. Although the Reeds unequivocally deemed this case a lynching of an innocent man, Windham and Figh vacillated. They reported that, according to some whites, lightning struck Wells dead, and the mob dispersed, "satisfied that the Almighty had meted out just punishment to a criminal."[29] These whites also scrubbed the lynching from their memories, choosing to interpret the face in the window as a reminder that God punished the Black man who burned down the courthouse rather than a reminder that the town of Carrollton had lynched an innocent man.

Other residents Windham and Figh interviewed said that the mob went ahead and lynched Wells despite his warning, and the following morning, a member of the lynch mob who saw the face in the window believed that the devil had appeared in the courthouse to haunt him. Still others told Windham and Figh that, on particularly stormy nights, you can sometimes hear Wells screaming from the courthouse.[30] Even those whites who admitted that a mob had killed Wells tried to rationalize the lynching of an innocent man. In Windham and Figh's version, the sheriff bent under considerable pressure from the citizens of Carrollton to find a suspect: they had waited two years since the arson for an arrest, so he charged Wells, who "had a bad name" since he got into fights and "was rumored [to] . . . always carr[y] a razor."[31] Nobody witnessed Wells committing the arson, but he allegedly was seen in town the morning of the fire, which the sheriff deemed sufficient grounds for charging him with the crime. Even if Wells had not committed the arson, he was, in their eyes at least, a suspicious and dangerous character, and therefore deserving of death by lynching. Windham and Figh alternated between describing Wells as a menace who "confronted [the mob], defiantly shouting at the top of his lungs" and a coward whose face was "distorted by fear" and "anguish and terror."[32] These depictions of Wells served to further rationalize his lynching but also reflected a palpable anxiety over white guilt, which the face in the window reminded white residents of every day when they walked through the center of town.

White collective memory was primarily concerned with the entertainment value of the story: they emphasized the novelty of the haunting itself, not the circumstances that led to it. This fascination with the ghost—but not the lynching—continues to this day in the form of a tacky sign attached to the courthouse itself with a large arrow pointing at the face in the windowpane. Between 1893 and 1917 the citizens of Pickens County lynched no fewer than ten people, which only made this deliberate attempt to reduce the site of a lynching to a tourist attraction all the more troubling.[33] To the Reeds, this piece of family lore represented far more than just another ghost story, for, as Katherine McKittrick argues in *Demonic Grounds*, "one way to contend with unjust and uneven human/inhuman categorizations is to think about, and perhaps employ, the alternative geographic formulations that subaltern communities advance."[34] Telling this ghost story about Williams, not Wells, was a "spatial act" that reimagined the meaning of the courthouse, which had been defined by white geographies and white ways of knowing, from a curiosity to a site of grave injustice.

Perhaps the best way to explain these competing historical memories of lynching is to read them in the context of Lost Cause mythology and white southern memories of Reconstruction. According to the stories white Alabamians published, Wells had destroyed a symbol of white southern resistance to Reconstruction. Windham and Figh explained that the 1876 fire "unleashed an emotional torrent that swept away both patience and reason" since, only eleven years earlier, federal troops had burned the original courthouse.[35] The new courthouse, which was built during the federal occupation, symbolized the white residents' "defiance of Yankee authority" and "a restoration of law and order."[36] Not only did this language of "defiance" and "restoration" reek of Lost Cause and Redemption rhetoric and gloss over of the terrorist tactics employed by Redeemers to end Reconstruction, but pinning the blame for the arson on an African American man also conveniently fit the narrative of tyrannical Republican (and therefore northern and Black) rule during Reconstruction. The perception of Reconstruction as "the tragic era" remained dominant among white southerners at least through the 1960s, and condemning Henry Wells only reinforced this deeply entrenched sense of white southern victimhood at the hands of dangerous African American men. The sting of this victimhood could only be repaired with the restoration of white dominance.[37]

One detail in the Reed family's version—that the face reappeared even after the window had been repeatedly replaced—captured the active attempts by whites to forget the lynching. *Replacing* the window over and over again was an attempt at *displacing* a persistent ghost, but just as Sethe saw the horrors of slavery permanently stamped onto the location of Sweet Home in *Beloved,* the courthouse itself seemed to be permanently afflicted. Whites in Pickens County recalled that at least one and maybe two severe hailstorms over the years shattered every pane of glass in the courthouse except the one with Wells's face. They also recounted how the sheriff was so distressed by the face in the window that he carried "buckets of water up the steep stairs to try to wash away the symbol of a town's guilt, but he only succeeded in making the picture more clearly defined. No amount of scrubbing, not even with gasoline, would remove the image from the windowpane."[38] The lynching victim's presence could not be exorcised from the courthouse—not by city workers replacing the window or by a sheriff scrubbing the pane or by the sky hurling hail at the building. That sheriff certainly seemed wearied by the ghost's dogged persistence. He knew all too well what the aptly named bluesman Sam "Lightnin' " Hopkins meant when he sang: "You better be careful 'bout what you do / I just want to [re]mind [you] the devil's watching you."[39]

Not every lynching site had a ghost lurking around to remind southern communities of the crimes perpetrated there. Sometimes a sense of hauntedness settled onto the sites themselves and wriggled its way into the imaginations and mythologies of local communities. In these ghostless hauntings, local memories remained fixed on the site of the lynching, which is unsurprising given the tendency of lynch mobs to repeatedly return to the same sites for subsequent lynchings.[40] The location of these rituals often held symbolic significance that was not lost on either white or Black communities. Black bodies swinging from trees at sites of white power and state power like the grounds of a courthouse, in front of city hall, or in the town square tacitly gave official sanction and social legitimacy to extralegal violence. The character of towns and collective identities of their residents were formed in public spaces where everything from the annual peach festival to campaign rallies took place, so even when a relatively small portion of the white community participated, the proximity of lynchings to public spaces imprinted that violence onto the character and identity of the town. Mobs that dragged dead bodies through Black neighborhoods or hanged bodies at the border of Black and white neighborhoods, in essence, laid claim to those streets and the people who resided there, unsettling the sense of security and autonomy among African Americans even in their own homes. As time passed, these crimes continued to mark these places as symbols of white supremacy and Black degradation.

A few hours south of Pickens County on the Mississippi side of the border is the town of Shubuta, which sits alongside the Chickasawhay River. Tucked away in the piney woods, the small town had been the site of a Choctaw settlement until a series of treaties in the early nineteenth century forced some of the Indigenous people onto a nearby reservation and condemned the rest to endure the Trail of Tears. With white incursions into the area in the 1830s came the first bridge across the Chickasawhay in the area, probably built by enslaved laborers for a South Carolina planter. The introduction of the railroad in the years leading up to the Civil War and the timber boom that swept the New South after the war brought speculators and then lumber mills that razed the giant pines by the thousands, and over the years, the railroad, new roads, and other bridges diverted much of the traffic from the original bridge.[41] Despite the influx of new industries and transient laborers, the bridge soon reclaimed its local notoriety.

Just a few days before Christmas in 1918, local whites snatched four African American murder suspects, two brothers and two sisters, both of the sisters pregnant, from the Shubuta jail and brought them to the bridge. The mob tied nooses around their necks and shoved them over the side of the bridge to their deaths. Maggie House, the older sister, refused to die easily. To silence her as she struggled and screamed that she was innocent, a member of the mob clocked her with a monkey wrench; the blows knocked out some teeth and left a large gash on her forehead. When they pushed her over the edge, she managed twice to grab onto the side of the bridge to break her fall before they successfully hanged her on the third try. The mob left the bodies of Andrew Clark, Major Clark, Alma House, and Maggie House hanging from the bridge's girders for the sheriff to cut down.[42] A couple of decades later, in October 1942, another mob returned to the bridge to lynch two fourteen-year-old boys, Charlie Lang and Ernest Green, accused of attempting to assault a thirteen-year-old white girl. In its new incarnation, what became known as the Hanging Bridge turned into the most visible and most powerful symbol of white supremacy in the area.[43]

The Hanging Bridge and Shubuta's violent reputation spread beyond the neighboring counties. When an African American man was suspected of attacking a white woman in Mobile, Alabama, in 1939, a member of the Mobile Branch of the NAACP wrote to the field secretary in the national

office: "If mob spirit should seem to be uncontrollable we shall make direct appeal to all law agencies of state, county and city, also to federal government. I think the present affair proves there is not ten minutes
difference between Mobile and other so-called liberal cities in the South
and Shubuta, Miss."[44] More than twenty years after the 1918 lynchings,
Shubuta remained so deeply lodged into national memory as a quintessentially backward and racist southern town that even the NAACP field
secretary in New York City recognized the reference.[45]

In 1918, local whites boasted about these displays of white power and
hatred, but as white public opinion on lynching shifted, many whites
stopped telling stories about the unpunished crimes perpetrated at the
bridge. Even though residents of Shubuta continued to refer to the bridge
as the Hanging Bridge, most white children born after the 1940s assumed
the name referred to the structure itself "hanging" over the Chickasawhay
River, not to the dead bodies left "hanging" from the beams by their own
family members and neighbors. As the civil rights movement chipped away
at the foundation of Jim Crow and the imperative among whites to obscure
and deny racial conflicts grew among all but the most staunchly racist
southerners, whites often chose to erase the memory of racial violence
from this landmark.[46]

Despite the willful forgetting of these lynchings among many whites,
African Americans in Shubuta passed on stories about the men, women,
and children lynched at the Hanging Bridge, but they did so out of earshot of their white neighbors, some of whom had been members of the
mobs. Black parents raising families in and around Shubuta often felt
they couldn't afford to spare their children from these stories, given the
persistent threat of racial violence. They told stories like the one that
Shubuta resident, Reverend Jim McRee, had heard from his nephew who
had been sitting in an adjacent jail cell that night in October 1942 when
a mob took Charlie Lang and Ernest Green from the county jail to lynch
the boys at the Hanging Bridge. McRee's nephew heard Lang and Green
desperately pleading with the sheriff to stop the mob from taking them
to the bridge. Instead, the sheriff dropped the keys to Lang and Green's
cell on the floor for the mob and left.[47] Ghosts weren't necessary to ter-
rify Lang and Green or McRee's nephew or, for that matter, generations
of Black children in the area. The stories about the lynchings and the
physical presence of the bridge itself provided bone-chilling reminders
to African Americans that some whites would readily resort to violence
to enforce the racial order of Jim Crow. The Hanging Bridge stood like a

specter on the outskirts of town, casting a long shadow upon the people of Shubuta.

Fear and silence were not the only responses to the lynchings in Shubuta—so was terrorist violence. Encouraged by the successes of the 1964 Freedom Summer, activists from the Mississippi Freedom Democratic Party (MFDP) set up shop in Shubuta in 1965 to organize the fledgling Head Start program, run voter education workshops, and organize a grocery co-op in a Black neighborhood. Confronting lynching was not explicitly on their agenda, though the lynching of three activists nearby in Philadelphia, Mississippi, the year before certainly loomed large, but they certainly understood their work to be combatting a white supremacist social order that condoned and often celebrated what had happened at the Hanging Bridge. The Klan, in keeping with the local tradition, responded to the MFDP's efforts with death threats and intimidation, sometimes in writing, sometimes from the barrel of a gun. In the civil rights era, these community organizers did not end up swinging from the Hanging Bridge, but carloads of whites fired shots into their offices and sent them bomb threats.[48] They even received a flyer that read: "All nigger's will be shot and killed if any demonstrations accure in Mississippi, All kinky headed darkies better stay on your guard, and kut out all this smart allic demonstration. . . . If you find your car windows dash in and it burn up, or your wife hanging on a light pole, or kids strung up in the outdoor toilet, it will be alright."[49] The Klan made thinly veiled allusions to the lynchings of James Chaney, Andrew Goodman, and Mickey Schwerner ("car windows . . . burn[ed] up"), Alma and Maggie House ("your wife hanging"), and Charlie Lang and Ernest Green ("kids strung up") to remind the African American community and other civil rights activists that the bridge remained a symbol of a racist system they were willing to preserve with violence if necessary.[50]

Shubuta was unexceptional among southern towns where lynchings had taken place, since most of these towns bore physical reminders of the violence with landmarks like the Hanging Bridge. In Kirven, Texas, that physical marker was a plow that sat on a vacant lot between the Methodist and Baptist churches in town. In May 1922, a mob of several hundred white men, women, and children watched as three Black men—John Cornish, Snap Curry, and Mose Jones—were bound by ropes to the plow, castrated, doused with several gallons of gasoline, and burned alive.[51] White residents left the plow on the vacant lot for nearly twenty years to remind Black people to "stay in their place," which was one of the many ways in which physical "places" and social "place" reinforced one another.

During World War II, a father and son who didn't realize the significance of the plow added it to a scrap heap that they sold to a junkyard, which infuriated many local whites. The iron plow was presumably melted down and cast into something else, likely for the war effort, but at least one white man didn't need the actual plow to feel its symbolic power. The man who castrated Curry and Cornish displayed six framed, professional photographs of the lynching on the wall above his bed because he "always wanted to remember it."[52] In 1922, that man had been a twenty-year-old farm laborer raising and butchering hogs, and, in his mind at least, castrating those Black men in the same way he butchered hogs was the way he proved his manhood. He was less forthcoming about his role in the lynchings in front of his family, but, grateful for the opportunity to talk about an experience that stayed with him for a lifetime, he proudly told a documentary filmmaker all the gory details in a series of phone calls he made in 2002. Until his death in 2006 at the age of 104, those photographs of the plow and the charred remains of the three men represented his domination over African Americans and served as a reassuring talisman that sustained this remorseless man to the very end.[53]

In Leesburg, Georgia, and Carrollton, Mississippi, the past stalked around, not in the shadows of black-and-white photographs, but in the branches of lynching trees. All five of the recorded lynchings in Leesburg occurred between February and July 1899, and the memory of those men hanging from tree limbs lingered in the community. Nearly one hundred years later, in 1994, Willie Jackson, at the age of 111, still worried he might be killed for discussing what he had seen all those years ago. Before revealing to an interviewer what he knew about the deaths of three of the victims, George Bivins, William Holt, and George Foot, he sighed, "There's so much [to] say, and so much you can't."[54] If those memories still made Jackson uneasy in 1994, they certainly stirred up anxieties in the early 1920s when a fourteen- or fifteen-year-old African American mechanic named John Henry Taylor punched a white teenager. With a group of white men looking for him, Taylor and his family worried that they might string him up from those trees as they had done to those men a couple decades earlier. Taylor was lucky, though. His mother, Dolly Raines, was a well-respected midwife in the community, so the sheriff helped smuggle him out of town on a train headed to Orlando where his father lived.[55]

About fifty years later, in 1972, Taylor finally returned home to Leesburg to retire with his wife, Robella. The lynching tree was still there.
His wife had harbored many apprehensions about moving to Georgia.
She explained to an interviewer, "Georgia was a terrible place. Even
Leesburg where [her husband's] home is now, there's a tree out there
now. They say, 'that's where they hung niggers.' . . . They'd hang them
and leave them hanging in the tree."[56] Robella Taylor was no stranger to
lynching, having grown up in Alachua County, Florida, where more than
twenty recorded lynchings had occurred, but since she was a newcomer
to Leesburg, locals made sure to warn her about the town's violent past
(or perhaps to intimidate her), using the lynching tree as shorthand for
what had made Georgia such a terrible place for African Americans. The
lynching tree remained a haunting reminder as well as a standing threat.

The lynching trees in Carrollton, Mississippi, also had a way of continually dragging the past into the collective consciousness of the local
African American community. When Mary Robinson was a little girl in
the 1910s, she attended a school at the base of a hill on the outskirts of
North Carrollton, the town just across the Little Sand Creek from Carrollton. One day the teacher took Robinson and the other schoolchildren
on a short field trip of sorts through the woods behind the school. Following their teacher's lead, the children made their way up the hill, snak-
ing their way between the trees. She never forgot what her teacher
showed her that day. Way up in the woods, the children came upon a few
trees with ropes hanging from the branches. Now, Robinson had probably heard older folks talk about lynchings in Carrollton—she undoubtedly knew about the three members of the McCray family, Betsy, Ida, and
Belford, who had been lynched just a few years earlier—but these stories
had always seemed disconnected from her own life and the places she
knew so well. Seeing those ropes dangling up above her head was enough
to make those stories tangible and real, so even though she had never witnessed bodies hanging in the trees, the feeling those trees evoked haunted
her. Robinson explained that "[her teacher] said she wanted us to see it,
but I didn't want to see it no more, even if it was true. I didn't want to see
it no more. I didn't want to see that anymore." Mary Robinson never
went up into those woods again. The palpable aura of hatred and death
that emanated from those trees kept her away for good.[57]

————————

Brooks County sits on the southern border of Georgia, just a few
dozen miles from Tallahassee, Florida. Named after Preston Brooks, the

infamous South Carolina congressman who in 1856 beat Senator Charles Sumner of Massachusetts with a cane on the floor of the US Senate, the county lived down to its namesake's violent reputation and his defense of white supremacy. By some counts, that county in southern Georgia recorded more lynchings than any other county in the United States. It was the county where mobs of white people lynched Mary Turner, her unborn baby, and between eleven and sixteen other African Americans during one week in 1918 alone. That lynching rampage, especially the brutal killing of Mary Turner and her baby, devastated the African American community in Brooks and neighboring Lowndes Counties, but faith in the righteousness of the Lord sustained them through that difficult time. Members of lynch mobs escaped legal punishment in this life, but many members of the African American community believed that nobody, not the sheriff or even the wealthiest planter, could elude God's judgment. The deathbed and the day of reckoning loomed like twin specters of eternal damnation over this county.[58]

Robert Hall, who grew up in Morven, a town just a few miles south of the site of Mary Turner's lynching, saw the physical materialization of that faith as a teenager in the early 1960s:

One day we was going to the store, my mother was along with us, and we were going to the store, and we would always see this old white gentleman. He walked slumped way over, and you know, kids being kids, we kind of laughed at him, you know. And momma told us, you know, "Don't laugh at him." And so we asked her, "Well what happened to him?" And then she went on to tell us that, "Do you remember me telling you all that, uh, the lady that was lynched and her baby was cut out of her stomach?" And we said, "Yes, ma'am." She said, "Well they said he's one of the ones that did it." And you know we got kind of tensed up at that time. And um, he wore a white shirt all the time, and the reason why he wore that white shirt [was] because, according to what my mother was saying, when he cut Mary Turner's stomach open, you know, her water broke, and so everywhere that water hit on their skin, a skin cancer came there. And that's why this old man wore these long-sleeve shirts, was to hide those cancer, but, you know, he had them all on his hands. And uh, that's what, you know, our mother told us. And when he died, he lived in a little shack alongside Highway 76 there in Barney. That's a little town, called Barney, Georgia. And when he got sick, you know, Black people, you know, took care of him 'cause he lived right next door to a Black family, so they would look in on him, give him, you know, food and stuff like this, and said when he died, he, they had to hold him down on the bed when he died, and said all he could say, all [that] was coming out of his mouth was, "Y'all get that nigger woman and that baby away from me." I guess he was having uh, um nightmares about it I guess. That's all he was saying until his last breath left him. "Y'all get that nigger woman and that baby away from me. Get that nigger woman and that baby away from me."[59]

Hall had seen the old man's sins marked upon his arms and hands, and even though that man may not have believed that those sores were physical reminders of his guilt, his desire to hide his disfigurement only reinforced the perception that his guilt and his shame had taken a physical form.

Hall told a variation of a story that circulated among Black people from neighboring towns for decades, and the idea at the core of that story—that lynchers would get their comeuppance—cropped up elsewhere in the South, too.[60] In 1917, a mob in Memphis tied Ell Persons to a log and burned him alive before taking "souvenirs," decapitating him, and dragging his body through the city streets. Persons had been falsely accused of murdering a white woman, and the man who actually had committed the crime, a white grocery store owner, had the gall to bring Persons's ear to his store to show off as a souvenir. Edmonia Taylor, a Memphis schoolteacher, recalled that "everything happened to somebody that had a part in lynching that man," including a white man whose car "jumped off the levee," killing his entire family.[61]

Like the African American community around Barney, Georgia, Taylor understood untimely deaths and other bad luck afflicting lynchers to be punishments. Telling those stories provided a modicum of comfort, yet they were not wholly comforting because punishment from without— careening off a levee, developing sores, and the like—did not require introspection, much less feeling guilty or taking responsibility. However, Hall's story about the old white man walking down Highway 76 included a powerful deathbed scene, which left open the possibility for self-reflection. Perhaps the generosity of his African American neighbors moved that man to feel the weight of his sins, or maybe the sheer barbarity of mutilating a dying, pregnant woman and murdering her baby made it plain that he should be worried about the fate of his soul. Alternatively, the mere presence of African Americans surrounding him on his deathbed may have forced him to confront the crime he had committed against the Turners and the Black community more generally. Regardless of what actually prompted him to dread the imminent final judgment of his sins, he clearly believed that after he drew his last breath, he would have to reckon with the ghosts of Mary Turner and her baby. In fact, they had already begun to torment his conscience as he lay dying. His deathbed confession left African Americans with the sense that some white people who had carried out or had been complicit in lynchings suffered and therefore would fully and consciously understand that what they had coming to them was punishment, not a random stroke of bad luck.

A couple of counties northwest of Barney and Morven, another elderly white man contemplated the prospects of his soul making it up to heaven. During his tenure as sheriff, Claude Screws had rarely hesitated to use violence to intimidate and demean African Americans in Baker County, Georgia. In 1943, he and two deputies arrested a local African American mechanic, Robert Hall (not to be confused with the Robert Hall from Morven), then beat him to death with a nightstick and dragged his lifeless body into a jail cell. Hall's death was, by most standards, a lynching, and certainly a murder, but Screws successfully appealed his case to the US Supreme Court. The Justice Department had argued that Hall's death violated civil rights legislation from Reconstruction that was intended to protect freedmen from draconian measures designed to curb their newfound freedom. The Supreme Court granted that the Justice Department had proven that Screws had intended to kill Hall, but since the government had not shown that Screws intended to violate Hall's civil rights, the case was overturned.[62] Screws was a "free" man, in one sense of the word, but African Americans in the area believed that his conscience was far from "free." In an interview, Shirley Sherrod, a civil rights activist from Baker County, recounted the sheriff's attempts to unburden his soul:

> Now I've heard some of my cousins talk about Screws. They say—and I don't know whether this is [an] old folk tale or whether it's true—but they said he had killed a number of Black people. And I guess, during his later years he lost his eyesight and I don't know what else was wrong with him. . . . He lived somewhere down there in Newton and he would, he would be saying,

he'd hear someone and say, "Is that a nigger? If that's a nigger, please come in here. Please." You know, he just wanted Black folk around him during the years when he was about to die. And they said he told the Gator [Warren Johnson, the new Baker County sheriff], said, "Whatever you do, don't kill a nigger."[63]

Facing death, Screws wanted absolution for taking Hall's life, but since he couldn't get absolution from the man he lynched, he figured any Black person passing by his home would do. He seemed to have hoped that, through a series of confessions, his soul could rest in peace. Sherrod remained skeptical of this repentant incarnation of Screws, probably because that image appeared to be so grossly out of character with the man who had killed Robert Hall and abused countless other African Americans for decades. Either way, the story resonated with Black dissatisfaction with human justice. When (or if) Screws begged for forgiveness, he revealed, at the very least, the extent to which he feared going to hell for his earthly crimes. His admission of guilt may not have indicated that he felt remorse—the fear of spending an eternity in hell and genuinely feeling remorseful are not the same—but for African Americans, the prospect of divine justice articulated in this story served to remind them that, with a Supreme Court that would let a known murderer go free, divine justice was their only option.[64]

For some African Americans who witnessed a lynching or lost a family member to a mob, the haunting was palpable. Traumatic memories, like ghosts, could intrude upon their everyday lives. For survivors, lynching was more than just a terrifying story. The horror and anguish of the past seeped into the present, and these psychological wounds still throbbed. Memories of the violence usually did not consume these survivors, but even decades later the pain was still raw, the sadness was still overwhelming, the sense of loss was still devastating. Survivors of trauma often lost control over fractured traumatic memories—after being stowed away, sometimes for years, these memories and the pain they caused could return unbeckoned, triggered by the faintest echoes of a traumatic event.[65] Haunting, for some, meant trying to keep painful memories at bay just long enough to avoid reliving the past.

Will Head was a thirty-year-old farm laborer when a mob of about three hundred white men in Brooks County, Georgia, lynched him on May 17, 1918. He was the first of the lynching victims in the killing spree that claimed Mary Turner's life. After getting him to confess to stealing the gun used to kill his white employer, the mob tied a rope around his neck, made him climb up a large oak tree, and, after fastening the other end of the rope around another tree, forced him to jump to his death. No member of the mob attempted to conceal his or her identity, and nobody faced prosecution.[66]

In its aftermath, the lynching of Will Head crept into the daily lives of the Head family. The fear that yet another young man in the family might suffer a similar fate stalked around in the backs of their minds. Fifty years after the family lost Will, Willie Head Jr., Will's grand-nephew, "sassed" Cordy Paris, the white vegetable buyer at the Thomas-ville market, by refusing to sell some butter beans at well below their market value. Right after Willie Jr. left with all his butter beans, Paris called Willie Sr., telling him that his teenaged son ought to show more respect to white folks. Willie Sr.'s mind flashed back to the family lore about what white people had done to his uncle, Will Head, and the moment Willie Jr. got home, his father took him out to his truck and drove him to his Uncle Rufus's farm for his safety. Willie Jr. demanded that his father take him home, insisting that he was overreacting, and although the older man eventually did turn around and head home, the fear that white folks would kill his son, too, lingered. When Willie Jr. arrived back at the house, he met the worried gaze of his mother, Jessie Mae Head. She warned him in a grave voice, "Son, they'll kill you. They'll kill you. It's a wonder they didn't kill you." Reflecting on that day in his home, which sits on the same land his grandfather had cleared and purchased, he said, "You would think that [Will Head's lynching] was long past them . . . but to them it was kind of fresh."[67]

The categories of past and present appeared to collapse for the older members of the Head family. Memories that perhaps should have yel-lowed and faded with time instead remained, as Willie Head Jr. put it, fresh. The immediate threat of violence had passed fifty years earlier, but the past had not loosened its grip. They couldn't know for sure whether they could trust that the white people of Brooks County had changed, and the memory of Will Head's lynching convinced them that the conse-quences of trusting white people were too high to risk it.

A few states over, in Mississippi, Minnie Weston grew up amid so many lynchings and so much racial violence that, even as a ninety-year-old woman, she struggled to fight off those traumatic memories. By the time Weston was fourteen years old, two of her brothers had been murdered, and some white men had visited her home in the dead of night to take her father and another brother out into the darkness, presumably to beat them. Around this same time, her family had run off from a plantation in Chickasaw County after a dispute at settling time with the white man they sharecropped for. From a very early age, she knew what whites in Chickasaw County thought about the value of Black life. Weston recalled that her father, after hearing that one of his sons had been murdered—drowned—by his white employer, went to see about his son: "We didn't know nothing about it [the murder] until it was done, but and then uh when my daddy went to him and ask him about that boy, only thing he said to, the white man said to him, 'Go ahead on and bury that nigger.' So that's all my daddy got out of him."[68] The family never knew what possessed that white man to commit the murder, and, unsurprisingly, no court of law ever bothered to look into the matter, either.

Raising children at the turn of the twentieth century, when racial violence was a part of everyday life in Mississippi, Weston's parents hid the "hanging, executing, just all kind of death among the Black [people]" under a shroud of secrecy. With three recorded lynchings of African American men in the county seat of Houston between 1904 and 1913, Black parents had plenty of violence to conceal.[69] As a child, Weston wondered what caused the pain she witnessed when her mother, aunts, and others would gather "over there [in] that old wood uh place there, in old shacky houses, [sitting] over [by] that old fireplace and crying . . . and whispering to each other,"[70] but she sensed that she shouldn't ask about the things that brought tears to her mother's eyes.

Weston suspected that her parents shielded their children from stories about racial violence out of fear that the children might say something out of turn in front of a white person, but her father's experience as a child pointed to other worries as well. Although her father was born free, his parents had been born enslaved. As a young boy, her father had heard a story about how his mother's enslaver would abuse her. He would build a large fire until the bricks in the fireplace got good and hot, then would force Weston's grandmother to stand on the bricks, burning her feet and legs. Listening to that story as a child, Weston's father wished that he could have helped his mother, but all he could do was try to suppress the impotent rage that welled up inside:

> That [story] made him hate because, you know, see, they told
> him when they shouldn't have told him. . . . He said when he

growed up, to get grown, he was, was going to kill people just as they come to it. But when he did grow up, God had fixed his heart. . . . He said he often thought about how his mother's legs were burned by slavery, but he forgive those people, and that's what he told, told us. . . . So that's the way that [we] come up.[71]

Even though her father had taught his children not to hate white people, "still something was raised up against them [his two murdered sons]," and no amount of forgiveness could bring peace to him or his daughter, Minnie.[72]

On the tape of the interview in which Weston recounted these stories, the pain in her voice cuts through in the recording. Moments earlier, she had been wistfully reminiscing about the generosity and kindness within the Black community during her childhood, but when the interviewer asked her about race relations during Jim Crow, she stopped. All of a sudden, words escaped her. Like her mother and aunts who had huddled around the fireplace in those shacks back in Chickasaw County, her voice shrank to an unsteady whisper. As she struggled to get out a few words— "Oh, well they didn't care [unintelligible] any time with the Black people. No, they didn't. No, they didn't allow any Black people [unintelligible] around there. Uh-uh. No. They would not."—she seemed to weigh how deep into those old wounds she would be willing to plunge. In time she revealed that one of her brothers had been drowned, but couldn't go further: "So, so that's all I would want to tell about my people."[73] The interviewer gently urged her to tell more, and she did, but every word seemed to push her deeper and deeper into a past she didn't want to revisit.

A few minutes later, the interviewer asked Weston whether she had heard stories about slavery as a child. Again, she hesitated as though she were girding herself for another wave of painful memories. With some more encouragement, though, she dove even deeper into those old wounds: "I never forget what my daddy told me about his mother. And I could never forget uh. . . . He was some related to, to us that my grandma told me that they hung him and put a chain around his neck. I just can't, I tried and tried to get, forget it. I can't forget."[74]

Weston paused before starting again. This time her whisper cracked, as though she were on the verge of tears. She then told the story about the three or four white men who visited her childhood home in the middle of the night. She began with an image, a fragment from the middle of the story: several children, herself included, sleeping on a pallet. The rest of her story unfolded in nonlinear fragments—a piece here and a piece there—but she always returned to that image of the sleeping children. Weston's reconstruction of that story mimicked the classic symptoms of trauma: vivid fragments of memory with gaps that made reconstituting the whole story seem impossible, returning to the same image repeatedly, and feeling the same panicked emotions that arose during the traumatic event. Some of that fragmentation resulted from never knowing what happened that night after those men took her father and older brother outside. The rest probably came from the intensity of her worry and fear that night, which disrupted her ability to process all that happened. As she lay on the pallet that night pretending to sleep alongside her brothers and sisters, she sensed that she should be afraid and keep quiet as her father and brother disappeared into the night. That fear stopped her from asking her parents the next day to explain what had happened, and that anxiety persisted some eighty years later. Weston ended that part of her conversation by reflecting on her struggle with those memories: "I think about it, that time. Now they run across my mind, but to think of it, I don't hold it. Now that's it. That's it."[75] She seemed to have seen enough of those ghosts for that day, and now was the time to lay them to rest once again.

CHAPTER FOUR

Violence

She kisses her killed boy.

    And she is sorry.

Chaos in windy grays

    through a red prairie.

—GWENDOLYN BROOKS, "The Last Quatrain of the Ballad
of Emmett Till"

AN EFFIGY DANGLED OUTSIDE the second-story window of Vardaman
Hall, a men's dormitory on the University of Mississippi campus, on October 3, 1962 (fig. 4.1). Its chin forced down against its chest from the
rope tightly wound around its neck, the limp figure was stuffed with
crumpled paper, tinder waiting for nightfall, preparing for flames. Students had painted its face black and added a sign that read "GO BACK TO
AFRICA WHERE _YOU_ BELONG," and for good measure they tucked a Confederate flag inside its collar. The effigy's mouth was simple—a piece of
masking tape that only magnified its silence—and its eyes, two cotton
balls crudely affixed with scotch tape, stared blankly at Baxter Hall, where
James Meredith, the man the effigy was meant to represent, lived.

The lynched effigy was the third to appear on campus in as many
weeks. The first showed up on September 13, even before Meredith had
enrolled at his home state's public university as its first African American

Figure 4.1. "An effigy of James Meredith, a recently admitted black student, hangs from a dormitory on the campus of Ole Miss in Oxford, Mississippi, October 3, 1962." (AP Photo/stf)

student. His white classmates strung up the second effigy on October 2. The sign draped around this second figure taunted Meredith, "We're gonna miss you when you're gone," and in the middle of the night, a crowd of students gathered outside Vardaman Hall to set the effigy aflame while they shot off firecrackers to intimidate Meredith with the sound of the explosions.[1]

The campus itself—its buildings, its grounds, its surroundings—was marked by Mississippi's long history of white supremacy. The dormitory where the last effigy was hanged took its name from James K. Vardaman, Mississippi's race-baiting governor and senator—a man who had openly endorsed lynching while in office in the early twentieth century.[2] The school's nickname, Ole Miss, was a nod to white nostalgia for slavery—a time when enslaved people performed deference to whites by calling enslavers "Ole Missus" and "Ole Massa." A cemetery and monument on campus honored the Confederate dead, and the Lyceum, the building in the center of campus where Meredith had registered for classes, had been constructed by enslaved people in 1848. The town of Oxford was the site not only of the university but also of several grisly lynchings in the late nineteenth and early twentieth centuries, which the white community had quietly swept under the rug by the 1940s. Though filled with cotton or crumpled paper, not flesh and blood, these carefully constructed effigies proudly carried on a tradition of lynching that celebrated white supremacy in Mississippi and throughout the South.

These effigies were far from empty threats. Meredith's "welcome" to campus began with a violent riot, put down by thousands of US marshals, that left two people dead and hundreds injured. For the remainder of the academic year, armed marshals accompanied Meredith almost everywhere he went to protect him from physical harm, though they could do little to deflect the almost daily verbal barbs and epithets hurled his way. In the weeks and months that followed the riot, Meredith received hundreds of death threats, many of which pointedly referenced lynching.[3] One letter from Troy, Alabama, signed "The Sovereign States of Alabama and Georgia," made a sorry attempt at poetry, practically shouting through the page in all uppercase letters:

ROSES ARE RED

VIOLETS ARE BLUE

I KILLED ONE NEGRO

I MAY MAKE IT *TWO*.[4]

The subsequent stanzas threatened that, if Meredith's "friends" set foot in Alabama or Georgia, "THEY'LL HANG BY THEIR BALLS"—presumably referring to Martin Luther King Jr., Medgar Evers, and Robert Kennedy. A letter signed simply "Buddy" predicted that someone would "pinch [his] head off" and make his wife a "black widow," and a postcard read:

> Dear Nigger bastard,
> I hope they hang your black ass from the biggest tree around. You fucking aborigini prick. You eight ball cocksucker. You prick cannibal. Your a mother-fucker you <u>black</u> <u>fuck</u>. Love, the WHITES[5]

For all their venom, these letters and postcards were acts of cowardice. Anxious about the social upheaval produced by the civil rights movement, these white southerners retreated toward what, for many, were comforting memories of a time when they wielded a near absolute right to use violence against African Americans. To boast of murdering a Black person and being willing to kill again, in a trite rhyme no less, seemed intended to reassure the letter writers of the power of their whiteness as much as it announced their murderous designs to Meredith. For decades, lynching had galvanized white southern identity and unified much of the white South under the mantle of white supremacy, and these letters signed "the WHITES" or "The Sovereign States of Alabama and Georgia" evinced the powerful social function of lynching for white southerners in the past as well as the continued potency of invoking lynching in the civil rights era.

Most of these death threats arrived in Meredith's mailbox printed on letters, postcards, and telegrams, but his fellow students hurled more than taunts and jeers at him. They also threw rocks, bottles, cherry bombs, and firecrackers. Once he even found a dead raccoon on the hood of his car—the epithet "dead coon" materializing in the flesh.[6] In a matter of weeks during that fall semester of 1962, the dead bodies had piled up. Alongside the dead racoon and three effigies were Paul Leslie Guilhard and Ray Gunter, who were killed in the riot, though, thanks in part to the marshals, Meredith was not among the dead. A local undertaker from Corinth, Mississippi, Bill McPeters, had other plans for Meredith. He sent Mississippi governor Ross Barnett a telegram offering to take Meredith and any other "troublemakers" off his hands free of charge. The telegram arrived a couple of weeks before Meredith enrolled at the University of Mississippi, and the offer to bury Meredith's corpse would not have seemed like much more than rhetorical chest-thumping had he not also boasted about "own[ing] the ground that the tree still stands on that was used about 55 years ago: when one got out of place."[7] Memories of what had taken place on the land he now owned trickled down to him through the years, and his possession of the lynching tree itself grounded him as he offered his undertaking services to the governor.

Meredith remained remarkably unflappable in public despite the daily onslaught of verbal and physical threats. When a reporter asked what he would like to say to his classmates, he answered, "I've noticed that a number of students looked like they're mad. I don't know what they're mad at, but if they're mad at me, I'd like to know about what."[8] He tended to give measured responses to reporters who asked about the violence and vitriol, the isolation and insults, but after his seventy-one-year-old father was awakened in the dead of night by shotgun blasts fired into his home, he wondered how much harassment he could stand to put his family through. In an article he wrote for *Look* magazine in 1963, he lamented that "hearts have now shown that they don't intend to change," but he also vowed to continue his fight for racial justice, despite trepidation about his family's safety.[9] In public, Meredith was unwavering in his fearlessness and defiance, but perhaps he worried about his own safety, too. During his time at the University of Mississippi, Meredith made only passing reference to the threats directed at him, which he seemed to brush off as undignified and shameful—more evidence of white Mississippians' well-deserved reputation for racist vitriol. These threats were a continuation of Mississippi's long history of anti-Black violence, and they exposed the desperation of white Mississippians like McPeters, who clung to memories of lynching for safety, reassurance, and comfort while their way of life slipped through their fingers, no matter how hard they grasped and clawed at it.

The history of the United States is, in many ways, a history of white supremacist violence. As the nation has cycled through various systems of white supremacy, one of the primary continuities of that history has been the deployment of violence to limit full citizenship to white people and to protect white people's stranglehold on power from threats and challenges to that racial order, whether slave insurrections, African American economic competition, or the enfranchisement of Black people. After emancipation, the brutality of enslavement—the whippings, rapes, iron collars, brandings, hangings, maimings—persisted and evolved. Lynching was but one of many forms that violence took, but by the early twentieth century, lynching had become emblematic of white supremacist terrorism and violence. Long before Meredith enrolled at the University of Mississippi and saw his classmates hang and burn him in effigy, the noose and pyre, more than other signifiers of anti-Black violence, perhaps with the exception of shackles and the Confederate flag, became the dominant signifiers of white supremacy and a shorthand for white power—one that simultaneously galvanized white identity and terrorized Black people.

Lynching became so intimately entangled with white southern identity because, through these communal and public rituals, masses of white southerners became invested in maintaining white supremacy. While often distinct from state-sponsored violence, lynching was both state-sanctioned and doing the work of protecting the racial state, even when agents of the state like elected officials or law enforcement were not actively involved. Under slavery, white citizens, whether enslavers or not, were, in essence, deputized by the state to use violence against Black people, especially on slave patrols but also in everyday interactions. After emancipation, the unofficial deputizing of all white people persisted.[10] By failing to charge and convict lynchers, the state empowered any white southerner to lynch African Americans with little to no interference from the law. Even on the rare occasions when white lynchers faced criminal charges, convictions were virtually unheard of.[11] All white southerners functionally became potential members of lynch mobs, which not only enforced white supremacy but encouraged all white southerners to buy into the power of whiteness. One popular adage among Black southerners during Jim Crow was, "You got to buy a license to kill everything but a nigger. We was always in season."[12]

Lynching rituals had white southerners step into their roles as the enforcers of white power, and bonding over stories about lynching, even decades after the fact, was a guiding light that provided many with a sense of community, purpose, place, and safety. In the civil rights era, with the foundations of Jim Crow beginning to crack and crumble, they revived memories of lynching through effigies and rhetorical invocations—and, of course, through acts of physical violence, including lynching—for the stakes of defending white supremacy were higher than ever, arguably higher than they had been during Reconstruction. As white southerners clung to white supremacy, memories of lynch mobs killing and terrorizing

Black people often became the filter through which they interpreted the destabilization of Jim Crow unfolding before them, even as their tried-and-true strategy of using excessive, ritualistic violence to intimidate African Americans seemed to be losing its potency. Bombing Black churches, assassinating NAACP leaders, and beating Black voters exacted a heavy toll on the Black community, but this violence did not completely discourage activists from protesting in the streets. In fact, this violence further eroded public opinion of Jim Crow and the white South more generally, and, for some activists, white supremacist terrorism strengthened their resolve to dismantle white supremacy. In acts of both desperation and fear, whites rearticulated collective narratives and rituals of lynching—through effigies, lynching rhetoric, and physical violence—to cope with the rapidly changing world around them.

In the wake of the Holocaust and as anticolonial independence movements gained traction around the world, however, white public opinion—both in the United States and abroad—had fractured somewhat and become less tolerant of the most extreme and visible manifestations of white supremacist violence, such as lynching. Large majorities of white people continued to uncritically embrace white supremacy and dismiss substantive challenges to its foundational place in the United States, but sadistic violence—associated with Nazis, European colonizers, and the vestiges of enslavement—was less socially acceptable.[13] Some white southerners preferred to silence and bury their memories of lynching, as a matter of either prudence or shame, for they knew that, if they were honest with themselves about lynching, they would have difficulty denying the merits of what the civil rights protesters demanded. But Jim Crow *was* maintained by violence. It was unjust. It was cruel and brutal and horrifying. Facing reality would mean that the myth that Black southerners were happy with their lot would collapse, as would the myth of white innocence.[14] However, those white southerners who returned to lynching through effigies, rhetoric, and violence were less bothered by the cruelty and brutality and horror than their counterparts who responded to the civil rights movement with silence and even introspection. To stave off criticism for being too outwardly racist, many of them strategically invoked the meaning and power of lynching, but in ways that often fell just short of lethal violence. Some might hang and burn effigies. Others might reminisce about past lynchings or mouth empty threats to lynch "rabble-rousers." The intent to terrorize remained, as did the desperate desire for their own reassurance.

Just as most white southerners did not personally participate in lynch mobs during the peak period of southern lynching, most white southerners after 1940 did not use figurative representations of lynching, and even fewer actually lynched Black southerners, but actual lynchings continued nonetheless, even as they went "underground," as the NAACP put it.[15] The lynch mobs of the post–World War II era tended to be much smaller and more secretive, and they often hid the victims' bodies, rather than display them at a crossroads or on a courthouse lawn. Gone were the days of posed photographs with lynched corpses and unmasked mass mobs in broad daylight—most of the time, anyway—but features of lynching from its heyday persisted. And the boasts and stories of lynchings and other racial terror killings still drifted through white communities, even if local whites remained tightlipped in the presence of outsiders inquiring about the widely known identities of perpetrators. In 1959, lynchers took Mack Charles Parker, a Black man charged with raping a white woman, from his jail cell in Poplarville, Mississippi, then shot him, before dumping his body into the Pearl River. The manner in which Parker died was indistinguishable from lynchings during the peak period, and even though the FBI sent investigators to Mississippi who identified the lynchers, neither state nor federal authorities pursued prosecutions.[16]

Other white supremacist violence in the South that was, at the very least, adjacent to lynching regularly made the national news in the civil rights era. Members of the Klan planted bombs in the homes of civil rights leaders and set fire to churches to terrorize Black communities. To preserve white political power, they ambushed and shot Black people who ran voter registration drives. They kidnapped, then killed and disfigured those committed to destroying Jim Crow. Fewer lynchings occurred, but the function of lynching—namely, to reproduce a white supremacist racial polity and maintain a white supremacist social and political order—shifted, and it shifted even more so into the legal workings of the state through the death penalty and other means.[17]

The changing character of lynching in the 1930s and 1940s was as much a matter of an evolving set of violent acts adapting to a changing racial landscape as a concerted effort among white liberals and moderates to downplay the persistence of white supremacist violence. As Ashraf Rushdy has compellingly argued, the "end-of-lynching discourse" has claimed, then and now, that lynching ended sometime in the 1940s, marking a clean break from the bad old days before the nation got a conscience.

Such discourse relied too heavily on the form that lynchings took after the early 1940s (and how closely that form resembled previous lynchings, which themselves were never uniform), and not enough on the motives of lynchers. It also sidestepped the enduring national culture that supported lynching and sustained the racial polity for decades, a culture that did not suddenly disappear with the threat of federal intervention, changing public opinion, or the beginning of the Cold War.[18] As lynching rituals changed and moved underground during the civil rights era, the South saw clear continuities between old and new white supremacist violence and terror, and Jim Crow's defenders saw in lynching something that provided them with the psychological reassurance they desperately needed, especially in a time of great social upheaval.

For Black survivors, the violence of lynching was not totalizing, nor was white supremacy, but the dividing line between the Black and white worlds—what Du Bois called "the veil"—was permeable. White supremacy impinged upon Black people's lives, even as they cultivated lives apart from the white world and white supremacy. White southern memories of lynching, and the figurative and literal repetition of the practice, altered the landscape against which Black people narrated (or not) and processed lynching memories. At times, Black southerners countered white supremacist invocations of lynching with denunciations of the practice and its aftermath. At other times, they went on with the work of mourning and living on their own terms or with the low din of the white world faintly audible in the distance.

In panel 15 from Jacob Lawrence's series of paintings, *The Migration of the Negro* (1940–41), a noose and the *absence* of a body mark the barren, washed-out landscape as a place burdened with the memory of a lynching (fig. 4.2). The mourning survivor bent over in the foreground is evidence enough that the noose left hanging from the branch had strained under the weight of a dead body. Against the bleakness of this spare landscape, the figure in red, though devastated by the loss of yet another life, somehow breathes—or perhaps sighs—life, and certainly pain and despair, into the painting. As he captured the journey of Black southern migrants to northern cities, Lawrence recognized the need to memorialize the grief and despair that followed lynching survivors up north and continued to haunt them well beyond the 1940s. The son of southerners who migrated to the Northeast around 1920, Lawrence made visible a violent history that pushed Black migrants up north, but he deliberately

Figure 4.2. Jacob Lawrence, *The Migration Series, Panel no. 15:* "Another cause was lynching. It was found that where there had been a lynching, the people who were reluctant to leave at first left immediately after this." 1940–41, casein tempera on hardboard, 12 × 18 inches (30.48 × 45.72 cm). Acquired 1942. (The Phillips Collection, Washington, DC; © 2021 The Jacob and Gwendolyn Knight Lawrence Foundation, Seattle / Artists Rights Society [ARS], New York)

removed the body from the scene, not to erase the violence of lynching, but to preserve the dignity of the dead and recognize the suffering of the living.[19]

Lawrence revisited lynching in other paintings and drawings during the 1930s and 1940s, and, as with panel 15, his art centered the Black community living in the midst and in the wake of lynching while always underscoring the barbarity of lynching. In *Subway* (1938), for instance, three seated Black women ride a subway in New York, each holding a handbag or shopping bag and keeping to herself (fig. 4.3). Hanging just above their heads are three white subway straps that resemble nooses— reminders that lynching was a specter that unexpectedly invaded the everyday even in New York City after a long day of errands and work. The noose remained a symbol of terror and violence, but, unlike white

Figure 4.3. Jacob Lawrence, *Subway*, 1938, tempera on illustration board, 20 × 15½ inches. (Art & Artifacts Division, Schomburg Center for Research in Black Culture, The New York Public Library; © 2021 The Jacob and Gwendolyn Knight Lawrence Foundation, Seattle / Artists Rights Society [ARS], New York)

supremacists who returned to the imagery of lynching to instill fear in Black people and reassure white people, Lawrence used the nooses as reminders of losses, both those already incurred and the real possibility of more to come.

Other contemporaries shared Lawrence's imperative to condemn and bring an end to lynching through their art, though, more often than not, their artwork focused on the viciousness of the mobs and the dead or dying bodies of their victims. Much of the art featured at rival antilynching exhibitions sponsored by the NAACP and the Communist Party in 1935 departed from Lawrence's approach and depicted lynched bodies and lynch mobs. These major exhibitions were intended to garner white liberals' support for antilynching legislation, and shocking the conscience through violent images of Black suffering and white bloodlust seemed to be an effective way to jostle them into action. Isamu Noguchi's sculpture titled *Death (Lynched Figure)* (1934) depicted a nearly life-size, contorted body constructed out of a nickel-copper alloy hanging from a rope around its neck. Modeled on a photograph of the 1930 lynching of George Hughes, the sculpture captured the sheer anguish of Hughes's final moments as he was burned alive in Sherman, Texas. In Prentiss Taylor's lithograph, *Christ in Alabama* (1932), a Black man with arms outstretched and face turned upward to the heavens stands with the faint outlines of a bright white cross behind him. To his left is a row of cotton; to his right is a Black woman, seated, with arms crossed, looking downward. The unmistakable reference to the crucifixion of Christ and the mourning of Mary expressed a hope for the redemptive suffering of lynching victims while condemning the un-Christian hypocrisy of white lynch mobs and their apologists. Whether intended to evoke horror or sorrow or a redemptive vision of lynching victims, these artworks reclaimed the humanity of the victims, countering the lynching photographs taken and distributed to reduce Black bodies to objects of ritualized violence, and instead turning images of lynching into protests against white supremacy. As civil rights organizations and Black newspapers had been doing for decades, these lynching photographs and artworks publicized these unpunished crimes and indicted the moral values of a racist nation.[20]

Despite antilynching appropriations of these images, visual representations of lynching that celebrated anti-Black violence were still pervasive during the civil rights era. Some white southerners kept photographs of lynchings in their homes, perhaps tucked away in the back of desk drawers or maybe even displayed on their fireplace mantel.[21] In public spaces, they often took representing lynching beyond two dimensions. Effigies like the ones hanging on the campus of the University of Mississippi in 1962 regularly appeared throughout the South during this period. Amid the earliest stirrings of the long civil rights movement, the Ku Klux Klan hanged a Black effigy from a telephone pole in Miami to intimidate African Americans who had registered to vote in 1939 (fig. 4.4). The bloodstain that spread from the effigy's heart ran down its torso and onto its legs, and across its chest was a sign announcing, "THIS NIGGER VOTED."[22] The effigy with its neck snapped back and to the side, its eyes bulging and staring blankly upward, and its missing right hand sent a stark warning that replicated the spectacle and terror of lynched bodies left hanging for days.

During the Montgomery bus boycott in 1956, two effigies, one Black and one white, appeared in Court Square, just blocks from Martin Luther King Jr.'s pulpit at Dexter Avenue Baptist Church (fig. 4.5). They dangled from a makeshift scaffold constructed by the local Citizens' Council, and perched above their mannequin heads were Confederate flags and black birds that appeared to have been killed and then stuffed. The Black effigy, dressed in a suit, was labeled "N.A.A.C.P."; the white effigy had "TALKED INTEGRATION" emblazoned across its torso. The city police had escorted to the square the white men who assembled the scaffold, giving tacit state sanction to the display of lynched effigies in the center of the city. With the symbol of the Confederacy physically looming above, the message was unmistakable: Black boycotters and white sympathizers had violated the racial code of Jim Crow and would face violent retaliation with the blessing of the state. Soon after, violence struck Montgomery's Black community as homemade bombs tore apart the homes of King, E. D. Nixon, and other local civil rights leaders, but the boycott continued. White fears mounted as the pressure from this well-organized and disciplined boycott strained the finances of the city's segregated bus system, and white racists reached for the powerful symbol of lynching to quell their fears and reassert white power.[23]

The mob outside Little Rock's Central High School on the morning of September 4, 1957, had a similar agenda. The NAACP had decided to test the Supreme Court's school desegregation decision, *Brown v. Board of Education* (1954), and the first Black child to arrive to integrate the school that morning was a shy but determined fifteen-year-old, Elizabeth Eckford. As she stepped off the Sixteenth Street bus stop that morning,

Figure 4.4. "KKK Warning That Failed," May 3, 1939. (Bettmann via Getty Images)

she was met by an angry white mob. Though the school was surrounded by National Guardsmen, white men and women spat on her and hurled racial epithets and insults at her as she approached the main entrance. Clutching her notebook, Eckford, a solitary Black child in a sea of enraged whites, steeled herself against the verbal onslaught and quickly

SEGREGATION SYMBOL SCUTTLED

This gallows was erected on Court Square yesterday to hang the NAACP and pro-integrationists in effigy. One of group of 12 men who erected the gallows said the purpose of the macabre ceremony was to show "how serious we feel about the segregation issue." The prank was reportedly the brainchild of the Committee on the Preservation of Segregation, a Montgomery group.

Figure 4.5. "Segregation Symbol Scuttled," August 5, 1956. (© *Montgomery Advertiser, USA Today Network*) walked back toward the bus stop. Somebody in the mob yelled, "Lynch her!" and others joined in: "Lynch her! Lynch her! Lynch her!" Shaking in terror and barely holding back tears, the high school student sat on the bus stop bench and waited. Only when the other eight Black students arrived at the school, escorted by local NAACP leaders and ministers, did most of the mob redirect its attention away from the lone Black girl on that bus stop bench.[24]

When Eckford's mother, Birdie Eckford, heard news coverage of her daughter's first day of school over the radio, the shouts of "Lynch her!" directed at her child must have resurrected frightening memories from growing up when lynching was a fairly regular occurrence. Back in 1927, a mob in Little Rock had brutally lynched a Black father of five named John Carter. After hanging him from a telephone pole until he was strangled to death, the mob pumped more than two hundred bullets into his lifeless body and then dragged his corpse behind a car for an hour. They dumped his body in Little Rock's Black neighborhood, and a mob of three or four thousand whites gathered to watch Carter's body burn for three hours.[25] The white classmates of the Little Rock Nine were far too young to have witnessed Carter's lynching, but they parroted the epithets and mimicked the violent rituals they had absorbed as children from their families and communities. On October 3, a month after the Little Rock Nine first entered the school, a group of white students walked out of their classes in the middle of the day, refusing to remain in the school with their Black classmates. With news cameras fixed squarely on Central High School, they hanged a Black effigy from a tree on the school's front lawn (fig. 4.6). Egged on by the adults in the mob while National Guardsmen stood by and watched, the students took turns pummeling the figure as it swung through the air, and they lit the effigy on fire just as another white mob in Little Rock had done to Carter's body thirty years earlier.[26]

In August 1963, three Black boys—high school students from Gadsden, Alabama—walked and hitchhiked to the March on Washington with only ten dollars among them, grazing on vending machine snacks and sleeping in bus terminals along the way. The final leg of their journey took them through the mountains of Virginia, where they passed by gas stations that flew Confederate flags and hung Black effigies from streetlights. Fifty years later, one of those young men, Robert Avery, recalled that the effigies were "sending a strong message. . . . They went to a lot of care to make them, to make sure [Black] people understood you can't stop here and buy gas."[27]

Figure 4.6. "A student at Little Rock Central High School had just punched and kicked an effigy of an African American hung in front of the school, after the students staged a walkout in protest of integration in Little Rock, AR, on Oct. 3, 1957." (AP Photo)

White supremacists invested time and energy in gathering the materials to construct each effigy and then, in a reversal of the taking of souvenirs at lynching rituals, assembled the bodies—stitching together (presumably their own) old clothing, stuffing the insides with rags or crumpled paper, making a head, tying the noose, deciding whether to write a message on the body, deciding whether to give the body shoes or hands or a face. Vividly aware that they had narrowly avoided physical danger, Avery and his friends safely made it to Washington, DC, unfazed and determined as ever to protest Jim Crow.

As the number of lynchings declined after World War II, the figurative bodies of effigies began to supplant literal dead bodies. Though most effigies, like the blood-stained one in Miami, resembled Black men, some whites were unsatisfied with purely figurative deaths, as the dead racoon left on Meredith's car attested. In 1965, Black residents of Holmes County, Mississippi, encountered dead black crows hanging from the stately oaks that lined the road to the town of Tchula. The 1965 Voting Rights Act, which had recently been passed over the loud protestations of southern congressional representatives, had dealt a severe blow to Jim Crow, and whoever methodically killed those crows, slipped nooses around their little necks, and strung them up from the limbs of the oak trees wanted to send a warning to Black people seeking to vote. Local African Americans like William J. Stewart certainly understood that warning. As Stewart peered up at the decaying bodies of the crows, he recognized this display as "an old intimidating tactic to frighten Blacks from going to the courthouse in Lexington to register to vote." The dead crows prompted recollections of other deaths to resurface. Stewart recalled, "After Emmett Till's murder, time and time again during the height of the civil rights movement, people were fished out of the Big Black River [near Durant, Mississippi]. Sometimes, the body's cut in two—one [part] in one burlap sack, one [part] in the other [sack] with a weight on it. Don't know where they came from."[28] Amid voting rights battles in the nation's capital and closer to home, the dead crows, gently swinging in the breeze, reminded the community that these were not idle threats—the crows whispered warnings of what might happen if African Americans walked up the courthouse steps and registered to vote.

Like the rest of the Delta, Holmes County had a Black majority; 72 percent of the county was Black in 1960. What set the county apart from others, though, was that Black people owned 50 percent of the land, in large part due to a Depression-era Farm Security Administration program designed to help tenant farmers and sharecroppers own the land they worked. Land ownership coupled with a cooperatively owned cotton gin gave many African Americans in Holmes County greater economic independence from white people and made them less vulnerable than sharecroppers to economic retaliation for civil rights organizing. In 1963, locals worked with the Council of Federated Organizations (COFO) to set up citizenship classes and organize a voter registration drive, but violent reprisals from the white community were swift. In the dead of night, white supremacists threw two firebombs into the home of Hartman Turnbow, the first Black person to register to vote, and, as he and his family ran outside to escape the flames, they were met with gunfire. Turnbow, armed with his rifle, returned fire until the shooters fled, and he stood guard over his home most nights after that. Two years later, with the promise of federal protections for Black voting rights, voter registration efforts continued, and soon after, the dead crows appeared, just south of Tchula.[29]

The correspondence between lawyers for the circuit clerk in Holmes County and Mississippi's senior senator, James O. Eastland, told quite a different story about new federal regulations of the franchise. Local whites hoped to keep the Justice Department from intervening in elections now that the Voting Rights Act mandated oversight over counties with voting irregularities. In 1965, Holmes County had far more African Americans than whites eligible to vote, so in the wake of the law's passage, the local registrar adopted a general policy of African American disenfranchisement while allowing a token number of African Americans to register. With white political control hanging in the balance, local white officials reported to Eastland that the clerk had registered more than one thousand African Americans, whom he repeatedly referred to with the derisive term "illiterates." They hoped these token registrations would be sufficient to satisfy Justice Department lawyers and to keep the federal government from administering local elections. Ever responsive to his white constituents' needs, Eastland called Attorney General Nicholas Katzenbach with the necessary reassurances that a federal registrar would be unnecessary.[30]

The attorney representing the Holmes County circuit clerk apologized for troubling Eastland with these local issues, writing, "We regretted so much to have to bother you about this matter, but it is really one of life or death to us here."[31] Though easily mistaken for hyperbole, his word choice was telling. Whites in Holmes County worried about relinquishing political power they had monopolized for centuries, and they recognized that sharing that power with a Black majority would sound the death knell for white supremacy, that is, for what they understood to be "the southern way of life." However, registering eligible Black voters was a matter of "life or death" in another sense, too. The Klan had already burned crosses on the lawns of local civil rights leaders organizing voter registration drives, and Klansmen had fired bullets into their homes. The Sanctified Church, where local African American activists had been meeting, burned to the ground in 1964, and in 1963, police dogs had attacked the handful of African Americans who attempted to register to vote at the courthouse. Whites across the state of Mississippi had murdered activists for registering Black voters for decades, so for

African Americans, voting had been a matter of "life or death," in essence, since the ratification of the Fifteenth Amendment.[32]

Though the dead crows brought back memories of dead Black bodies for African Americans like Stewart, many members of the Black community refused to be cowed by these renewed lynching threats. Around the same time the crows appeared hanging from tree limbs, a group of activists marched around the town square in Lexington, circling the county courthouse where the registrar had turned away potential Black voters. They walked past white-owned businesses that took money from Black customers but refused to hire them as employees. They passed by the spot on the town square where, forty years earlier, a Black man had been lynched. Several cars lined up along one side of the square with members of the Klan dressed in full regalia—white robes and hoods covering their faces—inside, watching the procession of protesters. A domestic worker named Bea Jenkins, who participated in the protest, recalled walking right up to one of the cars and saying to the Klansmen:

> I'm not afraid of you. . . . I just [as] soon to die today or tomorrow. . . . What you need to do [is] go somewhere. Pull those hoods and those robes off, and go back into your store. And then try to make you some money there if you can because those robes and things don't excite me.[33]

The Klansmen felt comfortable enough to occupy the town square in broad daylight while sitting in their own cars, which almost everyone in town recognized as theirs on sight. The hoods and robes they wore did not really conceal their identities, and though this garb was intended to intimidate the protesters—much like the dead crows—it also seemed to serve as a security blanket for the Klansmen, unsteadied by a changing world.

The repetition of lynched effigies—of James Meredith, NAACP activists, the Little Rock Nine, and others—were not mere throwbacks to Jim Crow terrorism at its worst. Despite the absence of flesh-and-blood Black bodies dangling from the ends of nooses, effigies were part of the evolution of lynching and still affirmed the power white southerners had enjoyed for centuries. They reinforced that whiteness was ensconced in anti-Black violence and represented the way things were in the Jim Crow South at a time when such reassurances were desperately sought by white southerners feeling cornered and vulnerable by the barrage of fierce attacks on their way of life.

"You ought to go to Old Abe Linco[l]n['s] Grave and Dig the old sun-fitch [*sic*] up and Burn him," wrote a white man named Willie J. Denson in a handwritten letter to Georgia senator Richard B. Russell in 1957. "The first Negro I Ever see Burn was in Parris [*sic*] Texas," he wrote, "and the next on[e] I saw Burn was in Tylar [*sic*] and the next two was Burn in Sulphur Spring[s] Texas so that['s] all the Negro I have Ever seen Burn up."[34] To Denson, witnessing public burnings of Black men estab-lished between himself and Russell his bona fides as a white supremacist: these lynchings proved that he was committed to defending white power in the South against threats both internal and external; burning Black men was a testament to his manhood. From his home in Shreveport, Louisiana, Denson casually reminisced about having joined four differ-ent Texas lynch mobs, before urging Russell to run for the presidency, impeach President Dwight Eisenhower, and burn the long-dead corpse of President Abraham Lincoln. Just a couple of weeks earlier, Eisen-hower had sent federal troops to Little Rock's Central High School to enforce the Supreme Court's school desegregation order, and by seam-lessly shifting from Eisenhower to that "old sunfitch" Lincoln, Denson collapsed one hundred years of history, tying together two historical mo-ments when US presidents had sent troops to the South to challenge white southern defiance of federal rule. When Denson urged Russell to exhume and burn Lincoln's body, he meant to literally and figuratively make him Black and therefore mark him as a race traitor who freed en-slaved people, and so by extension, Eisenhower was a race traitor too, de-serving of the same (or at least similar) treatment.

The pride with which Denson catalogued these deaths was shame-less and awful. It reflected the ease with which white southerners boasted of the abject destruction of Black life throughout the long civil rights movement and showed the enduring power of lynching to shape white southern identity. Presumably Denson did not actually expect Russell to dig up and burn the corpse of a celebrated US president, but blending memories of actual lynchings with a call to lynch Lincoln and opposition to school desegregation illustrated how lynching became a shorthand for white resistance to racial justice in both the mid-nineteenth and the mid-twentieth centuries. Other white southerners were more anxious about the future relationship between whiteness and power in the South when they invoked lynching memories during the civil rights era, but Denson's letter showed a steadfast assuredness that white southern defiance and white supremacist violence would once again expel the federal government from the South as they had during Reconstruction.

The prevalence and power of lynching rhetoric in the age of civil rights is difficult to fully appreciate without reading this language alongside collective memories of Reconstruction. Almost immediately after the surrender at Appomattox, former Confederates engaged in a struggle over the memory of the Civil War—a struggle that many of their descendants carry on to this day in "debates" over the motivations behind the war and the meaning of the Confederate flag. What became known as the Lost Cause constructed a mythology surrounding the war that denied that proslavery interests were the primary catalyst for secession and erased the brutality of enslavement itself. Instead, defenders of the Lost Cause, such as the United Daughters of the Confederacy, focused on the valor of Confederate soldiers and white southern suffering under Reconstruction, much of which was not suffering at all but rather bristling at a more racially just social order. Lost Cause boosters imagined Reconstruction to be a tragic era during which the white South became the victim of Republican tyranny and African American political corruption. Many even held up the violent tactics of the Ku Klux Klan and similar terrorist groups as the saving grace of the white South, while simultaneously maintaining the contradictory position that race relations had always been harmonious in the region. These well-organized campaigns of violence in the 1870s and 1880s eventually wrested political power from the Republican Party and African American voters, which led to the "redemption" of the Old South and the beginnings of Jim Crow. The Civil War ended in 1865, but the war and Reconstruction remained fresh wounds upon the white southern psyche, even a century later. These wounds ensured that the anti-Black violence of Redemption and Jim Crow became fundamental to preserving a white supremacist social order and white identity for generations, just as it had during slavery. In the 1950s and 1960s, on the cusp of a second Reconstruction, when white supremacy was once again under attack from African Americans and the federal government, many whites, like Denson, rehashed rhetoric that glorified lynching.[35]

The Supreme Court's *Brown v. Board of Education* decision and Eisenhower's order to send troops to Little Rock's Central High School three years later were instrumental in reviving bitter memories of Reconstruction for many white southerners. One year after the *Brown* decision, a white woman born and raised in the South nearly eighty years earlier, Mrs. Will Henry, lamented, "The Republicans and Communists are trying to destroy the South, and they are taking the only way they know how, through the negro, as they did during, and after the Civil War."[36] Though she would have been too young to remember Reconstruction, Henry proceeded to repeat a popular myth of white southern victimhood and suffering, a mythology that gave meaning to her place in southern society as a white person, as it did for so many other white southerners. This imagined white victimhood, during both Reconstruction and the civil rights movement, served to displace and deny African American victimhood, thereby absolving the white South of centuries of anti-Black violence, which was critical to preserving a sense of white southern innocence. Politicians from Henry's home state of Mississippi also drew parallels between debates over nullification and secession in the nineteenth century and contemporary debates over how to preserve segregation after the Supreme Court's school desegregation decision.[37] The knee-jerk impulse to collapse the political debates of the 1830s and 1860s with those of the 1950s and 1960s illustrated how a preoccupation with the racial politics of the nineteenth century blended seamlessly into the twentieth century.

Comparisons between Reconstruction and the civil rights movement often went beyond fondly reminiscing about violent nineteenth-century tactics used to curb the hard-won freedoms of African Americans in the past. Like Denson, some white southerners openly endorsed the terrorist violence that had ushered in Jim Crow in the 1870s and 1880s. After the desegregation "crisis" in Little Rock, one white Atlanta resident said, "Every advance in race relations in the South will go by the boards [and] the Ku Klux Klan will ride hard again and there will be anarchy in our land if the presidents forced methods are continued."[38] Six years later, in 1963, a Mississippi man ominously wondered: "Is it time for the KKK to come to the aid of our country?—again—"[39] A fellow Mississippian, Mabel B. Sheldon, warned her senator, James O. Eastland: "Please remind LBJ of all the South has done for the colored people since the Reconstruction days. And also in the 'hot summer' ahead, to plead with his 'pals'—Negro leaders,—to advise their people against leading ploitical meetings in their churches, to avoid another church bombing."[40] Sheldon wrote her letter less than a year after the Klan bombed Birmingham's Sixteenth Street Baptist Church, killing four Black girls who had just finished Sunday School, and she threatened more violence if African Americans continued to agitate for the vote, by invoking the supposed folly of

Black political power during Reconstruction. She believed that a campaign of terror like the one that had ended the first Reconstruction was the only way to maintain white supremacy and stamp out voter registration drives already underway as part of the Freedom Summer of 1964. Her letter proved to be devastatingly prophetic. The evening after she typed her letter, the Mount Zion Methodist Church in Neshoba County, Mississippi, burned to the ground. It was an act of arson committed by the Klan, and it would lead directly to the lynching of three civil rights workers five days later.[41]

With white racial anxieties running high, the Klan came to embody a final line of defense against the civil rights movement. A lawyer from Jackson, Mississippi, wrote: "If we don't fight to the finish now, we may as well arrange for our mulatto grandchildren. In less than a year from [now] we will have niggers and whites in the same school and nigger teachers for white children. My father rode with [the] KKK in 1875 and ran the scoundrels out. Now our leaders surrender."[42] In response to the imminent passage of the 1964 Civil Rights Act, another of Eastland's constituents, W. R. Rawls, threatened, "I am hoping the South will stick together and hold their Electoral votes, throw it back in the House, but should that not happen, and the Civil Rights bill is passed, looks like the South [will] have no alternative but to revert back to reconstruction (KKK)."[43] Eastland replied, "I agree with you that we are going through another tragic era in the south."[44] These letters conveniently ignored how, during the decades between Reconstruction and the civil rights era, the white South had consistently used lynching and other forms of terrorist violence to uphold Jim Crow, but even so, the return to the Reconstruction Klan was more than a matter of soothing abstract anxieties about white power with rhetorical bluster. Three days after Rawls sent his letter to Eastland, the Neshoba, Mississippi, Klan kidnapped and lynched James Chaney, Andrew Goodman, and Mickey Schwerner. What otherwise might have been dismissed as nostalgia for a much-longed-for past became real, as the Klan delivered what Rawls had wished for.

Lynching rhetoric often took far subtler forms, as was the case with the Citizens' Council, which was founded in the Mississippi Delta as a direct response to the Supreme Court's *Brown* decision. Primarily concerned with defending segregation and "states' rights," the council cultivated an image as the "respectable" and "law-abiding" alternative to the Klan. The organization defended the racial status quo, and its message of preserving what it called "racial integrity" reached millions of white southerners through its publications and extensive speaking tours.[45] Although its pamphlets, magazines, and speeches rarely, if ever, explicitly mentioned lynching, the Citizens' Council stoked white southern fears of "miscegenation," which had been one of the primary public justifications for lynching. One of the flyers quoted the race-baiting Mississippi politician, Theodore Bilbo, who had warned that "if the blood of our white race should become corrupted and mingled with the blood of Africa, then the present greatness of the United States of America would be destroyed and all hope for the future would be forever gone."[46] Bilbo was an outspoken apologist for lynching to the day he died in 1947, and, like many of his contemporaries, he had often used the specter of miscegenation to excuse and even commend lynch mobs for enforcing Jim Crow. These pamphlets left it to readers to connect lynching to antimiscegenation fears, but in reprinting Bilbo's words, the Citizens' Council defended the same white patriarchal rule that lynching had endorsed and protected for decades.[47]

Despite the Citizens' Council's carefully cultivated "respectable" image, the moderate white journalist Hodding Carter accused the organization of being a modern reincarnation of the Klan that would quickly devolve into "instruments of interracial violence." In response, Robert B. Patterson, the executive secretary of the Mississippi Councils, insisted that his organization was not "anti-Negro," nor did it foment racial hatred when it advocated for segregation. He also maintained that God condemned racial mixing both in schools and in the bedroom.[48] Patterson strategically dressed up his racist rhetoric in his response to Carter and, for that matter, in many of his public speeches, opting instead for a less outwardly crass version of white supremacy.[49] This supposedly kinder, gentler version of racism still reverted to the same arguments made to rationalize lynching: a fear of sex between Black men and white women, and white supremacy as the "natural" ordering of society. The Citizens' Council purported to condemn violent intimidation in favor of economic threats, political organizing, and the thinly veiled racist rhetoric of states' rights, but given the organization's propensity for quoting notorious pro-lynching white supremacists like Bilbo, the organization could draw only the finest of lines between its racist rhetoric and violence.[50]

Carter's observations that the Citizens' Council was reminiscent of the Klan and prone to violence turned out to be true.[51] Not only were many Klansmen also members of the Citizens' Council, but in Alabama two factions of the Citizens' Council publicly clashed over the role of violence in their organizing strategies. The Central Alabama Citizens' Council, which was led by a planter and former state legislator, Sam Engelhardt, maintained that political pressure and propaganda would stem the tide of integration, but the North Alabama Citizens' Council's Asa Earl "Ace" Carter took a more militant tack. While Engelhardt welcomed Catholics and Jews to the membership and corresponded with prominent southern politicians, Carter excluded Jews and alienated the upper-crust "Bourbons" by agitating for the forced retirement of the University of Alabama's president after the school desegregrated in 1963.[52] The differences between these two Alabama Councils went beyond membership restrictions and the alienation of white elites. In April 1956, members of the North Alabama Citizens' Council assaulted Nat King Cole as he performed in Birmingham, and the line between the North Alabama Citizens' Council and the Original Ku Klux Klan of the Confederacy, also based in Birmingham, quickly became blurred. In 1957, members of both white supremacist organizations performed a disturbing initiation ritual that involved the castration of an elderly African American man, a crime for which they were convicted later that year.[53]

Carter's expulsion from the Citizens' Council was prompted by actions that blatantly revealed direct connections to racial violence, but other, more covert relationships between violent white supremacists and the "respectable" set persisted. The Citizens' Council in Chattanooga, Tennessee, appeared to limit its activities to organizing prosegregation rallies and lectures, but one of its founding members and most enthusiastic boosters, Kate H. Steele, also subscribed to the National States Rights Party's newspaper, the *Thunderbolt*. A notorious neo-Nazi organization, the National States Rights Party advocated the extermination of Jews and the removal of African Americans from the United States, and the FBI suspected that the organization had close ties to the Klan. Steele probably knew that the National States Rights Party was reportedly behind dozens of bombings of synagogues and Black churches across the South, and that one faction in Kentucky attacked a group of Black people, which led to two deaths.[54] That she felt comfortable associating with both the Citizens' Council and a terrorist, neo-Nazi organization spoke to the fluidity between ostensibly "respectable" and "nonviolent" white supremacist groups and those that engaged in anti-Black terrorist violence.

As the civil rights movement made strides in ending segregation and transforming social relationships between whites and Blacks, white southerners from Denson and Henry to Ace Carter and Steele used ref-

erences to lynching as a means to register their opposition to racial justice and to appease their racial anxieties. During these tumultuous years,
African Americans found inspiration in an enduring protest tradition and
deep commitments to justice inherited from those who came before
them, but white southerners returned to memories of lynching, ritual elements of lynching, and parallel forms of anti-Black terrorism for comfort. With the uncertainty surrounding the future of white supremacy,
whites looked to tried-and-true methods of asserting control over African Americans, like lynching, methods they hoped would stem the tide of
a second Reconstruction.

"Have you ever smelled a nigger burn?" Again, a man's voice rang out
into the darkness of a late summer's night. "Have you had the privilege
of smelling a nigger burn?" Four semiconscious Black men lay in a pile
on a stage as a crowd of three hundred white men and women dressed in
Klan hoods and robes waited impatiently for someone to fetch some gasoline. Moments earlier, several Klansmen had pummeled the four men
with ax handles and baseball bats, knocking out teeth, cracking bones,
leaving deep gashes that bled out onto the stage. Some women in full
Klan regalia had egged them on, screaming, "Castrate the bastards!"
"Kick their balls out!" "Knock their heads off!" "Get the rope!" Before
the Klan could burn the four men alive as planned, the police arrived,
and the mob scattered. The four men had suffered serious injuries, but
they had made it through the night with their lives.[55]

This scene unfolded just outside St. Augustine, Florida, not in 1883,
but on September 18, 1963. The four men kidnapped by the Klan were
local NAACP activists who had parked close to the Klan rally in order to
catch a glimpse of the most reactionary opposition to their efforts to desegregate St. Augustine. Robert Hayling, one of the Black men left
bleeding on the stage, regained consciousness long enough to hear the
man with the microphone work the crowd into a frenzy as they waited
for the gasoline to arrive. Hayling, a local dentist, had been singled out
because of his leadership role in the desegregation struggle, and after
some of his white patients recognized him when he staggered onto the
stage, they told the men wielding the ax handles and baseball bats to
concentrate their blows on his right arm so he could no longer practice
dentistry.[56] Had a sympathetic white man in the crowd not contacted the
police in time, the Klan would probably have doused the four men in
gasoline and watched as they died, engulfed in flames.

What took place that night in St. Augustine was very nearly a mass lynching. By the 1960s, white southerners were far more likely to reference lynching in rhetoric than to leave a Black person hanging from a tree limb, but physical violence, including lynching, persisted. Scholars have nonetheless tended to confine lynching within the neat temporal bookends of 1880 to 1940.[57] The latter bookend, 1940, reflects the decline in the number of spectacle lynchings during and after the 1930s, but also speaks to the influence of white antilynching activists who were complicit in trying to define lynching out of existence.[58] In 1940, when several antilynching organizations met to settle on a common definition for lynching, the decidedly paternalistic Association of Southern Women for the Prevention of Lynching (ASWPL) repeatedly cast doubt on whether particular cases of lynching were "real," instead demoting many cases to the categories of "borderline lynchings" or "probable lynchings."[59] Not only did the ASWPL exclude African American women from its membership and oppose federal antilynching legislation, but its executive director, Jessie Daniel Ames, kept up friendly correspondence with some of the most ardent opponents of antilynching legislation, such as Hatton Sumners of Texas, who defended lynching on the floor of the House of Representatives as an understandable response to the rape of white women.[60] Ames was invested in cultivating an image of racial harmony in the South while largely maintaining the existing racial hierarchy, and though the ASWPL strongly rejected the narrative that lynching protected white womanhood, Ames viewed lynching primarily as a shameful blemish on the image of an otherwise genteel South. Throughout the 1940s, the ASWPL was quick to announce that no lynchings occurred in a given year, despite evidence to the contrary from the NAACP and Tuskegee Institute, because the triumph of declaring the end of lynching served the organization's ends.[61]

The tendency to impose such a firm historical boundary on lynching also reflects an assumption that the ASWPL and, more recently, some scholars have made: that the decline in the number of spectacle lynchings not only implied the inevitability of the end of lynching but also indicated that the definition of lynching remained fixed over time. Thus, the form that lynching often took in the late nineteenth and early twentieth centuries was implicitly viewed as the only "genuine" form it could take. Again, Ashraf Rushdy's insights, which echo the NAACP's argument in the 1940s that lynching adapted to new circumstances and went underground but did not disappear, are instructive:

Once we challenge the belief that the decline in the frequency of lynchings is in fact an inevitable prelude to the 'last' lynching ... we are better able to appreciate how lynchings have undergone significant transformation in their formal properties and ideological imperatives throughout the long history of extralegal, collective violence in America. We will then have a fuller, more accurate history of lynching that values the important and informative continuities in the practice, without denying the significant ways that the apparent discontinuities also reveal important truths about what lynchers thought and did.[62]

By emphasizing continuities in the practice of lynching over time, Rushdy does not flatten the clear historical differences between the post-Reconstruction South, the civil rights era, and the present. Instead, he recognizes that lynching was adaptive to evolving historical contexts, that as lynching became less socially acceptable in the form it had taken in the nineteenth and early twentieth centuries, lynchers changed its form, though not so drastically that it could no longer be identified as lynching.

In part, the desire to narrowly and rigidly define lynching reflected (and still reflects) a deeper desire to marginalize lynching, rendering it a regional problem, a throwback to preindustrial bloodlust, an aberration that doesn't contradict the narrative of American progress and the expansion of human liberty. The desire to disentangle lynching from modernity in the United States and the attendant argument that modernization itself ended the tensions at the root of lynching obscure what Jacqueline Goldsby describes as "lynching's normative relation to modernism's history over the last century."[63] African Americans continued to die at the hands of lynchers well after that 1940 meeting and well after the horrors of two world wars had devastated millions of people, often in ways that are indistinguishable in form and motive from lynchings of earlier eras.

Arguably the most notorious post-1940 lynching took place in Leflore County, Mississippi, in 1955, and it followed well-rehearsed scripts honed by generations of white southerners. Emmett Till, a fourteen-year-old boy from Chicago, was spending the summer with relatives in Money, Mississippi, when he was lynched for allegedly whistling at a white woman. Her husband, Roy Bryant, and her brother-in-law, J. W. Milam, wanted to teach Till a lesson about his place in the Jim Crow South, so they took him out in the dead of the night to scare him. The fourteen-year-old's refusal to submit and beg for mercy infuriated the two white men, who expected Black subservience. Their tactics of intimidation—the beating and torture, the threats and taunts—didn't work on Till, and in anger and frustration, they put a bullet in his head and then dumped his body into the Tallahatchie River.[64]

Till's mother, Mamie Till-Mobley, was the primary force behind publicizing the brutality of her son's death. Not only did she publish a photograph of her son's disfigured body in *Jet* magazine to "let the people see what they did to her boy," but she held an open casket funeral in Chicago that thousands of people attended.[65] The grisly photograph in *Jet* made it plain that Bryant and Milam had intended to do more than take Till's life. His body was so mangled from the beating that a ring bearing his father's initials was the only way his mother could positively identify him. His lynchers had poured their racist anger and social anxieties onto Till's fourteen-year-old body, trying to beat a Black boy into submission, trying to beat back the Supreme Court's *Brown* decision from a year earlier, trying to beat down the struggle for racial justice.

Despite the scrutiny of the national and international media, the all-white Mississippi jury deliberating Bryant and Milam's case returned a verdict of not guilty. That a grand jury indicted two white men for murdering an African American teenager in the first place seemed to violate the unspoken racial code of the South that allowed lynchers to avoid legal consequences for taking Black lives. In fact, many local whites came to the defense of Bryant and Milam to register their opposition to "outsiders" like the NAACP and national media interfering in local affairs, echoing the states' rights rhetoric used during the Civil War and in campaigns to block federal antilynching legislation. The broad support that the two men enjoyed took a different form from that of the mobs that had cheered as African Americans were strung up in trees, tortured, mutilated, and burned, but explicit and implicit public approval of Till's lynching bore a clear resemblance to the recent past when lynch mobs wore no masks and newspapers printed sensationalist accounts of their deeds. It was only after Bryant and Milam admitted to a journalist a few months after the verdict that they had indeed killed Till that whites in the Delta ostracized the two men and their families. In other words, it was only when their brazen boasts about murdering a child threatened to further erode Jim Crow by inviting additional outside scrutiny that they were turned into pariahs. The extreme physical violence of the lynching resembled the brutality of lynchings past, and its social function as a ritualized representation of white southern racial domination remained unchanged.[66]

Ritualistic, white supremacist violence resurfaced again and again after Till's lynching, but reporters and even civil rights activists and the victims' families were less likely to affix the lynching label than before as some features of lynching evolved. Klan members in Neshoba County, Mississippi, carried out a triple lynching of civil rights workers in 1964, but, more often than not, scholars and journalists have described the deaths of Chaney, Goodman, and Schwerner as murders, not lynchings.[67] The Klan in Neshoba County went to great lengths to hide the bodies and conceal the identities of perpetrators in order to hamper the FBI investigation, but the white supremacist message that these lynchings were intended to send to civil rights activists remained, as did the ritualistic, excessive violence. The Klan targeted these men for organizing local African Americans to start a voter registration drive and to set up Freedom Schools, and they intended for these lynchings to shut down the Mississippi Freedom Summer, to preserve white political dominance in Mississippi. Furthermore, the physical violence was indistinguishable from other lynchings. The two white New Yorkers, Goodman and Schwerner, died from single, close-range gunshot wounds, but when the FBI recovered Chaney's body, the physical deterioration of his body was noticeably more advanced. After conducting an autopsy at the request of Chaney's mother, the New York pathologist David Spain determined that Chaney "had been beaten to a pulp." The bones in his jaw and right shoulder were so completely shattered that Spain described them as looking as though Chaney had been in an airplane crash.[68] Local whites were tight-lipped when questioned by federal investigators about the lynchings, for their investment in white power and their fear of fracturing white racial solidarity still protected lynchers from prosecution. This was not just kidnapping and murder. This was a lynching.

Since slavery, Black bodies have been sites where white southerners demonstrate and perform their racial power, and this phenomenon continues in the present, in the age of mass incarceration, police killings of unarmed Black people, stop and frisk policies, burning of Black churches, and stand your ground laws. The term "lynching" has gone by the wayside since the 1950s, dropped in favor of phrases like "racially charged killing" or "murder," and, on those rare occasions when news outlets or social commentators apply the term to recent acts of violence, most Americans dismiss its usage as an anachronism or a throwback to a bygone era. Though lynching is a particular kind of murder, what sets lynchings apart from other murders is not when they happened or even the specific form that they took—for there was enormous variation in their form even in the peak period—but why they happened. White southerners lynched African Americans because they believed that ritual violence, terror, and domination were necessary to retain their power. Though the South has changed since Jim Crow, the desire to dominate has persisted as lynching has evolved. As activists dismantled Jim Crow, many white southerners returned to lynching to cope with this enormous social upheaval. In 1894, lynching reinforced a robust system of white supremacy. Seventy years later, in 1964, some white southerners returned to lynching in an attempt to cling to the past, to hold onto a system that was beginning to crumble and fall.

Given the persistence of literal and figurative lynchings, African American defiance of Jim Crow during the civil rights era is all the more remarkable. James Meredith certainly refused to be intimidated by the flurry of death threats following his admission to the University of Mississippi, and in 1966, only four years after being hanged in effigy on campus, he decided to embark on a one-man March Against Fear. Meredith began walking on Highway 51 from Memphis, Tennessee, to Jackson, Mississippi, as he put it, to "challenge that all pervasive fear that is so much a part of the day to day life of the Negro and to encourage the Negro to register to vote." He also wanted his march to inspire Black children to dream of opportunities beyond the cotton fields of Mississippi and to have the economic and social wherewithal to achieve those dreams.[69] As he walked along that barren roadside to challenge the fear that paralyzed so many Black Mississippians in their everyday lives, he greeted his supporters who lined the highway, ordinary Mississippians who saw in Meredith an inspiring symbol of defiance.[70]

Meredith made it through only one town. Just two miles south of Hernando, a white man from Tennessee, crouched in the wooded area alongside the highway, yelled, "James! James Meredith!" and fired three rounds of birdshot at him. The first shot hit his shoulder and knocked him to the ground. With a bloodstain spreading down his sleeve, he crawled to the other side of the highway, where he was hit with a second round in his back and the back of his neck. The third shot missed Meredith entirely, and the gunman ran off into the woods, pursued by state and county law enforcement. Meredith implored the members of the press snapping photographs of him bleeding on the ground: "Isn't anyone going to get me to a doctor?" Finally a supporter helped him.[71]

The shooter was identified as James Norvell, a white man from Memphis. In response, conspiracy theorists came out in force again, especially after newspapers printed photographs of the shooting, fueling speculation that the shooting was a publicity stunt and that the photographs were somehow staged.[72] These skeptics included J. R. Perry of Vicksburg, Mississippi, who penned a letter to Eastland: "You know as well as I do that if [Norvell] had wanted to kill Meredith he wouldn't have used bird shot. This man was no doubt paid a substantial sum to perpetrate this deed."[73] In response to a different constituent who was convinced that Norvell had been paid by a civil rights organization to shoot Meredith, Eastland only fed those suspicions: "The person who is accused of shooting [Meredith] has an Army medal for expert marksmanship with a rifle. One Eastern senator told me that when his name was called three times that was to give the photographers time to focus their cameras."[74] Racial anxieties lay at the heart of these conspiracy theories offered by Perry, Eastland, and others—anxieties fueled by the prospect of African Americans across the state of Mississippi fearlessly walking to the polls and casting votes as Meredith had envisioned.

While recuperating in a Memphis hospital, Meredith released a statement to the press in which he reflected on the shooting:

> Just the night before I went into Mississippi, I made that fateful decision—the decision was to carry a Bible instead of a gun. "What did I think while the man was shooting me?" I was thinking that I had made a mistake not to carry a gun with me. "How did I feel?" I felt embarrassed. Embarrassed because I could have knocked this intended killer off with one shot had I been prepared, but I was not. My father, who lived in Mississippi for 74 years and died there, would have been prepared.[75]

The nonviolent approach of Martin Luther King Jr. and much of the mainline civil rights movement had a profound influence on African American protest during this period, but armed self-defense was still a common response to white supremacy, and one that had deep roots in insurrections and Reconstruction militancy. During the early decades of the twentieth century, for instance, African Americans in the Arkansas Delta often turned to armed self-defense to protect their families from their white neighbors.[76] When rumors spread that a race riot could explode in Memphis in the 1920s or 1930s, Henrene Jenkins's father instructed her brothers to guard their home with shotguns. Her father had to leave town for a few days because of his job as a railway mail clerk, but he informed his sons, "When I come back . . . I expect to see your dead bodies across the doorstep. Defend them [their mother and sisters]."[77] In the early 1940s, a farmer in Shelby County, Tennessee, named Clifford Wilson, warned the white men who hired his teenaged sons not to raise a hand against his children or he would kill them. When some white men tied one of his sons to a tree and whipped him until he was unconscious, Wilson grabbed his shotgun and stormed over to the men, demanding that they "turn my child loose . . . right now or I'll kill everybody out here."[78] So when Meredith admitted his embarrassment for not carrying a gun during his abruptly curtailed March Against Fear, he uttered a long-standing belief about the importance of protecting not only his body but his dignity from white supremacists. And when he said that his father would have been prepared, he placed his protest in an African American tradition of defending oneself and one's community from harm with actual weapons.[79]

As news of Meredith's shooting broke, civil rights leaders from the Student Nonviolent Coordinating Committee (SNCC), the Southern Christian Leadership Conference (SCLC), and the Congress of Racial Equality (CORE) decided to continue Meredith's march, picking up from where he had been shot. These groups had collaborated on various campaigns and projects over the past few years, but by 1966 the ideological fissures within the movement began to show. After the police in Greenwood, Mississippi, arrested some protesters, including SNCC's Stokely Carmichael, the twenty-four-year-old activist announced, "This is the twenty-seventh time I have been arrested. I ain't going to jail no more. What we gonna start saying now is 'Black Power.'" Later that night, when Carmichael shouted out at the marchers gathered for a rally, "What do you want?" they responded with a thundering cry of "Black Power!"[80] As the call of "What do you want?" was answered with "Black Power!" again and again, these chants for Black self-determination echoed out into the Mississippi night, reverberating throughout Greenwood, where the Citizens' Council was founded and headquartered. White racists continued to draw upon lynching for inspiration and comfort when they perpetrated violent acts against civil rights activists like Meredith, but African Americans increasingly shed what Meredith called "that all pervasive fear" and stood up against these violent threats, even in the heart of Dixie.

CHAPTER FIVE

Protest

The trauma is repetitive. We weep. But we are still, even in our most anguished seasons, not reducible to the fact of our grief. Rather, the capacity to access joy is a testament to the grace of living as a protest.

—IMANI PERRY, "Racism Is Terrible. Blackness Is Not."

LILIAN WILLIAMS HAD NO love for Norway, South Carolina. Born there in 1885, in the shadow of slavery and the failed experiment of Reconstruction, she knew firsthand how quickly the promise of freedom had dimmed after emancipation. Even in freedom, her family lived behind the "big house" owned by the white family that had enslaved her mother, Sarah Donaldson. Williams's mother had nineteen children, and, for all but the oldest children, their father was a white man named John Evans. The Census and a handful of newspaper clippings contain faint impressions of her parents' relationship, which probably started in the mid-1870s. Even if the relationship was consensual—and the fact that John Evans publicly claimed his mixed-race children suggests that it may have been consensual—her parents lived within the unavoidable nexus of race, sex, and power that pervaded the South, as they flaunted the taboo of illicit sex across the color line that so often led to the violent deaths of

Black men and the routine yet routinely unpunished rape of Black women.[1] Vestiges of the most violent legacies of enslavement inveigled themselves into the Evanses' lives in other ways, too. In 1903, a mob lynched her brother Charles and hunted down another brother James, and then Lilian Williams left for good. Leaving Norway was as much an act of mourning as it was an act of defiance—a refusal to be subjected to the racism and violence of white people, many of whom resented the Evanses for being educated. As her daughter Ethel put it, the Evanses were " 'voiced people,' in other words, they didn't let [white] people run over them and they spoke their mind."[2] Defiance was in her blood, and that same defiant streak led to her brother Charles's death.

Norway had seen labor unrest in the years leading up to (and following) the lynching. Conflicts often arose between Black tenant farmers or sharecroppers and their white employers when Black people resisted physical abuse and "jumped" their contracts early, before the harvest and before "settling up" their debts with the farmers whose land they worked. Yet another labor dispute led to the lynching. A friend of the Evans brothers, Lorenzo Williamson, worked for a white man, Addie Phillips, who intended to punish Williamson with a whipping for having cursed at him. Whipping was a form of corporeal punishment used in the post-emancipation South that was as much about inflicting physical pain as it was about shaming and demeaning Black people, treating them as though they were enslaved again.[3] The Evans brothers tried to intervene, but after Phillips threatened them, they stalked away. Two evenings later, on June 29, as the Phillips family sat down to dinner, somebody fired shots through an open window of their home, wounding and eventually killing Addie Phillips's father. Soon after, two figures were spotted running through the adjacent cotton field.

Suspicion (at least among whites) fell upon the Evans brothers almost immediately, which is unsurprising given how deeply local whites resented the Evanses. As the children of a formerly enslaved Black woman and a white man whose name they shared, the Evanses, by their very existence, transgressed the South's vigilantly policed racial boundaries.[4] However, these "voiced people" went further to defy the racial mores of the time. They were more educated than many of their white neighbors—according to one newspaper account, they "had knowledge of literature and read a number of northern newspapers"—and they refused to tolerate the everyday mistreatment and degradation of Black people at the hands of white people.[5] With the murder of the elder Phillips—a white man and a one-armed Confederate veteran no less—their white neighbors had a convenient excuse to punish them for their irreverence toward racial norms and their insistence on their dignity as Black men.

After a frenzied manhunt, Charles Evans was apprehended on July 1 and taken to the local guardhouse (a makeshift jail), where a mob of armed white farmers soon congregated, poised for a lynching. A group of Black men gathered at the lumber planing mill just outside town, also armed with pistols. Though greatly outnumbered, these men, who were friends and neighbors of the Evanses, sent a messenger to town, daring the white mob to face them en masse. When the mob arrived at the outskirts of town, they demanded that the Black men put down their guns, and though most complied, three men in their group refused. For their defiance, these men were taken to the guardhouse and whipped nearly to death until they named Charles Evans as the killer and James Evans as his accomplice.[6]

Throughout the day, more and more whites, armed with shotguns and rifles, streamed into town from the surrounding area. As the white mob amassed outside, Evans must have grasped the danger of his situation—a trial was not likely to decide his fate, not after the whipping of his friends and neighbors within earshot of his cell.[7] He also must have worried about his younger brother, James, who still evaded capture by a white mob out for blood. When the lynch mob entered the guardhouse, Charles Evans denied his involvement and said he could find the real killer. Unmoved, the mob of three hundred white people hanged him from a tree near the Phillips home, and then, with two hundred guns, they pumped his lifeless body full of bullets. Until the end, he insisted on his innocence.

The Black community also believed he was innocent. They began to gather in the Black enclave, Freedman's Hill, just outside Norway, and, within a few days, hundreds of armed Black men from across Orangeburg County had assembled, looking to defend their people and avenge the lynching of Charles Evans. White newspapers alleged that these armed Black men had surrounded Norway and posted guards at the main roads leading to town, trapping its white residents, and that, led by Evans's white father, they planned to burn down the town and "promise[d] to exterminate the whites." The newspapers alleged that these Black men knew the identities of the five white businessmen who were the lynch mob's ringleaders and that those white men would most certainly die. Alarmed by the threat of armed retaliation, the white community sent word to the governor that an armed group of Black men was plotting

what they understood to be "the slaughter of the whites."[8] The governor
sent the militia to put down the alleged uprising, but the militia soon dispersed, having decided that the threat to wipe out the whole white population was overblown.[9]

The threat posed by that assemblage of armed Black men was no less
remarkable for the restraint they showed after one of their own had been
so brutally lynched. White anxieties about a "race war" and armed uprisings (especially one led by an apparent race traitor like the Evanses' white
father) often revealed more about their internalized guilt than the intentions of their Black neighbors, but in this case, the arsenal and the indignation and the sheer number of African Americans vying for a chance at
revenge were far from imaginary. And the Black community's desire for
vengeance certainly did not retreat with the militia's return to Columbia.
Just four years later, in 1907, another death sparked by yet another labor
dispute between a white farmer and a Black laborer threatened to revive
both the lynch mob and an armed response from local African Americans.
In what would become the first legal case argued by the NAACP, this resurgence of Black outrage reminded local whites that African Americans
would not put up with their abuse, much less a lynching.[10]

The trouble began when Pink Franklin no longer wanted to work on
the Thomas farm, located about ten miles from Norway near Cope, South
Carolina. He left in May 1907 and signed a new contract with another
white farmer. Franklin knew Thomas was not pleased that he had jumped
his contract—Thomas had barred him from coming back for his possessions, which left him and his wife to sleep on the floor in their new
home—but, by the middle of the summer, he figured Thomas had moved
on and dropped the issue. Just before dawn one day in late July, while
Franklin was still in bed, he heard a knock on his door. A man at the door
identified himself as "a friend," and as Franklin rose to get dressed and answer the door, the man barged in and started to shoot, hitting Franklin in
the shoulder with a bullet. Bewildered and in fear for his life, Franklin
grabbed the gun he kept under his pillow and shot the intruder, who he
later learned was Henry Valentine, a constable sent by Thomas to arrest
him for jumping his contract. Franklin fled to his in-laws, still confused
about the identity of the man who had shot him in his own home. Mean-
while, Valentine died from his wounds that night, and a posse formed to
find and kill Franklin. As with the Evans lynching, members of the posse
whipped and nearly killed a Black man who was suspected of aiding Franklin as they unsuccessfully tried to get information about the fugitive's

whereabouts. Franklin eventually turned himself in with the aid of a white man he knew—it was the only way to avoid being lynched by the posse. The sheriff in Norway quietly transferred Franklin to a jail in Columbia for his safety, and there he awaited his trial.[11]

This time, the Black community responded with a truly extraordinary letter left at local businesses owned by members of the posse. The letter laid out their intentions to retaliate after more than a decade of lynchings, whippings, murders, and exploitative labor contracts had pushed them to the brink.[12] Signed "the negroes of S.C.," the letter warned the white people of Cope: "You have been killing our people, and killing them and we said nothing about it, so now you all has gone too far and we are tired of it and can't take it any longer. Now you all has disgraced our women taken them and stripped them in public and whipped them severely. We are the negroes of the State and don't expect to put up with any such."[13] Dated just a week after Valentine forced his way into Franklin's home and shot him, the letter threatened: "We know every man that had something to do with the whipping . . . and we are going to . . . kill as we go and burn them out from one side of the State to the other." They would do this as payback in kind for what whites in the area had done to so many Black people, including Lawrence Brown in 1897 and Frazier Baker in 1898, both of whom were mentioned by name in the letter as lynching victims. Knowing full well that whites depended on Black labor to grow and harvest their crops, prepare their meals, wash their clothing, care for their children, and clean their homes, the letter writers threatened to withhold Black labor; after all, a labor dispute had sparked this most recent spate of violence, and the Black women who had been whipped appear to have worked in white homes. The letter writers warned that African Americans who continued to cook for whites would poison their food, and that "If we pick your cotton we will put matches in the cotton and burn you out." Any white person who barged into the home of an African American family, as Valentine had, would be killed immediately. They half-heartedly lamented, "We don't want to hurt the good white people, because it is not them doing all the devilment. It is those low class white ones, but we can't get after them without getting the good white people, so we will take as we go in order to get them all."[14]

The letter's promise to burn down white homes and murder those white men who "took our women [then] stripped and whipped them as though they were slaves" echoed the threats allegedly made by the armed

Black men who had gathered in Freedman's Hill four years earlier. It also staked out the meaning of freedom for African Americans just over four decades after emancipation. As bold expressions of protest, both the letter from 1907 and the gathering of armed Black men in 1903 threatened violent retaliation that never came to pass. The lynching of Charles Evans had spelled out in blood what could happen if these Black communities in Orangeburg County were to follow through with their threats, but, even so, they refused to conceal their condemnation of lynching. The letter writers narrated in detailed and unambiguous terms their intentions to burn down white homes and fields, poison white people's food, defend themselves against white intruders, and kill the men who had whipped and humiliated Black women. Rather than speaking through an intermediary like a ghost or through the cover of divine retribution, they announced in clear, unequivocal language that their vengeance was justified. Hewn out of the tragedy of lynchings and other anti-Black violence, these forceful critiques levied by African Americans in Orangeburg County boldly challenged Jim Crow, laying the foundations for the protests of the civil rights movement.[15]

Lynchings, like the one that claimed Evans's life, had long afterlives in the memories of survivors but also in the Black protest tradition. African Americans in Orangeburg County, who reacted to a lynching and a near-lynching with armed self-defense and outrage, were part of a long tradition of Black "race rebels" who challenged oppressive labor practices, the indignities of Jim Crow, and white violence from the periphery of organized social movements or political institutions. These race rebels protested against lynching, not as internationally recognized figures like Ida B. Wells or through an organized antilynching campaign orchestrated by a national organization like the NAACP (which in 1907 did not yet exist), but as members of a small Black community in the Deep South, living in the midst of lynching and yet refusing to keep their condemnation of lynching to themselves.

In *Race Rebels*, Robin D. G. Kelley argues for a new, more expansive definition of Black protest that encompasses organized political protests as well as small acts of sabotage and unorganized and often spontaneous protests on the margins of social movements—protest shaped by the everyday material and spiritual needs of working-class Black people.[16] Both the armed self-defense of the Black community in Norway and the letter promising vengeance in Cope challenge a narrow reading of Black protest, along the lines that Kelley suggests, for theirs are stories not often told about antilynching protest, unfettered as they are from the politics of respectability and rigid doctrines. Their militancy fits neatly into the resistance paradigm, especially with Kelley's broader definition of protest, but local Black responses to the lynching of Charles Evans and the near-lynching of Pink Franklin invite an even more expansive reading of resistance when the interiority of lynching survivors is examined as well. More often than not, African American southerners processed traumatic memories of lynching in covert and deeply private ways, and protest could also manifest as something quiet and introspective, as part of the inner lives of Black people and as expressions of care within the Black community. The antilynching movement, the defiance of race rebels, and subsequent protest movements largely directed their attention outward to the white world through public actions like marches, lobbying, threatening letters left at the doorsteps of would-be lynchers, and armed confrontations, real and imagined. But some forms of protest were not intended for white people's eyes or ears. While still resistive of white supremacy, these protests rhymed with the blues. They were intimate expressions of love and even joy mingled with sadness and anger. They were directed inward to the self through an affirmation of Black life, through mourning, through remembering the dead, through the necessary and often difficult work of making do and living.

The dominance of the resistance paradigm has contributed to the flattening not only of Black resistance but of Black life more generally. Literary scholar Kevin Quashie astutely observes, "[Blackness] is often described as expressive, dramatic, or loud. These qualities inherently reflect the equivalence between resistance and blackness. Resistance is, in fact, the dominant expectation we have of black culture."[17] Quashie points out that "all living is not in protest; to assume such is to disregard the richness of human life," but even protest itself, in certain instances, is not simply a matter of resistance, either.[18] A more expansive vision of protest that takes Quashie's point to heart must account for the impulse within the Black community to mourn and remember the dead. Lynch mobs intended public rituals of violence and the desecration of bodies to turn Black people into objects and object lessons, but mourning, whether through public memorials and art, or in private moments when sadness crept back in, was steeped in love—it was a process that was restorative for mourners and the mourned alike. It, too, was an act of protest. It, too, was *more than* just protest, for the tenderness and care that gave meaning and feeling to mourning were more capacious than mere protest. As Quashie reminds us, "As a concept, resistance is not capable of helping a viewer to notice all this beauty, all this heart-stirring loveliness. . . . Resistance may be deeply resonant with black culture and history, but it is not sufficient for describing the totality of black humanity."[19] As much as mourning provided a means to maneuver behind the definitions of the white world and to reclaim loved ones whose bodies and memories had been desecrated by lynch mobs, it was also the stuff of love and beauty.

Immediately before the lynching of Charles Evans, his community came to his defense, guns drawn, and immediately following his death, his people were armed and ready to defend themselves from further attacks and perhaps even prepared to avenge his death. But the enduring impact of the lynching among his family and friends was that they mourned his death, that they carried their grief for him—and their love for him—in their hearts for the rest of their lives. Many decades later, memories of his lynching deepened his sister Lilian Williams's resolve to never return to Norway, as her grief continued to weigh on her. The blues sensibility mingled her sadness and love for her brother with her refusal to pay any more mind to the white people who killed him. When she left Norway, she shut them out of her life, draining them of their power to take any more from her and claiming for herself the space to go on living. In the spirit of the blues, she forged ways to "make do" in the wake of horror, at once rendering the outside source of that horror invisible and taking care of her insides.[20]

A vision of protest that imagines Black life beyond the limits of the resistance paradigm can also open up unexpected possibilities for joy and laughter and delight, even when grappling with a subject as horrifying as lynching. Black ingenuity and wit often carried survivors through the devastation of lynching and its aftermath, for laughter and playful mockery had a way of sapping white supremacy of its power by flipping the script on lynchings that had thrilled generations of white southerners. Revenge fantasies and satires, for instance, reframed lynching narratives, figuratively meting out well-deserved punishment to white perpetrators and cackling at their foolishness and absurdity. They provided a measure of satisfaction when nothing could bring back the dead and when many whites remained unrepentant in their approval of lynching. Whether protesters took their grievances to the streets and to the doorsteps of white power or turned inward to grieve the dead or mock the absurdity of white supremacists behind their backs, these protests challenged white attempts to use violence to control African Americans, and they showed how justice and love were two sides of the same coin.

The myriad forms of protest that appear in this chapter, then, both expand and trouble the resistance paradigm. More overt, militant protestations like the ones in Orangeburg County occasionally burst through the surface, despite the dangers of openly challenging white supremacy in the era of Jim Crow, but most Black people did not take part in marches and grassroots organizing and armed conflicts with white supremacists, and even those who did often chose to direct their energies inward some of the time by shutting out the white world and tending to their insides. An expansive understanding of protest like the one envisioned here does the important work of embracing vulnerability and caring for oneself and loved ones, breaking free from the confines imposed upon Black life by the resistance paradigm. Resistance has often been used as a measure of the humanity of the oppressed, such that the only authentic act in the face of oppression is resistance—the more overt and spectacular, the better. The failure to rebel, then, becomes a failure to be heroic, to have agency, to be fully human.[21] Such expectations are grossly unfair, and they compound the dangers and burdens of surviving oppression for those who least deserve to shoulder them. A vision of protest that leaves room for tenderness and an ethic of care in the face of oppression—one that settles into these quieter moments of protest—insists on recognizing the grace necessary for Black survivors to make do in the wake of lynching and subvert white supremacy through an affirmation of Black life. This reading of protest hums the blues.

Many lynching survivors needed to channel their anger and frustration into action that targeted the sources of white supremacist violence. This could look like spontaneous protests such as the ones in Orangeburg County or formal ties to civil rights organizations like the NAACP. The antilynching movements of the late nineteenth and early twentieth centuries proved to be a training ground for generations of activists—they were an integral and early part of the long civil rights movement that provided the ideological and organizational foundations for the mass movement of the 1950s and 1960s.[22] The antilynching crusade of Ida B. Wells, the campaign to enact antilynching legislation led by the NAACP, and other national and international movements to end lynching honed protest strategies like silent marches, lobbying of Congress to pass legislation, and legal challenges in the courts that carried over into the civil

rights movement. Members of Black communities who survived lynchings often formed local NAACP branches in response, as had been the
case after the Jesse Washington and Mary Turner lynchings, and experience with grassroots organizing, even when branches disbanded after
only a few years, had lasting effects on civic life in these communities. At
other times, the memories of lynching that survivors carried would smolder like glowing embers waiting to spark a new wave of protest, just as
Emmett Till's lynching became the catalyst for a whole generation of African Americans who protested lynching and white supremacy more generally, a half-century after Evans's death propelled his community into
action. Not only did activists in the civil rights movement borrow and
adapt protest strategies from antilynching activists, but their movements
often overlapped and blended into one another.[23]

The NAACP's antilynching campaign, launched in 1916, was the
first major undertaking of the organization, which was founded in 1909.
But even in 1968, decades after federal antilynching legislation had
moved to the back burner of the organization's priorities, membership
cards included among the organization's purposes, "6. To end mob violence and police brutality."[24] The continued inclusion of antilynching activities was as much a recognition of the persistent threat that mob
violence posed as it was a nod to the importance of the antilynching
campaign in developing the organization's protest strategies. The addition of police brutality alongside mob violence reflected, not so much a
new phenomenon, but the changing nature of white supremacist violence during the civil rights era. Early antilynching efforts from the
1910s shaped both NAACP antilynching protests in the 1930s and civil
rights protests in the 1950s and 1960s. For instance, many members
of NAACP Youth Councils and College Chapters who organized antilynching protests in the 1930s continued to be active in the NAACP as
adults during the civil rights movement. In 1937, the Houston College
for Negroes Chapter raised money for the national organization by selling "Stop Lynching" buttons, and organized a mass protest against
lynching to bring attention to the issue a few months ahead of when the
Gavagan Anti-Lynching Bill was introduced to the House of Representatives.[25] The mass protest against lynching in Houston took a page from
one of the first mass demonstrations organized by African Americans in
the twentieth century, the Negro Silent Protest Parade of 1917, in which
between nine and ten thousand demonstrators silently marched down
Fifth Avenue in New York City holding placards decrying political inac-

tion on lynching. Many other protests followed, and, for years, the NAACP posted a banner that read "A Man Was Lynched Yesterday" outside its Manhattan offices the morning after a lynching. Arguably the most visible and iconic moments in the civil rights movement were mass protests in southern cities like Birmingham, Washington, DC, Selma, and Memphis, and the form that visibility took mirrored the activism of this earlier era.

Other strategies from the NAACP's antilynching campaign came to shape the organization's approach to civil rights: tracking lynching statistics, sending independent investigators to lynching sites, fundraising through branch activities, collaborating with artists to raise awareness of racial injustice, and publishing pamphlets on contemporary issues. Though the NAACP's legal victories garnered more attention than its grassroots organizing and mass protests, the organization's first major campaign, to pass federal antilynching legislation, honed its strategies for effecting change and elevated its presence as a political force on the national stage, especially after antilynching bills were passed by the House in 1922, 1937, and 1940. Similar strategies eventually led to the passage of the 1957 and 1964 Civil Rights Acts a generation later, and the legacies of the NAACP's antilynching campaign include the passage of the Hate Crime Statistics Act in 1990 under the stewardship of Representative John Conyers of Michigan.[26]

Local encounters with lynching gave rise to the protest of activists and mourners alike, but these intimate brushes with death often get lost in discussions of antilynching activism. African Americans, like those who lived in and around Norway, South Carolina, were at ground zero and had to live among lynchers every day. The NAACP's antilynching campaign itself depended on mobilizing its vast network of local branches, which often were spurred into action by local lynchings. Early grassroots organizing, more often associated with SNCC forty years later, had a long-term impact on these communities and subsequent social movements.[27] Correspondence from 1923 to 1925 between the NAACP Houston Branch and the national office in New York revealed how much autonomy local activists had in doing antilynching work—the national office wasn't simply handing down directives to the local branches. Letters from New York encouraged local contributions to the national antilynching campaign largely organized out of New York, while letters from Houston updated the national office about the legal case of Luther Collins, a Houston man who was falsely accused of assaulting a white woman and whose legal defense was funded by the Houston Branch. The Houston Branch's membership drive helped the national office lobby Congress to pass another antilynching bill, after the 1922 Dyer Anti-Lynching Bill failed to pass the Senate. The surge in membership also strengthened the case for mass support of the bill. At the same time, however, the Houston Branch provided legal counsel that, after three trials, prevented the legal lynching of Collins, who was initially sentenced to death but eventually was exonerated. Not only did the local branch raise thousands of dollars to cover Collins's legal fees, but it refused financial aid offered by the national office because it "declared it could and would finance the case itself."[28] Though the national office received more attention for its lobbying efforts in Congress, local chapters, especially those in major cities, worked in tandem with the national office to combat lynching, developing local protest strategies along the way that carried over into future campaigns against the white primary, disenfranchisement, and segregation.

For some survivors of lynching who lost family, friends, and neighbors to lynch mobs, protest provided an outlet to expel their grief and their rage. The possibility that legal justice would hold lynchers to account in the Jim Crow South was remote, and the impossibility of undoing the harm of the mob was inescapable and frustrating. Even so, protest could stave off the feeling of utter powerlessness. Activism inspired by the lives stolen through violence could help survivors make meaning out of tragedy and injustice, and work to ensure that lynching would end. Ida B. Wells, for instance, had been publishing editorials condemning lynching for years, but the lynching of her friend, Thomas Moss, in Memphis and her own narrow escape from a would-be lynch mob that destroyed the office of her newspaper, *Free Speech*, gave new, deeply personal meaning to her dedication to an antilynching campaign that she brought to the attention of the world.[29] Walter White, the executive secretary of the NAACP from 1931 to 1955, got his start in the organization investigating lynchings, including the lynching of Mary Turner.[30] Other survivors and their children also channeled their grief into political action.

Lilian Williams certainly never forgot what a mob had done to her older brother, Charles Evans, and she made sure her children knew of their uncle's death and his defiance. She may have been among the mourners who gathered to see her brother's body the next day, before the coroner finally cut his body down from the tree near the Phillips property, but soon after her brother's lynching, she left Norway and set out to become a teacher, attending the Colored Normal and Industrial Agricultural and Mechanical College of South Carolina (later known as South Carolina State University) in nearby Orangeburg, South Carolina. Her daughter, Ethel Williams, also attended South Carolina State University and taught in the public schools, but when Ethel got a teaching job in Norway nearly thirty years after Lilian had left that site of trauma behind, she didn't want her daughter to be there, much less work there. Ethel Williams, too, had the rebellious streak of a true Evans. Not only did she return to a place where her family had been persecuted, but several years later, when the school superintendent in Clarendon County refused to pay her, she sued. The Williamses were not directly involved in the NAACP since teachers, as state employees, were particularly vulnerable to retaliation just for being members, but they drew upon their righteous opposition to white supremacy that grew out of the lynching of Charles Evans to challenge unequal schools and other forms of racial discrimination.[31]

For others in Orangeburg County, memories of lynching shaped future protests in the civil rights era. When Geraldyne Zimmerman was eighty-three years old and returning to memories of racial violence from her childhood, she counted the lynching of Luke Adams in 1924 as "the only one that has been in my mind through the years, that I have really, [held] the horror of it. I even shudder now when I think about it."[32] Growing up in Orangeburg in the 1910s and 1920s, she lived just two houses down from the Adams family, and when news of his lynching reached the neighborhood, her parents and the other adults in the neighborhood gathered outside in the middle of the night, murmuring in low tones about what had happened. As was so often the case with lynchings of Black men, Adams was arrested after the alleged assault of a white woman. A mob took him from the jail in Norway in broad daylight and then, under cover of darkness, tied him to a sweet gum tree and shot him several times. The sheriff discovered his body the next day with a sign that read "Crucified by a Legion" on his back.[33] Zimmerman, who was just thirteen in 1924, couldn't remember how the community responded at the time, but, reflecting on her childhood later in life, she saw the lynching of Luke Adams as a precursor to the local white backlash against the civil rights movement. Whites in Orangeburg responded with violence when the local NAACP chapter organized protests after the Supreme Court's 1954 *Brown v. Board of Education* decision, including the 1960 sit-ins staged in downtown Orangeburg at the Kress Department Store's lunch counter. Zimmerman had seen this white fury before. This fury had killed Luke Adams.

Zimmerman's mother, Hazel Frederica Pierce, had sharper memories of Adams's lynching, and her opposition to Jim Crow was as direct as it was sustained over the course of her life. In 1932, Pierce brought her daughter to the board of elections so they could both register to vote, which they did after some hassling from the registrar. She joined the National Association of Colored Women in the 1940s and the NAACP during the 1950s, and she became the vice president of the Orangeburg Branch of the NAACP to advocate for school desegregation and to give African Americans access to businesses that only served whites. In 1955, the local Citizens' Council blacklisted NAACP members like Pierce, denying them credit, firing them from their jobs, refusing to rent homes to them, and even sending them death threats, just for demanding that the Supreme Court's school desegregation order be enforced. As Zimmerman remembers it: "They wanted to withhold credit and that sort of thing.... In my mother's case, they didn't have to withhold the credit—she withdrew it!"[34] On March 15, 1960, during the Kress sit-ins in Orangeburg, more than one thousand African American students at South Carolina State University and Claflin College marched to the downtown business district to protest the exclusion of African Americans. In a scene that would play out over and over again in the civil rights era, the mayor ordered the local police to fire tear gas and use fire hoses to disperse the protesters. That day, Zimmerman and her mother were shopping near the Piggly Wiggly in downtown Orangeburg, and as the student protesters approached, her mother, who was over seventy at the time but still eager to join the march, jumped out of the car. It took all of Zimmerman's strength to hold her mother back from running to the students who were being blasted with fire hoses and blinded by tear gas. Zimmerman was concerned about her mother's physical safety, but Pierce, having seen how destructive white supremacists could be, especially to the lives of young Black people, wanted to grab the fire hoses away from the police. When that white mob lynched Luke Adams in 1924, he was only twenty-five years old, just a couple of years older than the students marching through downtown Orangeburg to end segregation in 1960. Pierce could not stand the thought of white supremacists hemming in the lives of yet another generation of young Black people. She lunged toward the hoses, but her daughter held tight. From the car, they watched the students get blasted into the gutters by the powerful fire hoses, wishing they could do something more to protect them.[35]

Generations of African American survivors of lynching redirected the pain and anger of lynching memories into the struggle to dismantle white supremacy. John M. Adkins, the branch secretary for the Houston NAACP during the 1920s, had faced lynch mobs three times and survived, and even amid a social climate in which the threat of Klan violence was heightened, he worked tirelessly for the NAACP, railing against "the braying of Southern Jackasses in the Senate" who blocked federal anti-lynching legislation in 1922.[36] A fellow member of the Houston Branch wrote to the NAACP's national office, "We do not fear to do right. Our secretary [Adkins] is a man who has three times faced a mob. No wonder that he sometimes swears when folks are indifferent or cowardly."[37] Adkins's fearless commitment to justice grew out of and alongside having faced down three lynch mobs. Three decades later, Medgar Evers, the NAACP field secretary in Mississippi, cited lynching as a major reason for dedicating his life's work to racial justice. When he was a child, a lynch mob killed a family friend for insulting a white woman, and they left his bloodied clothing for over a year at the foot of the tree where he died. When asked why he joined the NAACP, he would tell the story of sitting at his dying father's bedside in a segregated hospital ward, trying to offer him comfort, while a rowdy lynch mob yelled taunts outside. That night he cried, but when a mob lynched Mack Charles Parker in 1959, he nearly boiled over with rage and exasperation. He told his wife, Myrlie Evers, "I'd like to get a gun and just start shooting."[38] These close personal brushes with lynching produced outrage but also propelled Wells and Pierce and Adkins and Evers, like so many others, into the world of Black activism.

On the national level, the lynching of Emmett Till in 1955 had a profound impact on activism among African Americans, but especially with children growing up in the 1950s who saw something of themselves, whether their race, gender, southern roots, or age, in the fourteen-year-old Black child brutally murdered in Mississippi. Cleveland Sellers, who grew up not far from Norway, South Carolina, and later joined SNCC, recalled that Till's lynching was all that people in his town talked about for days, perhaps because his lynching revived stories of Luke Adams, Pink Franklin, Charles Evans, and others.[39] In many respects, the outrage at Till's lynching and the ease with which a Mississippi jury acquitted his killers spurred the mass movement for civil rights during the 1950s and 1960s, which had already been energized by the *Brown v. Board of Education* decision one year earlier.⁴⁰ Till's mother, Mamie Till-Mobley, knew the public needed to see what his killers had done to him. She went to the press and authorized the publication in *Jet* of photographs of his mangled body, and at her request, his casket was open at his funeral. Thousands of people came to the funeral in Chicago, and an estimated one hundred thousand more viewed the body in the days that followed. The name of Emmett Till was immortalized; his mother had made sure of that.⁴¹

Among the thousands who waited in line outside the Rayner Funeral Home and later at the Roberts Temple of the Church of God in Christ in Chicago to solemnly pay their respects to Till was Jesse Pennington, who had escaped a lynch mob in the Mississippi Delta only one year earlier. Pennington's memories of that day were still vivid fifty-six years later:

> I'll never forget that day his body was displayed in that church. Lord have mercy, that was the most grievous day of my life. . . . I mean, it was like the whole world had ended. It was incredible. One of the saddest days. I think that's the best thing that she [Till-Mobley] could have done. She opened that casket. People were just, I remember people were crying and crying. I remember we were all waiting in line trying to see him. I finally got, you know, I didn't see him because people were just, people were crying and screaming, passing out. Oh god it was horrible. Ooh, my god.⁴²

Alongside this anguish was real anger in Chicago, and in the weeks that followed, Pennington witnessed the first rumblings of a mass movement for Black liberation, a movement rooted in the sentiment, as Pennington put it, "We gotta get the guns" and "I'm not going to take this shit." This move toward armed resistance harkened back to the gathering of hundreds of armed Black men in Norway, South Carolina, back in 1903. Pennington, however, chose to take the path of education. He got a law degree from Howard University and in 1969 returned to Mississippi to practice law. For Pennington, being a lawyer was not a matter of money or fame. After surviving an attempted lynching himself, and after seeing Till's body, he felt called to help others: "I remembered what had happened to me, and this whole time, there was nobody. You couldn't get anybody to help you. Nobody. There was no, there was nobody there for you . . . nobody in authority or power there for you. So when I came back, my raison d'être for coming back after law school was to be there [for others]."[43]

Till-Mobley's remembrance of her son reached millions of people, galvanizing support for the NAACP in the immediate aftermath of his death, but his lynching had a far deeper impact on the Black freedom struggle. For many civil rights activists, but in particular those who were children in 1955, his lynching was a flash point in the development of their political identity, his death both illustrating the precarity of their lives in a white supremacist society and motivating them to dismantle the systems of oppression at the root of that precarity. When Rosa Parks refused to move to the back of a bus in Montgomery, Alabama, in 1956, she was thinking about Till. Just a few days earlier, she had attended a lecture by T. R. M. Howard in which he urged the attendees to take action against Jim Crow and described the Till lynching in detail. For Minnijean Brown-Trickey, who was one of the Little Rock Nine, Till's lynching illustrated the destructiveness of racism. His death hit her particularly hard because they were the same age and, had he lived, Till also would have been entering eleventh grade in 1957 when she and the other eight children desegregated Central High School in Little Rock, Arkansas. Student activists who initiated the Greensboro, North Carolina, sit-ins in 1960, like Ezell Blair Jr. (later known as Jibreel Khazan), and the Freedom Rides in 1961, like SNCC's John Lewis and Julian Bond, cited Till as both the impetus for their activism and the person in whose memory they protested Jim Crow.[44]

Lynchings left memories that throbbed and gave past wounds renewed immediacy time and again. These memories often remained raw and tender, scabbed over but never quite healed. Though most survivors of lynching gave private expression to these memories, some found that channeling traumatic memories into explicit protest against racial injustice helped them process the trauma they lived with for the rest of their lives. African Americans across the South had lived through the horrors of white depravity, and yet they imagined what justice and liberation would look like in the midst of lynching and in the wake of lynching.

Mourning is living through loss—getting through days and weeks and years without those we hold dear and struggling with the pain left in their absence. Mourning is an act of love—keeping the dead alive in memories and remembering them as they lived, not just as they died.

And for the families and friends of lynching victims, in particular, mourning became a matter of restoration. This heart-wrenching blend of love and loss rhymed with the blues, with the impulse of the blues to remember as a means to make it through the pain. In the aftermath of lynch mobs physically and narratively mangling their loved ones— turning them into terrifying monsters to destroy, trophies to display, nameless bodies to disfigure—families and friends and communities re- claimed narrative control over victims' lives through mourning rituals, at funerals and wakes, in memorials, and with art. Remembrance was a matter of survival, love, and restoration. Mourning was protest.[45]

Mourning took many forms and was often stunted and delayed, re- sponding, as it did, to the unpredictable traumatic reverberations of lynching memories that unfolded and refolded over time. Among chil- dren touched by lynching, that unpredictability was often even more pronounced because the traumas they experienced tended to go unex- plained and unprocessed until decades later. When Elijah Muhammad (born Elija Pool) was a small child at the turn of the twentieth century, a white man in Cordele, Georgia, approached the little boy, smiling, hold- ing something special to show him. The man opened his fist to reveal a severed ear resting on his palm, a souvenir from a lynched Black man's body. Behind his cruel smile was a clear warning: that dead body could be yours someday. In 1903, another Black man was lynched in Cordele, and though Muhammad was spared from witnessing the lynching itself, it so traumatized him that he started wetting the bed. He was only six years old, and these embarrassing accidents continued until he was twelve.[46] Just a few years later, in 1912, another lynch mob in Cordele killed one of his closest friends, Albert Hamilton. Before hanging Hamil- ton from a tree in the Black section of town, the mob beat him nearly unconscious. While he still struggled for breath as he dangled from the end of the rope, the lynchers shot him three hundred times. Members of the Black community were too terrified to cut down the body, so Hamilton's corpse remained hanging like "strange fruit" until the coro- ner took it away. Muhammad's tears mingled with a fury raging inside, and then the nightmares returned. The image of his friend's lifeless body, bloodied and riddled with bullet holes and hanging from that tree, haunted Muhammad for the rest of his life. Many years later, as founder of the Nation of Islam, he paid tribute to Hamilton by displaying in every mosque an image of a tree with a Black body hanging from one of its branches.[47]

Yet another lynching spurred Muhammad's decision to leave the South when he was in his twenties, and he eventually settled in Detroit. Not only did he fear for the safety of his family, but had he remained in Georgia, where African Americans were lynched with such brutality and with no legal consequences for the perpetrators, he worried that his rage against white people would grow even deeper and more corrosive. Such a stifling environment might lead him to kill or be killed.[48]

Mourning the violent death of his friend was painful enough, but living in a place where white people could commit heinous crimes and yet still walk the streets, Muhammad had to bottle up his disgust, making it nearly impossible to fully and openly process all of his traumatic memories. And yet new traumas were heaped upon old traumas. While Muhammad processed his grief, he encountered daily reminders of Hamilton's death. He knew that some of the white people he passed on the streets of Cordele had lynched his friend and that some might have purchased photographs of his friend's lynched body. In moments when he felt Hamilton's absence most sharply, he might have wondered about the terror of his final moments, about which of these white folks he saw around town gazed upon those photographs with relish, about the life his friend would have led had he lived past age eighteen. From the relative safety of the Midwest, Muhammad's tribute to Hamilton—the images he hung in every Nation of Islam mosque—allowed him to return to painful memories of the past on his own terms and remember his friend in peace.

The lynching images in the Nation of Islam mosques, like the photographs of Hamilton's lynched body, were public gestures, though the images in the mosques and the photographs gestured in radically different directions. In the mosques, these images served as memorials to more than just Hamilton, for thousands more victims like Hamilton had lost their lives to lynchers and many thousands more survivors, like Muhammad, were left to mourn in the wake of these deaths. Though he could have displayed a portrait of his friend, he chose an image of an anonymized lynched Black body hanging from a tree. These images of death reminded African Americans who viewed them in the mosques that lynching and white supremacy loomed, but stopped just short of tearing open old wounds, or so one hopes. Muhammad reframed these images of anti-Black violence as memorials, not because they were any less graphic, but because they were thoughtfully placed in Black sanctuaries effused with love and genuine care, in places largely untouched by the white world. In viewing these memorials, pain and anger nestled up against remembrance and love in quiet, introspective moments bathed in the spirit of the blues. In these spaces, Muhammad could reclaim the image of lynching, not to shed from it the inescapable violence of the mob, but to condemn and mourn the destruction of Black life.

Despite the wide range of ways in which lynching survivors channeled their traumatic memories into protest, they all shared a desire to make meaning out of deaths that were undeserved—deaths that came too soon and were too brutal, deaths that came without due process of the law, deaths with no legal consequences for the killers. Knowing full well that lynchings could not be undone, many survivors sought ways to prevent future injustices that took members of their families and communities from them. They mourned the dead, and memorialized them for the sake of the living. These acts of protest were, at their heart, acts of love, memorials to the dead that helped to dull the sharpness of pain and temper the fires of anger.

Artists of all stripes, too, memorialized lynching victims, giving public expression to the losses felt by Black communities across the nation. Most art and literature about lynching focused on condemning lynch mobs. These artists sought to reveal what drove white people to lynch African Americans and how white perpetrators grappled with the long-term social and psychological impacts of lynching, as in James Baldwin's short story, "Going to Meet the Man."[49] Like Baldwin, W. E. B. Du Bois excoriated white lynchers in "Jesus Christ in Texas," a short story that exposed the thinness of white Christian love and the hypocrisy of their faith in a just and loving God. When Jesus wanders into Waco, Texas, African Americans immediately beg for forgiveness for their sins, but whites eye the olive-skinned stranger, whose face is framed in dark curls, with suspicion, unable to recognize him as the son of God. These white Christians brutalize their Black neighbors and exploit their labor, and when a white mob lynches an innocent Black man accused of attempted rape, it is the lynched, not the lynchers, whom Jesus redeems.[50] Other African American artists, however, diverged from these works focused on white perpetrators, instead placing Black families and communities at the center of their creative visions. Some saw in the deaths of lynching victims the redemptive suffering of God's sacrifice of his son, Jesus, on the cross, while others focused on African American mourning and remembrance, as Muhammad had.[51]

Some artists did both, comparing lynching to the crucifixion of Jesus and capturing the deepest wells of collective loss and mourning.

Richmond Barthé's sculpture, *The Mother* or *Mother and Son* (1939), alluded to Michelangelo's *Pietà* (1498–99), but, instead of depicting Jesus and Mary, he captured a quiet moment of grief: a Black mother holding the limp body of her dead son whose neck bears the marks of a noose (fig. 5.1).[52] The mother's gaze is fixed not on the body of her son—a body that she clutches to her own, a body whose weight she once again bears—but somewhere off in the distance. Her expression is pained, as though she is looking beyond her son's body for a sign that his death is somehow redemptive, that his suffering is somehow a pathway to hope, that his lynching in this world might be followed by the promise of peace in the afterlife. Barthé's reference to the crucifixion resonated with African Americans because, as James Cone explained, "in the United States, the clearest image of the crucified Christ was the figure of an innocent black victim, dangling from a lynching tree."[53] Barthé captured a belief held by many African American Christians that, as Cone put it, "just knowing that Jesus went through an experience of suffering in a manner similar to theirs gave them faith that God was with them, even in suffering on lynching trees, just as God was present with Jesus in suffering on the cross."[54] Artists like Barthé expressed mourning in the afterlife of lynching in ways that captured *collective* grief, and because Americans could view works like *The Mother* at the 1939 World's Fair or the American Negro Exposition in 1940, his sculpture gave *public* expression to the possibility that Black suffering could be redemptive.[55]

The seated woman in panel 16 of Jacob Lawrence's *The Migration of the Negro Series* (1940–41), also grieves—the absence of the lynched body in the painting only deepens the loss and devastation that Lawrence captures, and redirects attention to the mourner left in a lynching's wake (fig. 5.2). The woman, collapsed on a table, buries her face in her right forearm while her limp left hand nearly grazes the floor. Her hand and hair cascade downward like the flowing of her unseen tears, this private moment providing an intimate glimpse into grief, not for voyeuristic consumption, but to reveal in her pain the imprint of a life now absent, missed, and forever loved. The caption of this panel provides a narrative bridge between the injustice of lynching and the Great Migration out of the South and into urban centers in the Northeast and Midwest. Amid their grief in the aftermath of a lynching, African Americans—women like Lilian Williams who left Norway, South Carolina, after her brother's lynching—drew from wells of love for the ones they had lost and the ones that remained, and they resolved to refuse the devastation of lynching and to leave.

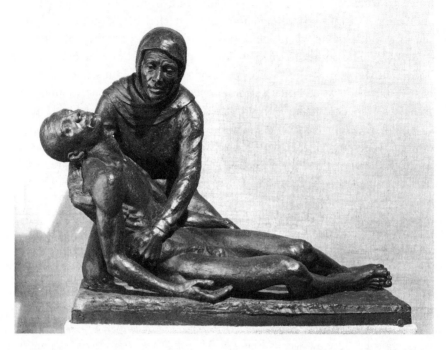

Figure 5.1. Richmond Barthé, *The Mother*, 1939. (National Archives, photo no. 200-HN-BAR-58)

Lawrence's painting is a statement of reclamation, redemption, and refusal, one that centers Black life rather than the spectacle of Black death.[56]

In giving expression to the mourning of lynching survivors, artwork like Barthé's *The Mother* and Lawrence's panel 16 reconfigured lynching narratives by centering African American victims and survivors rather than white perpetrators. Through these representations of mourning, they restored the full picture of those lives lost and expanded the temporal boundaries of lynching. Rather than reinforcing the notion that a lynching was a discrete event bounded by the formation and the dissolution of the white lynch mob, these artists reclaimed victims as whole people who had been cherished and loved by their families and communities *in life* and *in death*, and thereby captured the long afterlives of lynchings. Survivors like Muhammad and Williams carried these losses for the rest of their lives and lived through the traumatic aftershocks of

Figure 5.2. Jacob Lawrence, *The Migration Series, Panel no. 16:* "Although the Negro was used to lynching, he found this an opportune time for him to leave where one had occurred. After a lynching the migration quickened." 1940–41, tempera on gesso on composition board, 18 × 12 inches (45.7 × 30.5 cm). (Digital image © The Museum of Modern Art / Licensed by SCALA / Art Resource, NY; © 2021 The Jacob and Gwendolyn Knight Lawrence Foundation, Seattle / Artists Rights Society [ARS], New York)

lynching that haunted them, and they kept those lost to mob rule alive through their love and remembrances.

The connections between mourning and the blues went beyond blues songs occasionally broaching the subject of death and loss. Mourning mingled deathliness with aliveness, just as the blues blended despair and joy. Something in these seeming contradictions was reinvigorating and life-giving, for the blues exorcised everyday troubles, and mourning confronted the painful reality of death but ultimately celebrated life.[57] That "something" made possible by this ironic intermingling becomes more legible when considering Black life as it relates to anti-Blackness. Quashie observes in *Black Aliveness, or A Poetics of Being:* "Antiblackness is part of blackness but not all of how or what blackness is. Antiblackness is total in the world, but it is not total in the black world."[58] What Quashie identifies here is the irreducibility of Blackness to anti-Blackness, which recognizes the inherent beauty of Blackness—that enduring joy, love, laughter, and vulnerability that cannot be touched by the world. This same sentiment imbues the funeral sermon in James Baldwin's novel, *Another Country,* when Reverend Foster tells the mourners: "Don't lose heart, dear ones—don't lose heart. Don't let it make you bitter. Try to understand. Try to understand. The world's already bitter enough, we got to try to be better than the world."[59] It is this irreducibility to anti-Blackness, this refusal to let the world's bitterness enter one's own heart, this urge to hold close memories of those most dear even when they're gone that gives mourning its celebratory notes and lets blues singers crack a smile despite their tears.

Reading that 1907 letter signed "We are the negroes of S.C." in the twenty-first century is an indulgence in the satisfying pleasure and even catharsis of imagining lynchers getting their comeuppance—their fields and homes reduced to cinders, their faces ashen from a hot meal laced with rat poison, their days numbered. Revenge fantasies like that letter have figured into artistic representations of lynching, too, and for the same reasons the Black residents of Orangeburg County, South Carolina, penned that letter. In Mario Van Peebles's neo-western film, *Posse* (1993), for instance, the hero vanquishes the literal white devils who lynched his father and tried to steal the land from a Black town in the West. Depictions of Black vengeance against white violence, like Foxy Brown (Pam Grier) taking on the mafia to avenge the death of her boyfriend in the Blaxploitation classic *Foxy Brown* (1974), tap into a visceral sense of satisfaction achieved through righteous and punitive violence against evil white men who are getting their just deserts. But other revenge fantasies are far less straight-faced—they come with a smirk and a chuckle. Take, for instance, a *Chappelle's Show* sketch from 2004, "The Time Haters," in which the "player haters" time-travel to the antebellum South to call an enslaver a "cracker."[60] One of the "player haters," played by Dave Chappelle, shoots an enslaver, right after saying, "Nice whip. This here is a pistol. Reach for the sky, honky!" Originally that sketch had been cut from a previous show for being "too controversial" for television because it showed him shooting an enslaver four times on a loop. After playing the clip on a show of previously cut sketches, Chappelle, who is doubled over laughing, adds, "If I could, I'd do it every episode," much to the amusement of his live audience. Like *Posse* and *Foxy Brown*, that sketch from *Chappelle's Show* critiqued anti-Black violence through a revenge fantasy, but with Chappelle's comedic approach, the effect of that critique was different. Satire and humor provided not just righteous satisfaction but also real pleasure by unmasking the horrors and absurdity of white supremacy.

Given the gravity of the subject matter, artists have less frequently turned to satire and humor when representing lynching, but *Pittsburgh Courier* journalist and thorn-in-the-side provocateur, George Schuyler, did just that in his absurdist satire, *Black No More*, published in 1931 at the tail end of the Harlem Renaissance.[61] The novel explores the phenomenon of racial passing (from Black to white *and* white to Black) by way of science fiction, and it ends with a scene in which a white mob in Mississippi lynches two prominent "white" men who have been revealed to have Black ancestry. This scene turns the history of white mobs lynching Black men on its side, revealing the absurdity of clinging to the myth of racial purity and the hypocrisy of many white Christians in the South.[62]

Black No More destabilizes the supposed rigidity of racial categories, not through righteous or retributive violence, but through buffoonery and farce. The premise of the novel is that a Black scientist, Dr. Junius Crookman, wreaks havoc upon the American racial landscape by developing a medical procedure that transforms Black people into white people. That the doctor develops the procedure after studying in Germany is no mere accident since his procedure makes a clear nod to eugenics, which was popular on both sides of the Atlantic during the 1920s and 1930s. Crookman's intention, however, is not to eliminate the Black race per se, but to further "mix" an already racially mixed nation. (In fact,

Crookman never undergoes his own procedure, which makes his company, Black No More, millions of dollars.) With millions of African Americans "passing" into white social circles and neighborhoods after undergoing this new procedure, an angry white backlash gains momentum. This backlash includes a populist faction, the Knights of Nordica, which closely resembles the Klan, and an elite faction, the Anglo-Saxon Association of America, led by characters who are thinly veiled references to the eugenicist and statistician Walter Plecker and John Powell, founder of the Anglo-Saxon Clubs of America. These two white supremacist factions grudgingly unite during the presidential election with the Imperial Grand Wizard of the Knights of Nordica at the top of the ticket and the founder of the Anglo-Saxon Association of America, Arthur Snobbcraft, as his running mate. During the campaign, Snobbcraft's eugenicist and statistician friend, Dr. Samuel Buggerie, unearths extensive genealogical data to expose recently whitened Black people with the help of the meticulous research of the whitened version of Dr. Shakespeare Agamemnon Beard, himself a thinly veiled allusion to Du Bois. Much to their surprise, however, Snobbcraft and Buggerie, these self-proclaimed defenders of white purity, have Black ancestors, and when word of their racial impurity leaks to the press, they flee for Mexico, but not before literally crapping their pants in fear.

Unfortunately for them, their plane runs out of fuel over Mississippi. As they are about to crash, they reason that nobody would be able to identify them if they were disguised as a pair of Black men, so in a panicked frenzy, they slather black shoe polish onto their skin and attempt to "pass" as Black. Now in disguise, they abandon their crashed plane and approach a revival, foolishly remarking, "We can be sure those folks will treat us right. One thing about these people down here they are real, sincere Christians."[63] Little do they know, they have stumbled upon the all-white town of Happy Hill, Mississippi, which is known for "its inordinately high illiteracy and its lynching record."[64] Through an absurd yet amusing cascade of buffoonish mishaps, they find themselves pleading with a Mississippi lynch mob to spare them as they insist they are, in fact, white men "passing" in blackface. The disappointed mob halts the lynching, but only until the lynchers get wind of news that their captives/guests are Snobbcraft and Buggerie, two racially impure con artists on the lam. Satisfied that these two self-avowed white supremacists are Black men by their own one-drop rule, the mob seizes them again, mutilates their bodies, and burns them alive.[65]

The lynching of Snobbcraft and Buggerie in *Black No More* is largely self-inflicted, caused by a bungled attempt to escape from the United States. But on a deeper level, their deaths ultimately result from their own painstaking statistical and genealogical research, and, of course, a one-drop definition of Blackness they had invented and publicly championed. They are unable to correctly read the "good Christians" at the revival, for they lack what Du Bois called "second sight," among other things, like good sense.[66] Even after their Black ancestry comes to light, they still cannot understand themselves as anything other than white, and their performance of Blackness is, to put it mildly, unconvincing. For men from a supposedly superior stock of Anglo-Saxons, they appear to be preternaturally dim-witted. Schuyler lampoons the likes of Snobbcraft and Buggerie because, in mocking their earnest veneration of whiteness, he reveals their utter ignorance. After all, Schuyler opens the novel with a sarcastic dedication to "all the Caucasians in the great republic who can trace their ancestry back ten generations and confidently assert that there are no Black leaves, twigs, limbs or branches on their family trees."[67]

Schuyler also vanquishes white supremacists while keeping Black people's hands clean—African Americans are not even remotely implicated in Snobbcraft's and Buggerie's lynchings.[68] Even the two or three "whitened Negroes," as Schuyler calls them, who find themselves in the Mississippi mob "would fain have gone to the assistance of the two men but fear for their own lives restrain them," and they "were looked at rather sharply by some of the Christ Lovers because they did not appear to be enjoying the spectacle as thoroughly as the rest."[69] By removing African Americans from the act of revenge, Schuyler invites his readers to chuckle at the notion of white superiority in light of Snobbcraft's and Buggerie's idiocy, and to reconsider biological notions of race since Schuyler shows race to be a performance and primarily a proxy for power. His caricatured portrayals of his contemporaries, John Powell (Snobbcraft) and Walter Plecker (Buggerie), might compel white introspection, for white readers have nowhere left to look but at themselves. Or, as is so often the case, they can choose to look away—from Schuyler's satirical barbs and from who they really are.

Schuyler's satire resists the pitfalls of sentimentality, much like a blues song that brings in just enough irony and pleasure to avoid becoming consumed by anger or despair. Rather than pegging characters as either righteous and good or heartless and evil, Schuyler is far more ambivalent. The doctor who develops the whitening procedure, Dr. Crookman, is somewhere between a mad scientist and a genius prophet. One Black character becomes white and joins the Knights of Nordica to pursue a love interest, the daughter of the Imperial Grand Wizard, and another works for the Anglo-Saxon Association of America to trace the racial ancestry of every American, though with the intention of leaking the findings. The white supremacist leaders spew hateful speech and condone racist violence, but the lot of them are buffoons, including Snobbcraft and Buggerie, so they are as much objects of pity as of scorn. In Schuyler's hands, this ambivalence is not intended to downplay the horrors of racism, nor does it. However, he refuses to cast even the most distasteful characters as pure, distilled evil.

As a satirist and general contrarian, Schuyler writes against the protest novel tradition, which Baldwin describes as "an accepted and comforting aspect of the American scene, ramifying that framework we believe to be so necessary. Whatever unsettling questions are raised are evanescent, titillating; remote, for this has nothing to do with us . . . so that finally we receive a definite thrill of virtue from the fact that we are reading such a book at all."[70] Protest novels insist on pitting good against evil, making identification with evil nearly impossible for the reader and identification with goodness all but guaranteed. Even if questions about white supremacist violence are raised, a reader of protest novels is made to feel satisfied and even virtuous for not only reading about evil being vanquished but by siding with the good guys. *Black No More* is very intentionally unsettling because a reader encounters a violent lynching scene that is inflected with absurdity and humor. Just as the "whitened Negroes" in the lynch mob wince as they "[remember] what their race has suffered in the past," the history of anti-Black lynching cannot help but intrude upon the page, no matter how unsympathetic Snobbcraft and Buggerie are as characters.[71] At the same time, Schuyler's razor-sharp wit peels back the layers of absurdity draped upon the idea of race in the United States—the one-drop rule, the indiscriminate veneration of whiteness, claims of superiority and purity—and exposes whiteness for what it is: a powerful myth, but a myth nonetheless.

Fictional narratives of lynching and visual representations of its aftermath could wrest narrative control over lynching from unsympathetic or even aggressively antagonistic white voices. Faced with an onslaught of lynching postcards and newspaper accounts sensationalizing lynching after decades of white southerners publicly defended the practice, these narrative reclamations by Black artists were acts of protest. They spelled out Black condemnation of lynch mobs. They gave expression to the love and loss felt by Black families and communities mourning the deaths of their kinfolk, their friends, and their neighbors. They provided a release valve for pent-up frustrations by fantasizing about revenge and laughing to keep from crying.

All these stories of protest—from the generation of activists politicized by Emmett Till's lynching to the art of mourning—share the intermingling of seemingly discordant sentiments: defiance and despair, love and grief, laughter and disgust. These layers of joy and anguish, which have deep roots in the African American experience, recognize that life is not lived one note at a time or in perfect harmony but often in blue notes stretched and bent across pitch and time. Generations of Black southerners have navigated the dual inheritance of a nation set on their debasement and a Black southern culture steeped in love and joy, and this dual inheritance undoubtedly informs the sensibility of the blues, a sensibility in which people breathe joy through and beyond suffering. Imani Perry, when describing the relationship between these inheritances, explains that "[Black joy is] actually a disposition of constantly accessing the depth and breadth of our humanity as Black folks. . . . When I'm talking about joy, it's never an evasion of the depth of the wounds. It is literally the sustaining life force."[72] So, too, does the blues sensibility refuse to evade the terror of anti-Black violence or to strike a singular note of anger, sadness, fear, or vengeance in reaction to white violence. For tangled with these notes is a fierce affirmation of Black love, of Black joy, of Black life.

Even the most direct and public protests contended with this dual inheritance. Armed self-defense, for instance, was as much a matter of protecting those you loved as it was a necessity born out of the persistent precarity of Black life in a white supremacist nation. When Lester Gibson would tell the story of his family taking up arms to defend one of their own from a lynch mob in 1922, he was filled with great admiration for the bravery and steadfast convictions of his people. In his telling, the story began decades earlier with several hundred acres of land in Simsboro, Texas, that his formerly enslaved great-grandparents had purchased after emancipation—land that his family still owns. His people were proud—they were self-sufficient, they established their own schools, and they refused to work for white people—and, as he put it, "they would bite you back."[73] When a mob descended upon the family farm to lynch

Leroy Gibson, the family protected their people and their land. Leroy's uncle, Floyd Gibson, was an expert marksman who had fought in World War I, and, as his great-niece, Lutisia Gibson, told it, "he fell on his stomach and started shooting, as he'd been trained, and wasn't missing a lick. He only stopped because he ran out of shells."[74] Floyd picked off several members of the mob, forcing the rest to retreat.

This story of self-defense and defiance later became a point of family pride, but their armed resistance came at a devastating cost. Leroy and his nephew, Allie, died during the shootout and Floyd had to slip away to Washington state for his own safety. The members of the family who remained in Simsboro knew that, though they might take out a few racists along the way, they couldn't protect every member of the family from a mob, not even on their own property. And they were afraid. When word of the shootout spread, hundreds of armed white men gathered nearby to put down what they considered a Black uprising. Black families also converged upon Simsboro, posting armed Black men behind barricades along the road into town in preparation for the onslaught. Further bloodshed was avoided only when white officials called for peace.[75]

Lester Gibson, who was born almost thirty years after the lynchings, inherited the vestiges of these losses, the fortitude to affirm and protect his people, and that family tradition of protest. As a McLennan County (Texas) commissioner, he proposed a resolution in 2002 to officially apologize for lynchings in the county, whose victims included Sank Majors (1905), Jesse Washington (1916), Elijah Hayes (1917), and Jesse Thomas (1922).[76] The other commissioners, all of whom were white, watered down the resolution to a "condemnation" of lynching, but it eventually passed in 2006. Defying the rest of the commissioners, he displayed the resolution next to a mural in the McLennan County Courthouse in Waco that included a lynching tree and noose—a mural that he had unsuccessfully attempted to take down in 2002. The appropriately named sheriff, Larry Lynch, twice ordered the removal of the antilynching resolution from the courthouse, but Gibson persisted and displayed it in the County Records Building down the hall from the other commissioners' offices.[77] Like his family before him, he insisted on honoring the dead and tending to the living. Amid the devastating aftermath of lynchings and the continued attempts of white Wacoans to evade their history, he struck a blue note—finding light in the dignity of lynching victims and survivors, including his own kin, while knowing he was still very much in the storm.

CHAPTER SIX

The Blues

In the days when a man
would hold a swarm of words
inside his belly, nestled
against his spleen, singing.

In the days of night riders
when life tongued a reed
till blues & sorrow song
called out of the deep night:
Another man done gone.
Another man done gone.

—YUSEF KOMUNYAKAA, "Blue Dementia"

WHAT WOULD IT COST a man to "hold a swarm of words / inside his belly, nestled / against his spleen, singing"?[1] And how long could he contain that swarm and bear its painful barbs, even while giving expression to some whisper of the swarm in song? The capacity to absorb and contain the horrors of a traumatic episode, much less the accumulated horrors of a traumatic era like Jim Crow, is difficult to measure, especially when the stakes of a single word in that swarm straying from the rest and slipping out could be no less than death. For African American southerners in the era of Jim Crow, the imperative to contain the swarm was a daily reality. And yet stories about containing the swarm survived. Even at the nadir, the essence of these traumatic stories crept out, at times in the "worrying exhale of an ache," as Claudia Rankine put it, and sometimes in a blues singer's moan.[2]

In one such story, Riley King, a Black boy who spent his childhood in the shadow of Jim Crow, was delivering clean laundry for his stepmother when he cautiously circled the town square of Lexington, Mississippi, snatching furtive glimpses at the dead body of a Black man hanging from a makeshift scaffold. Decades later, King recalled how, at the sight of the body and the white mob that gathered around, that swarm of words Komunyakaa spoke of hovered within his belly:

> Deep inside, I'm hurt, sad, and mad. But I stay silent. . . . What do I have to say and who's gonna listen to me? . . . My anger is a secret that stays away from the light of day because the square is bright with the smiles of white people passing by as they view the dead man on display. I feel disgust and disgrace and rage and every emotion that makes me cry without tears and scream without sound. I don't make a sound.[3]

That such a young child knew to remain silent reveals how, long before that afternoon in 1938, he knew the precarity of Black life and the destructiveness of white violence. His innocence had already been stolen, soiled by previous humiliations and hardened by grave lessons in survival. Why else would he already have known to keep his anger a "secret" when he saw white faces smile up at the Black corpse? Why else would his instinct have him stay away despite his burning curiosity to see what novel attraction stirred up such a commotion?[4] He already knew to swallow his anger, stifle his tears, and silence his screams, for even the softest grumble or the slightest flash of anger in his eyes might be interpreted by white folks as insolence.[5]

The sight of the dead man's body took what remained of King's childhood. He had already heard about the horrors of enslavement from his maternal great-grandmother, and he knew about the frequent lynchings and cross burnings that happened elsewhere in the Delta. This time, however, he witnessed firsthand the brutality of southern racial violence.

That day in the square, King wore a deferential mask to conceal the tangle of emotions that raged below; the dead man's contorted face, by contrast, wore the anguish of his final moments—his eyes frozen wide open, his mouth agape—and King's anguish, too. As he snuck a few glances at the dead man, he saw himself in that Black man's face and in that Black man's fate. He knew that Mississippi offered no refuge for Black boys like him.

King made it through those times, enveloping his grief and anger in silence, burying it somewhere deep inside, but he carried his memories of the dead body and the contorted expression on the dead man's face for the rest of his life. By the mid-1940s, King had grown weary of sharecropping in the Mississippi Delta, so he packed his guitar and moved to Memphis, unaware that one day he would be crowned "king of the blues."

As a child, B. B. (for "Blues Boy") King stuttered, as did his Uncle Major and his maternal great-grandfather, whom he called "Pop." It required intense concentration to remove the invisible barriers blocking him from getting past a letter or a syllable, which he likened to an internal battle in which silenced injuries and rage tried to burst free: "Sometimes I wondered about Pop's stuttering, which, like Uncle Major's, frustrated him like crazy. I wondered if a speech impediment has something to do with boiled-up fury inside."[6] Pop, "a stutterer who talked with his shotgun and liked to ride his mule while swigging moonshine whiskey out of a jug," had accumulated a significant backlog of anger and resentment after living through slavery and Jim Crow.[7] King wryly recalled one afternoon when a white landowner demanded that Pop's daughter return to work on his farm. Pop emerged from his cabin with his Winchester rifle and, after ordering this trespasser off his property, fired two warning shots at the enraged (and then bewildered) white man.[8] A feisty old man, Pop struggled to contain the "boiled-up fury inside" trapped behind his stutter, and sometimes it blasted out the barrel of a gun.

Unlike his rifle-toting great-grandfather, King coped with the traumatic memory of that lynching in 1938 and other hardships through singing and playing the blues. Music had long sustained his family and community through great adversity. His maternal great-grandmother had told him stories about enslaved people singing work songs, and from those stories he understood that "singing about your sadness unburdens your soul. But the blues hollerers shouted about more than being sad. They were also delivering messages in musical code.... The blues could warn you what was coming. I could see the blues was about survival."[9] Even before King was old enough to work in Mississippi cotton fields, he had heard "shouting in the fields" or "music meant to take the ache out of our backs and the burden off our brains."[10] He eventually joined his family in the fields, doing the backbreaking labor of sharecropping, and after a hard day's work, he would listen to jazz, gospel, and the blues on his aunt's Victrola. When his mother died suddenly when he was just ten, he spent hours listening to blues songs to comfort himself in his grief and loneliness: "Something in the music kept pulling me in. The blues was bleeding the same blood as me. The blues didn't have to explain the mystery of pain that I felt; it was there in the songs and voices of singers like Lonnie Johnson and Blind Lemon Jefferson, in the cries of their guitars."[11]

Eventually the blues became not just a refuge but also an antidote to silence—a way to give expression to painful memories and "unburden [his] soul" just as his enslaved ancestors and his relatives had while toiling in the cotton fields of the Mississippi Delta.[12] The solitary child who stuttered and who "scream[ed] without sound" let his soul speak through the sound of his voice and guitar, giving generations of listeners an outlet for expressing and working through their own troubles.[13] King learned to capture the essence of the blues without words, letting his beloved guitar, Lucille, do much of the singing:

> By bending the strings, by trilling my hand—and I have big fat hands—I could achieve something that approximated a vocal vibrato. I could sustain a note. I wanted to connect my guitar to human emotions. By fooling with the feedback between my amplifier and instrument, I started experimenting with sounds that expressed my feelings, whether happy or sad, bouncy or bluesy. I was looking for ways to let my guitar sing.[14]

After hours upon hours of patient experimentation, King could cry and scream, laugh and swoon, express hope and excitement, and convey the anger and disgust that he had "[kept] away from the light of day" all those years earlier on a sunny summer afternoon in Lexington, Mississippi.[15]

The blues music that King played occupies one corner of the African American cultural tradition, but the blues *sensibility* encompasses far more within that tradition than simply performing or listening to blues music.

Ralph Ellison, in bestowing upon Bessie Smith the title of "priestess" within the Black community, wrote that, among Black people, "the blues were part of a total way of life."[16] The blues sensibility is, as Ellison makes clear, best understood as a posture toward living—one that transcends genre and form, too. For instance, the folklore that produced tricksters who could slip the yoke and the spirituals that provided a path to transcend the pain of this world both spoke dialects of the blues sensibility.[17] Through the blues sensibility, a person could simultaneously articulate hope and sorrow without contradiction. The blues also possessed the agility—a wink and a nod—necessary not just to survive the seemingly impossible, but to land on one's feet with grace while protecting the soul from destruction in an oppressive society. According to James Cone, "The blues tell us how black people affirmed their existence and refused to be destroyed by the oppressive environment; how, despite white definitions to the contrary, they defined their own somebodiness."[18] And although the African American experience is far richer and more varied than a litany of tragedies, this cultural tradition, hewn out of the African American experience, has a remarkable capacity to process the tragedies and traumas of the past four hundred years of US history, including the historical trauma of southern lynching.

Scholars have been reluctant to introduce trauma theory into discussions of the African American experience, in large part because of an understandable anxiety that discussions of African Americans as victims of trauma are prone to insidious distortions that are degrading to Black culture and communities. The likes of the 1965 Moynihan Report and the retrogressive trope of "Black cultural pathology"—of a people and culture damaged by the traumas of enslavement, lynching, convict leasing, and so on—stalk the discourse around African Americans and trauma. But the erasure of the traumatic nature of lynching is indefensible, too, for it does further violence to the victims and survivors of lynching. To talk about trauma does not inevitably lead to a discussion of "Black cultural pathology," especially if we are honest about where in American society the pathology lies. As the journalist Ta-Nehisi Coates observes, "There is no evidence that black people are less responsible, less moral, or less upstanding in their dealings with America nor with themselves. But there is overwhelming evidence that America is irresponsible, immoral, and unconscionable in its dealings with black people and with itself."[19] In fact, Coates notes that the nation's anti-Black brutality and injustice produced resilience, a "warrior spirit," and the blues.

Talking about trauma also carries risks of being reductive, of making African American history entirely a story of struggle and oppression while ignoring Black joy and pleasure. However, an honest and, quite frankly, long overdue acknowledgment of lynching victims as victims (and lynching survivors as survivors) in the United States writ large can still leave room for laughter and love, hope and ingenuity, refusal and resistance in Black life.[20] The interior lives of African Americans *were* touched by the trauma of lynching—the weight of those memories was a daily reminder of loss for most survivors and a crushing burden for others. To deny the traumatic effects of lynching is to endow African Americans with a nearly superhuman capacity to endure pain that strips from them the ability to hurt and suffer and to be vulnerable. For more important than recognizing the trauma of lynching *as trauma* is the task of recovering how the blues sensibility provided Black people with a way to survive and with the beauty and ingenuity to live, love, and create through and beyond trauma.[21]

To theorize lynching as a historical trauma requires more than a simple application of the existing scholarship on trauma theory to the particular historical case of lynching in the United States. Much of that literature comes out of Holocaust studies and uses Freud as a model for understanding how individual survivors and societies "work through" traumas. According to Freud, survivors needed to narrate or represent their traumatic memories in order to make sense of an often fragmented, painful, and seemingly incomprehensible event. In this same vein, Dominick LaCapra, who has written extensively on trauma theory, has argued that "writing trauma" involves "processes of acting out, working over, and to some extent working through in analyzing and 'giving voice' to the past—processes of coming to terms with traumatic 'experiences.' "[22] Narration, however, was but one component of the process of "working through." The psychoanalyst Dori Laub, whose work with Yale University's Genocide Studies Program includes recording and preserving Holocaust survivor testimonies, has pointed out that, in addition to "giving voice" to traumatic memories, survivors need others to bear witness to those memories. A Holocaust survivor himself, Laub argues that survivors struggle to act upon their compulsion to tell their stories, and that "[memories] become more and more distorted in their silent retention and pervasively invade and contaminate the survivor's daily life ... so much so that the survivor doubts the reality of the actual events." Witnesses help make those memories "real" again, so public witnessing of testimony allows survivors to "reclaim" and "repossess" their experiences.[23] To work through trauma, Laub contends, requires willing and sympathetic witnesses.

Although some aspects of the Holocaust map onto the historical trauma of lynching, the white response to lynching in the United States has been a far cry from the vigorous responses of the post–World War II West German state and civic organizations to prosecute perpetrators, pay reparations to survivors, record survivor testimony, and memorialize victims. West German citizens tended not to pass on stories about their role in the Holocaust to the postwar generation, especially among family members, but because of the visibility of the Holocaust in the public sphere—in museums, films, memorials, art, school curricula, political discourse, and so on—even postwar generations were relatively fluent in the discourse of Holocaust memory and claims for justice.[24] In the US South, both during and after the peak period of lynching, the social consensus among whites tended toward silencing and suppressing a public discussion of lynching or, among the more unrepentant, glorifying and celebrating lynching. The South was (and, in many spaces, still is) teeming with unwilling and unsympathetic white witnesses. Decades after the peak period of lynching, the threat of economic and physical reprisals remained real for African American southerners who dared to openly "give voice" to the trauma of lynching, to borrow LaCapra's language, so instead, they often repressed those memories or revealed them only to their closest confidants or resorted to more indirect forms of expression.

The US context demands a homegrown metaphor for "working through" trauma—one that resonates with the cultural sensibilities of a people who lived through centuries of enslavement and Jim Crow, and one that reflects the particular historical context and social realities of the United States—a metaphor with the capacity to both express and conceal, like the blues, both the music and the sensibility. Unlike the comparatively transparent narrative of a memoir or museum exhibit or published interview, the blues provide a veiled, if not intentionally opaque, narrative. They refuse simplistic closure and resolution, and resist catharsis; they carry within them a history of ingenuity and struggle; and they articulate a message both through and beyond language. When King described the blues as "bleeding the same blood as me," he recognized that the meaning of blues music, in part, transcended the lyrics and contained in its blue notes and sighs and rhythms a mystery that touched and seamlessly blended with his own pain.[25]

King's blues songs, too, encapsulated that same emotional depth and complexity. When he hummed the first bars of "Nobody Loves Me But My Mother," his long moans ached with loneliness and despair, most especially when he sang or played blue notes—when he slid past an expected pitch to build tension and skimmed the very edges of pain. But the slightly lilting rhythm of the piano accompanying his moans lent a playfulness to the song, hinting at the lighthearted chuckle that followed his moaned lament. The lyrics, though spare, explained the source of his blues and yet also made light of those blues—nobody loves him but his mother (and, wait for it, the punchline) "and she could be jiving too." As he sang the lyrics, he sang the pitches straight—no sliding or fiddling with the melody—which made the initial humming tinged with blue notes all the more striking. The intensity of feeling conveyed without lyrics made for a kind of narrative that has a narrator but no language except that of a moan. Unlike "screaming without sound," as King had done when he witnessed the dead Black man's body hanging in the Lexington town square, his blue notes captured and expressed his pain without language. Words weren't necessary. Language merely filled in the details of his blues.[26]

The lilting piano accompaniment, the blue notes, and the moans in King's song did more than lend an emotional complexity to his music. When he and other blues musicians stretched time signatures and pitches, they massaged the rigid boundaries of formal Western music theory and opened up new spaces (and styles of expression) within the sound. Ralph Ellison described a similar bending of sonic conventions in the prologue to *Invisible Man*. The protagonist, stoned and listening to Louis Armstrong sing "Black and Blue," says: "The unheard sounds came through, and each melodic line existed of itself, stood out clearly from all the rest, said its piece, and waited patiently for the other voices to speak. That night I found myself hearing not only in time, but in space as well. I not only entered the music but descended, like Dante, into its depths."[27] The protagonist, who at that point is no longer living within but rather beyond the reach of American society, then descends into a bewildering flashback and hallucination that reveal glimpses of his journey to his underground room.[28] This descent into his subconscious and the unresolved corners of his psyche is full of promise as he prepares for the liberatory act of confronting his past and then reconfiguring his present.

What the protagonist calls "the slightly different sense of time" that he experiences in his invisible state might, with practice, be controlled in order to step out of time, away from the gaze and temporal limits of the white world. Indeed, he already seems to have become aware of the potential for this other sense of time. He explains that, with invisibility, "instead of the swift and imperceptible flowing of time, you are aware of its nodes, those points where time stands still or from which it leaps ahead. And you slip into the breaks and look around."[29] In those breaks and leaps in time, what he calls "the unheard sounds"—shards of forgotten or silenced memories, memories unutterable to oneself and to the white world—surface. The blues that both King and Armstrong sang opened up cracks in time and pitch, and collapsed past and present, conscious and subconscious, but rather than tumbling into the more terrifying corners of their minds against their will, their descents allowed them to bring a sliver of their pain to light, to give voice to an echo of their trauma.[30]

Perhaps with the prologue of *Invisible Man* in mind, Jeffrey B. Ferguson uses language similar to Ellison's "slip[ping] into the breaks" to describe the inner workings of the blues: "Rather than rely on God, or any outside source of comfort or deliverance, the self-reliant blues singer attempted to make suffering *livable* in part by entering into its folds and crevices."[31] In the wake of something as traumatic as lynching, playing or listening to blues music could not improve material conditions or transform a society steeped in oppression, but as a musical form and sensibility, the blues could make the afterlife of lynching *livable*, such that "making suffering livable" would mean more than mere survival. Or, as Ferguson puts it, the blues seek to "[exploit the] opportunities that a fractured world offers to experience moments of joy and freedom."[32] Entrance into breaks or folds or crevices or fractures could open up both a momentary escape from a hostile world and an introspective descent deep inside an individual, for the blues singer, to quote Ferguson again, commanded "the highest and most native powers of the naked soul facing the alternately exhilarating and disappointing events of this life solely through the creative use of its own resources, without otherworldly support. . . . In some ways a rhythmic confessional, productive of a truth at times both terrible and exhilarating, the blues sought an enchantment of this life in all of its contradictions as it transformed prayerful and ecstatic religious moods into a secular but bracing and transportative alternative to religious doctrine and attitude."[33]

The pursuit of "enchantment in this life" and the "transportative" potential of the blues reframes the simplistic binary into which most narratives of African American life fall: either unimaginable suffering or heroic resistance. This binary and the resultant overemphasis on resistance gives outsized attention to external sources of oppression and obscures the richness of Black interiority—aspects of Black life like love, vulnerability, tenderness, laughter, and collective survival.[34] Elsewhere, Ferguson offers a generative alternative to resistance, namely, *escape*. If the blues sensibility is transportative, then escape suggests where it might take you. Defined by Ferguson as "making the oppressor disappear," escape opens up new possibilities for naming what is actually a common way of being for Black people—"not so much free as unfettered, not so much resistant as inaccessible to power." Escape provides a way to think about what "making suffering livable" might have looked like for Black southerners in the oppressive context of Jim Crow and beyond, for escape—whether going underground or migrating out of the South or reveling in the joy and beauty of a Black world or slipping into the breaks with the blues—"derived its power from its assertion of a hidden black potential that could coincide with the worst oppression and yet, at the same time, live outside of it."[35] Just as the blues sensibility borrows elements of more overtly resistant forms of expression, escape bears some similarities to revolutionary acts of resistance but offers greater safety, especially in environments in which open acts of rebellion are lethal. As a refuge from anti-Blackness, escape recenters Blackness, making life livable and enabling Black people to *be* on their own terms.

Escape also clarifies how to productively modify Laub's conception of witnessing to better fit the US context.[36] Laub identifies three levels of witnessing: "being a witness to oneself within the experience," "being a witness to the testimonies of others," and "being a witness to the process of witnessing itself." He argues that, for survivors, "survival takes place through the creative act of establishing and maintaining an internal witness, who substitutes for the lack of witnessing in real life," and that the latter two levels provide trauma survivors a community to help them process the aftermath of a traumatic event by assuring them that they are not alone. The blues sensibility provides lynching survivors a means to bear witness to their own traumas, not as a temporary and inadequate bandage in the absence of other witnesses, but as a self-propelled will to confront and subdue pain, and find amid that pain some kernel of hope to keep on living. And yet, although blues music is a highly personalized form of expression (and the blues sensibility provides a means to confront the self), both the music and the sensibility provide collective release, not only through what Laub understands as the second and third levels of witnessing, but also through a shared experience of pain since, as acts of terror, lynchings typically targeted Black people as a collective. Whereas Laub imagines that the second and third levels of witnessing extend to the broader public of Jews and non-Jews, the community of witnesses to Black southern lynching survivors was usually confined to the Black world or even smaller pockets within the Black world—a world made possible, quite often, through Ferguson's sense of the word "escape."[37] So when Eva Hall confined conversations about the Mary Turner lynching to her closest friends and a handful of trusted (adult) family members, a kind of selective witnessing limited to a sliver of the Black world could happen safely. When Jacob Lawrence expressed with a brushstroke the pain of mourning the death of a lynching victim, his art bound together myriad experiences of mourning and, through its display in museums and galleries, provided the conditions for something approximating collective grief and collective relief among Black viewers.

In an essay titled "Richard Wright's Blues," Ellison described the blues as "an impulse to keep the painful details and episodes of a brutal experience alive in one's aching consciousness, to finger its jagged grain, and to transcend it, not by the consolation of philosophy but by squeezing from it a near-tragic, near-comic lyricism."[38] The blues sensibility, according to Ellison, leaves open the possibility of personal transcendence over adversity, by "squeezing" from that pain something beautiful to ease a troubled mind.[39] What Ellison called "transcendence" the blues musician Mississippi Fred McDowell expressed in more ambivalent terms as keeping the blues "off my mind." In a track from his record *I Do Not Play No Rock 'n' Roll*, McDowell explained how the blues worked. As he lightly glided a bottleneck over guitar strings, he mused, "the more you play, the bluer you get, until you get to it.... When I got satisfied I put [the guitar] down.... You see, [the blues] was off my mind. But it's a worrisome thing, man."[40] Like Ellison, McDowell recognized that returning to a painful memory, though unpleasant, was necessary for "getting satisfied," but playing the blues did not provide a neat resolution for McDowell. The blues were *off* his mind but not *out of* his mind. Another writer, Ellison's good friend Albert Murray, agreed with McDowell that the blues as such were much more difficult to shake:

[The blues] do not appear and disappear. They are there because they have already come, and they linger somewhat as if clinging with tentacles, and they go, mostly when driven. But never soon enough. Nor do they ever seem to go far enough away even so. Once they have been there they only shift from the foreground to the background, and maybe you forget about them for the time being, but only for the time being.[41]

The blues sensibility may begin with the assumption that "life is a low-down dirty shame," but it holds out hope that, with a touch of irony and cleverness, people can keep the blues as such at bay just long enough to allow them to breathe and make it through the chaos of life.

"Working through," to the extent that it was possible according to the blues sensibility, meant revisiting painful memories until the feeling of despair dissipated enough that a person felt "satisfied," but those memories and that pain never fully vanished from consciousness. "Satisfaction" lacked the permanence and finality of transcendence. But the blues sensibility should not be misunderstood as passive or pessimistic, resigned to inaction. With lyrics like "I was sitting by my window when I saw my man walk by / he was with another woman and I felt like I wanted to cry," blues music might seem easy to reduce to sad songs that wallow in self-pity and passivity, but blues musicians considered their music to be a form of confrontation, albeit an indirect confrontation at times.[42] Big Mama Thornton, who sang those lyrics about a cheating lover, paired that devastation with an upbeat dance rhythm, so, in essence, the mind could speak of the blues without succumbing to them, since the body was simultaneously trying to shake them off.

Similarly, the blues piano player Memphis Slim said that the blues were "kind of a revenge." As an African American man living in the South, he often felt restricted in what he could say or do to white people when he was frustrated, angry, or insulted, so when he couldn't say something, he would sing it, as he put it, "you know signifying like."[43] His friend, the bluesman Big Bill Broonzy, told a story about a man who, rather than confront his boss directly, took out his frustration on a mule in song:

> I've known guys that wanted to cuss out the boss and he was afraid to go up to his face and tell him what he wanted to tell him, and I've heard them sing those things—sing words, you know—back to the boss, just behind the wagon, hooking up the horses or something or another—or the mules or something.

And then he'd go to work and go to singin' and say things to the horse, you know, horse—make like the mule stepped on his foot—say, "Get off my foot goddam it!" or something like that, you know, and he meant he was talkin' to the boss. "You son of a bitch, you." Say, "You got no business on my ... stay off my foot!" and such things as that—that's the point.[44]

The stories African American southerners told about courthouses haunted by lynching victims and lynchers haunted by the ghosts of their victims not only became a part of local lore, thus allowing them to reclaim control over lynching narratives from local whites, but also exacted a similar sort of indirect revenge. The audiences—witnesses, if you will—to these stories were almost exclusively Black people as a matter of security and privacy, since the threat of retaliation lingered for decades, even after the end of legal segregation, just as the legacies of lynching lingered. These narratives, told through the ventriloquy of speaking through vengeful ghosts, used the slight misdirection of the ghosts to demonstrate that Black people who retold these stories placed their faith not in the US legal system or white southerners, both of which had consistently been shown to be morally compromised, if not morally bankrupt, but in a sense of justice that existed among a society of moral peers. White southerners who had long silenced their complicity—if not their outright participation in lynchings—or had threatened African Americans who reminded them of these crimes, did not seem ready to be witnesses in the way Laub imagined in the context of Holocaust testimony. The blues sensibility provided protection and a means to act—that action being the creation of narratives—and a modicum of revenge, animated not by malice so much as by the patience needed to protect oneself from a people prone to lashing out, a people who were not ready to face their history or themselves.[45]

Like the man berating his mule rather than his boss, Big Bill Broonzy also aired his grievances, whether against cheating women or Jim Crow, not by berating mules but through his music. In "Black, Brown, and White,"[46] he sang about his personal experiences with racial discrimination: a bar refusing to serve him, the employment office never calling his number, being paid fifty cents for the same work another man got paid a dollar for, building the foundations of a country that denied him opportunities, and fighting wars for a nation that told him to "get back." Broonzy's direct critiques of Jim Crow and the hypocrisy of racial

discrimination against Black veterans fighting for "freedom" were somewhat unusual for their transparency and overtly political message.[47] Most
blues songs cloaked these complaints and laments in metaphor or humor,
like another Broonzy song, "Diggin' My Potatoes," that took up a less
controversial subject.[48] In the most literal interpretation of the lyrics, this
is a song about stolen vegetables, a trampled garden patch, and the farmer's plan to catch the thieves, but Broonzy is actually talking about infi-
delity. Although a "bed" can be a patch of land for planting potatoes and
cabbages, Broonzy playfully uses double entendre to indicate that what
has been stolen isn't produce from the garden but his lover from his bed
and what has been trampled isn't a vine but his manhood. The intentionally slippery nature of signifyin(g) and the irony of Broonzy's blues made
light of betrayal through double entendre and humor, and softened the
blow of heartbreak.

The blues could convey love and joy, condemnation and anger, but
most blues musicians took a far too ironic posture and were generally
too skeptical and cautious to risk exposure to the potentially devastating
consequences of full transparency. Blues musicians often combined
seemingly contradictory elements—Thornton's lyrics about betrayal and
an exuberant dance beat, or King's song about loneliness that he punctu-
ates with a joke—and, in part, this was in order to save for oneself the
trapdoor of plausible deniability in case the painful memories cut too
close to one's heart or the boss man came within earshot of one's song.
In the Jim Crow South, protection was a matter of common sense and
survival—of wearing a congenial mask, as King had in front of whites in
the Lexington town square, or of cloaking the object of scorn, as
Broonzy's friend had.

These elements of blues music—the ironic blending of joy and sorrow, the subversive bending of blue notes, the calculated manipulation of
time, the depth of expression captured without words, the relief from the
blues as such, the undermining of the powerful, the potential for sweet
revenge, the playfully deceptive double meaning of the lyrics—surfaced
in the lynching memories of victims and survivors. The blues sensibility
also shaped the emplotment and articulation of those memories, whether
as family lore or paintings or memorials. Even when families withheld or
selectively passed on these memories, we see the protective cover that
the blues sensibility provided to the most vulnerable and to those whose
lives were shattered by lynching. We see their ethic of care and their tenderness and their grace. We see how, in the face of unspeakable horrors

and unwilling witnesses, the blues sensibility provided a pathway to make it through the afterlife of lynching.

Albert Murray, Amiri Baraka, James Cone, and others have anointed the blues as the emblematic form of ironic Black expression, and though some might question the continued relevance of the blues sensibility as more direct avenues to challenging white supremacy have emerged during and after the civil rights era, it endures. In part, the durability of the blues sensibility reflects the ways that it extends beyond—both before and after—the period when the musical genre was most popular. Forged, in part, out of what Imani Perry describes as a social necessity for enslaved people to "ma[k]e selves inside, under the flesh, that could hold the anchor even as the storms knocked them down," the foundational elements of the blues sensibility—the cloaking, the hopefulness in the face of despair, the hoped-for release, the bulwark of a robust inner life—emerged long before blues music itself.[49] Spirituals written and sung by enslaved people, as well as trickster tales, humor, and the everyday masking of one's true self, all took a page from the blues sensibility, even as the conditions of Black life changed.[50] This sensibility is as enduring as the troubles it dispels, for it centers the inner lives of Black people and Black communities, which remain vital for making it through a world steeped in anti-Blackness.

W. E. B. Du Bois believed the spirituals, which he called "the Sorrow Songs," were the most beautiful cultural expression of human experience the United States had to offer the world. He celebrated these "weird old songs in which the soul of the black slave spoke to men" because they told "of death and suffering and unvoiced longing towards a truer world, of misty wanderings and hidden ways."[51] Written by enslaved African Americans who endured dreadful suffering in their everyday lives, the spirituals carried a message of hope that a more just world might come to pass—or that they might pass into a more just world after death. Du Bois captured the force and beauty of the spirituals, rightly underscoring their concern with justice: "Through all the sorrow of the Sorrow Songs there breathes a hope—a faith in the ultimate justice of things. The minor cadences of despair change often to triumph and calm confidence. Sometimes it is faith in life, sometimes a faith in death, sometimes assurance of boundless justice in some fair world beyond."[52]

The blues, which Cone called "a secular spiritual," emerged out of an African American cultural tradition that frequently combined tragedy with humor or hope. "They [the enslaved]," wrote Howard Thurman, "made a worthless life, the life of chattel property, a mere thing, a body, *worth living!*" and they expressed that defiance, hope, and affirmation of life alongside sadness and suffering in the spirituals, as their children and grandchildren would do with the blues.[53] After lamenting how "white Americans seem to feel that happy songs are *happy* and sad songs are *sad*," James Baldwin explained the complexity and nuance of blues expression:

> I think it was Big Bill Broonzy who used to sing "I Feel So Good," a really joyful song about a man who is on his way to the railroad station to meet his girl. She's coming home. It is the singer's incredibly moving exuberance that makes one realize how leaden the time must have been while she was gone. There is no guarantee that she will stay this time, either, as the singer clearly knows, and, in fact, she has not yet actually arrived. To-night, or tomorrow, or within the next five minutes, he may very well be singing "Lonesome in My Bedroom," or insisting, "Ain't we, ain't we, going to make it all right? Well, if we don't today, we will tomorrow night."[54]

Even in a song bursting with joy like "I Feel So Good," the memory of "leaden" times quietly intruded, and even the melancholy "Lonesome in My Bedroom" left room to hope for something better tomorrow night.

Hope and faith for eventual justice in the afterlife were usually insufficient when enslaved people stared down brazen injustice every day, so spirituals, like the blues, used coded language to give voice to their desire for freedom, helping enslaved people survive the psychological and physical brutality of enslavement. The spiritual "Steal Away," for instance, cleverly disguised a more incendiary message with words that white enslavers might assume to be a pious affirmation of Christian faith:

> Steal away, steal away, steal away to Jesus
> Steal away, steal away home
> I ain't got long to stay here.

Within a more literal religious framework, the lyrics suggested that the singer find solace in dying and going to heaven to be with Jesus, but those same lyrics could also announce the singer's intention to run away to the Promised Land of the North. Big Bill Broonzy's double meaning for the word "bed" had roots in a sacred and secular tradition that played on ambiguity to conceal subversive messages. Whereas Broonzy used signifying as a salve for the pain of heartbreak, his ancestors had used coded language to avoid being caught running away to freedom.

Like the spirituals and work songs that preceded them, the blues were also concerned with getting through hard times, and they always left room for hope, whether hope for freedom, hope for the workday to end, or hope for a good man to come knocking on your door. Take, for instance, the cautiously optimistic chorus to the blues standard, "Trouble in Mind":

> Trouble in mind, I'm blue
> But I won't be blue always
> 'Cause the sun is going to shine in my backdoor someday.

These three lines encapsulated what Ellison meant when he described the attraction of the blues as "at once express[ing] both the agony of life and the possibility of conquering it through sheer toughness of spirit."[55] The verses, "the agony," sandwiched between the hoped-for sunshine of the chorus, "the possibility," tempered the optimism of the song, though even tragic verses occasionally had a sense of humor. In a version of "Trouble in Mind" that Sister Rosetta Tharpe sang, which begins with the Broonzy verse above, the desperation and rawness came through:

> Trouble in mind, I'm blue,
> I almost lost my mind,
> So when you see me laughing and laughing, laughing just to keep
>   from crying.
>
> I'm gonna lay, lay my head
> On some lonesome railroad line [spoken: Must I do it?]
> Let the 2:19 train pacify my mind.[56]

The only thing holding her back from letting a train "pacify" her mind was the possibility of better days ahead, but looking forward didn't magically erase the pain of the past or the present. Being "satisfied" meant living with these troubles, or perhaps living despite these troubles.

The blues are not mired in despair or self-pity, nor are they resigned to defeat, but there is a danger in conflating what Ellison calls "the possibility of conquering [the agony of life]" with blind optimism. Hope divorced from reality and history can be dangerous, especially for people who have historically been vulnerable to becoming the victims of violence. Instead, the hope expressed in the blues sensibility is cautious, tempered by a long history of struggle. That same sensibility reverberated through the final pages of Baldwin's *The Fire Next Time:*

> I know that what I am asking is impossible. But in our time, as in every time, the impossible is the least that one can demand—and one is, after all, emboldened by the spectacle of human history in general, and American Negro history in particular, for it testifies to nothing less than the perpetual achievement of the impossible.[57]

Baldwin, writing in the midst of the civil rights movement, asked the nation to live up to its own creed, which it had consistently failed to do since its inception, and yet, despite these failures, he drew inspiration from the "perpetual achievement of the impossible" by African Americans to imagine a more just society. What Baldwin described as "an ironic tenacity" at the core of the blues tradition and the African American experience spoke to the creative agility of Black people, the emotional complexity and nuance of the blues sensibility, and the capacity to imagine liberation in the face of impossible odds.[58]

However, much has been made of the limitations of the blues as a meaningful cultural touchstone in the postsoul age. Back in 1988, Nelson George announced that rhythm and blues was dead, the victim of commercial interests that, in placing value on crossing over to mainstream white audiences, had diluted the political weight of the music for the Black community.[59] The blues presumably had crossed the River Jordan long before 1988. After all, the blues needed resurrecting—or perhaps just a little resuscitating—during the folk revival of the 1960s. The hip-hop generation has moved on too, apparently, and, according to some, for these young bloods the blues are an anachronism, merely a fading memory of their Jim Crowed grandparents who, like King, had to hold "a swarm of words inside" or face near-certain death.[60] In the haze of what Komunyakaa called "blue dementia," the grandparents of the hip-hop generation might still battle with the ghosts of Jim Crow—what daily indignities stole from them, what they lost in their attempts to keep themselves whole—but, to some, their strategies for coping and defiance have seemingly lost their relevance.

Imposing such a clean break from past generations, however, is as artificial as it is unrealistic, especially when the trauma and violence of lynching are ongoing and passed on.[61] Just as blues music is at the root of virtually all American popular music, including hip-hop, the sensibility of the blues is foundational to African American culture, perhaps most noticeably in African American humor and storytelling. Even though boasting, playing the dozens, swapping lies, and telling jokes have been remixed countless times over the centuries, one constant in African American humor is its utility as a tool for levying critiques of US society and simultaneously disarming a potentially hostile audience with laughter.[62] Just as Big Mama Thornton combined heartbreak with a spirited dance beat in her music to help shake out the blues troubling her listeners, African American humor was rarely mere lighthearted silliness. When the comedian Dick Gregory said, "If I've said anything to upset you, maybe it's what I'm here for," he understood his humor to be an art form that elicited both laughter and unsettling realizations about the world he inhabited.[63] Far from diminishing the sheer pleasure of sitting around and swapping lies (and, ideally, belly-laughing until it hurt), the hard truths at the heart of these stories (and Gregory's jokes, for that matter) only deepened an appreciation for the skill required to lie with finesse and made this collective release from everyday white foolishness all the more satisfying.

Much of humor, like much of the blues, relies on the veil of plausible deniability that the literal provides to obscure the figurative. The need to cloak one's true meaning may admittedly be less a matter of life and death for the hip-hop generation than it was for earlier generations, but the swarm of words and the need to expel the tumult of feelings has continued unabated, not only because the United States has yet to wake up from its racial nightmare but because so many Americans still refuse to recognize white supremacist violence as a daily feature of Black life. Like their great-grandparents before them, the parents of Black children, out of necessity, still try to train them to read minds—to anticipate the responses of white people who can't "police their imagination," as Claudia Rankine put it, to reassure white people that they are not a threat.[64] The constant stream of anti-Black violence, the character assassination of Black victims of police violence, the demonization of the Black poor, white gaslighting and white denial—all of that demonstrates that Black people must still convince the white world that their pain is real. The indignities and the violence persist, as does the swarm trapped within, which is why the hip-hop generation can still sing its own version of the blues.[65]

Now, as in the days of King's childhood and the long travail of enslavement, the hip-hop generation still needs to find ways to expel and disperse the swarm of words they hold inside and to anchor the selves they maintain inside. For, as Ferguson reminds us, "the blues, conceived of as a method for making a troubled life livable by entering into its terms, no longer addresses the predominant way most black Americans think of their needs, though a simple glance below the poverty line or into the racially skewed population of a prison block might suggest to an outside observer the continuing relevance of a blues sensibility."[66] Direct opposition to white supremacy may still be inaccessible or too dangerous for some, and leaning upon the blues sensibility—that is, "making a troubled life livable by entering into its terms"—is not an act of surrender, but an affirmation of life while living with your head in the lion's mouth.[67]

To understand how the blues as a metaphor make trauma and justice legible in the African American experience requires a return to both the blues as such—the heavy, near-despair produced by life's troubles, large and small—and the blues sensibility as a posture toward life. Traumatic events have stalked African Americans for centuries, and out of this collective experience Black people have forged what Thurman called "tools of the spirit ... to cut a path through the wilderness of their despair."[68] These tools include the blues sensibility. Perry calls these tools a precious inheritance that guides Black people as they "learn not only to grieve but also to chat with death," "turn over this reality [of loss] in your hands, mix it into the clay of your living," and "learn to live with the ache."[69] Perry warns of the destructive potential of trauma, grief, and the daily onslaught of racism that, like a chronic disease, lingers and nags and flares up. Harboring the swarm for too long can lead to lashing out with violence, bearing the toll of unprocessed grief in one's body, burying pain with drugs and other escapes, and succumbing to soul-crushing despair. Only by coming to terms with the blues as such can people get to the more important stuff of living.

On the level of individual trauma and community trauma, the blues sensibility has offered Black people "tools of the spirit" for processing traumatic events: the lynching of a relative, the terror that lasted for generations in a community, the structural inequalities entrenched by lynching and white supremacy more generally. The very narrative structure and mood of the African American lynching memories recovered in this book have been steeped in the blues sensibility. In one way or another, they say to the powerful, to those set on the destruction of Black people, "you may try to destroy me, but I will create beauty out of this horror you perpetrate."[70] African Americans sought out the protective cover of the blues sensibility when, like Jesse Pennington, they repressed memories of lynchings or harrowing escapes from lynch mobs to keep their souls intact, or when, like the Head family, they shielded their children from the most disturbing details of local lynchings. The masked double meanings and adept evasions of the blues found expression in the supernatural stories that families passed down, whether about the ghost of a lynching victim haunting an Alabama courthouse or sores that spread on the arms of a known lyncher. When memories of lynching and murder became too much for Minnie Weston to bear, she knew how to keep the pain at bay, echoing the blues hollerers who shouted away their troubles. The assertion of dignity in the face of practiced humiliations in the blues could be detected in Judge Head's refusal to give up his dream of farming his own land after his brother's horrific death by lynching. And blue notes enveloped artistic renderings of Black mourning with affirmations of the preciousness of Black life.

Lynching as a form of terrorism targeted entire Black communities and touched Black people across the nation, and, though traumatic events don't necessarily inflict the greatest or the longest lasting harm upon those nearest to lynching victims, the pain was often sharpest and most devastating for those who knew and loved them.[71] Survivors and witnesses further removed from the victim—neighbors, grandchildren born decades after a lynching, people from neighboring towns passing through and seeing a lynched body, strangers hundreds of miles away reading about lynching in the news—also could experience intense traumatic reactions to lynching, though, in general, they could more readily find the words to bring their memories to the surface. Mary and Hayes Turner's great-grandchildren rarely heard their grandmother (and the Turners' only daughter) speak of their lynchings, much less the pain she endured living in the wake of their deaths, but they could see their grandmother's suffering when they asked about her parents. They saw her become withdrawn and silent. They saw their grandfather swoop in to shield her from their questions. Her pain was too much to disclose, especially to such young children, curious but unprepared for the burden she carried. Though only these faint outlines of her trauma reach us in the present, her grandchildren's memories reveal the family's protective love and the strategies she cultivated for stowing away these traumatic memories, most of the time anyway, where they were undetectable to her grandchildren.[72] Would she have said her strategies for living with and through the trauma of her parents' lynchings drew from the blues sensibility? Probably not, but she seemed fluent in the language of the blues, in making the afterlife of lynching livable.

At the heart of the blues sensibility was an ethic of care that soothed traumatic injuries and protected the self, the family, and the community. Monroe Saffold Jr. was born in Lexington, Mississippi, in 1948 but grew up in Chicago, and he used to beg his grandfather, Jeffrey Saffold, to take him along on his annual trips down south. His grandfather always hedged and found some excuse to leave him behind, and he later learned that "it was for my protection because I was from the north. . . . He was saving me." Jeffrey Saffold knew all too well what Mississippi could do to Black boys. When he was a young man in 1926, his brother's friend was killed by a city marshal. His brother wanted to avenge his friend's death, and he spent all evening and all night talking his brother out of looking for the killer. It was all he could do to save his brother from being lynched, too. During one of those trips home, a couple he was friends with died when their house was burned to the ground by white people. Around this time, two white men lynched Emmett Till, a Black boy from Chicago with Mississippi Delta roots, just like his grandson. The murders and lynchings were too much for Jeffrey Saffold, so, as his grandson told it, "my grandfather said, 'when I die, I don't want to be taken back to Mississippi.' " The Saffolds passed on these and other stories—stories of coming across trees in Lexington with the remnants of nooses and of police harassment, arson, and beatings—to explain why they had to get out of Lexington and go north. Of his grandparents and parents, the younger Saffold said: "They forged a life amid the atrocities. They knew what to do [to navigate Jim Crow] and how to protect the children."[73] The family's intimacy with fear and loss and their brushes with lynching haunted Jeffrey Saffold until he died, but, amid the traumatic reverberations emanating out of Mississippi, he and his family passed on these lynching narratives—only when the time was right—to protect one another from the worst of white supremacy, to keep his grandson alive.

These and other lynching narratives perform the work of the blues in particular families and communities touched by local lynchings, but on the level of the nation as a whole, the existence of these blues-inflected narratives speaks to the need for a collective reckoning with lynching and its legacies. But, like any real reckoning with racial violence in the United States, these efforts must bridge the personal and the collective with the structural. Just as racism encompasses far more than individual prejudice and indeed flourishes because systemic forces of oppression produce and reinforce injustice, the legacies of lynching are vaster than the individual pain of victims and survivors, as immense as that pain is. As the blues sensibility makes clear, the imperative to remember and revisit must be paired with an equal move to confront the sources of suffering through actions that lead to justice for Black people. Without justice, memorials become sites of despair, not healing. Without justice, public apologies remain hollow words and self-congratulatory pats on the back, not policy. Without justice, museums and historical studies risk unearthing stories that are frustratingly irrelevant to the vast majority of Americans, rather than issue warnings that the not-too-distant past may be rhyming grotesquely with the racial violence of the present.

The meaning of justice in this context, however, is difficult to define, as is the meaning of healing. Not only has racial justice eluded the United States for the entirety of its history, but justice becomes murkier for lynchings in which the direct perpetrators and survivors are long dead. Even if we could travel back in time, the notion of justice outside the retributive "justice" of legal punishment is difficult to achieve. One descendant of Will Head, a Black man lynched in 1918 in southern Georgia, said regarding racial reconciliation after a lynching:

> There is no immediate reconciliation—there is none. If there is any long-term reconciliation—[pause] Some things you can't reconcile, you know what I mean. Let's be realistic, you know. That's just like killing a man and bringing him back, you know what I'm saying. [If] you killed him, you can't bring him back, you know what I mean. You can go put flowers on his grave or talk about him after his death, but you can't bring him back. . . . So there's no reconciliation for some things. You just have to live beyond it, you know, and hope it doesn't raise its ugly head again.[74]

For Will Head's great-grandnephew, Willie Head Jr., the finality of death —and the enormity of the loss that brings on the blues as such—made restitution incalculable, indeed impossible. What he called "immediate reconciliation," or reconciliation between the survivors and perpetrators of lynching in the immediate aftermath of the killing, simply was not possible. In a sense, Head echoed Mississippi Fred McDowell's sense of keeping the blues "off my mind" to survive when he spoke of "liv[ing] beyond" the pain and "hop[ing] it doesn't raise its ugly head again," but in his case the fierce hostility of some of his white neighbors toward his continued ownership of land and his very presence in their town has soured even contemporary prospects of reconciliation. Reconciliation itself places a deeply unfair burden upon victims and survivors of lynching, especially in a nation that expects Black forgiveness, even for unspeakable atrocities, and for nothing in return. Lynching is an ongoing trauma, an open wound that renews itself daily in our times, a chapter still being written that precludes closure. We remain in its wake.[75]

White refusal to acknowledge local lynchings was discouraging, and yet by expressing the need to "live beyond" the pain of the blues, Head— the great-grandnephew, that is—deployed the strategies of the blues, a return to a painful family secret to dismantle injustice in the present. He went on to say that, even though death is irremediable, "what you do [is] you don't continue to oppress the oncoming generations. You give them the opportunity that you didn't give his father or his mother, you see. You don't incarcerate them. You don't profile them in the street."[76] The distinction Head draws between "immediate reconciliation" and "long-term reconciliation" hinges not only on the temporal (the immediate or the long term) but also on that gap between the personal and the structural. For Head, the personal was virtually irreconcilable, especially for family members who bore the losses caused by lynching so acutely, but to explain where the potential for justice and reconciliation lay, he then cited the continued criminalization of Blackness, racial profiling, and the War on Drugs, all of which have turned Black people into the targets of the carceral apparatus.[77] Pointing to structural inequalities produced by incarceration and other forms of anti-Blackness, he saw the dismantling of this racialized system of control as necessary for achieving long-term reconciliation and real racial justice, because as much as lynching was about terror—and it most certainly was—it was ultimately about protecting white power.

That Head identified structural racism as an ongoing legacy of lynching should come as no surprise given his experiences farming the land in southern Georgia his grandfather worked so hard to purchase just a few years following the lynching of Will Head. The family's resilience was all the more remarkable in light of ongoing white supremacist terror, segregation, exclusion from all-white farm cooperatives, and discrimination in applying for Department of Agriculture loans, all of which made clear how the courts, the state, economic institutions, and their white neighbors threatened the family's financial and physical security for generations. In the 1990s, he joined hundreds of other Black farmers in a class-action lawsuit against the Department of Agriculture, and, in *Pigford v. Glickman* (1999), the courts awarded more than $1 billion in damages for decades of blatant and systematic discrimination against Black farmers in the granting of loans and relief. Receiving damages from a faceless government agency decades after many Black farmers had already lost their farms may seem to be a far cry from justice or closure, but that the *government* paid restitution for racial discrimination marked a recognition—though partial and much delayed—of both the systemic nature of white supremacy and the collective responsibility for racial oppression.[78] In essence, Head pointed to the persistence of structural racism to explicitly expand the scope of complicity for lynching and other forms of racial oppression beyond the direct perpetrators to include its beneficiaries, namely, white Americans then and now.[79]

Few of Head's white neighbors, however, have expressed interest in reconciliation, and some have shown outright hostility toward renewed calls to reckon with the dozens of lynchings that took place in the area.[80] They have preferred to forget and avoid the past. Even if local whites—or the nation, for that matter—apologized for lynching, the true measure of any apology's sincerity is whether it came with the action Head called for: a recognition of national complicity in anti-Black racism, the dismantling of those systems and social perceptions that criminalize Black people and "justify" inflicting violence upon Black bodies, ending of practices that keep African Americans at an economic disadvantage, removal of voting restrictions, fostering of a sense of social responsibility built on compassion, and the like. In a sense, Head expressed the very essence of the blues sensibility. He warned against collective amnesia as avoidance and dismissed easy bromides for intergenerational trauma as unrealistic and pat. Instead, he called not only for returning to the collective trauma of lynching, but also for creating out of that pain something regenerative and liberatory. Head wasn't asking for a literal blues song, but for a moral reckoning that issued from the blues. Out of these painful memories of lynching, he cautiously hoped, might emerge a revolution in values wrapped in love that would fundamentally restructure the United States into a genuinely just society.[81]

Komunyakaa's poem "Blue Dementia" ends with the narrator encounter-
ing three "dark-skinned men / discussing the weather with demons / &
angels." The narrator pauses on the street to glance at his own reflection
and wonders what might have pushed these men over some invisible
ledge into a "blue dementia"—into a dream world, a place that steals or
wounds some elemental piece of them, a place where they reason with
ghosts. These men remind the narrator of Lucky Thompson and Marion
Brown, the great jazz saxophonists who knew and lived the blues all
those years ago before Alzheimer's took Thompson and a string of ill-
nesses claimed Brown. The narrator knows some of the same ghosts that
these "dark-skinned men" converse with—the night riders, both literal
and figurative, and the heartbreak, too. But Thompson, Brown, these
"dark-skinned men" with "a blue dementia," the narrator, and presumably a great many more African Americans share something else: the expressive gift of the blues, the saxophone reed that "called out of the deep
night: / Another man done gone. / Another man done gone," the bottleneck bending and sliding over the catgut strings of a guitar until the hurt
subsided.[82]

The blues sensibility binds wounds. It binds communities and generations, too. And it binds the dead and the living through the traumatic
afterlife of lynching.

Epilogue

they ask me to remember

but they want me to remember

their memories

and i keep on remembering

mine

—LUCILLE CLIFTON, "why some people be mad at me sometimes"

PEOPLE DON'T USUALLY STUMBLE upon Glendora, Mississippi. They either seek out the tiny all-Black Delta town because it's part of the Mississippi Civil Rights Trail, or they are among the handful of people who actually live there. The town is surrounded by vast fields that every fall are covered in thick, white cotton bolls, but the mechanization of cotton cultivation has taken its toll, shrinking the town down to a few dozen homes and a population that hovers around two hundred. A quiet town, save for the occasional freight train cutting through or the crunching of gravel under car tires, Glendora has an almost peaceful air about it, but just under the surface, embedded somewhere in the soil or the trees or the river bottom, something vaguely sinister stirs. For on a late August night in 1955, two white men tortured and lynched Emmett Till at the cotton gin in town and, after tying a cotton gin fan to his body, threw him in the Tallahatchie River to sink into oblivion.

When I visited Glendora, Tracey Rosebud, a local activist and tour guide at the Emmett Till Historic Intrepid Center (ETHIC), met me in town and offered to give me a tour of the area, which he has known since childhood and his family has known for more than four generations. Rosebud has a disarming and generous spirit, and his tour was steeped in the personal as much as it was rooted in the historical. I drove; he navigated. He told me the story of his town and the story of Till, which was so engrossing that I had trouble keeping my eyes on the road, so he would interrupt himself every so often to save me from flying over car-sized potholes that rendered the occasional speed bump wholly redundant. I had not yet settled into the pace of Glendora—its steady yet deliberate patience, its observant quiet, like the slow and gentle rolling of my tires over every bump and crevice.

Our first stop was the bridge where Till's body had been dumped. A sparse cypress grove stood in the slow-moving Black Bayou below. The water was opaque and brown, and offered no sign of the violence that had taken place there more than a half-century earlier. On the other side of town, along the unpaved road that skirts the Tallahatchie River, Rosebud pointed out a tree, the only remaining marker of his childhood home left on the land. In its place was a cotton field that left no trace of the house bulldozed years ago.

As my car slowly rolled alongside the Tallahatchie River and as every bump and groove in that dirt road took its toll on my car's poor suspension, I asked Rosebud if his family ever talked about the Till lynching when he was growing up in the 1980s. Directly, no, they had not, but he remembered a warning from his grandparents: if he was walking home after dark and saw headlights in the distance, he should crouch in the ditch along the road, just in case white folks were in the approaching car. His grandparents' warning reminded me of John Henry Johnson's oral history, which I had listened to in the Duke University archives a few months earlier. Johnson grew up near Glendora in Itta Bena, Mississippi, and not only did he remember when Till disappeared and later when his body was discovered, but he was a distant relative of Till's. For Johnson, that lynching was a cautionary tale to be passed on even in 1995:

> I mean, you just knew that you didn't, some things you just didn't do, didn't say to white women, unless you wanted to die. And like I said, the Emmett Till thing is, even to this day, is talked about because I know with my son, when I started talking

to him, you know, because he went to an integrated school!—
Greenwood High is integrated—and, and I told him the story
of Emmett Till 'cause he needs to know. Actually 'cause in
white America ain't too much changed between then and now.
White folks still don't want to see no Black man with no white
woman . . . you relay the stories to them [African American chil-
dren]. You know. Sure is relevant. That [will?] be relevant forever
in my mind. When I have grandsons, I'm going to tell them
about it.[1]

Johnson's son was a teenager in the 1980s—just a few years older than
Rosebud—and three decades after Till's lynching, African American parents still worried that what had happened to Till could happen again and
strike even closer to home. In private conversations between Black parents and Black children in the Delta—private in that they were never
spoken in the presence of whites—these memories of Till's lynching still
informed, whether explicitly or implicitly, the ways parents protected
their children decades later. The intergenerational passage of lynching
memories and the intergenerational passage of the hypervigilance necessary for surviving what Christina Sharpe calls "the weather" persisted as
lynching and other anti-Black violence evolved after Jim Crow.[2]

A few more minutes down the road from where Rosebud's childhood
home had once stood, he showed me the spot where a man fishing on the
banks of the Tallahatchie River had discovered Till's decomposing body
poking up from the riverbed. I pulled over, and staring at the shallow,
dull-brown water from my car, I thought about how and why Rosebud's
family and community had selectively silenced memories of an event that
had happened so close to home and arguably had been the catalyst for
the civil rights movement. The trees along the banks, their branches bare
this late in the year, cast ghostly reflections on the muddy river, and
those trees and their reflections that darkened the waters seemed to hold
the answer. For even though the Rosebuds had not spoken about the Till
lynching to their grandchildren, the specter of Till's lynching was still
there—it still cast a shadow over the community and carved worry lines
into the brows of parents and grandparents. The violence of the past
seemed poised to snap back into the present and claim yet another Black
child. When Rosebud was growing up and when Johnson was raising his
son, the community was still mourning Till, still searching for the words
to make sense of his death, still worried it might happen again.

In most narratives of the Till lynching, the nearby towns of Money and Sumter loom large: Money was where the fourteen-year-old allegedly whistled at Carolyn Bryant in the general store she owned with her husband, Roy Bryant, and Sumter was where the two white men who lynched Till were acquitted while the nation watched. Glendora had largely avoided the national spotlight during the trial, even though one of Till's killers, J. W. Milam, lived in town. However, in the past decade or so, residents of Glendora, led by their longtime mayor, Johnny B. Thomas, decided to embrace the spotlight and reclaim the cotton gin building where Till had been brutally beaten in 1955, the same building from which Milam and Bryant had taken the cotton gin fan that was wrapped around Till's neck when his body was recovered from the Tallahatchie River.[3] In 2011 the town opened ETHIC inside the old cotton gin building. In a blues-inflected twist, the town transformed a space haunted by the brutal killing of a Black child into a museum, memorial, and community space.[4] Through its exhibits and programming, the museum confronts the history of lynching, rewriting the historical narrative of the Delta by placing Till's lynching and the acquittal of his lynchers at the center of its history, while reappropriating a site of Black torture and death that represented the full force of white supremacy under Jim Crow. After decades of relative silence regarding Till's lynching, the people of Glendora have created in ETHIC a memorial that embraces the confrontational spirit of the blues sensibility.

Over the past couple of decades, public discourse about the personal and collective tragedy of lynching has become more pronounced across the United States as the blues sensibility has continued to resonate, though now at louder volumes than most African Americans deemed prudent during Jim Crow. With museums like ETHIC and the steady proliferation of exhibits, memorials, historical markers, academic books, fiction, and art about lynching, African American lynching narratives, though still often intended for Black audiences, are increasingly aimed at whites and other non-Blacks. These narratives echo earlier protest traditions with their dual emphasis on memorializing and mourning the dead as well as demanding justice and reparation for the survivors of that trauma. At the same time, debates over *how* to best confront the traumatic afterlife of lynching have also been drawn into the public sphere.

In the final months of 2000, Emory University held a series of public forums to receive feedback from the community about plans to co-sponsor an exhibit of one hundred lynching photographs collected by James Allen.

Titled *Without Sanctuary*, the proposed exhibit, which was first shown in New York earlier that year, elicited a variety of reactions. Many in Atlanta thought the exhibit would finally force Americans (and white southerners in particular) to face their history. Like critics who viewed the exhibit in New York the previous year, some worried that a gallery full of spectators gazing at lynched Black bodies would inadvertently reproduce the spectacle of lynching, objectify African Americans once again, and reinscribe white power (and even provide relief to non-Blacks for being exempt from that violence). Some visitors might even take sadistic pleasure in viewing the Black death on display. Other critics opposed the exhibit for inflaming racial tensions by dredging up unpleasant memories that they believed should remain buried in the past. Among the hundreds of people who weighed in at these public forums was Judy Willis from nearby Decatur, Georgia. Willis's grandfather, Richard Willis, had been lynched decades before she was born, when her father was just a child. During the public comment portion of the forum, she walked up to the microphone and said:

> I just humbly ask that we can see these images so that the pain that I feel still in my heart can be healed.... My father ... just revealed [that my grandfather had been lynched], and he was in his elder stages. I was a grown woman at that time, so it made me feel that there was a part of him that was hidden. There was a family secret, you know, that had an effect on me that I couldn't even really fully understand because I didn't know. And still there was shame because he didn't speak further about it. But I've taken it upon myself to honor my grandfather, to look more at the power that my ancestors have, and I know that my grandfather wants to—his memory wants to be brought forward.... I know that for me it's important for me to express the anguish that it had and how it's still a very painful part, and it's still— when I look at my father, I still see the sadness of not having a father when he came up. I know how I felt about not having a grandfather. I know how my daughter feels about not having a great-grandfather, and all the things that he could have shared with us and all the moments of compassion he could have shown my father, who never knew him.[5]

The pain in her voice was palpable. At first choking back tears until she regained her composure, Willis spoke with a deep and abiding love for a grandfather she had never known as she explained that exhibiting *Without Sanctuary* would finally honor his suffering and pain. With legal justice no longer an option, since members of the lynch mob were probably long dead, she urged the committee from Emory to record and make public oral histories from the descendants of lynching victims and the descendants of lynching perpetrators. Using South Africa's Truth and Reconciliation Commission as a model, she asked that these stories, from both "sides" as she put it, be brought out into the open.

Willis made it clear that "express[ing] the anguish" that spanned four generations was necessary for her to process this family tragedy and that telling her grandfather's story would both memorialize his suffering and remove the shame that had caused her father's silence in the first place. As she put it, "his memory wants to be brought forward." The exhibit had the potential to memorialize victims like Richard Willis and to drag an ugly, painful history out from the shadows and expose it to what Martin Luther King Jr. called "the light of human conscience and the air of national opinion."[6] King saw the exposure of injustice as a necessary step on the path to liberation, and, in that same vein, perhaps the curators hoped that the collective experience of Atlantans of all races bearing witness to these lynching photographs would shift the visitor's gaze away from the spectacle of Black death and turn it inward. In the spirit of the blues sensibility, the return to these painful lynching memories would open up spaces for introspection and maybe even something like relief for survivors. And so, rather than reinscribing the objectification of lynching victims, the exhibit might provide a space for visitors who crowded into the King Center to publicly condemn crimes that had gone unpunished by the courts and collectively mourn the dead.

At the same time, becoming a witness to lynching by viewing these photographs could itself be traumatic and could risk reobjectifying victims in disturbing and damaging ways.[7] Artists like Kerry James Marshall and Ken Gonzales-Day have addressed this potential for reobjectification by shifting the gaze of viewers away from Black corpses and toward white perpetrators. Marshall's *Heirlooms and Accessories* (2002), for instance, is a triptych composed of three copies of the widely circulated photograph of Abe Smith and Tommy Shipp's 1930 lynching in Marion, Indiana, but rather than drawing attention to Smith's and Shipp's bodies, he encircles the faces of three white women in the lynch mob with keepsake frames attached to necklace and watch chains. The rest of the photographs, including the bodies of two young men hanging from a tree, is so faint, so nearly white, that only by leaning in closer to the image can you can make out the whisper of the lynching scene. As its title suggests, this piece captures how white families and communities treasured and then passed down lynching mementos and lynching memories, while marking these white women and the rest of the mob as accessories to a crime. Marshall, by forcing viewers to stare at the three white women staring back at them, prompts white viewers to reckon with this inheritance rather than gawk at the spectacle of Black death.

In the *Erased Lynching Series*, Gonzales-Day, too, shifts the viewer's gaze away from victims to perpetrators, but does so by fully erasing dead bodies from historical photographs of lynchings. He removes not only the bodies of victims but also the ropes and chains used to kill them, leaving bare the tree limbs, beams, and telephone poles in the photographs, leaving scaffolds empty. What remains is the land, the spatial repository of memory, and the perpetrators, the social repositories of memory.[8] With these erasures, however, comes a commitment to recovery, for Gonzales-Day's scholarship on the lynching of ethnic Mexicans, other Latinx people, Native Americans, and Chinese immigrants fundamentally challenges the geographical and temporal boundaries of lynching through the recovery of previously ignored (or erased) lynchings in the US West.[9] As much as these artistic choices to erase lynched bodies seek to temper the most voyeuristic and dehumanizing elements of the practice, the emphasis on perpetrators by both Marshall and Gonzales-Day leaves unexamined African American stories—stories of survival, stories of mourning, stories of defiance, and stories that tell what it means to live in the wake of lynching.

Confronted with either being trapped in the voyeuristic reverberations of lynching, like the curators of *Without Sanctuary*, or centering the perspectives of perpetrators, as in the works of Marshall and Gonzales-Day, some lynching memorials and other memory projects have found a third way to represent lynching that inspires critical introspection while inflicting less harm on victims and survivors. Those who walk among the pillars suspended from the ceiling of the recently opened National Memorial for Peace and Justice (more colloquially known as the national lynching memorial) in Montgomery, Alabama, feel the weight of these unmistakable symbols of lynching, but without being surrounded by lifelike (but dead) hanging bodies. Opened in April 2018 by the Equal Justice Initiative, the memorial's design forces a recognition that lynching is a national crime that still remains largely unexamined, but ultimately is

aimed at combatting the legacies of that violence in the present—
whether the death penalty and mass incarceration or police brutality and
the criminalization of Black bodies—through remembrance of the dead.

Located on a hill that overlooks a starkly divided and incoherent memorial landscape that includes both the first White House of the Confederacy and the Freedom Rides Museum, the memorial differs from
most museums and exhibits in the city because it's a fully immersive experience: each visitor becomes enmeshed in the physical space of the
memorial itself as a witness/mourner/participant. After literally walking
up from slavery—by the entrance, you pass a sculpture of enslaved people in chains experiencing the anguish of forced separation, as you walk
up the hill—you come face to face with enormous steel pillars suspended
from the ceiling by metal poles, one for each county where a lynching
was recorded, the names of African American victims and dates of lynchings engraved on their rusted surfaces. As you walk among the pillars,
each corner you turn takes you deeper underground, as though you are
slowly descending into a grave, and the pillars, now hanging above you,
resemble more clearly rigid, dark, cold bodies. In this space, where the
victims of lynching loom overhead, haunting the space and settling into
your bones, the horror of lynching is made viscerally apparent, but as
you squint up at these steel pillars, your eyes witness not literal dead
bodies (or photographs of dead bodies) but names. Though names alone
can't tell the victims' stories, the memorial is an invitation to seek out
their stories, to contemplate the victims' lives and deaths, to mourn
them, to seek justice. The final wall of the memorial has water slowly
rolling down its face, evoking tears of pain and mourning as much as the
cleansing waters of rain, and it bears an inscription that is at once a call
to remember and a call to act: "For the hanged and beaten. For the shot,
drowned, and burned. For those abandoned by the rule of law. We will
remember. With hope because hopelessness is the enemy of justice. With
courage because peace requires bravery. With persistence because justice
is a constant struggle. With faith because we shall overcome."

On the other side of the memorial is a field with pillars, replicas of
the ones that hang in the memorial, neatly resting on the grass like cof-
fins and waiting to be claimed and brought home to their respective
counties. In the spirit of that inscription on the wall of the memorial, the
Equal Justice Initiative has been working with communities to claim
their pillars, thereby spreading these stories and a reckoning with this
history throughout the nation. The few empty spaces in the field left by

claimed pillars speak to the enormous challenge of confronting the legacies of lynching at the local level, for the unclaimed pillars that remain
reflect a refusal among white Americans to lay claim to this history of
white supremacy and perhaps a continued reluctance among some African Americans to bring these memories to the surface. In explaining the
intent of the memorial, the Equal Justice Initiative's director, Bryan Stevenson, wrote, "Our nation's history of racial injustice casts a shadow
across the American landscape. This shadow cannot be lifted until we
shine the light of truth on the destructive violence that shaped our nation, traumatized people of color, and compromised our commitment
to the rule of law and to equal justice."[10] Stevenson echoes the sensibility
of the blues by building a memorial that returns to painful memories of
lynching in order to confront its legacies, though whether the shadow he
speaks of can be lifted remains an open question.

These various attempts to place lynching at the center of the national narrative—ETHIC, *Without Sanctuary*, and the National Memorial for Peace and Justice—are all oriented toward healing wounds from
the past *and* inspiring political action in the present. ETHIC serves as a
community space for confronting not only the unresolved lynching of
Till but also the legacies of racial violence and white supremacy writ
large in the Delta. Several of the exhibition spaces where *Without Sanctuary* was shown made explicit connections between the lynchings depicted
in the photographs on the walls taken at the height of Jim Crow and
more recent hate crimes and police violence.[11] The Legacy Museum:
From Enslavement to Mass Incarceration, which is a companion to the
memorial in Montgomery, places lynching along the continuum of the
history of white supremacy and alongside the parallel history of the African American freedom struggle, ending with the inhumanity of the death
penalty and the emergence of the carceral state. Remembering, in all
three cases, is more than a matter of recovering the past; like the blues,
revisiting the trauma of lynching is ultimately inspired by a drive to rec-
tify injustices both past and present.

Under the strictures of Jim Crow, the blues sensibility provided an outlet
for unleashing biting social critiques and indulging in revenge fantasies;
cloaking one's true face under the masks of metaphor, double entendre,
and humor; or even using strategic silences for self-protection. Nearly
sixty years after the dismantling of Jim Crow, these narrative strategies
remain relevant. Black people continue to live under the threat of white

supremacist violence as evidenced by the spate of African Americans killed by police officers, stand your ground laws used to rationalize the murder of African Americans, the disproportionate use of the death penalty in cases involving Black defendants, the targeting of Black Lives Matter activists, and the like. Despite the desire to neatly compartmentalize lynching as a Jim Crow relic, lynchings also still occur. During my first research trip for this book project in 2011, James Craig Anderson was lynched in Jackson, Mississippi. As I finished revisions on the final manuscript in 2020, Ahmaud Arbery and Breonna Taylor died at the hands of the lynchers who walk among us in our times. Ashraf Rushdy points out in *The End of American Lynching* that lynching has evolved in form over time, but that the white supremacist motives that animate lynchers have remained constant.[12] The myriad strategies of the blues sensibility to endure and survive as well as to expose injustice and foolishness remain relevant given the lived reality of anti-Black violence in the wake of lynching.

These violent legacies of lynching even invade the very memorial spaces intended to bring attention to this history. Along the stretch of Georgia Highway 122 between Barney and Hahira in Brooks County, just past the bridge at the Little River, sits an official historical marker from the Georgia Historical Society. Most of the historical markers that dot the countryside of Georgia celebrate the incorporation of a county or the bravery of Confederate soldiers; this marker reads "Mary Turner and the Lynching Rampage of 1918." Ninety-two years after that lynching, in May 2010, the descendants of the Turners joined members of a community organization called the Mary Turner Project and the local branch of the Southern Christian Leadership Conference to dedicate the marker just a few yards from the place where Turner and her baby had been killed. They gathered to publicly mourn the suffering of lynching victims and to remember the anti-Black violence that plagued their county. They vowed to combat racial injustice in the present and to pass these stories on to their children and grandchildren. However, some residents of Brooks County resented these efforts to remember and mourn, and about one and a half years later, somebody shot up the sign. Vandals returned in 2013 to further desecrate the marker with five more bullet holes, leaving an unmistakable reminder that the violence of lynching and the battle over its memory are far from confined to the past.

The desecration of memorials to lynching victims has been widespread. In Mississippi alone, people have stolen and vandalized the Emmett Till

Memorial Highway sign in LeFlore County, Mississippi, as well as historical markers about the Till lynching at Bryant's Grocery in Money and at
the site along the Tallahatchie River where Till's body was recovered in
Glendora. The sign in Glendora had been shot up, stolen, and thrown into
the river so many times that it was replaced with a bulletproof sign.[13] Vandals have also repeatedly desecrated the grave of James Chaney, one of the
three civil rights workers lynched near Philadelphia, Mississippi, in 1964.
Not only was his gravestone ripped out of the ground and smashed to
pieces in 1989, but after it was repaired, vandals destroyed the small picture
of his face etched on the new gravestone, blasting it with bullets in an attempt to extinguish the enduring memory of his sacrifice for the movement.[14] When the NAACP sued the Hanging Bridge Hunting and Fishing
Club in Shubuta, Mississippi, in the 1980s, its members thought it was sufficient to paint over the "Hanging Bridge" part of their sign that still marks
the bridge where six African Americans had been lynched.[15] Lynching memorials and those who publicly condemn lynching continue to remain vulnerable to actual attacks, and the very exposure that so many in these Black
communities hoped to avoid through strategic silences and misdirection
during Jim Crow remains risky. As important as these public memorials are,
blues-inflected narratives on the lower frequencies remain necessary for
some as a matter of safety.

Despite efforts by many communities to memorialize local lynching
victims, these measures have remained largely marginal to the lives of white
southerners, many of whom still refuse to acknowledge the impact of
lynching on the past and the present. In response to an official resolution
apologizing for the 1916 lynching of Jesse Washington in Waco, Texas, one
white teenager wrote to the local newspaper in 2006, "Bringing up issues of
this sort only makes things worse. It divides people, and this is not what we
need in order to be a functional nation." Having already erased the white
supremacist intent from lynching by declaring that "lynching is not a race
issue," this high school student deemed all forms of racism from the past
"obsolete."[16] Many other white Wacoans joined him in opposing an official
apology from the mayor and city council for Washington's lynching. One of
the most vocal opponents was Patsy Kilgore, a distant relative by marriage
to the woman Washington allegedly murdered. She told the local organization demanding the public apology, "Yeah, maybe law enforcement should
have handled the situation better at the time, but if he hadn't raped and
murdered her, he wouldn't have been where he was. . . . To me, when you
break the law, you deserve what you get."[17] Kilgore saw no need to issue an

apology for the actions of the lynch mob or the city leaders—she did not think Washington's sham trial, his attorney who declined to launch a defense at his trial, and even his lynching were wrong. Not only were these views a provocation that dismissed the long history of white supremacist violence as frivolous complaints about racist acts that were supposedly not racist to begin with, but they spoke to the need for museums like ETHIC, memorials like the National Memorial to Peace and Justice, public lectures by scholars of lynching, and other historical and artistic work on lynching.[18]

Memory projects like these, however, are simply a precondition for honest, productive introspection and significant structural change. As the unfinished business of the civil rights movement so plainly illustrated, the struggle to expose the injustice of Jim Crow and to eliminate discrimination from the letter of the law was certainly important, but the critical change necessary for racial justice had to occur in the hearts and minds of white Americans. Ralph Ellison pointed out that "[the blues] fall short of tragedy only in that they provide no solution, offer no scapegoat but the self," but sadly the most formidable obstacle to confronting lynching and its legacies is the general reluctance among whites to look inward and examine the collective conscience of the nation.[19] And if, as James Baldwin intoned in *The Fire Next Time*, racial justice can be achieved only when "[African Americans], with love, shall force our [white] brothers to see themselves as they are, to cease fleeing from reality and begin to change it," then perhaps this reluctance to face the history of lynching is another iteration of that age-old problem, the pervasive fear among whites of truly seeing themselves for who they are.[20]

These denials have been replicated on the national level. In 2005, the US Senate passed a resolution "apologizing to the victims of lynching and the descendants of those victims for the failure of the Senate to enact anti-lynching legislation" after repeatedly blocking antilynching bills over the course of the twentieth century.[21] The resolution passed on a voice vote since seventy-nine senators co-sponsored the resolution, and within three days of the vote, another eight senators added their names to the list of co-sponsors. Then Senate majority leader Bill Frist refused to hold a roll-call vote, which allowed the eight Republican senators who opposed the measure to avoid going on the record as voting against the resolution.[22] When asked why he refused to co-sponsor the resolution, Senator Thad Cochran, who represented Mississippi, the state with the highest number of lynchings, said, "I don't feel that I should apologize for the passage or the failure to pass any legislation by the US Senate.

But I deplore and regret that lynchings occurred and that those committing them were not punished."[23] Cochran's excuses make the possibility of a meaningful reckoning with the past seem bleak. More recently, in 2022, the Emmett Till Antilynching Act, introduced by Representative Bobby Rush of Illinois, became a federal law, but like the largely symbolic 2005 Senate Resolution, the law fails to confront the root causes of lynching.[24] Not only do these public gestures have no mechanism for seeking justice or providing reparations for lynching victims and survivors, but they ignore the newest iterations of lynching—and the newest victims and survivors of lynching—during a time when lynching rhetoric, especially in the realm of politics, has seen an ugly resurgence.[25]

The persistence of lynching—in rhetoric, in violence that targets Black people, in its myriad and lasting legacies—leaves us with much to despair over, as do so many other emblems of white supremacy that infect the present, but if anything, the blues counsel patience and hope. For even in the wake of a lynching rampage, African Americans in Valdosta, Georgia, formed a local NAACP branch in 1919, and Eva Hall placed the protection of her children above revealing to them the violence their white neighbors had perpetrated. Even amid the tragedy of her son's death, Mamie Till-Mobley published photographs of his lynching that inspired a mass movement for racial justice. Even under the threat of death, Jesse Pennington, who, as a child, had barely escaped the clutches of a lynch mob, channeled his own feeling of powerlessness into establishing a civil rights law practice in Mississippi. Even under the shadows of lynchings past, Minnie Weston had called up those traumatic memories just long enough to make a record of them for posterity. And even in the depths of despair a blues singer can muster up the words: "Trouble in mind, I'm blue / But I won't be blue always / 'Cause the sun is going to shine in my backdoor someday."

Notes

Introduction

1. The definition of "lynching" has been the subject of lively debate. In 1940, several prominent antilynching organizations, including the National Association for the Advancement of Colored People (NAACP), the Tuskegee Institute, and the Association of Southern Women for the Prevention of Lynching (ASWPL), met to create a consensus definition of lynching. Though the definition remained unsettled after that meeting and remains so today, my usage of the term generally follows the definition that the participants in that meeting agreed to: unlawful death(s) caused by a "group acting under pretext of service to justice, race, or tradition." This definition, while unable to capture every nuance of lynching as the practice emerged and transformed over centuries, accounts for both the form of and motive behind lynching, thus encompassing the vast majority of southern lynchings that targeted African Americans. Also, although lynching occurred throughout the United States, I have chosen to focus on the US South where most lynchings of African Americans took place. "Summary of the Conference on Lynching and Reports on Lynchings, Tuskegee Institute, Alabama," 14 December 1940, Box 5, Folder 93, Arthur Franklin Raper Papers #3966, Southern Historical Collection, Wilson Library, University of North Carolina at Chapel Hill. For more on disagreements over the definition of lynching, the stakes of defining lynching narrowly, and whether to emphasize continuity or change in defining and periodizing lynching, see my discussion in the epilogue, as well as Christopher Waldrep, "Hate Crimes," in *African Americans Confront Lynching: Strategies of Resistance from the Civil War to the Civil Rights Era* (Lanham, MD: Rowman & Littlefield, 2009), 113–27; Christopher Waldrep, *The Many Faces of Judge Lynch: Extralegal Violence and Punishment in America* (New York: Palgrave Macmillan, 2003), 1–8, 127–50, 185–91; Ashraf H. A. Rushdy, *American Lynching* (New Haven: Yale University Press,

2012), 5–21, 123–55; Ashraf H. A. Rushdy, *The End of American Lynching* (New Brunswick, NJ: Rutgers University Press, 2012), 97–100, 128–59, 174–75.

2. As Jesse beats the man in jail, this same feeling of joy creeps back in, which prompts "something deep in him and deep in his memory . . . [to be] stirred, but whatever was in his memory eluded him." Baldwin then connects the beating of the protest leader to the lynching memory he recalls a few pages later. James Baldwin, "Going to Meet the Man," in *Going to Meet the Man* (1965; repr., New York: Vintage International, 1993), 247, 233.

3. Much of the existing scholarship on lynching falls into two categories: studies that focus on what white people did to Black people during and in the immediate aftermath of lynchings and studies that examine antilynching activism. Scholars in the former category have described the ritual of lynching, the spectacle of lynching, the imagery of lynching, lynching culture, and the commodification of lynching. Indispensable as those monographs are for understanding this history, privileging the experiences of white southern perpetrators has tended to reduce African Americans to objects of white violence rather than historical subjects in their own right. Those scholars who fall into the latter category emphasize the enduring presence of the Black protest tradition, but in doing so, they place disproportionate emphasis on the most vocal Black responses to the trauma of lynching. To counteract tendencies to amplify white perspectives and focus on a singular Black perspective, this book centers African American narratives and unearths a wide range of ways in which people experienced the traumatic afterlife of lynching. The scholarship in lynching studies is vast, but I list here some critical studies in the field that examine southern lynching: Sandy Alexandre, *The Properties of Violence: Claims to Ownership in the Representations of Lynching* (Jackson: University Press of Mississippi, 2012); Dora Apel, *Imagery of Lynching: Black Men, White Women, and the Mob* (New Brunswick, NJ: Rutgers University Press, 2004); Dora Apel and Shawn Michele Smith, *Lynching Photographs* (Berkeley: University of California Press, 2007); Amy Kate Bailey and Stewart E. Tolnay, *Lynched: The Victims of Southern Mob Violence* (Chapel Hill: University of North Carolina Press, 2015); W. Fitzhugh Brundage, *Lynching in the New South: Georgia and Virginia, 1880–1930* (Urbana: University of Illinois Press, 1993); W. Fitzhugh Brundage, ed., *Under Sentence of Death: Lynching in the South* (Chapel Hill: University of North Carolina Press, 1997); William D. Carrigan, *The Making of a Lynching Culture: Violence and Vigilantism in Central Texas, 1836–1916* (Urbana: University of Illinois Press, 2006); Philip Dray, *At the Hands of Persons Unknown: The Lynching of Black America* (New York: Modern Library, 2003); Jacqueline Goldsby, *A Spectacular Secret: Lynching in American Life and Literature* (Chicago: University of Chicago Press, 2006); Trudier Harris, *Exorcising Blackness: Historical and Literary Lynching and Burning Rituals* (Bloomington: Indiana University Press, 1984); Tameka Bradley Hobbs, *Democracy Abroad,*

Lynching at Home: Racial Violence in Florida (Gainesville: University Press of Florida, 2015); Koritha Mitchell, *Living with Lynching: African American Lynching Plays, Performance, and Citizenship, 1890–1930* (Urbana: University of Illinois Press, 2011); Cynthia Skove Nevels, *Lynching to Belong: Claiming Whiteness through Racial Violence* (College Station: Texas A&M University, 2007); Rushdy, *American Lynching;* Sarah L. Silkey, *Black Woman Reformer: Ida B. Wells, Lynching, and Transatlantic Activism* (Athens: University of Georgia Press, 2015); Stewart E. Tolnay and E. M. Beck, *A Festival of Violence: An Analysis of Southern Lynchings, 1882–1930* (Urbana: University of Illinois Press, 1992); Waldrep, *The Many Faces of Judge Lynch;* Waldrep, *African Americans Confront Lynching;* Amy Louise Wood, *Lynching and Spectacle: Witnessing Racial Violence in America, 1890–1940* (Chapel Hill: University of North Carolina Press, 2009); Robert L. Zangrando, *The NAACP Crusade against Lynching, 1909–1950* (Philadelphia: Temple University Press, 1980).

    I use the term "survivors" here to mean not only the lucky few intended victims of lynching who were not killed by lynch mobs, either by evading capture or escaping or being released, but also the families of lynching victims and survivors, and African Americans in the communities where lynchings occurred. Lynch mobs terrorized entire Black communities for the (sometimes imagined) transgressions of a few individuals. Leon Litwack describes lynching as a "public ritual," "collective experience," and "voyeuristic spectacle" intended to affirm the power of whiteness for white southerners and to strike fear and horror into the hearts of African Americans throughout the South. Because the targets of this racial terrorism were not simply Black victims but their families and communities, the survivors of lynching encompass the families and communities that survived to live in the wake of lynching. Leon F. Litwack, *Trouble in Mind: Black Southerners in the Age of Jim Crow* (New York: Vintage Books, 1998), 288–91, 285.

4. As a corollary to Jesse seeking refuge in memories of lynching, African American memories of lynching may have fueled the desire among the protesters singing freedom songs in the jail to defy Jim Crow by registering to vote. The trauma of lynching and responses to that trauma did not manifest in a singular way within the Black community, but protest against white supremacy was certainly one major response, which I discuss at length in chapter 5.

5. Southern memorials often include "both sides" in the same memorial spaces in an attempt to be conciliatory and to suspend judgment of the past, thereby avoiding any real reckoning with the role of white supremacy in southern history and ignoring the contradictions between, for instance, memorials for civil rights heroes and those for Confederate generals. Even so, bringing Black and white southern memories into a single frame makes an important intervention in the memory studies literature about the US South since so often southern memorial spaces and museums themselves remain segregated.

6.   The literature on memory and the African American experience is vast. The following books are particularly helpful in articulating the broader stakes of memory as a subject of study: David W. Blight, *Race and Reunion: The Civil War in American Memory* (Cambridge, MA: Belknap Press, 2001); W. Fitzhugh Brundage, "No Deed But Memory," in *Where These Memories Grow: History, Memory, and Southern Identity*, ed. Brundage (Chapel Hill: University of North Carolina Press, 2000), 1–28; Geneviève Fabre and Robert O'Meally, eds., *History and Memory in African-American Culture* (New York: Oxford University Press, 1994); Avery Gordon, *Ghostly Matters: Haunting and the Sociological Imagination* (Minneapolis: University of Minnesota Press, 2008); Jonathan Scott Holloway, *Jim Crow Wisdom: Memory and Identity in Black America since 1940* (Chapel Hill: University of North Carolina Press, 2015); Nathan Irvin Huggins, "The Deforming Mirror of Truth," in *Black Odyssey: The African-American Ordeal in Slavery* (New York: Vintage Books, 1990), xi–lxx; Christina Sharpe, *In the Wake: On Blackness and Being* (Durham, NC: Duke University Press, 2016). As many scholars of memory point out, both individual and collective memories are constructions of the past, not reproductions of the past, and on the collective level, memory helps to shape popular perceptions of the past and group identity, usually in a way that actively purifies the past of the shameful and ugly. Brundage describes this process of negotiation and sharing as "the active labor of selecting, structuring, and imposing meaning on the past rather than the mere reproduction of inherent historical truths" ("No Deed But Memory," 5). Clashes over historical memory determine who wields the power to shape the political, economic, and social structure of a region or nation. Adherents to the dominant historical memory gain the authority, privilege, and status to further entrench their vision of the past through memorials, textbooks, commemorative events, museums, and historical novels.

7.   James Baldwin, "White Man's Guilt," in *The Price of the Ticket: Collected Nonfiction 1948–1985* (New York: St. Martin's Press, 1985), 410.

8.   This book builds upon existing scholarship on lynching and memory. See Julie Buckner Armstrong, *Mary Turner and the Memory of Lynching* (Athens: University of Georgia Press, 2011); Bruce E. Baker, "Under the Rope: Lynching and Memory in Laurens County, South Carolina," in *Where These Memories Grow*, ed. Brundage, 319–45; Jonathan Markovitz, *Legacies of Lynching: Racial Violence and Memory* (Minneapolis: University of Minnesota Press, 2004); Evelyn M. Simien, ed., *Gender and Lynching: The Politics of Memory* (New York: Palgrave Macmillan, 2011); Jason Morgan Ward, *Hanging Bridge: Racial Violence and America's Civil Rights Century* (New York: Oxford University Press, 2016).

9.   Though Sharpe's framing of the afterlife of slavery through "the wake" provides helpful language to describe the afterlife of lynching, I depart from her description of anti-Blackness and deathliness as totalizing since doing so forecloses too much from Black people and grants too much to white

people. Sharpe, *In the Wake*, 8–9. For historical analysis of Black responses to white supremacist violence specifically during Jim Crow, see Kidada E. Williams, *They Left Great Marks on Me: African American Testimonies of Racial Violence from Emancipation to World War I* (New York: New York University Press, 2012).

10. Sharpe, *In the Wake*, 18.

11. Traditionally, books on lynching in the South date the "peak period" of lynching as roughly 1880 to 1940, but this periodization depends on a definition of lynching that excludes lynchings in the South during Reconstruction and enslavement. Such a temporal and geographic boundary also obscures connections between southern lynchings and lynchings in the US West, many of which were bound up with US colonialist violence against Native Americans and ethnic Mexicans before 1880. That being said, because memories of lynchings that occurred before 1880 are usually less accessible in sources from the mid-twentieth century, the lynchings discussed in this book largely happened after 1880. For more about lynching in the West, see William D. Carrigan and Clive Webb, *Forgotten Dead: Mob Violence against Mexicans in the United States, 1848–1928* (New York: Oxford University Press, 2014); Ken Gonzales-Day, *Lynching in the West, 1850–1935* (Durham, NC: Duke University Press, 2006); Nicole M. Guidotti-Hernández, *Unspeakable Violence: Remapping U.S. and Mexican National Imaginaries* (Durham, NC: Duke University Press, 2011); Monica Muñoz Martinez, "Recuperating Histories of Violence in the Americas: Vernacular History-Making on the U.S.–Mexico Border," *American Quarterly* 66, no. 3 (September 2014): 661–89; Monica Muñoz Martinez, *The Injustice Never Leaves You: Anti-Mexican Violence in Texas* (Cambridge, MA: Harvard University Press, 2018); Nicholas Villanueva Jr., *The Lynching of Mexicans in the Texas Borderlands* (Albuquerque: University of New Mexico Press, 2017).

12. Sharpe, *In the Wake*, 104; Kevin Quashie, *Black Aliveness, or A Poetics of Being* (Durham, NC: Duke University Press, 2021), 8.

13. For more on the dominance of the resistance paradigm and alternatives to its vision of Black life as either suffering or resistance, see Jeffrey Ferguson, "Race and the Rhetoric of Resistance," *Raritan* 28, no. 1 (Summer 2008): 4–32; Quashie, *Black Aliveness*; Kevin Quashie, *The Sovereignty of Quiet: Beyond Resistance in Black Culture* (New Brunswick, NJ: Rutgers University Press, 2012).

14. I include within the resistance paradigm not just overt forms of resistance but also what James C. Scott calls "hidden transcripts" and infrapolitics—the everyday transgressions by the relatively powerless that often went undetected by the targets of these transgressions. James C. Scott, *Domination and the Arts of Resistance: Hidden Transcripts* (New Haven: Yale University Press, 1992).

15. Ralph Ellison, *Invisible Man* (1952; repr., New York: Vintage International, 1995), 581.

16. The recovery of silence is far more difficult than the recovery of protest for the obvious reason that searching for what went unsaid is more difficult than locating what was said and done. However, the impulse to silence these memories often softened over time, and the further one was from the epicenter of the trauma itself. The children and grandchildren of survivors felt the impact of the traumatic afterlife of lynching but usually in ways that left more room for opening up in public about these memories.

17. Kiese Laymon, "Perpetual Reckoning: An Interview with Kiese Laymon," *New Ohio Review* (Summer 2019), https://newohioreview.org/2019/04/16/an-interview-with-kiese-laymon/.

18. Laymon, "Perpetual Reckoning."

19. Ken Mandel, dir., *Bluesland: A Portrait in American Music* (DVD) (Munich: Toby Byron/Multiprises, 1993).

20. Many of the formative texts in trauma studies focus on Europe in general and the Holocaust in particular, including the following: Cathy Caruth, ed., *Trauma: Explorations in Memory* (Baltimore: Johns Hopkins University Press, 1995); Cathy Caruth, *Unclaimed Experience: Trauma, Narrative, and History* (Baltimore: Johns Hopkins University Press, 1996); Dominick LaCapra, *Writing History, Writing Trauma* (Baltimore: Johns Hopkins University Press, 2001); Ruth Leys, *Trauma: A Genealogy* (Chicago: University of Chicago Press, 2000). For a pointed critique of the Eurocentric approach of much of trauma studies, see Mark Rothberg, "Decolonizing Trauma: A Response," *Studies in the Novel* 40, nos. 1 and 2 (Spring and Summer 2008): 224–34. Recent studies have taken up Rothberg's critique and have examined trauma in new contexts, in particular the Global South and nonwhites in the West. See, for instance, Monica J. Casper and Eric Wertheimer, eds., *Critical Trauma Studies: Understanding Violence, Conflict and Memory in Everyday Life* (New York: New York University Press, 2016); Soyica Diggs Colbert, Robert J. Patterson, and Aida Levy-Hussen, *The Psychic Hold of Slavery: Legacies in American Expressive Culture* (New Brunswick, NJ: Rutgers University Press, 2016); Gordon, *Ghostly Matters;* Kelly Oliver, *Witnessing: Beyond Recognition* (Minneapolis: University of Minnesota Press, 2001); Tanya L. Sharpe, "Understanding the Sociocultural Context of Coping for African American Family Members of Homicide Victims: A Conceptual Model," *Trauma, Violence, and Abuse* 16, no. 1 (2015): 48–59; Erica Still, *Prophetic Remembrance: Black Subjectivity in African American and South African Trauma Narratives* (Charlottesville: University of Virginia Press, 2014).

21. The lyrics to Skip James's "I'm So Glad," for instance, capture the irony and humor at the heart of the blues. In the first verse, he sings, "I'm so glad," no fewer than four times in a row before admitting that the true source of his newfound joy is just that he has grown weary of crying over his most recent heartbreak. Read in isolation from the upbeat and intricate three-finger picking of James's guitar, the lyrics seem to convey that, in his misery, he is all but willing himself to be happy by repeating over and over again that

he's glad, despite mourning the loss of someone close to him. The guitar's cheerful licks, however, belie the sadness of the lyric and hint that, in fact, he may be "glad" and hopeful that someday he won't be "weepin' " and "moanin' " and "groanin' " over this loss, but that he still hasn't let go of that feeling of sadness in the last two lines of the verse. Skip James, "I'm So Glad," recorded 1966, track 1 on *Blues from the Delta* (CD, Vanguard 79517–2, 1998).

22. Billie Holiday, "Body and Soul," recorded 1957, *Body and Soul* (CD, Verve Records 314 589 308–2, 2002).

23. Many blues songs take up the theme of revenge or supernatural justice, whether Memphis Slim's "Mother Earth," Lightnin' Hopkins's "Devil Is Watching You," or John Lee Hooker's "I'm Bad Like Jesse James." Narrating revenge and justice in song provided the satisfaction of airing one's anger and frustration, whether directly as the singer or vicariously as the listener. These songs were rarely sung in the presence of their intended targets because blues songs ultimately were about introspection and making oneself right again. Similarly, the blues sensibility is tethered to an ethic of care— care for oneself, care for one's family, care for one's community—in the face of a hostile world. Ellison contended that the blues "fall short of tragedy only in that they provide no solution, offer no scapegoat but the self." Even in its most outward-facing iterations (like outright protest against injustice), the blues sensibility is fueled by a desire to reach the point of satisfaction, which is not to say that satisfaction provided a clear sense of resolution, necessarily, but rather that satisfaction was about living through adversity while knowing that something of that adversity might always linger. Memphis Slim, "Mother Earth," recorded 1961, track 10 on *All Kinds of Blues* (CD, Prestige/Bluesville Records 1053, 1990); Lightnin' Hopkins, "Devil Is Watching You," recorded 1962, track 4 on *Lightnin' Strikes* (CD, Collectables 7128, 2000); John Lee Hooker, "I'm Bad Like Jesse James," recorded 30 August 1966, track 8 on *The Best of John Lee Hooker 1965 to 1974* (CD, MCA 10539, 1991); Ralph Ellison, "Richard Wright's Blues," in *The Collected Essays of Ralph Ellison* (New York: Modern Library, 2003), 143.

24. James Baldwin, *Giovanni's Room* (1956; repr., New York: Delta Trade Paperbacks, 2000), 5; Lawrence W. Levine, *Black Culture and Black Consciousness: Afro-American Folk Thought from Slavery to Freedom* (1977; repr., New York: Oxford University Press, 2007), 221, 223, 237; Jeffrey B. Ferguson, "A Blue Note on Black American Literary Criticism and the Blues," *Amerikastudien/ American Studies* 55, no. 4 (2010): 706.

25. Through a series of conversations with Clifton Granby, I have come to appreciate the limits of the historian's craft regarding the excavation of traumatic histories. Many historians insist on a near limitless duty to recover stories of unimaginable horror. Ignoring the trauma of lynching would be unconscionable, but writing about anti-Black trauma can turn Black suffering into an object of fascination—a sort of torture porn—and self-interested

benefit. All historians, on some level, benefit from the stories they tell, whether it is through book sales, professional reputation, or tenure and promotion. This kind of "exploitation" is inevitable for any kind of historical writing, but some stories may be too awful to pass along because they cease to contribute to the ends of justice and may inflict more harm than good upon those who bore the brunt of suffering in the first place. For more on the conversation around representing anti-Black violence, see Saidiya V. Hartman, *Scenes of Subjection: Terror, Slavery, and Self-Making in Nineteenth-Century America* (New York: Oxford University Press, 1997); Fred Moten, "Resistance of the Object: Aunt Hester's Scream," in *In the Break: The Aesthetics of the Black Radical Tradition* (Minneapolis: University of Minnesota Press, 2003), 1–24; Teju Cole, "Death in the Browser Tab," in *Known and Strange Things* (New York: Random House, 2016), 201–6; Mari N. Crabtree, "The Ethics of Writing History in the Traumatic Afterlife of Lynching," *Rethinking History* (1 December 2020), https://doi.org/10.1080/13642529.2020.1846968.

26. Communities across the United States have memorialized lynching victims with plaques, historical markers, and statues, but perhaps the best known memorial is the National Memorial for Peace and Justice, which the Equal Justice Initiative opened in Montgomery, Alabama, on April 26, 2018. Recent hearings on reparations in the US Congress, as well as the Justice for Victims of Lynching Act of 2018, introduced by Sens. Cory Booker and Kamala Harris, have briefly directed national attention to lynching, but these hearings and this legislation relegate lynching to the past, making lynching into something we might shudder to think about but also something that no longer occurs.

27. Joseph Goldstein and Nate Schweber, "Man's Death after Chokehold Raises Old Issue for the Police," *New York Times*, 18 July 2014; Allyson Chiu, "Nooses, Confederate Flags and Monkey Imagery: 19 Black UPS Workers Say Company 'Encouraged a Culture of Racism,' " *Washington Post*, 14 March 2019; Benjamin Fearnow, "Black General Motors Employees: 'Whites Only' Signs, Hanging Nooses Weren't Investigated by GM, Lawsuit Says," *Newsweek*, 29 November 2018; Jerry Mitchell, "Ole Miss Students Pose with Guns in Front of Emmett Till Sign. They Could Face Investigation," *Clarion Ledger* (Jackson, MS), 25 July 2019.

28. The epilogue discusses in more depth these and other contemporary references to lynching. Amy B. Wang, "Lawmaker Apologizes after Saying Leaders 'Should be Lynched' for Removing Confederate Statues," *Washington Post*, 22 May 2017; Molly Roberts, "Walmart Stocked a Shirt That Suggested Lynching Journalists. This Isn't New," *Washington Post*, 1 December 2017; Cindy Boren, "Missouri Bar Owner Denies Sending a Racial Message with 'Lynch, Kaepernick' Jerseys as Doormat," *Washington Post*, 28 September 2017; "Two Arrested for 'Hanging Effigy of Barack Obama from a Tree,' " *Telegraph* (UK), 31 October 2008; Associated Press, "N. Idaho Sign

Advertises Obama 'Public Hanging,' " *Seattle Times*, 13 November 2008; "Barack Obama Effigy Hanged in Georgia," *Guardian* (UK), 4 January 2010.

29. The soul still witnesses what one cannot fully remember or chooses to conceal or cannot put into words. James Baldwin, *The Evidence of Things Not Seen* (1985; repr., New York: Henry Holt, 1995), xv.

Chapter One.　An Anatomy of Lynching

1. "Mob Takes Negro from Court House, Burns Him at Stake," *Waco Times-Herald* (hereafter cited as *WTH*), 15 May 1916; James M. SoRelle, "The 'Waco Horror': The Lynching of Jesse Washington," *Southwestern Historical Quarterly* 86, no. 4 (April 1983): 526; Patricia Bernstein, "An 'Exciting Occurrence,' " in *The First Waco Horror: The Lynching of Jesse Washington and the Rise of the NAACP* (College Station: Texas A&M University Press, 2005), 87–118.

2. The monthly magazine of the NAACP, the *Crisis*, published a supplement about the Washington lynching in 1916, based on a report by a white suffragist, Elisabeth Freeman. According to the supplement, Washington was asked for his thoughts on the mob (which mob is unclear in the text). He said, "They promised they would not [lynch me] if I would tell them about [the murder]." Some scholars speculate that Washington was intellectually disabled, based on his former teacher telling Freeman that he had difficulty learning to read, and he appeared to be first confused and then indifferent when he was informed at his trial that a guilty plea could result in the death penalty. However, his responses in court and his actions while in custody indicate that he understood that people intended to lynch him. He clearly did not write his confession, which he signed with an "X," so his signing the confession was probably some combination of strategic calculation on his part and compulsion by the sheriff. At the trial he testified, "I ain't going to tell them nothing more than what I said—that's what I done. I'm sorry I done it." He did not confess until after he was moved to Hillsboro to evade the first lynch mob from Robinson, which suggests that he believed that the confession provided his only means to avoid a lynching. "The Waco Horror," supplement to *Crisis* 12 (July 1916): 2–3; "Negro Confesses to Terrible Crime at Robinsonville," *WTH*, 9 May 1916; SoRelle, "The 'Waco Horror,' " 520–22, 526; "Mob Takes Negro," *WTH*.

3. SoRelle, "The 'Waco Horror,' " 522–23.

4. "Mob Takes Negro," *WTH*.

5. A significant portion of lynching victims in Texas were ethnic Mexicans and Native Americans who were killed as part of colonialist and white supremacist projects to consolidate Anglo political power and to violently wrest land from nonwhites. Carrigan and Webb, *Forgotten Dead*; Martinez, "Recuperating Histories of Violence"; Martinez, *The Injustice Never Leaves You*; Villanueva, *The Lynching of Mexicans in the Texas Borderlands*.

6. "Lynching in Waco," *Dallas Morning News* (hereafter cited as *DMN*), 9 October 1905.

7. Carrigan, *The Making of a Lynching Culture*, 185.

8. According to the report in the supplement to the *Crisis*, Washington was castrated, but the text does not clearly indicate whether this occurred while he was being dragged from the courthouse to the grounds of city hall or once he was at city hall. I suspect that he was "unsexed" when his ears were cut off as souvenirs since the report says, "Someone cut his ear off; someone else unsexed him. A little girl working for the firm of Goldstein and Mingle told me that she saw this done." Also, the clipping from the *Waco Times-Herald* suggests that he was castrated right before he was burned—I assume that is what is meant by "when they had finished [taking souvenir body parts] with the negro his body was mutilated." "The Waco Horror," *Crisis*, 4; "Mob Takes Negro," *WTH*.

9. "Mob Takes Negro," *WTH*; SoRelle, "The 'Waco Horror,' " 526–28; "The Waco Horror," *Crisis*, 2–4.

10. In contrast to the Washingtons, the white, land-owning Fryers remained in Robinson for generations and are easily located in the Census and other public records.

11. Armstrong, *Mary Turner and the Memory of Lynching*, 25–43; Christopher C. Meyers, " 'Killing Them by the Wholesale': A Lynching Rampage in South Georgia," *Georgia Historical Quarterly* 90, no. 2 (Summer 2006): 214–35, especially 224; Walter White, *Rope and Faggot: A Biography of Judge Lynch* (1929; repr., Notre Dame, IN: University of Notre Dame Press, 2001), 27–29; Walter White, "The Work of a Mob," *Crisis* 16, no. 5 (September 1918): 221–23.

12. "Woman Lynched by Brooks Co. Mob," *Atlanta Constitution*, 20 May 1918.

13. "Death Dealt to Man and Wife," *Savannah Morning News*, 20 May 1918.

14. Walter White, "I Investigate Lynchings," in *Witnessing Lynching: American Writers Respond*, ed. Anne P. Rice (New Brunswick, NJ: Rutgers University Press, 2003), 255.

15. White, "I Investigate Lynchings," 255.

16. Brundage, *Lynching in the New South*, 119.

17. In reference to the 1899 lynching of Sam Hose in Newman, Georgia, the last line of Ida B. Wells's pamphlet "Lynch Law in Georgia" reads, "With these facts I made my way home, thoroughly convinced that a Negro's life is a very cheap thing in Georgia." The Black Lives Matter Movement today echoes this sentiment by asserting the value of Black lives in the face of systemic racism that treats Black people as intrinsically less valuable than white people. Ida B. Wells-Barnett, *Lynch Law in Georgia* (Chicago: Chicago Colored Citizens, 1899), 18.

18. *George Fryer v. Paul Quinn College*, case no. 1194, Case Files of the 74th Judicial District Court, McLennan County Archives, Waco, Texas; Carrigan, *The Making of a Lynching Culture*, 201n63.

19. SoRelle, "The 'Waco Horror,' " 530–31; Carrigan, *The Making of a Lynching Culture*, 201.

20. For many African Americans, the integrity of the justice system had been corroded by thousands of lynchings, countless unpunished crimes committed against African Americans, and baldly discriminatory laws. This pattern of injustice was widely chronicled in local lore about mob violence, Black newspaper coverage of lynchings around the country, Ida B. Wells's crusade against lynching, and the NAACP's lobbying for federal antilynching legislation. Racist juries, judges, and sheriffs deeply undermined the African American community's faith in the due process of the law, and false accusations and the lynching of innocent people, often for minor offenses or transgressions of white supremacist norms, raised more doubts about the "justice" upheld by the courts. Smith's suspicions about George Fryer Sr. must be read in light of this well-warranted skepticism that pervaded the Black community, though Smith's accusation was not substantiated with concrete evidence to my knowledge. For more information on contemporary Black perceptions of lynching, see Ida B. Wells, *Southern Horrors and Other Writings: The Anti-Lynching Campaign of Ida B. Wells, 1892–1900*, ed. Jacqueline Jones Royster (Boston: Bedford/St. Martin's, 1997); Ralph Ginzburg, *100 Years of Lynchings* (1962; repr., Baltimore: Black Classic Press, 1988); W. E. B. Du Bois, "Jesus Christ in Texas," in *Darkwater: Voices from within the Veil* (New York: Harcourt, Brace & Howe, 1920), 123–33; White, *Rope and Faggot*.

21. "Wrong Negro Caught," *DMN*, 16 July 1905.

22. "Negro Killed by Father of Victim: Body Is Later Burned by Waco Mob," *DMN*, 27 May 1922.

23. "Negro Whipped by Vigilance Committee," *WTH*, 10 August 1905; Carrigan, *The Making of a Lynching Culture*, 201n62.

24. "Lynching at Waco," *DMN*, 9 August 1905.

25. Smith had difficulty securing legal representation, and, according to Richard D. Evans, an African American attorney in Waco who represented Smith, many members of the Black community were afraid to help Smith and afraid for Evans, too. SoRelle, "The 'Waco Horror,' " 531.

26. Elisabeth Freeman, "The Waco Lynching," Box I:C370, Folder 14: "Lynching, Waco, Tex., 1916," National Association for the Advancement of Colored People Papers, Manuscripts Division, Library of Congress (hereafter cited as NAACP LoC); SoRelle, "The 'Waco Horror,' " 530n25.

27. Levine, *Black Culture and Black Consciousness*, 206.

28. The threat of violent (and economic) retaliation against African American leaders as well as their communities more generally hemmed in more radical rhetoric throughout the South, at least in front of whites. In fact, NAACP branches in the South routinely requested that the national office send correspondence in unmarked envelopes as a safety precaution. Eventually, at the behest of "our 'City dads' " who worried that the lynching tarnished Waco's image, Gildersleeve stopped selling souvenir photographs

of Washington's death, and two weeks after the Washington lynching, the faculty at Baylor University issued a belated resolution, "declar[ing] that we abhor and deplore the violent acts of the mob, although we do not condone the dastardly offense of which the said negro made confession." The Baylor faculty revealed their deeper motivations for issuing the resolution in stating, "we apprehend that the incident will evoke from the outside world reproaches unmerited by the majority of the people of our fair city and county." Freeman, "The Waco Lynching," NAACP LoC; SoRelle, "The 'Waco Horror,'" 530n25; "The Waco Horror," *Crisis*, 6; Resolution of the Baylor University Faculty, 27 May 1916, [Waco] Community Race Relations Coalition Records, Texas Collection, Baylor University.

29. Reverend Strong was the first president of the Waco Branch, and both he and Reverend Jenkins served on the executive committee. Application of Charter of the Waco, Texas Branch of the National Association for the Advancement of Colored People, 16 June 1919, Box I:G205, Folder 14: "Waco, Texas," NAACP LoC. A man named R. H. Hines had expressed interest in starting a branch in Waco in January 1916, but no record of a 1916 charter exists in the NAACP Records. R. H. Hines to NAACP, 18 January 1916, Box I:G205, Folder 14: "Waco, Texas," NAACP LoC.

30. Author's interview with Robert Hall in Valdosta, Georgia, 28 January 2012.

31. Memo from Walter F. White to John R. Shillady Re: Interview with George U. Spratling at Quitman, Ga., 12 November 1918, Box I:C355, Folder 9, NAACP LoC; Memo from Walter F. White to C. P. Dan, 16 November 1918, Box I:C355, Folder 9, NAACP LoC; Brundage, *Lynching in the New South*, 231. For more on how the NAACP publicized the lynchings in their immediate aftermath to lobby both the governor of Georgia and the president of the United States to condemn lynching and prosecute lynchers, see Armstrong, *Mary Turner and the Memory of Lynching*, 43–69, 231.

32. Robert W. Bagnall to George F. Porter, 19 March 1923, Box I:G201, Folder 25, NAACP LoC.

33. The 1920 Federal Census for Colquitt County, Georgia, listed Conie L. Manning as an adopted girl and Otha Manning as an adopted boy in the household of James and Viola Godfrey. (Leaster Grant affectionately called her aunt, Aunt Ola.) Those entries were recorded on 12 January 1920. The Godfreys moved to Barney, Georgia, a couple of months later, where they showed up in the 1920 Federal Census for Brooks County, Georgia, which was recorded on 10 April 1920. The Barney entries listed Conny Manning as a niece and Ophy Manning as a nephew in the Godfrey household. Since the Godfreys raised Leaster, "Conie L." or "Conny" were probably aliases for Leaster, perhaps another precaution to protect her.

34. The *Crisis* published Walter White's investigation of the lynchings in Brooks and Lowndes Counties, and the NAACP frequently cited the case in its campaigns to end lynching and pass federal antilynching legislation. Armstrong, *Mary Turner and the Memory of Lynching*, 43–64.

35. Oral History of J. Charles Jones, 16 June 1993, from *Behind the Veil: Documenting African-American Life in the Jim Crow South*, Center for Documentary Studies, David M. Rubenstein Rare Book and Manuscript Library, Duke University (hereafter cited as *Behind the Veil* Duke).

36. " 'Unknown Parties' Who Lynched Three in South Carolina Known," *New York Amsterdam News*, 3 November 1926.

37. At least seven other pregnant Black women were lynched, and news of these lynchings often circulated more widely and gained more notoriety due to the politics of protection, rendering the lynching of mothers and children particularly disturbing to the public. Crystal N. Feimster, *Southern Horrors: Women and the Politics of Rape and Lynching* (Cambridge, MA: Harvard University Press, 2009), 174.

38. Ida Legett Hall, "History of the Negro in Waco, Texas," *Waco Heritage and History* 14, no. 3 (Spring 1984): 34; Carrigan, *The Making of a Lynching Culture*, 202. Hall's article was originally an assignment for a sociology course at Baylor University in 1928.

39. Although Eliza Jane Owens's granddaughter, Alice Owens Caulfield, did not know for certain whether her grandparents had been born enslaved when she was interviewed in 1993, the 1900 and 1910 Census records for McLennan County, Texas, confirm that both Robert and Eliza Jane Owens were born in Georgia in 1834 and 1845 respectively, so they were probably born enslaved. Oral Memoirs of Alice Owens Caulfield, 22 January and 15 and 18 February 1993, Baylor University Institute for Oral History, Baylor University, 2–4, 138–40 (hereafter cited as Baylor Oral History).

40. Oral Memoirs of Alice Owens Caulfield, 3.

41. W. E. B. Du Bois, *Black Reconstruction in America 1860–1880* (1935; repr., New York: Free Press, 1998), 124.

42. Oral Memoirs of Marcus Langley Cooper Jr., 8 August 1980, Baylor Oral History, 127.

43. I have resisted writing a more concrete estimate of the total number of lynchings because such a figure is difficult to determine with any certainty. Also, the definition of lynching is so fluid and contested that many documented acts of violence encompassed by even the most commonly invoked definitions have not yet been counted. Recent studies of lynching have undertaken the painstaking work of uncovering and documenting more lynchings, especially in the US West, but even those lists are incomplete. For more information on lynching records and demographics, see the University of Washington's Center for Studies in Demography and Ecology lynching database compiled by Amy Kate Bailey, E. M. Beck, and Stewart E. Tolnay (hereafter cited as CSDE Lynching Database), as well as the Equal Justice Initiative's report, *Lynching in America: Confronting the Legacy of Racial Terror*.

44. Gonzales-Day, *Lynching in the West*; Carrigan and Webb, *Forgotten Dead*; Martinez, "Recuperating Histories of Violence in the Americas."

45. I borrow the term "anatomy" from James R. McGovern, *Anatomy of a Lynching: The Killing of Claude Neal* (Baton Rouge: Louisiana State University Press, 1982).

46. People from out of town began to congregate on the courthouse lawn the night before the trial in anticipation of the lynching, so the lynching was far from spontaneous. "The Waco Horror," *Crisis*, 3.

47. "The Waco Horror," *Crisis*, 6.

48. Goldsby's term, "cultural logic," is particularly generative since it offers a way to understand lynching outside the bounds of southern white supremacy (that is, not just as the product of region and racial animosity alone but also in terms of other forces like gender, class, and modernity) and as a cultural phenomenon that evolved in concert with the historical changes propelled by modernity (by which she means the period of industrialization in the United States starting in roughly 1880). Lynching was not antimodern but rather quintessentially modern. She argues that "the 'cultural logic' of lynching enabled it to emerge and persist throughout the modern era because its violence 'fit' within broader, national cultural developments." Goldsby, *A Spectacular Secret*, 4–9, 12–42, 282–88, quote on 6. See also Carrigan, *The Making of a Lynching Culture*, 10–14.

49. After centuries of white southerners enslaving African Americans and passing a battery of laws and customs designed to control free and freed Black people, identity formation among white southerners was already intimately entangled with anti-Black violence by the late nineteenth century when southern lynching was at its peak.

50. The 1910 and 1920 Census records list the population of Waco at 26,425 and 38,500 respectively, and assuming that the rate of growth was steady during that decade, SoRelle estimates that the 1916 population was around 33,760. In 1910 and 1920, African Americans made up 23.0 percent (6,067 people) and 20.1 percent (7,726 people) of the population of Waco respectively, and the corresponding numbers for whites were 76.9 percent (20,333 people) and 77.3 percent (29,762 people). Note that during this period, the number of Mexican-born residents of McLennan County grew from 17 in 1900 to 496 in 1910 to 1,502 in 1920. Based on these figures, even if people poured in from the surrounding towns, the mob of 15,000 probably included more than half of the white population of Waco. SoRelle, "The 'Waco Horror,' " 518n4; Carrigan, *The Making of a Lynching Culture*, 171, 174; "The Waco Horror," *Crisis*, 1.

51. "The Waco Horror," *Crisis*, 5.

52. "The Waco Horror," *Crisis*, 4.

53. "The Waco Horror," *Crisis*, 5.

54. "The Waco Horror," *Crisis*, 3.

55. None of the people involved in the 1918 lynching rampage in southern Georgia faced grand juries, much less prosecutions or convictions, nor were they ostracized by their white neighbors. Many died old men and women,

having lived for decades with no fear of legal repercussions for their roles in these deaths. Even with Gildersleeve's photographic evidence identifying members of the lynch mob, nobody was held accountable for Washington's lynching either.

56. "Mob Takes Negro," *WTH.*

57. I have decided not to reprint photographs of lynchings in this book, aside from the photographs of effigies that appear in chapter 4. However, I describe some lynching photographs when necessary for my analysis.

58. In his investigation of the Brooks County lynching spree, the NAACP's Walter White wrote, "Since the lynchings, more than five hundred Negroes have left the immediate vicinity of Valdosta alone and many more have expressed the determination that they too were going to leave as soon as they could dispose of their lands and gather their crops. This wholesale migration occurred in spite of threats made that any Negro who attempted to leave the section would thus show that he was implicated in the murder of Smith and would be dealt with accordingly. Hundreds of acres of untilled land flourishing with weeds and dozens of deserted farm-houses give their own mute testimony of the Negroes' attitude toward a community in which lynching mobs are allowed to visit vengeance upon members of their race." White, "The Work of a Mob," *Crisis*, 223. The data collected in the Agricultural Census support White's observations about a mass Black exodus. The Agricultural Censuses of 1910 and 1925 record a decline in Black and other nonwhite farm owners in Brooks County from 332 to 260 (72 fewer) and in Black and other nonwhite farmers from 1,369 to 978 (391 fewer), while the numbers for white farm owners and white farmers stayed nearly the same. The figures for Lowndes County show an even more dramatic decline: the number of Black and other nonwhite farm owners decreased from 366 to 217 (149 fewer), and the number of Black and other nonwhite farmers decreased from 1,125 to 648 (477 fewer). However, whites in Lowndes County benefited greatly from their Black neighbors fleeing the area: the number of white farm owners increased from 711 to 1,107 (396 more) even though the number of white farmers decreased from 1,190 to 1,128 (62 fewer). Unfortunately, the Agricultural Census of 1920, which would provide a more useful comparison, did not include county-level numbers. Department of Commerce and Labor, *Thirteenth Census of the United States Taken in the Year 1910: Agriculture 1909 and 1910*, vol. 6 (Washington, DC: Government Printing Office, 1913), 331, 338, 345, 352; Department of Commerce, *United States Census of Agriculture 1925*, pt. 2 (Washington, DC: Government Printing Office, 1927), 405, 414.

59. "The Waco Horror," *Crisis*, 5–7. The *Crisis* supplement reprinted several photographs of Washington's lynching taken by Gildersleeve, including photographs in which the faces of several members of the mob are clear enough to identify them, and among the faces are those of young white boys.

60. Big Bill Broonzy, Memphis Slim, and Sonny Boy Williamson, *Blues in the Mississippi Night* (CD, Alan Lomax Collection, Rounder Records 82161–1860-2). The quote, taken from track 16 ("Conversation Continues"), is from a story that Broonzy tells about working on a levee camp probably during the 1910s or 1920s.

61. Oral Memoirs of Joseph Martin Dawson, 17 February 1971, Baylor Oral History, 53. Dawson said the mob was five thousand people, not the fifteen thousand reported by local newspapers the day after the lynching. Carrigan notes that estimates white people made for the size of the mob decreased both in the days after the lynching and in the decades that followed, as shame about the barbarity of Washington's death set in. Carrigan, *The Making of a Lynching Culture*, 193.

62. During the interview Dawson recorded at Baylor University in 1971, he explained that a committee of Klan leaders and members had approached him about joining the Klan, and he declined their invitation. The interviewer also asked if any members of his congregation led the lynching, and he answered no. He noted that, although the Klan may have instigated the violence and participated in the burning, "the lowest order of people in the City of Waco" actually led and carried out the lynching. Oral Memoirs of Joseph Martin Dawson, 52–53, 55–57, quote on 56. Bernstein claims that the Klan did not arrive in Waco until 1920, though Dawson's memories of being solicited to join their ranks suggests either that the Klan may have arrived earlier or that Dawson misremembered the timing of this exchange. Bernstein, *The First Waco Horror*, 179–80, 182.

63. Oral Memoirs of Joseph Martin Dawson, 54. SoRelle notes that Dean John L. Kesler of Baylor University responded to criticism from Oswald Garrison Villard (owner of the *Nation*, founding member of the NAACP, and grandson of the abolitionist William Lloyd Garrison) by saying that Waco ministers, including Caldwell and Dawson, denounced lynching from their pulpits. At the same time, the supplement to the *Crisis* indicates that Caldwell was the only Waco pastor to speak out. Perhaps the line Caldwell drew between condemning lynching and betraying his expected role as a white southern man compelled him to stop short of signing Dawson's resolution. SoRelle, "The 'Waco Horror,' " 532; "The Waco Horror," *Crisis*, 8.

64. In reference to the lynchings of Jesse Washington and others in Waco, the *Houston Informer* referred to Waco as "Barbecueville" in two January 1923 articles. Also, Armstrong notes that local white newspapers in southern Georgia downplayed the 1918 lynchings by reducing the number of lynchings, shrinking the size of the mobs and then calling them small vigilance committees, claiming the mobs came from outside Brooks and Lowndes Counties, denying that tensions existed between white and Black residents, and even denying that lynchings had occurred. With greater outside condemnation came eventual white silence, at least in public, but the size of these mobs—which rose to several hundred in some cases—and the brazen

boasting about the lynchings spoke to a deep sense of pride regarding lynching, not circumspection. Carrigan, *The Making of a Lynching Culture*, 198; Armstrong, *Mary Turner and the Memory of Lynching*, 42.

65. Lynching studies that describe the composition and assemblage of lynch mobs include Brundage, "Mobs and Ritual," in *Lynching in the New South*, 17–48; Michael J. Pfeifer, "The Making of Mobs: The Social Relations of Lynchers," in *Rough Justice: Lynching and American Society, 1874–1947* (Urbana: University of Illinois Press, 2004), 38–66; Tolnay and Beck, *A Festival of Violence*.

66. Donald G. Mathews, *At the Altar of Lynching: Burning Sam Hose in the American South* (New York: Cambridge University Press, 2018), 263–68.

67. Among the many cases in which lynch mobs indiscriminately killed Black people unconnected to the intended lynching victim were the murder of a Black worker by the leader of a lynch mob impatiently waiting for the bloodhounds to arrive for the manhunt of Luther Holbert and his wife in Sunflower County, Mississippi, in 1904 and the lynching of a Black minister, Lige Strickland, for supposedly being involved in the murder of a white man in Coweta County, Georgia, in 1898. Chris Myers Asch, *The Senator and the Sharecropper: The Freedom Struggles of James O. Eastland and Fannie Lou Hamer* (Chapel Hill: University of North Carolina Press, 2008), 24; Litwack, *Trouble in Mind*, 282–83. The people who lynched Chime Riley went to the trouble to hide his body, which suggests that, though they attempted to rationalize his death by somehow connecting him to Smith's murder, they may have worried that the white community would look at his death as categorically different from the others.

68. Walter White, "I Investigate Lynchings," 255.

69. Armstrong notes that, after a week or so, whites in Brooks and Lowndes Counties did not appear to speak about the lynching spree, which may be because the lynching spree relieved their racial anxieties enough that they could return to "normal" life. I suspect some lynchers continued to talk about their role in the lynchings and what they witnessed among themselves, especially when threats to the white supremacist hierarchy reemerged. These memories may have helped some whites in the area quell their racial anxieties. Armstrong, *Mary Turner and the Memory of Lynching*, 5–6, 41–43.

70. Several scholars have written about lynching photographs, which were often sold as postcards so that members of the mob could send them to their family and friends. James Allen, *Without Sanctuary: Lynching Photography in America* (Santa Fe, NM: Twin Palms Publishers, 2000); Apel, *Imagery of Lynching*; Apel and Smith, *Lynching Photographs*; Courtney R. Baker, "Introduction" and "Framed and Shamed: Looking at the Lynched Body," in *Humane Insight: Looking at Images of African American Suffering and Death* (Urbana: University of Illinois Press, 2015), 1–17, 35–68; Goldsby, "Through a Different Lens: Lynching Photography at the Turn of the

Nineteenth Century," in *A Spectacular Secret*, 214–81; Leigh Raiford, "No Relation to the Facts about Lynching," in *Imprisoned in a Luminous Glare: Photography and the African American Freedom Struggle* (Chapel Hill: University of North Carolina Press, 2011), 29–66; Wood, "The Spectator Has a Picture in His Mind to Remember for a Long Time: Photography" and "We Wanted to be Boosters and Not Knockers: Photography and Antilynching Activism," in *Lynching and Spectacle*, 71–111, 179–221.

71. "The Waco Horror," *Crisis*, 6; "Mob Takes Negro," *WTH*.

72. Oral Memoirs of James Kuykendall Evetts, 23 May 1977, Baylor Oral History, 33. Evetts's father as well as the chief of police had tried to prevent the lynching, and Evetts told the story to illustrate his father's commitment to principles and justice. I was unable to identify a 1912 lynching in Bell County, where Killeen is located. However, Evetts may have been referring to the 1910 lynching of Henry Gentry in Belton, Texas, also in Bell County. Carrigan, *The Making of a Lynching Culture*, app. A.

73. James Baldwin, "To Crush a Serpent," in *The Cross of Redemption: Uncollected Writings*, ed. Randall Kenan (New York: Pantheon Books, 2010), 165.

74. James H. Cone, *The Cross and the Lynching Tree* (Maryknoll, NY: Orbis Books, 2011), 3. Artists, from fiction writers and poets to painters and sculptors, have flipped the script on the intended impact of lynching rituals on the white community, turning an affirmation of white power into a condemnation of white immorality. To criticize the hypocrisy of white southern Christians, Du Bois published a short story about a Georgia lynch mob that hangs a Black convict whom Jesus then redeems, "Jesus Christ in Georgia," in the December 1911 issue of the *Crisis*. He later published the story in *Darkwater* (1920) under the title "Jesus Christ in Texas." See also Langston Hughes's poem, "Christ in Alabama," which is discussed in Apel, *Imagery of Lynching*, 113–14. See also Mathews, *At the Altar of Lynching*, 259–71; Wood, "A Hell of Fire upon Earth: Religion," in *Lynching and Spectacle*, 45–68.

75. For more on the ritual aspects of lynching, see Brundage, "Mobs and Ritual"; Harris, "Ritual and Ritual Violence in American Life and Culture," in *Exorcising Blackness*, 1–28; Wood, "They Want to See the Thing Done," in *Lynching and Spectacle*, 19–44.

76. Ida B. Wells, *Southern Horrors*, 52.

77. George M. Fredrickson, *The Black Image in the White Mind: The Debate on Afro-American Character and Destiny, 1817–1914* (1971; repr., Hanover, NH: Wesleyan University Press, 1987), 276.

78. Whereas Fredrickson asserted that the trope that rendered Black men as "beasts" was a "projection of unacknowledged guilt feelings derived from their own [whites'] brutality towards blacks," Winthrop Jordan argued that white anxieties about not measuring up to the abilities of Black people underlay racism and the corresponding fear of racial equality. Similarly, whites projected sexual licentiousness onto Black people because they feared the unrestrained animal within themselves. Apel, *Imagery of Lynching*, 24, 26–29;

Fredrickson, *The Black Image in the White Mind*, 282; Winthrop D. Jordan, *White over Black: American Attitudes toward the Negro, 1550–1812* (Chapel Hill: University of North Carolina Press, 1968), 154–63, 577–82.

79. Jordan, *White over Black*, 154–58, quote on 157.

80. For more on accusations of rape and lynching, see Apel, *Imagery of Lynching*, 23–28; Brundage, *Lynching in the New South*, 58–72; Feimster, *Southern Horrors*, 73–79, 88–103. During the lynching of Claude Neal in Greenwood, Florida, on October 27, 1934, the white men who tortured and killed him cut off his penis and testicles then forced him to eat them. Neal's torture vividly demonstrates the extent of white men's anxieties about Black male sexuality. McGovern, *Anatomy of a Lynching*, 80–81. For more on how lynching and rape intersect, see Patricia Hill Collins, *Black Sexual Politics: African Americans, Gender, and the New Racism* (New York: Routledge, 2004), 63–66, 216–23.

81. Many southern white women, most notoriously Rebecca Felton, embraced elements of the white patriarchy due to the racial benefits they reaped as a result, and they often deployed the rhetoric of "protecting white womanhood" in their defenses of lynching. Feimster, "New Southern Women and the Triumph of White Supremacy," in *Southern Horrors*, 125–57. One notable exception was the ASWPL, which was a segregated organization that used direct appeals to southern politicians and law enforcement to prevent lynchings. The exclusion of Black women from the ASWPL and the organization's opposition to federal antilynching legislation were but two of the organization's many limitations, but the ASWPL directly disavowed "the claim of lynchers and mobsters that they were acting solely in the defense of womanhood. In light of the facts, this claim can no longer be used as a protection to those who lynch." *Death by Parties Unknown* (pamphlet), January 1936, Box 5, Folder 6, Jessie Daniel Ames Papers #3686, Southern Historical Collection, Wilson Library, University of North Carolina at Chapel Hill (hereafter cited as Ames Papers UNC). For more analysis of the ASWPL and its founder, Jessie Daniel Ames, see Jacquelyn Dowd Hall, *Revolt against Chivalry: Jessie Daniel Ames and the Women's Campaign against Lynching*, rev. ed. (New York: Columbia University Press, 1993). For a more general overview of women's organizations in the Jim Crow South, see Glenda Gilmore, *Gender and Jim Crow: Women and the Politics of White Supremacy in North Carolina, 1896–1920* (Chapel Hill: University of North Carolina Press, 1996); Evelyn Brooks Higginbotham, *Righteous Discontent: The Women's Movement in the Black Baptist Church, 1880–1920* (Cambridge, MA: Harvard University Press, 1993). For more on the politics of protection as it pertains (or not) to African American women, see Kali Nicole Gross, "African American Women, Mass Incarceration, and the Politics of Protection," *Journal of American History* 102, no. 1 (2015): 25–33; Sarah Haley, " 'Like I Was a Man': Chain Gangs, Gender, and the Domestic Carceral Sphere in Jim Crow Georgia," *Signs* 39, no. 1 (2013): 53–77.

82. White, *Rope and Faggot*, 56–57; Brundage, *Lynching in the New South*, 68. The ringleader of the first Robinson mob that attempted to lynch Washington expressed the grave importance of his role as a protector of white women, telling the sheriff that wives, daughters, and sisters "kissed us good bye and told us to do our duty" before they set out for the county jail to retrieve Washington. SoRelle, "The 'Waco Horror,' " 521; Bernstein, *The First Waco Horror*, 96.

83. "Negro Confesses," *WTH*.

84. "Along the Color Line," *Crisis*, July 1911, 99–100. Like Nelson, Julia Baker, an infant who was lynched in Lake City, South Carolina, in 1898, died because a mob looking for her father set fire to their home while the family was sleeping, and to prevent the family from fleeing their burning home, the mob shot into the home, killing her and her father. Similarly, Bertha Lowman died at the hands of a mob near Aiken, South Carolina, in 1926 because of an earlier incident involving law enforcement officers looking for her father, whom they suspected of bootlegging. In both cases, they were victims of lynching due to their proximity to a male family member who was the primary target. John L. Dart, *The Famous Trial of the Eight Men Indicted for the Lynching of Frazier B. Baker and His Baby, Late U.S. Postmaster in Lake City, S.C. in the U.S. Circuit Court at Charleston, S.C. April 10–22, 1899*, John L. Dart Family Papers, Avery Research Center, College of Charleston, Charleston, SC (hereafter cited as Avery CofC); " 'Unknown Parties' Who Lynched Three in South Carolina Known," *New York Amsterdam News*, 3 November 1926.

85. "Woman Raped and Lynched by Mob of Southern White Men," *Chicago Defender*, 18 December 1915; Feimster, *Southern Horrors*, 174n67.

86. The most comprehensive analysis of the lynching of Black women is Feimster's *Southern Horrors*, and she suggests that the prevalence of rape as part of lynching rituals was more extensive than the printed historical record captured. Feimster, "The Lynching of Black and White Women," in *Southern Horrors*, 158–85. Also see Armstrong, *Mary Turner and the Memory of Lynching*; Simien, *Gender and Lynching*.

87. "Negro Woman Is Hanged by Brooks County Mob," *Atlanta Journal*, 20 May 1918.

88. In pointing out the lack of protection granted Black women, I am not implying that patriarchal, and frankly infantilizing, protection from men is what women of either race desired. As Black feminists from bell hooks to Kimberlé Crenshaw have made clear, a truly just society would not simply give groups previously excluded from power structures access to those structures but rather reimagine those structures such that they led to liberation. Rather than seeking a form of protection steeped in patriarchal control over women, a reimagined sense of protection would be couched in basic citizenship rights, justice, and the value of preserving human dignity.

89. The three men hanged or burned on the grounds of the Camp Ground Methodist Church during that deadly week in May 1918 weren't the first to

be lynched at that church, nor would they be the last. Other victims included an unidentified man in the 1950s, whom I discuss in chapter 2. As recently as 2013, a Black student named Kendrick Johnson died under
mysterious circumstances at Lowndes High School in nearby Valdosta. His
dead body was found inside a rolled-up gym mat, and an autopsy arranged
by his parents showed fatal injuries from being struck. His family and members of the community successfully pressured the state of Georgia to reopen
the investigation into his death with the assistance of the US Justice Department, though his death is still considered an accident and his parents were
forced to pay the legal fees of defendants in their civil suits alleging a cover-
up. The *Valdosta Daily Times* has the most comprehensive coverage of the investigation into Johnson's death, but also see Jordan Conn, "A Death in
Valdosta," Grantland (blog), 6 September 2013, http://grantland.com;
Christian Boone and Mark Niesse, "Mystery Surrounds Valdosta Student's
Strange Death," *Atlanta Journal-Constitution*, 13 October 2013; Alan Binder,
"Federal Review Opened in Georgia Death," *New York Times*, 31 October
2013; "Kendrick Johnson's Parents Will Exhume His Body—Again," *Atlanta
Journal-Constitution*, 20 June 2018; "New Federal KJ Suit Filed," *Valdosta
Daily Times*, 24 January 2020.

90. Oral Memoirs of Carrie Skipwith Mayfield, 22 December 1989, Baylor Oral
History, 16.

91. Oral Memoirs of Carrie Skipwith Mayfield, 14–16.

92. Oral Memoirs of Carrie Skipwith Mayfield, 15.

93. For more on "spatial acts" that reclaim spaces that have been defined by
white geographies and white ways of knowing, see Katherine McKittrick,
Demonic Grounds: Black Women and the Cartographies of Struggle (Minneapolis: University of Minnesota Press, 2006).

94. Paul Laurence Dunbar, "The Haunted Oak," in *Witnessing Lynching: American Writers Respond*, ed. Anne P. Rice (New Brunswick, NJ: Rutgers University Press, 2003), 90–91.

Chapter Two. Silence

Excerpt from "Terminus" from *Far District* by Ishion Hutchinson. Copyright © 2010, 2021 by Ishion Hutchinson. Reprinted by permission of Farrar, Straus and Giroux. All Rights Reserved. Reprinted by permission of
Faber and Faber Ltd.

1. Author's interview with Jesse Pennington in Jackson, Mississippi, 5 November 2011.

2. In December 1946, Harris Jesse Fields shot and killed in cold blood two
Black men, David Jones and Simon Toombs, just a few towns south of
Greenville in Anguilla. Some members of the Fields family said that Harris
Fields and his brothers Bill and Tom had gotten into a fight with a Black
man who had taken a company car without permission after hours to pick

up some machinery, but instead of returning the car afterward, he went to a juke joint to get drunk. Fields did not face any legal consequences for the double murder. The similarities between the consequences of "joyriding" in 1946 and 1954 are eerie. Molly Walling, *Death in the Delta: Uncovering a Mississippi Family Secret* (Jackson: University of Mississippi Press, 2012), 3–4, 10–11, 27–28, 55–56.

3. The white supremacist backlash against the *Brown v. Board of Education* (1954) decision was swift and intense, and even though the lead case was from Kansas, white southern outrage at the decision led to a spike in anti-Black violence and eventually to the founding of the Citizens' Council, a white supremacist civic organization. The near-lynching of Pennington, just one month after the case was decided, was part of this backlash.

4. William Bradford Huie, "Whole State Condones It: The Shocking Story of Approved Killing in Mississippi," *Look*, 24 January 1956, 46–49. In this chapter, I examine the conspiratorial thinking among white southerners in reaction to Till's death and the trial that followed, but I also bring the Till case into my analysis in chapter 4, where I consider the persistence of lynching after 1940. Some key works on Till include Elliott J. Gorn, *Let the People See: The Story of Emmett Till* (New York: Oxford University Press, 2018); Christopher Metress, *The Lynching of Emmett Till: A Documentary Narrative* (Charlottesville: University of Virginia Press, 2002); Dave Tell, *Remembering Emmett Till* (Chicago: University of Chicago Press, 2019); Mamie Till-Mobley with Christopher Benson, *Death of Innocence: The Story of the Hate Crime That Changed America* (New York: One World, 2003); Timothy B. Tyson, *The Blood of Emmett Till* (New York: Simon & Schuster, 2017).

5. Laymon uses the phrase "swinging back" to capture when the pent-up frustration of being expected to comply with racist social mores—a part of what he terms "slowly killing yourself"—boils over into acts of self-defense and anger. These bursts of defiance carry dangerous, and often deadly, consequences for Black boys and men from Till to Trayvon Martin and to Laymon himself. Kiese Laymon, "How to Slowly Kill Yourself and Others in America," in *How to Slowly Kill Yourself and Others in America: Essays* (Chicago: Bolden Books, 2013), 35–48.

6. Author's interview with Jesse Pennington.

7. John Griffin Jones, ed., "Shelby Foote: August 16, 1979," in *Mississippi Writers Talking* (Jackson: University Press of Mississippi, 1982), 44–45.

8. Jones, ed., "Shelby Foote: August 16, 1979," 45–46.

9. The following individuals were lynched in Washington County, Mississippi: Green Jackson (Greenville) on February 5, 1891; Louise Stevenson (Hollandale) on September 27/28, 1891; Grant White (Hollandale) on September 27, 1891; Wesley Gould (Leland) on July 7/12, 1898; William Edwards (Deep Creek Bridge) on March 27, 1900; Vincent Serio and John Serio (Erwin) on July 11, 1901; John/Robert Dennis (Greenville) on June 4, 1903; [first name unknown] Clark and [first name unknown] Van Horne (Trail

Lake) on June 3, 1904; [first name unknown] Mayfield (Trail Lake) on June 4, 1904; unknown African American (Helm Station) on March 5, 1905; William Robinson (Greenville) on August 12/17, 1909; Minter Moore (Greenville) on May 5/7, 1912; Samuel Petty (Leland) on February 24, 1914. Ginzburg, *100 Years of Lynchings*, 263–65; CSDE Lynching Database.

10. John M. Barry, *Rising Tide: The Great Mississippi Flood of 1927 and How It Changed America* (New York: Touchstone, 1997), 102–3, 111–20, 143–55, 303–35. After emancipation, W. A. Percy leased land on his plantation to sharecroppers, a practice often described as debt peonage. LeRoy Percy, the son, also owned vast expanses of land sharecropped by Italian immigrants and African Americans; muckraking journalist Mary Quackenbos threatened to expose his illegal contracts and the squalid living conditions of his sharecroppers until President Theodore Roosevelt intervened on his behalf. A few decades later, during the Mississippi Flood of 1927, LeRoy Percy tried to prevent further damage to the levees near Greenville by forcing Black people at gunpoint to reinforce the levee for no pay. Rather than evacuate Black people suffering without potable water and sufficient food or shelter, he decided that the preservation of his labor force and his land outweighed their well-being. Also note that Barry claims that only one lynching occurred in Washington County (122) and that the Percys had "always prevented such happenings [as lynchings]" in Greenville (330). Barry not only considers the lynching of two Italian immigrants, John and Vincent Serio, to be murders but also champions W. A. Percy's prevention of a lynching in the 1870s (103). As Barry's own writing illustrates, the production and preservation of silences in the historical memory of lynching continued well into the late twentieth century.

11. Michel-Rolph Trouillot, *Silencing the Past: Power and the Production of History* (Boston: Beacon Press, 1995), 27.

12. James Baldwin, *No Name in the Street* (1972; repr., New York: Vintage International, 2007), 33.

13. Goldsby's analysis of lynching as a "cultural secret" is also helpful for understanding white silences. She argues that the move to push lynching to the margins of modernity (that is, lynching as a blemish on modernity-as-progress narratives) rather than to understand lynching as a product of modernity contributes to its secret nature. Also, many thanks to Mostafa Minawi for suggesting that I use the phrase "white noise" to signal both the white supremacist politics that these silences served and the way this collective denial attempted to drown out white culpability for thousands of lynchings. Goldsby, *A Spectacular Secret*, 6, 27.

14. C. W. Sherlock to Harry S. Truman, 23 December 1947, Subgroup C, X: Civil Rights, A: Anti-Lynch, Box 1, Folder 4, Richard B. Russell, Jr. Collection, Richard B. Russell Library for Political Research and Studies, University of Georgia Libraries, Athens (hereafter cited as Russell Collection UGA).

15. For more on the 1946 lynchings of George Dorsey, Mae Murray Dorsey, Dorothy Malcom, and Roger Malcom in Monroe, Georgia, see Laura Wexler, *Fire in a Canebrake: The Last Mass Lynching in America* (New York: Scribner, 2003).

16. F. P. Bennett to Richard B. Russell, 31 July 1946, Subgroup C, X: Civil Rights, OO: Supreme Court, Box 201, Folder 4, Russell Collection UGA.

17. At the trial of Roy Bryant and J. W. Milam for the 1955 lynching of Till, witnesses like county sheriff H. G. Strider and deputy sheriff James Cochran disputed that the badly disfigured and decomposed body was Till's. In fact, in his closing arguments at the trial, Milam and Bryant's defense attorney, John Whitten, speculated, "If these people [the NAACP] had the opportunity to create a commotion to stir up a trial such as this and focus national attention on Mississippi and focus national attention on the strained relations here, they would do it. . . . They would not be above putting a rotting, stinking body in the river in the hope he would be identified as Emmett Till." A white physician from nearby Greenwood, Mississippi, L. B. Otken, examined Till's corpse, and two years later wrote a letter to Mississippi senator James O. Eastland, describing the body as "that of a man 55 to 60 years old, practically white, with dirty reddish blond hair." Clearly, white Mississippians were willing to perform elaborate mental gymnastics in order to hide the truth of white supremacist violence. John Herbers, "Till's Mother Due to Testify: Will Dispute Claim Body Wasn't Son's," *State Times* (Jackson), 21 September 1955; James L. Kilgallen, "Wright Tells Story of Negro's Kidnapping," *Commercial Appeal* (Memphis), 21 September 1955; Huie, "Whole State Condones It"; "Mississippi Jury Acquits White Men in Slaying of Negro Boy of Chicago," *Norfolk Ledger-Dispatch and the Portsmouth Star* (Norfolk-Portsmouth, VA), 24 September 1955; Paul Hendrickson, "Mississippi Haunting," *Washington Post Magazine*, 27 February 2000, 26.

18. The state WPA officials in Mississippi, for example, held back materials deemed too inflammatory (that is, those that featured overt discussions of white slaveholders' violence against enslaved people) from the WPA slave narratives so they would not be included in the Library of Congress collection. George P. Rawick, ed., *The American Slave: A Composite Autobiography*, suppl., ser. 1, vol. 6, *Mississippi Narratives: Part 1* (Westport, CT: Greenwood Publishing Co., 1977), xxi–xxii, xxvi.

19. Quashie uses the term "quiet" to describe "the expressiveness of the inner life, unable to be expressed fully but nonetheless articulate and informing one's humanity," which partly accounts for these Black silences. However, he distinguishes between "silence" and "quiet" because "silence often denotes something that is suppressed or repressed, and is an interiority that is about withholding, absence, and stillness." Although unspeakable memories are "unable to be expressed fully" like the quiet that Quashie describes, the inability to put those memories into words usually stems from suppression or

repression, making them silences. In general, memories usually include an element of quiet in that they are embedded in the interior life and often push up against the limits of language and other forms of expression, and quiet certainly speaks to many aspects of the blues sensibility, which is ultimately about contending with oneself and one's blues to find peace and joy. Quashie, *The Sovereignty of Quiet*, 24, 22.

20. Oral History of Cleo Jeffers, 11 July 1995, *Behind the Veil*.

21. Baldwin, *No Name in the Street*, 190.

22. For a related discussion of the politics of refusal, see Sarah Haley, *No Mercy Here: Gender, Punishment, and the Making of Jim Crow Modernity* (Chapel Hill: University of North Carolina Press, 2016).

23. Author's interview with Robert Hall in Valdosta, Georgia, 28 January 2012.

24. Author's interview with Robert Hall.

25. Author's interview with Robert Hall.

26. As a boy, Rufus Morrison, whose family owned the land abutting the site of Mary Turner's lynching, witnessed the lynching. He and his family hid in the fields near their home in case the mob came for them, and he witnessed the entire gruesome spectacle carried out by his white neighbors.

27. Author's interview with Robert Hall. See also Goldsby's discussion of lynchings as "unspeakable acts" that had the capacity to "traumatize survivors into silence, leaving gaps of knowledge in its wake," and what Jennifer D. Williams calls the "unrepresentability" of lynching. Goldsby, *A Spectacular Secret*, 35; Jennifer D. Williams, " 'A Woman Was Lynched the Other Day': Memory, Gender, and the Limits of Traumatic Representation," in *Gender and Lynching: The Politics of Memory*, ed. Evelyn M. Simien (New York: Palgrave Macmillan, 2011), 86, 88–89, 92.

28. Author's interview with Audrey Grant in Adel, Georgia, 20 May 2013.

29. Author's interview with Audrey Grant. Leaster Grant's silence undoubtedly was caused by the trauma of losing both parents to lynch mobs, for, as Goldsby states, "a significant but untold dimension of lynching's force as a tactic of white supremacy derives from its capacity not just to terrorize but to traumatize survivors into silence, leaving gaps of knowledge in its wake." Goldsby, *A Spectacular Secret*, 35.

30. Author's interview with Audrey Grant. When members of the Black community talked about the lynching of Mary Turner, they often referred to her simply as "the lady who had the baby cut out of her." The Grant family referred to Mary Turner by her maiden name, Hattie Graham, which is why Audrey Grant did not know her great-grandmother was Mary Turner until a community organization began to hold public meetings about the 1918 lynching rampage in the early 2000s. (The 1900 Federal Census for Brooks County, Georgia, listed her as Hattie Graham.) A. D. and Leaster Grant owned land adjacent to Rufus Morrison, who in 1918 had witnessed the lynching of Mary Turner as a young boy. The Morrisons were close friends of the Grants, and in the late 2000s, Rufus Morrison's daughter, Esther, told

Audrey Grant the details of the lynching, which she had heard from her father's firsthand account.

31. Author's interview with Willie Head Jr. in Pavo, Georgia, 29 January 2012.

32. Author's interview with Willie Head Jr.

33. Head indicated that Frank Head (b. 1840/50) was Judge Head's (b. 1875/81/82) brother, but according to the 1900 Census, Frank Head was Judge Head's father and Will Head (b. 1888) was Judge Head's younger brother. Despite some discrepancies between Census records regarding Frank and Judge Head's birth years, because Judge's younger brother Edson is listed as a son of Frank on the 1900 and 1910 Censuses, I concluded that Frank was Judge's father.

34. Author's interview with Willie Head Jr.

35. For a comprehensive analysis of white southern responses to the end of Jim Crow, see Jason Sokol, *There Goes My Everything: White Southerners in the Age of Civil Rights, 1945–1975* (New York: Vintage Books, 2006).

36. Between 1882 and 1951, members of Congress proposed 257 antilynching bills, three of which passed the House of Representatives but were blocked by the Senate. Zangrando, *The NAACP Crusade against Lynching*, 162, 165; Waldrep, "NAACP: Organized Resistance," in *African Americans Confront Lynching*, 59–91.

37. In a flourish of unapologetic denial, Burnette also claimed that, among the many lies spread about lynching in the South, was the "myth" that mobs would harvest and sell the fingers and ears of lynching victims as souvenirs. Maud Burnette to Tom Connally, 30 April 1940, Part 1, Box 126, Folder Anti-Lynching Bill—Correspondence—1930–1944, Tom Connally Papers, Library of Congress Manuscripts Division (hereafter cited as Connally Papers LoC).

38. G. D. Meredith to Luther A. Johnson, 22 February 1940, Part 1, Box 126, Folder Anti-Lynching Bill—Correspondence—1930–1944, Connally Papers LoC.

39. 81 Cong. Rec. H3532 (15 April 1937) (remarks by Hatton Sumners). Sumners's constitutional argument conveniently omitted any consideration for the constitutional rights of US citizens to a trial.

40. 81 Cong. Rec. H3534 (15 April 1937) (remarks by Hatton Sumners). Sumners never specified the race of the rapist, but he didn't have to, given the tacit understanding among sympathetic listeners that the man was Black.

41. 83 Cong. Rec. S874 (21 January 1938) (remarks by Theodore Bilbo). Bilbo's son claimed his father's racial views were "greatly misunderstood," but he betrayed his effort to construct a more palatable memory of his father when he explained that his father opposed interracial marriage because "mingling" the blood would degrade the white race. He added, "There are certain physical and mental differences that just can't be overcome." Oral History of Theodore G. Bilbo Jr., vol. 151, 1979, Mississippi Oral History Program, University of Southern Mississippi, 13.

42. R. B. Zeller to James O. Eastland, 23 April 1948, Box 32, Folder 1948 Civil Rights 1 of 3, James O. Eastland Collection, University of Mississippi Library (hereafter cited as Eastland Collection UMS).

43. President Harry Truman issued an executive order desegregating the military and included a civil rights plank in the 1948 Democratic Party platform. The civil rights bill introduced in 1948 was the first legislation of its kind to be seriously debated since Reconstruction.

44. White southerners trotted out arguments against civil rights legislation that hinged on the prospect of Black-on-white rape and "mongrelization"—precisely the same excuses invoked to justify lynching. One year after the 1957 Civil Rights Act passed, a minister from Russellville, Alabama, Willie Duboise, warned of the nation's demise in an impassioned letter to Eastland: "And do you not see that in a course of time, the Black Race through the Communist will soon multyply and take over—then this will be a nation of mixed, atheist, embiciles and moral degenerates, and perverts. . . . God never did intend for the nations to be conglomerated in any such mess." Underneath Duboise's grim prophecy about "conglomerated" races was a fear that racial justice would destroy a social order that artificially elevated whites economically, politically, and socially. Willie Duboise to James O. Eastland, 7 October 1958, Box 37, Folder 1958 Civil Rights, Eastland Collection UMS.

45. In an interview in 1964, the Imperial Wizard of the Ku Klux Klan of America, Robert Shelton, bragged that each of Mississippi's eighty-two counties could boast a local chapter. Kenneth Toler, "Trio 'Up North or in Cuba'? Could Be Governor Thinks," *Commercial Appeal* (Memphis), 27 June 1964.

46. James O. Eastland, interview by Mike Wallace (CBS, 28 July 1957), from the University of Texas at Austin, Harry Ransom Center, *The Mike Wallace Interview*, video and transcript, http://www.hrc.utexas.edu/multimedia/video/2008 /wallace/eastland_james_t.html.

47. Steele had ties to a neo-Nazi group, the National States Rights Party, which she asked Eastland about in her letter. Kate H. Steele to James O. Eastland, 24 June 1963, Box 42, Folder 1963 Civil Rights 3 of 4, Eastland Collection UMS.

48. Evers often appears in histories of the civil rights era at the moment of his assassination, overlooking his years of activism as the NAACP field secretary for Mississippi. Charles M. Payne, *I've Got the Light of Freedom: The Organizing Tradition and the Mississippi Freedom Struggle* (Berkeley: University of California Press, 2007), 48, 50.

49. "Coming Back Home to 'Home Sweet Home,'" *Jackson Daily News*, 31 July 1957.

50. This clipping enclosed with the letter from W. R. Haynie did not have any publication information. The letter mentioned that Haynie got the clipping from the "Miss. Co. Op. paper," and Maxie was a porter in the building that housed the Mississippi Federated Cooperatives. W. R. Haynie to James O. Eastland, 18 January 1957, Box 37, Folder 1957 Civil Rights 3 of 5, Eastland Collection UMS.

51. Hoyt Bass (Mrs. I. H. Bass) to James O. Eastland, 19 July 1957, Box 37, Folder 1957 Civil Rights 3 of 5, Eastland Collection UMS.

52. James O. Eastland to Mrs. I. H. Bass, 31 July 1957, Box 37, Folder 1957 Civil Rights 3 of 5, Eastland Collection UMS.

53. Wilmer C. Johnston to James O. Eastland, 18 January 1946, Box 32, Folder 1946 Civil Rights 2 of 2, Eastland Collection UMS; Press Release from Richard B. Russell, 24 September 1957, Subgroup C, X: Civil Rights, P. Little Rock, Box 133, Folder 6, Russell Collection UGA.

54. J. Todd Moye, *Let the People Decide: Black Freedom and White Resistance Movements in Sunflower County, Mississippi, 1945–1986* (Chapel Hill: University of North Carolina Press, 2004), 3–18; Asch, *The Senator and the Sharecropper,* 69, 23–32; Ginzburg, *100 Years of Lynchings,* 62–63.

55. John S. Boyette to James O. Eastland, 25 May 1961, Box 39, Folder 1961 Civil Rights, Eastland Collection UMS.

56. Boyette was born in Ruleville, Mississippi, in 1903, just one year before the senator was born, and though he would have been an infant at the time of the lynchings, his familiarity with what happened in Doddsville in 1904 suggests that the lynchings were common knowledge among whites. Boyette to Eastland, 25 May 1961, Eastland Collection UMS.

57. Asch, *The Senator and the Sharecropper,* 33.

58. Ruby Sheppeard Hicks to James O. Eastland, 1 October 1962, Box 41, Folder 1962 Civil Rights 5 of 6, Eastland Collection UMS. In 1976 Hicks published a nostalgic, romanticized memoir about growing up in the Delta, in which she almost entirely ignores the existence of African Americans. Ruby Sheppeard Hicks, *The Song of the Delta* (Jackson, MS: Howick House, 1976).

59. After the Evers assassination on June 12, 1963, many whites convinced themselves that it was an inside job perpetrated by African Americans. In a letter to Eastland, a resident of Jackson, Mrs. W. Q. Sharp, wrote, "We think this . . . murder that was done in our city is to *discredit us.* We have our own theory that Evers was not successful in contaminating *enough* of our negro population." Slim Gilmore wrote to Eastland, "[Evers's assassination] was a squeeze to bring out Kennedy's new legislature bills to pass. . . . Sometimes I think perhaps that communists are behind the Negro movements." Eastland even received a letter supposedly sent by a Black woman named "Mary" in Baton Rouge, Louisiana, who claimed that, when her husband was talking in his sleep, he admitted to accepting five thousand dollars from President Kennedy and a US marshal to assassinate Evers. "Mary" also said that a white southern man would be falsely blamed for the murder. Mrs. W. Q. Sharp to James O. Eastland, 13 June 1963, Box 41, Folder 1963 Civil Rights 1 of 4, Eastland Collection UMS; Slim Gilmore to James O. Eastland, 20 June 1963, Box 41, Folder 1963 Civil Rights 1 of 4, Eastland Collection UMS; Mary to Richard B. Russell forwarded to James O. Eastland, 14 June 1963, Box 41, Folder 1963 Civil Rights 2 of 4, Eastland Collection UMS.

60. Attempts to connect civil rights activists to communism intended to discredit the movement as un-American, and in doing so, these opponents of civil rights implied that white supremacy and racial injustice were fundamentally American. James O. Eastland to L. L. Price, 17 April 1968, Box 45, Folder 1968 Civil Rights, Eastland Collection UMS.

61. Seth Cagin and Philip Dray, *We Are Not Afraid: The Story of Goodman, Schwerner, and Chaney and the Civil Rights Campaign for Mississippi* (New York: Nation Books, 2006), 1–14, 35–41, 395–401.

62. Toler, "Trio 'Up North or in Cuba'? Could Be Governor Thinks."

63. 110 Cong. Rec. S16596 (22 July 1964) ("Communist Infiltration into the So-Called Civil Rights Movement" by Sen. Eastland).

64. James O. Eastland to Rose Wilder Lane, 31 July 1964, Box 43, Folder 1964 Civil Rights 2 of 6, Eastland Collection UMS.

65. Thomas J. Reed, a white Presbyterian minister from Natchez, Mississippi, told Eastland that he owed the families of the three lynched men an apology for dismissing their deaths as a hoax, and James Ballard from Piney Woods, Virginia, sent Eastland a postcard that simply asked, "Dear Mr. Eastland: Still think it's a hoax?" The vast majority of letters sent to the senator about the lynchings supported the sentiments expressed in his speech. Thomas J. Reed to James O. Eastland, 6 August 1964, and James Ballard to James O. Eastland, 7 August 1964, both in Box 43, Folder 1964 Civil Rights 2 of 6, Eastland Collection UMS.

66. A. Klingerof (?) to James O. Eastland, 26 June 1964, Box 42, Folder 1964 Civil Rights 2 of 6, Eastland Collection UMS.

67. Ann Parker to James O. Eastland, 23 July 1964, Box 43, Folder 1964 Civil Rights 3 of 6, Eastland Collection UMS.

68. Denials like Parker's blamed the national media and civil rights organizations for the supposed hoax of the Till lynching, but she ignored the public admission from Till's killers that they committed the crime.

69. A particularly zealous white woman from Millington, Tennessee, sent Eastland an annotated, spiral-bound scrapbook of clippings about the North with lurid headlines about ruthless mobsters, depraved rapists, and roving gangs of juvenile delinquents. A Miami man sent Senator Richard B. Russell of Georgia a March 1949 column penned by syndicated journalist Westbrook Pegler that claimed northern unions lynched more people than the Klan. He scrawled above the clipping's headline, "N.B. 'The Klan' punishes guilty persons, rapists, wife-beaters, etc. Labor Union Racketeers beat and murder innocent citizens," both condemning unions as murderous "goons" and defending southern lynch mobs as an extension of the justice system. A clipping from the *Jackson Daily News* that Eastland received featured two photos side by side: Black and white women standing on a corner patiently waiting for the traffic lights to change on the left and a car engulfed in flames with firefighters scurrying around it on the right. The caption printed below read "Racial Harmony Prevails in Jackson while Riots Rage in Chicago." In floor debates, southern senators and

representatives routinely rattled off crime statistics about the North to argue against antilynching legislation that targeted the South and to claim that integration would cause the crime rate to skyrocket. Agnes Whitman to James O. Eastland, 3 March 1960, Box 38, Folder 1960 Civil Rights 1 of 2, Eastland Collection UMS; L. A. McLaughlin to Richard B. Russell, 7 April 1949, Subgroup C, X: Civil Rights, A: Anti-Lynch, Box 1, Folder 1, Russell Collection UGA; Jackson Daily News to James O. Eastland, 29 July 1957, Box 36, Folder 1957 Civil Rights 1 of 5, Eastland Collection UMS.

70. J. A. Sasser to Henry Jackson bcc James O. Eastland, 30 July 1957, Box 37, Folder 1957 Civil Rights 3 of 5, Eastland Collection UMS.

71. Judy Barnett to James O. Eastland, 28 July 1957, Box 36, Folder 1957 Civil Rights 1 of 5, Eastland Collection UMS.

72. As recently as March 17, 2013, the South Carolina Division Children of the Confederacy rededicated the Crozier monument on the one-hundredth anniversary of the dedication with members of the Calvin Crozier Chapter, United Daughters of the Confederacy and members of the John M. Kinard Camp, Sons of Confederate Veterans attending. In both 2013 and 1913, remembering the Confederate dead came with a conspicuous erasure of enslavement and racial oppression. "Children of the Confederacy Rededicate Calvin Crozier Monument," *Newberry Observer* (Newberry, SC), 1 April 2013. For more information on Confederate memory, see Karen L. Cox, *Dixie's Daughters: The United Daughters of the Confederacy and the Preservation of Confederate Culture* (Gainesville: University Press of Florida, 2003).

73. "Buggy Collision Incites Mob to Lynch Ala. Negro," *Montgomery Advertiser* (Montgomery, AL), 11 November 1912; "Two Saved from First Mob Are Lynched by Second Mob," *Atlanta Constitution*, 30 September 1916; "Negro Killed by Mob after Slaying Three / Downed by Machine Gun Fire after 15-Hour Chase," *Dallas Evening Journal*, 15 December 1923; "Courthouse, Negro Burned / Mob Destroys Three Blocks in Negro Part of Sherman," *Ennis Daily News* (Ennis, TX), 10 May 1930.

74. Louis W. Cotton to James O. Eastland, 21 May 1961, Box 39, Folder 1961 Civil Rights, Eastland Collection UMS.

75. Adam Fairclough, *To Redeem the Soul of America: The Southern Christian Leadership Conference and Martin Luther King, Jr.* (Athens: University of Georgia Press, 1987), 77–82; Henry Hampton and Steve Fayer with Sarah Flynn, *Voice of Freedom: An Oral History of the Civil Rights Movement from the 1950s through the 1980s* (New York: Bantam Books, 1990), 73–96.

76. "After the Violence," *Washington Post*, 27 May 1961.

77. Walter Sillers to James O. Eastland, 21 June 1961, and Melvin T. Weakley to James O. Eastland, 3 June 1961, both in Box 39, Folder 1961 Civil Rights, Eastland Collection UMS. Weakley railed against the Freedom Riders for "inflam[ing] the citizenry," and he beseeched Eastland to continue his fight to prevent the destruction of American freedom and the "enslavement of our people" without even an inkling of irony.

78. Telegram from Arthur J. Hanes to John McClellan, 12 May 1963, Box 42, Folder 1963 Civil Rights 2 of 4, Eastland Collection UMS.

79. Some of the more radical groups participating in the march, like SNCC and CORE, had hoped for a show of civil disobedience that would shut down Washington, but by early July the organizers had decided to limit the activities to a rally on the National Mall. Fairclough, *To Redeem the Soul of America*, 152.

80. Mrs. Frank M. Bianca to James O. Eastland, 23 August 1963, Box 42, Folder 1963 Civil Rights 3 of 4, Eastland Collection UMS.

81. William K. Martak to Estes Kefauver, 2 August 1963, Box 42, Folder 1963 Civil Rights 3 of 4, Eastland Collection UMS. Because Congress had called a recess during the march, Mr. and Mrs. J. V. Pace Jr. of Forest, Mississippi, lamented, "This Republic has truly become a Democracy controlled by masses of mobs, which in reality is a 'mobocracy.' " Mr. and Mrs. J. V. Pace Jr. to James O. Eastland, 27 August 1963, Box 42, Folder 1963 Civil Rights 3 of 4, Eastland Collection UMS.

82. Another useful pair of events to analyze is the 1962 riot at the University of Mississippi and the 1968 uprisings following the assassination of King. Many white Mississippians preferred to describe the white rioters as a "crowd" persecuted by federal marshals rather than as a "mob," but they were quick to condemn Black "rioters" in 1968 as disruptive, violent mobs. Although white southerners sometimes described white behavior with the rhetoric of mob violence, their tendency to describe whites as members of a crowd and Blacks as members of a mob revealed the depths of white denial and their opposition to Black protest.

83. Taylor Branch, *Parting the Waters: America in the King Years 1954–63* (New York: Simon & Schuster, 1988), 889–92. Alabama governor George Wallace placed the blame for the bombings in "Dynamite Hill" at the feet of civil rights protesters who wanted to "create internal strife and turmoil." He failed to explain what would motivate protesters to target Black people who were sympathetic to the movement. Telegram from Armistead Selden to James O. Eastland, 13 May 1963, Box 42, Folder 1963 Civil Rights 2 of 4, Eastland Collection UMS.

84. William M. Spencer to Richard B. Russell, 1 October 1963, Subgroup C, X: Civil Rights, AA: Racial—Out of State, Box 155, Folder 8, Russell Collection UGA.

85. Gene Oliver to Richard B. Russell, 20 September 1963, Subgroup C, X: Civil Rights, AA: Racial—Out of State, Box 155, Folder 8, Russell Collection UGA.

86. Martin Luther King Jr., "Eulogy for the Young Victims of the Sixteenth Street Baptist Church Bombing," in *A Call to Conscience: The Landmark Speeches of Dr. Martin Luther King, Jr.*, ed. Clayborne Carson and Kris Shepard (New York: Grand Central Publishing, 2001), 97.

87. Timothy V. Kaufman-Osborn, "Capital Punishment as Legal Lynching?" in *From Lynch Mobs to the Killing State: Race and the Death Penalty in America*,

ed. Charles J. Ogletree Jr. and Austin Sarat (New York: New York University Press, 2006), 20–54; Naomi Murakawa, *The First Civil Right: How Liberals Built Prison America* (New York: Oxford University Press, 2014), 31–44.

88. Author's interview with Robert Hall.

89. Author's interview with Jesse Pennington.

90. When the exhibit headed south, Joseph R. Jordan became the curator, and this version of *Without Sanctuary* was the one Pennington saw in Jackson. Jordan made significant changes to the exhibit to transform the exhibit spaces into sanctuaries for Black visitors: painting the walls black and keeping the carpet red, adding display cases that highlighted antilynching activism, and playing recordings of spirituals interspersed with the hum of insects on a summer night in the South. Even with the care that Jordan put into centering Black experiences and Black viewers, some critics, such as Hilton Als and Michael Eric Dyson, took issue with the spectacle of Black death on display. Apel, *Imagery of Lynching*, 7–15; Baker, *Humane Insight*, 48–55.

91. Anthony W. Lee, introduction to *Lynching Photographs*, by Dora Apel and Shawn Michele Smith (Berkeley: University of California Press, 2007), 3–6.

92. Author's interview with Jesse Pennington.

Chapter Three. Haunting

1. The Huaco (or Hueco or Waco) people are part of the Wichita and Affiliated Tribes, based in Anadarko, Oklahoma, but before US colonial violence forced them onto a reservation, their homeland was in what is currently central Texas. My re-creation of the tornado myth synthesizes fragments of stories from several oral histories and books about the Waco tornado of 1953. Oral Memoirs of Kneeland H. Clemons, 21 October 1988, Baylor Oral History, 33; Oral Memoirs of Maggie Langham Washington, 18 April 1988, Baylor Oral History, 51; Author's interview with Lester Gibson in Waco, Texas, 24 February 2012; Mike Cox, *Texas Disasters: True Stories of Tragedy and Survival* (Guilford, CT: Insiders' Guide, 2006), 145–54; Gene Fowler, *Texas Storms: Stories of Raging Weather in the Lone Star State* (Mankato, MN: Capstone Press, 2011), 56–67; Louis Mazé, "Radio and the 1953 Waco Tornado," KWBU-FM in Waco, from *Living Stories*, 3:38, aired 10 May 2011, http://www.baylor.edu/livingstories/index.php?id=82072.

2. Maggie Washington's oral history includes a description of the tornado's path, which she says is where Jesse Washington's body had been dragged. The route she describes is through East Waco, a Black neighborhood located just across the Brazos River from downtown Waco. The tornado touched down on the downtown side of the Brazos River then jumped the river to East Waco. Newspaper accounts of Washington's lynching in 1916 and Jesse Thomas's lynching in 1923 indicate that their bodies were dragged through downtown but not in East Waco. The tornado destroyed several

Black-owned businesses located on the part of Bridge Street that was on the downtown side of the river, which would have been only one block from the square where the lynchings took place, but these businesses may not have been located there in 1916 and 1923. Despite these discrepancies, the underlying sentiment behind this story and its variations reveals how the lynching lingered in the Black community's folklore and consciousness. Oral Memoirs of Maggie Langham Washington, 51.

3. Oral Memoirs of Maggie Langham Washington, 51.

4. Author's interview with Lester Gibson. Thirty people died when the Dennis Building, located across the street from the ALICO Building, collapsed, and, though the ALICO Building did not slam into the parking lot and return to an upright position, the strong winds of the tornado caused the building to sway so violently that people working on the top floors were thrown against the walls.

5. In the immediate aftermath of the 1916 lynching, some whites believed burning, mutilating, and dragging Washington's body exceeded the limits of decency even for a lynching. Many of these same people, however, did not oppose lynching in general. Even so, guilt and shame seeped into pockets of the white community, especially after the 1923 lynching of Jesse Thomas, who was later cleared of wrongdoing. As far as I can tell, white Wacoans did not associate the tornado with the lynchings that occurred downtown.

6. The folklore around Pecos Bill, a legendary cowboy who lassoed a tornado in Kansas and rode it to California, offers a productive counterpoint to the Waco tornado/lynching story. According to legend, Pecos Bill tamed and controlled nature to create the Grand Canyon, and although the actual "taming" and "controlling" of the West exacted a devastating death toll upon Indigenous peoples, the legend celebrates the imperialist project of white settlement in "untamed" Indigenous lands as a time of creation rather than destruction. By contrast, the story of God's vengeance in Waco served as a powerful indictment of racial violence.

7. Oral Memoirs of Kneeland H. Clemons, 25–27; Oral Memoirs of Maggie Langham Washington, 51–52; Oral History of Ada Ateman, 20 June 1994, *Behind the Veil* Duke. Ada Ateman and others from Memphis, Tennessee, used the term "pigeon roost" to describe the Jim Crow section of movie theaters. The term "buzzard roost" was common elsewhere in the South.

8. Harry Estill Moore, *Tornadoes over Texas: A Study of Waco and San Angelo in Disaster* (Austin: University of Texas Press, 1958), 35; Cox, *Texas Disasters*, 152–53. The $51 million figure is in 1953 dollars. In 2022 dollars, that figure is around $542 million. In addition to the tornado, an urban renewal project, growth of suburbs, and the construction of Interstate 35 displaced many homes and businesses, and contributed to the decline of the neighborhood.

9. Levine, *Black Culture and Black Consciousness*, 63.

10. Gladys-Marie Fry discusses related forms of Black subversion in the face of white terror. She argues that, despite attempts by white southerners to

terrorize African Americans with the specter of supernatural night riders to prevent them from gathering at night, African Americans feigned fear for these supernatural beings and gathered under the cloak of darkness anyway. Gladys-Marie Fry, *Night Riders in Black Folk History* (Chapel Hill: University of North Carolina Press, 2001).

11. Norman R. Yetman, *Life under the "Peculiar Institution": Selections from the Slave Narrative Collection* (New York: Holt, Rinehart & Winston, 1970), 289; Levine, *Black Culture and Black Consciousness*, 79n73.

12. Levine, *Black Culture and Black Consciousness*, 79, 79n76; Lewis Clarke, "Questions and Answers," in *Interesting Memoirs and Documents Relating to American Slavery, and the Glorious Struggle Now Making for Complete Emancipation* (1846; repr., Westport, CT: Negro Universities Press, 1970), 87. Another source discussing supernatural phenomena, such as ghosts knowing where to find buried money and owls being a sign of an imminent death in the family, is the Oral History of Daniel Swanigan, 12 July 1995, *Behind the Veil* Duke.

13. Clarke, "Questions and Answers," 91. Clarke also told the story of an enslaved man named George whose dying enslaver told him that he would reward George by arranging for him to be buried alongside him and other (white) church leaders. George liked the idea of being buried in a nice coffin, but he told his enslaver some of his reservations: "Well, I fraid, massa, when the debbil come take you body, he make mistake, and get mine." Although this isn't a ghost story, Clarke humorously points out that, after a life of sin, even the most "pious" of enslavers would get what they had coming to them—a special place in hell with the devil.

14. Edward C. L. Adams, "Ole Man Rogan," in *Congaree Sketches: Scenes from Negro Life in the Swamps of the Congaree and Tales by Tad and Scip of Heaven and Hell with Other Miscellany* (Chapel Hill: University of North Carolina Press, 1927), 49–51; Sterling Stuckey, *Slave Culture: Nationalist Theory and the Foundations of Black America* (New York: Oxford University Press, 1987), 10n17. For another example of a cruel enslaver coming back to haunt her enslaved people, see the WPA narrative of Jane Arrington in George P. Rawick, ed., *The American Slave: A Composite Autobiography*, ser. 1, vol. 14, *North Carolina Narratives: Part 1* (1941; repr., Westport, CT: Greenwood Publishing Co., 1972), 46; Levine, *Black Culture and Black Consciousness*, 79n74.

15. Arrington, *North Carolina Narratives*, 46.

16. Oral History of Theresa Pearson, 13 July 1995, *Behind the Veil* Duke.

17. Oral History of Cleo Jeffers.

18. For the specific stories about these ghosts, see Oral History of Cleo Jeffers; Oral History of Mary Robinson, 26 June 1995, *Behind the Veil* Duke.

19. Gordon, *Ghostly Matters*, xvi.

20. "A Conversation with James Baldwin," 24 June 1963, WGBH, American Archive of Public Broadcasting, https://americanarchive.org.

21. In other texts, Baldwin sends a more explicit warning about divine vengeance. He opens *The Fire Next Time* with, "God gave Noah the rainbow sign / No more water, the fire next time!" James Baldwin, *The Fire Next Time* (1963; repr., New York: Vintage International, 1993).

22. White southerners also had a rich tradition of telling ghost stories. The structure and themes of those stories often mirrored the tales told among African Americans, but because ghost stories reflected the cultural values of a particular community, some of the themes and portrayals of white and Black characters differed considerably. For instance, one ghost story from Pontotoc, Mississippi, involved a faithful enslaved man who protected his enslaver's family during the Civil War. Uncle Eb, as they "affectionately" called him, patrolled the grounds of the plantation at night carrying a lantern, and after his death, people periodically saw the light from his lantern bobbing through the woods. This story reeked of the paternalism that white southerners often deployed to justify and defend slavery, which certainly did not resonate with the historical memory and cultural values of African Americans. Kathryn Tucker Windham, *13 Mississippi Ghosts and Jeffrey* (Tuscaloosa: University of Alabama Press, 1974), 9–17.

23. Howard Thurman captured these distinct moral universes: "The fact was that the slave owner was regarded [by the enslaved] as one outside the pale of moral and ethical responsibility. The level of high expectation of moral excellence for the master was practically *nihil*. Nothing could be expected from him but gross evil—he was in terms of morality—amoral." Howard Thurman, *The Negro Spiritual Speaks of Life and Death*, in *Deep River and The Negro Spiritual Speaks of Life and Death* (Richmond, IN: Friends United Press, 1975), 30.

24. Toni Morrison, *Beloved* (New York: Knopf, 1987), 43–44.

25. Author's interview with James Reed in Jackson, Mississippi, 9 November 2011.

26. Although James Reed couldn't recall the precise circumstances that led to the lynching, the face in the window may have belonged to James Williams, who had been accused of "miscegenation" and lynched on January 19, 1893, in Pickens County.

27. Mrs. C. P. McGuire Sr. and the Birmingham Genealogical Society, *Records of Pickens County, Alabama* (Tuscaloosa, AL: Willo Publishing Co., 1959), 12.

28. Kathryn Tucker Windham and Margaret Gillis Figh, *13 Alabama Ghosts and Jeffrey* (Huntsville, AL: Strode Publishers, 1969), 65. Although Windham and Figh don't say that they collected these ghost stories from white sources, they drop several hints suggesting as much. In almost all the stories they compiled, the protagonists are white, and they celebrated white southern culture from plantation estates and southern belles to Confederate veterans and white southern honor. At one point, Windham included this line: "Almost before their honeymoon was over, the War Between the States (call it the Civil War, if you must) had erupted." I read their version of the

Pickens County Courthouse haunting as reflective of white lore. Windham, *13 Tennessee Ghosts and Jeffrey* (Tuscaloosa: University of Alabama Press, 1977), 143.

29. Windham and Figh, *13 Alabama Ghosts*, 66.
30. Windham and Figh, *13 Alabama Ghosts*, 63–69.
31. Windham and Figh, *13 Alabama Ghosts*, 64, 65.
32. Windham and Figh, *13 Alabama Ghosts*, 65, 63, 66.
33. According to Ginzburg's records and the CSDE Lynching Database, the following seventeen African Americans were lynched in Pickens County, Alabama: 3 unknown African Americans (Pickens County, town unspecified) on October 21, 1886; James/David Williams (Pickens County, town unspecified) on January 19, 1893; Joe Floyd (Pickens County, town unspecified) in August 1893; Paul Archer, William Archer, Emma/Ellen Fair/Fant, Ed Guyton, and Paul/Polk Hull/Hill (Carrollton) on September 14/15, 1893; John Marritt (Pickens County, town unspecified) on March 26, 1897; Bud/Andy Beard (Carrollton) on December 17, 1897; Will Roberts (Pickens County, town unspecified) on July 9, 1904; John Lipsey (Pickensville) on August 27, 1907; Lemuel Weeks (Pickensville) on July 1, 1916; unknown African American (Reform) on July 16, 1917; Poe Hibbler (Pickens County) on July 23, 1917. The town of Carrollton is spelled "Carrolton" in Ginzburg, but I assume that "Carrolton" refers to Carrollton. Also, Ginzburg has no record of the Wells lynching. Ginzburg, *100 Years of Lynchings*, 253–55; CSDE Lynching Database.
34. McKittrick, *Demonic Grounds*, xix.
35. Windham and Figh, *13 Alabama Ghosts*, 63.
36. Windham and Figh, *13 Alabama Ghosts*, 63–64.
37. Du Bois's final chapter of *Black Reconstruction*, "The Propaganda of History," offers a comprehensive and biting critique of Reconstruction historiography, which sadly held until after the civil rights era, when white scholars finally took seriously Du Bois's interpretation of Reconstruction—reading "the attempt to make black men American citizens" as "a splendid failure." Until then, the Dunning School, which derided Black voters as inept and Black politicians as corrupt, dominated the scholarship and white memory (North and South) of Reconstruction. At times Dunning and his disciples defended Klan violence and other forms of intimidation, and this defense of terrorist violence to protect white political, economic, and social interests from Black and northern power bled into the rhetoric deployed to defend lynching throughout the early twentieth century. Du Bois, "The Propaganda of History," in *Black Reconstruction*, 711–29, quote on 708. For more about the Lost Cause and white southern memory, see Blight, "The Lost Cause and Causes Not Lost," in *Race and Reunion*, 255–99; Cox, *Dixie's Daughters*. For more on Redemption, see Eric Foner, "Redemption and After," in *Reconstruction: America's Unfinished Revolution, 1863–1877* (New York: Perennial Classics, 1988), 564–601; Steven Hahn, "Of Paramilitary Politics," in *A Nation under*

Our Feet: Black Political Struggles in the Rural South from Slavery to the Great Migration (Cambridge, MA: Belknap Press, 2003), 265–313.

38. Windham and Figh, *13 Alabama Ghosts*, 69. McGuire also referenced attempts to remove the image from the windowpane, writing, "Through all the years, in spite of hail and storm, which destroyed all other windows in the Courthouse, that particular pane, with the striking image, remains. The glass has been scribbed with soap and gasoline as well as other means, but still that pane has met all tests and to this day, (August 1959) the face remains unchanged." McGuire, *Records of Pickens County*, 12.

39. Lightnin' Hopkins, "Devil Is Watching You," recorded 1962, on *Lightnin' Strikes* (LP, Vee-Jay LP1044).

40. For more on ghostless hauntings, consult Judith Richardson, *Possessions: The History and Uses of Haunting in the Hudson Valley* (Cambridge, MA: Harvard University Press, 2003), 5.

41. Gayle Graham Yates, *Life and Death in a Small Southern Town: Memories of Shubuta, Mississippi* (Baton Rouge: Louisiana State University Press, 2004), 67–71. The violent displacement of the Choctaw and other Indigenous people accelerated in the 1820s and 1830s as wealthy white enslavers from the Upper South expanded cotton cultivation into Mississippi, Alabama, and territory west of the Mississippi River. Edward E. Baptist, *The Half Has Never Been Told: Slavery and the Making of American Capitalism* (New York: Basic Books, 2014); Walter Johnson, *River of Dark Dreams: Slavery and Empire in the Cotton Kingdom* (Cambridge, MA: Belknap Press, 2013).

42. The murdered man had likely impregnated Alma House, who was sixteen years old and eight and a half months pregnant, and her older sister Maggie House, who was twenty years old and five months pregnant. Andrew Clarke, the older of the two brothers, had been seeing Maggie House and did not like that the white farmer had been having sex with her. Walter White, Extract from Confidential Report on Shubuta Lynchings, 19 January 1919, Box I:C337, Folder 6, NAACP LoC; Ward, *Hanging Bridge*.

43. According to the *New York Times*, the alleged attempted assault happened on the Hanging Bridge itself. Cases involving Black men, white women, and alleged assaults often led to lynchings, but perhaps the violation (an attempted assault) of this symbol of white supremacy (the bridge) made their lynching even more likely. "2 Negro Boys Lynched," *New York Times*, 13 October 1942, Box II:A408, Folder 5, NAACP LoC.

44. J. L. LeFlore to William Pickens, 22 June 1939, Box I:G3, Folder "Mobile, Ala. 1939," NAACP LoC.

45. In addition to local coverage of the 1918 lynchings in Shubuta by the *Meridian Star*, regional newspapers in Jackson, Mobile, Memphis, New Orleans, Houston, and St. Louis, and national newspapers in New York, Washington, DC, and Los Angeles broadcasted Shubuta's crimes to the nation. The *Crisis* ran an extensive report on the lynchings based on an investigation conducted by the assistant secretary to the NAACP, Walter White, so the case

was widely known to NAACP members. Newspaper clippings, Box I:C360, Folder 41, NAACP LoC.

46. For decades, a local hunting lodge called the Hanging Bridge Hunting and Fishing Club proudly displayed a sign bearing its name on the bridge until a judge ordered the club to remove the word "Hanging" from the sign after the NAACP filed a suit in the 1980s. Rather than replacing the sign, the club simply painted over the offending word, making even more explicit the grudging acceptance of the post–Jim Crow way of life. The monument to notorious segregationist Strom Thurmond on the grounds of the South Carolina state capitol, which lists the names of his children, raised similar questions in 2005 when the South Carolina General Assembly added the name of his biracial daughter, Essie Mae Washington-Williams, to the monument. Because the text of the monument had been etched in stone, the process of filling and recarving the text left a stain. The belated inclusion of her name and its separation from her half-siblings' names only highlighted her marginal status both in the family and in South Carolina society. Joseph Crespino, "The Scarred Stone: The Strom Thurmond Monument," *Southern Spaces*, 19 April 2010, http://www.southernspaces.org/.

47. Jeneane Jones, "Mississippi Looks Back, Forward after Inauguration," United Methodist News Service, 27 January 2009, http://www.umc.org. The white community claimed that the mob had forcibly taken the keys from the sheriff, thrown a blanket over him, and pinned his hands behind his back. Many lynchings investigated by the NAACP turned up similar discrepancies. Law enforcement officers didn't want to face criticism for failing to uphold their responsibilities, especially after public opinion began to turn against lynching. Some sheriffs legitimately tried to prevent lynchings, but many more remained complicit. "2 Negro Boys Lynched," *New York Times*, 13 October 1942, NAACP LoC.

48. In Mississippi, civil rights activists took these threats very seriously since so many among their ranks had been beaten and killed. Just among the leadership of the NAACP in Mississippi, the death toll included Reverend George W. Lee in 1955, Herbert Lee in 1961, Medgar Evers in 1963, and Vernon Dahmer in 1965.

49. Yates, *Life and Death in a Small Southern Town*, 155.

50. Yates, *Life and Death in a Small Southern Town*, 152–56. After one woman with the MFDP was assaulted by a member of the Klan, the local hospital in Quitman refused to treat her, so another MFDP member had to drive her to Meridian for medical attention, which carried its own risks since a Black man driving a white woman in a car could invite even more violence.

51. According to a relative of John Cornish, members of the mob cut off Cornish's, Curry's, and Jones's fingers so they could not untie the ropes and escape, and these fingers along with some tongues were preserved in a pickling jar and displayed in a Kirven storefront for years. Monte Akers, *Flames after Midnight: Murder, Vengeance, and the Desolation of a Texas Community*, rev. ed.

(Austin: University of Texas Press, 2011), 204–5. Although Akers's interviews shed new light on the collective memories of the lynching, I take issue with his tendency to be skeptical of the reliability of his Black interviewees. At one point he admits that, during an interview with a Black woman named Bertha Williams, "in my ignorance, I believed she was merely repeating some myth about the event that had grown up in the black community to exculpate the lynching victims. I paid lip service to what she was saying, but promptly returned to my original line of questions" (92). Williams's story was more likely to be accurate than what he calls "the traditionally accepted account of Eula's murder," by which he means the white memory of the murder that sparked the lynchings (103). Akers only began to take Williams seriously when he came across a report by a white NAACP investigator that corroborated her story. He similarly dismissed the relative of Cornish who offered information about the jar of body parts at a 1999 book signing in Teague, Texas. He prefaces that exchange by writing, "occasionally a person [at a book signing] came forward claiming special, dubious knowledge" (204). The morbid practice of preserving "souvenir" body parts from lynchings was common in the South, and Akers provided no reasonable explanation for disparaging that "claim" as "dubious." Because Akers quotes reports, articles, and interviews at length, his sources can be analyzed without being tainted by his interpretive bias, so I have cautiously drawn on these sources in this chapter and other parts of the book.

52. Akers, *Flames after Midnight*, 214.
53. Akers, *Flames after Midnight*, 188–90, 213–15. Akers did not reveal the identity of the man who castrated Cornish and Curry because the man's son didn't want to make his father's story public. The father secretly called documentary filmmaker Gode Davis when his family was away or asleep. Davis noted that in one of his later phone conversations, the man seemed ever so slightly more circumspect about the lynchings. Davis wouldn't describe the man as remorseful, but he mentioned that he would give African Americans extra peaches without them knowing that they had come from him. Still, the prominent display of those photographs undercuts these belated attempts at generosity.
54. Oral History of Willie Jackson, 15 June 1994, *Behind the Veil* Duke.
55. Oral History of John Barry Taylor, 19 June 1994, *Behind the Veil* Duke. John Barry Taylor is the son of John and Robella Taylor. Although he grew up in New York City, he spent summers in Leesburg and Albany, Georgia, and he moved to Albany as an adult.
56. Oral History of Robella Sally Taylor, 30 June 1994, *Behind the Veil* Duke.
57. Oral History of Mary Robinson. As an adult, Robinson was a casket decorator.
58. During a 2000 public forum in Atlanta about the *Without Sanctuary* exhibit, David Smith said that, during his career as a nurse in Florida, older white patients often confided to him that they were haunted by memories of attending lynchings. These deathbed confessions seem to indicate that they

were seeking absolution from Black people. "Thee Smith Notes," Box 1, Folder 9, Without Sanctuary Project Files, Stuart A. Rose Manuscript, Archives, and Rare Book Library, Emory University (hereafter cited as Without Sanctuary Emory).

59. Author's interview with Robert Hall. Wexler recounts a similar set of stories about the vengeful ghosts of lynching victims that circulated in the Black community around Monroe, Georgia, after the quadruple lynching in 1946. These stories included haunting deathbed scenes and accidental or tragic deaths caused by vengeful ghosts taunting and punishing the white community for participating in the lynchings. Wexler, *Fire in a Canebrake*, 206.

60. Willie Head Jr. also saw that man walking in Barney and asked his father about the sores on this man's hands, which, his father explained, marked where Mary Turner's blood had splashed on his arms. Author's interview with Willie Head Jr.

61. Although Taylor does not mention the name of the lynching victim, the date and details appear to match the May 18, 1917, lynching of Ell Persons. Oral History of Edmonia Taylor, 26 June 1995, *Behind the Veil* Duke; Oral History of Margarette Edmond, 22 June 1995, *Behind the Veil* Duke; Ginzburg, *100 Years of Lynchings*, 112–13.

62. Branch, *Parting the Waters*, 408–9.

63. Oral History of Shirley Sherrod, 30 June 1994, *Behind the Veil* Duke. Warren "Gator" Johnson shot, but did not kill, civil rights activist Charlie Ware in 1963.

64. A more optimistic reading of Screws, in which he actually felt remorse, would make the prospect of redeeming the nation more likely. Like Sherrod, I am skeptical of such a reading.

65. Mark Wolynn, *It Didn't Start with You: How Inherited Family Trauma Shapes Who We Are and How to End the Cycle* (New York: Penguin Books, 2016), 15–16.

66. Meyers, " 'Killing Them by the Wholesale,' " 222, 219.

67. Author's interview with Willie Head Jr.

68. Oral History of Minnie Weston, 8 August 1995, *Behind the Veil* Duke.

69. Weston (b. 1905) and her family moved from Chickasaw County to the Mississippi Delta around 1919. She would have been born a year after the Jesse Tucker lynching on July 10, 1904, and alive during the lynchings of Henry Sykes on October 22, 1907; Robby Buskin on February 9, 1909; and Andrew Williams on February 7, 1913. Ginzburg, *100 Years of Lynchings*, 263, 265; CSDE Lynching Database.

70. Oral History of Minnie Weston.

71. Oral History of Minnie Weston.

72. Oral History of Minnie Weston.

73. Oral History of Minnie Weston.

74. Oral History of Minnie Weston.

75. Oral History of Minnie Weston. When Weston refused to "hold" those memories in her mind, she refused their hold on her, too, though she could

not force them completely out of her mind. Her refusal is a "formation of an oppositional geography," as McKittrick might say, but, whereas the Reeds and Robinson reclaimed the meaning of *physical* geographies of violence, Weston reclaimed *metaphorical* space in her consciousness, while recognizing that those traumatic memories could run across her mind if she called them up from its deeper recesses. Her hold on those memories struck me as more tenuous than that of the Reeds and Robinson, for the pain that surfaced in retelling those memories seemed to wound her as though they were fresh, but she had found a way to put away those memories, and keep the past in the past, if only temporarily. McKittrick, *Demonic Grounds*, xi.

Chapter Four. Violence

Gwendolyn Brooks, excerpt from "The Last Quatrain of the Ballad of Emmett Till." Reprinted by consent of Brooks Permissions.

1. Charles W. Eagles, *The Price of Defiance: James Meredith and the Integration of Ole Miss* (Chapel Hill: University of North Carolina Press, 2009), 284, 372; McCandlish Phillips, "Meredith Lonely But Will Remain," *New York Times*, 3 October 1962; "Effigy Hanging Breaks Calm at Ole Miss," *Bellingham Herald* (Bellingham, WA), 3 October 1962.

2. Neil R. McMillen, *Dark Journey: Black Mississippians in the Age of Jim Crow* (Urbana: University of Illinois Press, 1989), 224.

3. I first became aware of these effigies while reading a letter to Meredith from a fifteen-year-old white girl from Audubon, New Jersey, named Eileen Pots. She wrote that, after hearing about the burned effigy, "for the first time I could really imagine what was going on there [in Oxford, Mississippi]." Later I came across a newspaper clipping of the photograph reproduced here. Eileen Potts to James Meredith, 3 October 1962, Box 97.25.3, Folder 11 "Meredith Letters of Support October 3, 1962," James Howard Meredith Collection, University of Mississippi Library (hereafter cited as Meredith Collection UMS).

4. "The Sovereign States of Alabama and Georgia" to James Meredith, undated 1962, Box 97.25.6, Folder 13 "Negative Letters, 1962 (mostly undated)," Meredith Collection UMS.

5. "Buddy" to James Meredith, 13 October 1962, Box 97.25.6, Folder 4 "Anti-Integration Corr 10–14 Oct 1962," Meredith Collection UMS; "the WHITES" to James Meredith, undated 1962, Box 97.25.6, Folder 3 "Meredith-Negative Letters 1962 Oct 5–9," Meredith Collection UMS.

6. Eagles, *The Price of Defiance*, 391.

7. The three early twentieth-century lynchings recorded in Alcorn County, where Corinth is located, did not involve hanging the lynching victim from a tree, but McPeters may have been referring to the 1900 lynching of Jack Betts, who was hanged from a telegraph pole in the town square, or the 1902 lynching of Thomas Clark, who was burned alive in a cemetery. Bill

McPeters to Ross Barnett, 19 September 1962, Western Union Telegram Collection, University of Mississippi Library.

8. Phillips, "Meredith Lonely But Will Remain."

9. James Meredith, "I Can't Fight Alone," *Look*, 19 April 1963, 70–78.

10. I draw upon insights from Mills and Kaufman-Osborn. Lynching falls in the category of acts that Charles Mills describes as "informal illegal or quasi-legal practices effectively sanctioned by the complicity of silence and government failure to intervene and punish perpetrators." In essence, civilians are empowered to carry out the racial state's work of protecting white supremacy with the full support of the state. Kaufman-Osborn expands upon Mills's ideas, explaining that "many lynchings … should be located not in the domain of the illegal or the extralegal but, rather, near the heart of a more comprehensive structure of racial control, one that vested informal police powers in members of the white race and that encouraged vigilantism as a necessary complement to its weak agencies of formally authorized political discipline." Charles Mills, *The Racial Contract* (Ithaca, NY: Cornell University Press, 1997), 21, 86; Kaufman-Osborn, "Capital Punishment as Legal Lynching?" 33.

11. A contemporary example of how the state deputizes whites to regulate the activities of Black people is the recent spate of highly publicized cases of white women calling the police on African Americans who are not engaged in illegal activity but are perceived to be a threat by virtue of being in the "wrong" place. Jennifer Schulte, who called the police on a group of Black people barbecuing in Oakland in 2018, felt empowered by her whiteness to act as an extension of the racial state, and although she has become amusing fodder for the meme "BBQ Becky," had the police responded with more force, the consequences for those Black people simply having a barbecue could have been fatal. Jordan Davis, however, wasn't so lucky. In 2012, a white man, enraged by how loudly Davis was playing music in his friend's parked car, shot at the teenaged Davis nine times, killing him. The killer was convicted of his murder and the attempted murder of his friends only after the first trial ended in a mistrial.

12. William Ferris, *Give My Poor Heart Ease: Voices of the Mississippi Blues* (Chapel Hill: University of North Carolina Press, 2009), 154.

13. Mary Dudziak, "Coming to Terms with Cold War Civil Rights," in *Cold War Civil Rights: Race and the Image of American Democracy* (Princeton, NJ: Princeton University Press, 2000), 18–46.

14. I discuss silences among white southerners at length in chapter 2. Sokol, " 'Our Negroes' No More," in *There Goes My Everything*, 56–113.

15. *Lynching Goes Underground: A Report on a New Technique* (NAACP, 1940), Box II:A395, Folder: "Lynching, 'Lynching Goes Underground,' 1941," NAACP LoC.

16. The intervention of the FBI in this case was due to both public outcry and the likelihood that Parker was taken across state lines during the lynching

ritual. Howard Smead, *Blood Justice: The Lynching of Mack Charles Parker* (New York: Oxford University Press, 1986).

17. Kaufman-Osborn argues that, rather than understanding the decline in the number of spectacle lynchings as a sign of progress—that due process given legitimacy by state institutions replaced extralegal and private violence—we need to recognize the ways in which the death penalty continues to do the white supremacist work of spectacle lynchings after they became rare. Borrowing from Hall's usage of the "underlaw" and Mills's concept of the Racial Contract, he reasons that, because the "underlaw" (that is, the local white customs that reinforce white supremacy and are given legal sanction by local law enforcement) of the death penalty remains committed to upholding the Racial Contract, the death penalty renders anti-Black violence a rationalized procedure (by electric chair and lethal injection) that is both legal and ostensibly race-neutral. In effect, under the veneer of "humane" and race-neutral justice meted out by the state, the Racial Contract remains intact, but this veneer of fairness makes the white supremacist violence less legible and therefore more difficult to root out. Only by dismantling the Racial Contract can we truly have racial justice. Kaufman-Osborn, "Capital Punishment as Legal Lynching?" 23, 36–49; Goldsby, *A Spectacular Secret*, 288; Hall, *Revolt against Chivalry*, 140–41; Mills, *The Racial Contract*, 11–14.

18. Rushdy, *The End of American Lynching*, 98, 139, 166–67, 172, 174. Some contemporary accounts of lynchings that occurred during the long civil rights era labeled them lynchings. Newspaper accounts of the quadruple lynching at Moore's Ford, Georgia, in 1946 and the lynching of Mack Charles Parker in Pearl River County, Mississippi, in 1959, for instance, frequently used the language of lynching in their coverage, as did the NAACP. For many other cases, including the lynching of Till in 1955, the lynching label was less consistently used, even though the NAACP and Till's mother, Mamie Till-Mobley, called his death a lynching. The triple lynching of the civil rights workers in 1964 rarely carries the label of lynching even though the manner in which they were kidnapped and killed resembled countless other lynchings that unquestionably carried the lynching label. For more on how the white supremacist violence of lynching shifted into the work of southern police departments, and the connections between lynching and hate crimes, see Waldrep, *African Americans Confront Lynching*, 93–111, 113–27.

19. For three excellent discussions of this painting and Lawrence's artistic representations of lynching more generally, see Apel, *Imagery of Lynching*, 160–61; Farah Jasmine Griffin, *"Who Set You Flowin'?" The African-American Migration Narrative* (New York: Oxford University Press, 1995), 13–15; Patricia Hills, *Painting Harlem Modern: The Art of Jacob Lawrence* (Berkeley: University of California Press, 2009), 112, 136–41, 164–67.

20. Apel, *Imagery of Lynching*, 83–131; Zangrando, *The NAACP Crusade against Lynching*, 125–26. One NAACP official was arrested for passing out pamphlets that included an image of a teenager named Rubin Stacy who was

lynched in 1935 by a Fort Lauderdale, Florida, mob. See also Wood, *Lynching and Spectacle*, 179–221; Mitchell, *Living with Lynching*; Baker, *Humane Insight*, 41–47.

21. The self-described "southern picker," James Allen, amassed a collection of more than one hundred lynching photographs, often purchasing them directly from people who had been holding onto them for decades in their homes.

22. Anonymous from Hot Springs, AR, to James O. Eastland, 25 January 1946, Box 32, Folder 1946 Civil Rights 2 of 2, Eastland Collection UMS. The enclosure with this letter was an article from the 11 September 1944 issue of *Life*, titled "P.A.C.: CIO's Political Action Committee Raises a Storm," that included the photo and description of the effigy hanged in Miami in 1939.

23. *The Papers of Martin Luther King, Jr.*, ed. Clayborne Carson, vol. 3, *Birth of a New Age, December 1955–December 1956* (Berkeley: University of California Press, 1994), 357; Robert S. Graetz, *Montgomery: A White Preacher's Memoir* (Minneapolis: Fortress Press, 1991), 88–89. The "Built by Union Labor" sign in front of the makeshift scaffold referred to the decision among some southern locals of the AFL-CIO to ignore the national union's order to integrate.

24. Elizabeth Jacoway, *Turn Away Thy Son: Little Rock, The Crisis That Shocked the Nation* (New York: Free Press, 2007), 2–6; David Margolick, *Elizabeth and Hazel: Two Women of Little Rock* (New Haven: Yale University Press, 2011). A *New York Times* reporter, Benjamin Fine, sat next to Eckford on the bus stop bench to comfort the rattled teenager, telling her not to let her tormenters see her cry, and for this, the mob threatened to lynch and castrate him. A Jewish New Yorker, Fine was an easy target for those white southerners who distrusted white outsiders, especially Jews, who supported the civil rights movement. Although African Americans made up the vast majority of lynching victims in the South, lynch mobs also targeted white ethnics whom many other white Americans perceived to possess only liminal whiteness.

25. Jacoway, *Turn Away Thy Son*, 1; Margolick, *Elizabeth and Hazel*, 17–19.

26. "WSB-TV newsfilm clip of African American students—the 'Little Rock Nine'—integrating Central High School and white students burning an effigy in protest in Little Rock, Arkansas, 1957 October 3," Civil Rights Digital Library, Digital Library of Georgia, University of Georgia Libraries.

27. Michele Norris, "Determined to Reach 1963 March, Teen Used Thumb and Feet," NPR, podcast audio, 14 August 2013, https://www.npr.org.

28. Oral History of William J. Stewart, 7 August 1995, *Behind the Veil* Duke.

29. In an act of utter absurdity, the sheriff arrested Turnbow for firebombing and shooting up his own home but later dropped the charges. Among Mississippi's civil rights activists, Holmes County became a safe haven because Black homes and meeting spaces were so well guarded. Payne, *I've Got the Light of Freedom*, 278–82; Akinyele Omowale Umoja, *We Will Shoot Back: Armed Resistance in the Mississippi Freedom Movement* (New York: New York

University Press, 2013), 74–75, 104–5; Charles E. Cobb Jr., *This Nonviolent Stuff'll Get You Killed: How Guns Made the Civil Rights Movement Possible* (Durham, NC: Duke University Press, 2016), 10, 138, 142.

30. Edwin White to James O. Eastland, 2 November 1965, Box 18, Folder Holmes County, MS Civil Rights, Eastland Collection UMS.

31. Edwin White to James O. Eastland, 2 November 1965.

32. Cagin and Dray, *We Are Not Afraid*, 135, 152–54.

33. Oral History of Bea Jenkins, 17 January 2000, "Civil Rights Documentation Project: The Holmes County Movement," Center for Oral History and Cultural Studies, University of Southern Mississippi.

34. Willie J. Denson to Richard B. Russell, 14 October 1957, Subgroup C, X: Civil Rights, P: Little Rock, Box 132, Folder 1, Russell Collection UGA.

35. Blight, *Race and Reunion*; Cox, *Dixie's Daughters*; Hahn, "Of Paramilitary Politics," in *A Nation under Our Feet*, 265–313; Foner, "The Challenge of Enforcement" and "Redemption and After," in *Reconstruction*, 412–59, 564–601.

36. Mrs. Will Henry to James O. Eastland, 6 June 1955, Box 34, Folder 1955 Civil Rights 2 of 2, Eastland Collection UMS.

37. W. B. Alexander to James O. Eastland, 15 December 1955, Box 34, Folder 1955 Civil Rights 2 of 2, Eastland Collection UMS.

38. William L. Brady to Richard B. Russell (telegram), 28 September 1957, Subgroup C, X: Civil Rights, P: Little Rock, Box 133, Folder 6, Russell Collection UGA.

39. Louis G. Hoffman to James O. Eastland, 5 July 1963, Box 41, Folder 1963 Civil Rights 1 of 4, Eastland Collection UMS.

40. Mabel B. Sheldon, 15 June 1964, Box 43, Folder 1964 Civil Rights 3 of 6, Eastland Collection UMS.

41. Sheldon's return address was in Biloxi, Mississippi, so she was probably unaware of the Klan activity planned for the following day in Neshoba County when she predicted the destruction of Black churches involved in civil rights agitation. Cagin and Dray, *We Are Not Afraid*, 1.

42. Archibald S. Coody to James O. Eastland, 29 August 1956, Box 35, Folder 1956 Civil Rights 1 of 3, Eastland Collection UMS.

43. W. R. Rawls to James O. Eastland, 18 June 1964, Box 43, Folder 1964 Civil Rights 3 of 3, Eastland Collection UMS.

44. The supposed tragedy of the "tragic era" of Reconstruction was that Black political power briefly disrupted white rule in the South. Although the "tragic era" also refers to the postwar ruin of the plantation economy, the term clearly reflects a worldview in which white supremacy rather than racial justice is the ideal to aspire to protect. James O. Eastland to W. R. Rawls, 30 June 1964, Box 43, Folder 1964 Civil Rights 3 of 3, Eastland Collection UMS.

45. The official logo for the Association of Citizens' Councils of Mississippi included a US flag next to a Confederate battle flag circled by the phrases,

"Citizens' Councils," "states' rights," and "racial integrity." The phrase "racial integrity" was probably borrowed from Virginia's Racial Integrity Act of 1924, which codified the one-drop rule to make interracial marriage illegal. This and other antimiscegenation laws remained legal until the *Loving v. Virginia* (1967) decision, which struck down these statutes for violating the equal protection and due process clauses of the Fourteenth Amendment.

46. "Famous Quotations" (flyer), M99, Box 1, Folder 31, Citizens' Council/ Civil Rights Collection, Historical Manuscripts, Special Collections, University of Southern Mississippi Libraries.

47. White fears about sex between Black men and white women were at the center of prolynching rhetoric, and though rape accusations and the "protection of white womanhood" were the most repeated and inflammatory phrases used to justify lynching, the potential for miscegenation (illicit interracial sex), interracial marriage, and mixed-race children was also invoked to articulate their fears—fears that actually were about Black economic competition, Black political power, and social equality. Apel, *Imagery of Lynching*, 24–28; Martha Hodes, "Murder: Black Men, White Women, and Lynching," in *White Women, Black Men: Illicit Sex in the Nineteenth-Century South* (New Haven: Yale University Press, 1997), 176–208. For more on the political and economic interests that underpinned fears about miscegenation and interracial marriage, see Peggy Pascoe, *What Comes Naturally: Miscegenation Law and the Making of Race in America* (New York: Oxford University Press, 2009).

48. The *Times-Picayune* reprinted some of Carter's quotes that originally appeared in *Look*. "Patterson Hits 'Klan' Comment: Blasts Editor on Article in National Magazine," *Times-Picayune* (New Orleans), 9 March 1955.

49. One Citizens' Council pamphlet, for instance, included this line: "We intend to carry on the peaceful relations we have had with our colored citizens, to help them to help themselves and to try to help instill in them a sense of pride in their race as we have in ours." What I'm describing as crassness is relative to the outright endorsement of burning African Americans alive, and by no means am I saying that his racism was not crass. "The Citizens' Council" (pamphlet), Box 1, Folder 31, Citizens' Council Civil Rights Collection, McCain Library and Archives, University of Southern Mississippi.

50. McMillen argues that, despite the violent activities of some council members and leaders (most notoriously Byron de la Beckwith, who murdered Medgar Evers), the Citizens' Council "eschewed the rope, fagot, and whip" and "forswore lawlessness and pledged itself to strictly legal means of defiance." He largely distances anti-Black violence from the council by blaming acts of violence on individuals, and though the leadership largely maintained a public stance against physical violence, the tolerance for violent elements within the organization casts doubt on this neat separation between the national leadership and its members. Neil R. McMillen, *The Citizens' Council:*

Organized Resistance to the Second Reconstruction 1954–64 (Urbana: University of Illinois Press, 1994), 360.

51. The economic pressure that the councils placed on African Americans involved in (or suspected of being involved in) the civil rights movement included firing activists and their family members, denying them loans, and demanding that they immediately pay existing loans in full. Because so many members of the council controlled local economies as employers and bankers, these tactics were devastating to grassroots organizing efforts in the Black community.

52. Without even a hint of irony, one member of the Citizens' Council of Alabama, Alston Keith, warned against allowing antisemitism to taint the organization, chiding, "There is no place for prejudice . . . in this movement." McMillen, *The Citizens' Council,* 50.

53. McMillen, *The Citizens' Council,* 47–57.

54. In 1963, amid congressional debates over civil rights legislation, Steele sent Eastland pamphlets and newspaper clippings he could read into the *Congressional Record* during a filibuster, including the *Thunderbolt* and articles from the *Citizen,* the council's monthly publication. FBI, "White Extremist Organizations: Part II National States Rights Party," May 1970, http://vault.fbi .gov; Kate H. Steele to James O. Eastland, 24 June 1963, Box 42, Folder 1963 Civil Rights 3 of 4, Eastland Collection UMS.

55. David R. Colburn, *Racial Change and Community Crisis: St. Augustine, Florida, 1877–1980* (New York: Columbia University Press, 1985), 51–53.

56. Hayling's right arm was badly injured, but he recovered and eventually returned to his practice. A similar near-lynching occurred in Cuthbert, Georgia, in 1967, when a mob stripped Winfred Rembert, hung him up by his ankles, stabbed him, and nearly castrated him. Oral History of Robert B. Hayling, 14 September 2011, "Civil Rights History Project," Southern Oral History Program, Smithsonian Institution's National Museum of African American History and Culture and the Library of Congress; Jud Esty-Kendall, "He Survived a Near-Lynching. 50 Years Later, He's Still Healing," NPR, podcast audio, 15 November 2019, https://www.npr.org; Winfred Rembert with Erin I. Kelly, *Chasing Me to My Grave: An Artist's Memoir of the Jim Crow South* (New York: Bloomsbury Publishing, 2021).

57. Using "murder" in place of "lynching" when discussing lynchings after 1950 often has the effect of marking clear progress in crushing white supremacy, implying that (white) community support for lynching dramatically shifted after 1940. For instance, though Brundage is careful to acknowledge many post–World War II lynchings, he labels the lynchings of Chaney, Goodman, and Schwerner in 1964 "murder" and talks about "the disappearance of lynching by 1950" and "the passing of one of the most significant rituals of black degradation." Brundage argues that "small, secretive mobs" in the 1940s, 1950s, and 1960s operated like the "terrorist mobs" that preceded them but then distinguishes between civil rights era racial violence and

lynching because the public element of "mass mobs" had largely disappeared. Brundage explains that lynching by "terrorist mobs" and "private mobs" in the earlier period "count" but similar mobs in the civil rights era don't "count" because popular sentiments among white southerners had changed. The recurrent usage of prolynching rhetoric during the civil rights era and the white community shielding Klan members from prosecution for crimes well into the 1990s, however, casts doubt on whether popular sentiments regarding lynching had truly changed or had simply gone underground as a matter of basic prudence. Brundage, *Lynching in the New South*, 252, 257–58.

58. Most histories of lynching place the beginning of southern lynching around 1880, but doing so erases lynchings in the South during the antebellum and Reconstruction periods. Mari N. Crabtree, "Lynching in the American Imagination: A Historiographical Reexamination," in *Reconstruction at 150*, ed. Orville Vernon Burton and J. Brent Morris (Charlottesville: University of Virginia Press, forthcoming 2023).

59. Despite discord between these antilynching organizations during that 1940 meeting, the participants settled on a common definition of lynching: an unlawful death or deaths caused by a "group acting under pretext of service to justice, race, or tradition." "Summary of the Conference on Lynching and Reports on Lynchings, Tuskegee Institute, Alabama," 14 December 1940.

60. Although the ASWPL lobbied southern politicians and sheriffs to prevent lynchings, the group opposed federal antilynching legislation on the grounds that states should be left to enforce laws without federal intervention, and Ames even applauded the southern Democrats' filibuster of an antilynching bill in 1938. A note that Ames probably wrote in reference to alleged lynchings in 1938 included the rather underhanded comment: "since both these organizations [the NAACP and Tuskegee Institute] are working for the passage of a Federal AntiLynching Bill (which the ASWPL does not endorse) they have a patri[o]tic interest in seeing that lynching continue." "Summary of the Conference on Lynching and Reports on Lynchings, Tuskegee Institute, Alabama," 14 December 1940; Memo pasted to letter from Tuskegee, 28 May 1937, Subseries 1.1, Box 1, Folder 6, Ames Papers UNC; Roy Wilkins to Marian Wilkinson, 3 February 1938, Subseries 1.1, Box 1, Folder 6, Ames Papers UNC. Hall, *Revolt against Chivalry*; Feimster, *Southern Horrors*, 231–32.

61. Rushdy, *The End of American Lynching*, 97–105.

62. Rushdy, *The End of American Lynching*, 167.

63. Goldsby, *A Spectacular Secret*, 5–6, 24–27, 283–84, 286, 288–89, 288n14, quote on 6. What Goldsby calls "the modernization thesis," which points to the mechanization of farm labor, secularization, a growing intellectual class, and other markers of modernity as the causes for lynching's decline, appears in Edward L. Ayers, *Vengeance and Justice: Crime and Punishment in the Nine-*

teenth-Century South (New York: Oxford University Press, 1984), 270, 275–76; Brundage, *Lynching in the New South*, 249–51, 257–58; Dray, *At the Hands of Persons Unknown*, 406–7, 459–61; Tolnay and Beck, *A Festival of Violence*, 213–33. Waldrep recognizes the difficulties of defining lynching, though his distinction between lynchings and hate crimes (or other racist violence) largely hinges on popular support, which glosses over how lynching evolved as historical circumstances changed over time. Waldrep, *The Many Faces of Judge Lynch*, 1–12, 177–83, 185–89.

64. Huie, "Whole State Condones It," 46–49. Mamie Till-Mobley often described her son's death as a lynching, though she used language like "hate crime" or "murder" as well. Some notable studies on Till's lynching include Devery S. Anderson, *Emmett Till: The Murder That Shocked the World and Propelled the Civil Rights Movement* (Jackson: University Press of Mississippi, 2015); Baker, "Emmett Till, Justice, and the Task of Recognition," in *Humane Insight*, 69–93; Gorn, *Let the People See*; Davis W. Houck, *Emmett Till and the Mississippi Press* (Jackson: University Press of Mississippi, 2008); Darryl Mace, *In Remembrance of Emmett Till: Regional Stories and Media Responses to the Black Freedom Struggle* (Lexington: University Press of Kentucky, 2014); Metress, *The Lynching of Emmett Till*; Tell, *Remembering Emmett Till*; Till-Mobley, *Death of Innocence*; Tyson, *The Blood of Emmett Till*; Stephen J. Whitfield, *A Death in the Delta: The Story of Emmett Till* (New York: Free Press, 1988).

65. Baker, *Humane Insight*, 77–87; Goldsby, *A Spectacular Secret*, 294–307; Gorn, *Let the People See*, 1.

66. Huie, "Whole State Condones It."

67. Cagin and Dray's meticulous reconstruction of the 1964 civil rights lynchings shies away from using the term "lynching," preferring "conspiracy" or "killings" or "assassinations" instead. Like Brundage, they argue that a lynching required a mob that didn't have to worry about being convicted of a crime because they had public opinion and "the law" on their side. To say that "the lynch mob by 1964 was an anachronism" strikes me as dismissive of the racist motivations behind the "conspiracy" and the wall of silence FBI agents encountered when investigating the lynchings. John Dittmer, in contrast, calls their deaths "lynchings." Cagin and Dray, *We Are Not Afraid*, 284–85; Dray, *At the Hands of Persons Unknown*, 457–63; John Dittmer, *Local People: The Struggle for Civil Rights in Mississippi* (Urbana: University of Illinois Press, 1994), 247, 251–52.

68. Dittmer took Spain's report seriously as evidence that Chaney had been severely beaten by the Klan, but Cagin and Dray conclude that, because the FBI witnesses never mentioned beating Chaney, those injuries must have been caused by the bulldozer. John Dittmer, *The Good Doctors: The Medical Committee for Human Rights and the Struggle for Social Justice in Health Care* (New York: Bloomsbury Press, 2009), 58–59; Cagin and Dray, *We Are Not Afraid*, 406–8.

69. Notes by James Meredith about the March Against Fear, undated, Box 97.25.14.3, Folder 4 " 'Walk to Jackson, MS' June 1966," Meredith Collection UMS; James Meredith, "Statement: My Walk from Memphis to Jackson," 31 May 1966, Box 97.25.14, Folder 2, Meredith Collection UMS.

70. Even the act of publicly supporting Meredith was quite daring for those who cheered him on along the highway. Hernando had been the site of at least six lynchings between 1889 and 1935, so Black residents were certainly aware of the dangers involved in refusing to "stay in their place." Ginzburg, *100 Years of Lynchings*, 263–65; "A Negro Fiend Lynched," *Washington Post*, 13 October 1889; "ILD Lynch Report of 24 Is Four Higher Than Tuskegee," *Chicago Defender*, 11 January 1936.

71. "Sniper Halts Meredith with Shotgun Blasts; Shelby Countian Held," *Commercial Appeal* (Memphis), 7 June 1966.

72. C. C. Alexander from Kosciusko, Mississippi, wrote to Eastland: "There is something 'Phony' about the picture as reports state that he (Norvell) gave a warning." C. C. Alexander to James O. Eastland, 5 July 1966, Box 45, Folder 1966 Civil Rights, Eastland Collection UMS.

73. J. R. Perry to James O. Eastland, 14 June 1966, Box 45, Folder 1966 Civil Rights, Eastland Collection UMS.

74. James O. Eastland to H. C. VanZant Sr., 24 June 1966, Box 45, Folder 1966 Civil Rights, Eastland Collection UMS.

75. James Meredith, "Statement on the Walk to Jackson, Mississippi," 7 June 1966, Box 97.25.14.3, Folder 4 " 'Walk to Jackson, MS' June 1966," Meredith Collection UMS.

76. Oral History of LeRoy Boyd, 19 and 22 June 1995, *Behind the Veil* Duke.

77. Oral History of Ada Ateman. Although the interview is filed under Ateman's name, her older sister, Henrene Jenkins, also participated in the interview and provided the testimony cited here.

78. Clifford Wilson and his wife, Elizabeth Wilson, were strict disciplinarians in their home, but they refused to allow whites to humiliate and punish their children in the manner that enslavers had punished enslaved people, namely, through whipping. According to their daughter, Earline McDowell, Clifford Wilson told the white men who employed his sons, "I'm their daddy. Ain't nobody going to discipline them but me and their momma. . . . One thing I do not allow is no white folk whooping my children." The son who was whipped had refused to load some sacks of dry goods into a general store because the white man who owned the store did not intend to pay him for his labor. Even as an elderly man, he carried thick scars across his back from that beating, which knocked him unconscious. Oral History of Earline McDowell, 30 June 1995, *Behind the Veil* Duke.

79. For more on Black self-defense in the civil rights era, see Cobb, *This Nonviolent Stuff'll Get You Killed;* Timothy B. Tyson, *Radio Free Dixie: Robert F. Williams and the Roots of Black Power* (Chapel Hill: University of North Carolina

Press, 2020); Umoja, *We Will Shoot Back;* Robert F. Williams, *Negroes with Guns* (1962; repr., Detroit: Wayne State University Press, 1998).

80. Manning Marable, *Race, Reform, and Rebellion: The Second Reconstruction in Black America, 1945–1990,* 2nd ed. (Jackson: University Press of Mississippi, 1991), 84.

Chapter Five. Protest

1. The nature of Sarah Donaldson and John Evans's relationship is hazy. Their children took his last name, but their granddaughter, Ethel Williams, when asked about her grandparents said, "I guess my grandmother—I'm not trying to defend her—she didn't have [unintelligible], she didn't have enough, but anyway, she had children by the, what, the slave master you call them?" Donaldson and Evans were born in the 1850s, and Evans was probably the nephew or some other relation of Andrew J. and Eliza S. Evans, who lived a few houses away from Donaldson with their son, William W. Evans. The 1880 Census lists Sarah Donaldson as the head of her household, and though all seven of her children share her last name, only the oldest four are identified as Black like their mother. The youngest three children, born after 1876, are identified as "mulatto," including an unnamed two-year-old boy, who is probably Charles Evans. In the 1900 Census, all nine of Donaldson's children living in her household have the last name Evans. The census taker from 1880, William W. Evans, was a single white man who lived with his parents, and their household in 1880 included two "mulatto" servants named S. Jackson Evans (age sixteen) and Andrew Evans (age ten). Those "servants" may have been William W. Evans's children or half-brothers. If so, multiple men in the white Evans family had children with Black women and gave their mixed-race children their last name. Oral History of Ethel Williams, 18 July 1994, *Behind the Veil* Duke.

2. Oral History of Ethel Williams. My reconstruction of the manhunt and lynching is largely based on local newspaper coverage: "Maddened Citizens Avenge the Crime," *Newberry Herald and News* (Newberry, SC), 3 July 1903; "Lynching at Norway," *Yorkville Enquirer* (York, SC), 4 July 1903; "An Assassin Dies," *Times and Democrat* (hereafter cited as *TD;* Orangeburg, SC), 8 July 1903; "An Assassin Dies," *Manning Times* (Manning, SC), 8 July 1903; "Lynching in Orangeburg," *Intelligencer* (Anderson, SC), 8 July 1903; "Suspected Murderer Lynched," *Bamberg Herald* (Bamberg, SC), 9 July 1903; "Norway Negroes Arrested," *TD,* 15 July 1903; "$1,500 in Rewards," *TD,* 19 August 1903.

3. Although newspaper accounts of the lynching call the Evanses' friend Lorenzo Williams, he is listed in the 1880 Census for Willow Township in Orangeburg County, South Carolina, as Lorenzo Williamson.

4. The resentment toward the Evanses was rooted in their mixed-race background. Local newspaper accounts of the lynching made more than one

mention of Charles Evans's complexion, in particular his "yellow face," in-
sinuating that, because of his proximity to whiteness, he believed he was de-
serving of the social status that came with whiteness.

5. Lilian Williams and her daughter, Ethel Williams, were teachers and college
graduates. In the antebellum South, whites feared Black literacy precisely
because it undermined white supremacy, and those associations between
Black education, radical northern influences, and a danger to the racial
order persisted well after emancipation. "An Assassin Dies," *TD.*

6. The *Atlanta Constitution, Chicago Daily Tribune,* and *New York Times* reported
that four, not three, Black men were taken to the jail and beaten just before
the lynching of Charles Evans, and the *Chicago Daily Tribune* and *New York
Times* coverage indicated that two of those men eventually died from their
injuries. "Armed Blacks Marching to Burn Carolina Town," *Atlanta Constitution,* 5 July 1903; "Blacks Hold Town," *Chicago Daily Tribune,* 5 July 1903;
"Negro Uprising in South Carolina," *New York Times,* 5 July 1903. One of
the men taken into custody and beaten, John Felder, may have been the
same John Felder lynched in 1912, also in Norway.

7. All three of the men arrested and whipped were from Willow Township, a
neighborhood just southeast of Norway where the Evanses lived. After the
lynching, ten other Black men were arrested on suspicion of being accessories to the Phillips murder, and all of them were from Willow Township as
well, including the Evanses' uncle, William Donaldson. "More Trouble at
Norway," *Atlanta Constitution,* 9 July 1903.

8. "Negro Uprising in South Carolina," *New York Times.* A *Times and Democrat*
article quoted a local deputy sheriff who speculated that whether James
Evans would continue to evade capture "will depend on how much money his
father can raise to give him to travel with." "Norway Negroes Arrested," *TD.*

9. The *Atlanta Constitution* reported that "at least five hundred negroes" were
assembled just outside Norway, but the *New York Times* indicated the number was two hundred. "Armed Blacks Marching," *Atlanta Constitution;*
"Blacks Hold Town," *Chicago Daily Tribune;* "Negro Uprising in South Carolina," *New York Times;* "By White Man Armed Blacks Are Being Led," *Atlanta Constitution,* 6 July 1903; "Negroes Threaten Town," *Sun* (Baltimore),
6 July 1903. Thirty to forty Black workers at the sawmill and the planing
mill just outside Norway refused to work after the lynching, causing both
businesses to temporarily cease operations. This work stoppage occurred
while local law enforcement continued to search for and arrest at least ten
Black men whom they suspected of being accomplices to Charles Evans in
the murder of Phillips. This work stoppage has clear resonances with the
Black workers in Waco who refused to work after the lynching of Sank
Majors in 1905. "An Assassin Dies," *TD.*

10. *Pink Franklin, Plff. In Err., vs. State of South Carolina,* 218 U.S. 161 (1910).
The NAACP was not founded until 1909, two years after the incident between Franklin and Valentine.

11. "Dastardly Affair," *TD*, 1 August 1907; "Got Him Safe," *TD*, 8 August 1907; "Farmers Aroused," *TD*, 8 August 1907; "Causes Trouble," *TD*, 15 August 1907.

12. "We are the Negroes of S.C." to Cope residents, 8 August 1907, Avery CofC. This letter has not been processed by the Avery Research Center yet. A brief article referencing the letter appeared a week after the date printed on the letter, noting, "one of the merchants at Cope got a letter postmarked Orangeburg and signed 'The Negroes of South Carolina' on last Saturday containing the most incendiary language. The writer of the letter said the negroes intended to poison and burn out all the white people in the State." "Playing with Fire," *TD*, 15 August 1907.

13. The local newspaper, the *Times and Democrat*, did not mention white men in Cope stripping and whipping Black women in public after Valentine's death, but given the frequency with which Black men in the area had been whipped to extract information and to punish them, the letter's reference to whipping and stripping Black women is hardly surprising. In fact, the lynching of Reuben Elrod in Piedmont, South Carolina, within days of the Evans lynching in 1903 involved white men whipping Black women and lynching Elrod for attempting to protect them from the assault. "Killed in His Own Home," *Keowee Courier* (Pickens, SC), 15 July 1903; "Mob Killed Negro," *TD*, 8 July 1903.

14. "We are the Negroes of S.C." to Cope residents.

15. Pink Franklin evaded the lynch mob, but at his trial he was sentenced to death. Though he lost his appeal, pressure from Booker T. Washington, the NAACP, and others convinced one South Carolina governor to commute his sentence and another to issue a pardon. I suspect that the author or authors of that letter didn't act on their threats, since the Valentine brothers weren't run out of Cope. In fact, a general store and cotton gin established in Cope just a few years after the near-lynching of Pink Franklin still bear the Valentine family name.

16. Robin D. G. Kelley, *Race Rebels: Culture, Politics, and the Black Working Class* (New York: Free Press, 1996), 3–9.

17. Quashie, *The Sovereignty of Quiet*, 3.

18. Quashie, *The Sovereignty of Quiet*, 9.

19. Quashie, *The Sovereignty of Quiet*, 26.

20. Ferguson's incisive analysis of the blues opens up new possibilities for thinking about the relationship between the blues, escape, and resistance, but his assertion that the blues takes a "fundamentally apolitical posture" and is "anti-resistant" relies on a rather narrow understanding of "the political." Though the blues doesn't offer political solutions to suffering in the narrow sense of "the political" (electoral politics, organized political protests, fighting against the root causes of white supremacy, and so forth), it embraces the political acts of refusing the terms of life set by the more powerful, of finding something in the midst of lynching to sustain life, of placing the self

and the people most precious to you at the center of your life. Ferguson, "A Blue Note," 699, 706.

21. Ferguson, "Race and the Rhetoric of Resistance," 17–18.

22. Key studies on the long civil rights movement include Tomiko Brown-Nagin, *Courage to Dissent: Atlanta and the Long History of the Civil Rights Movement* (New York: Oxford University Press, 2011); Dittmer, *Local People;* Robin D. G. Kelley, *Freedom Dreams: The Black Radical Imagination* (Boston: Beacon Press, 2002); Marable, *Race, Reform, and Rebellion;* Aldon D. Morris, *The Origins of the Civil Rights Movement: Black Communities Organizing for Change* (New York: Free Press, 1984); Payne, *I've Got the Light of Freedom;* Barbara Ransby, *Ella Baker and the Black Freedom Movement: A Radical Democratic Vision* (Chapel Hill: University of North Carolina Press, 2003).

23. Scholars tend to frame anti-lynching activism as something confined to the peak period of southern lynching, between roughly 1880 and 1940. Zangrando, for instance, placed bookends on the NAACP's antilynching activities based on the organization's formal campaigns, but Waldrep extends the timeline to include hate crimes legislation passed in 1994. Zangrando, *The NAACP Crusade against Lynching;* Waldrep, *African Americans Confront Lynching.*

24. NAACP membership card, 1968, Box IV:C7, Folder 1: "Augusta Branch 1966–1969," NAACP LoC.

25. Roy Leland Hopkins to Juanita Jackson, 8 February 1937, Box I:G203, Folder 22: "Houston College for Negroes, Houston, Texas 1936–1937," NAACP LoC.

26. Between 1882 and 1951, members of Congress proposed 257 antilynching bills, three of which passed the House of Representatives but were blocked by the Senate: H.R. 13, 67th Cong. (1922); H.R. 1507, 75th Cong. (1937); and H.R. 801, 76th Cong. (1940). Between 1941 and 1951 alone, members of Congress introduced sixty-six antilynching bills and held several antilynching hearings. Williams, *They Left Great Marks on Me,* 181–220, 224; Zangrando, *The NAACP Crusade against Lynching,* 26–42, 162, 165; Waldrep, *African Americans Confront Lynching,* 59–91, 121.

27. Zangrando, Waldrep, and Hobbs, for instance, do the important work of chronicling efforts to raise the public outcry against lynching, pass anti-lynching legislation, and prosecute lynchers, but other forms of protest, especially on the local level and in ways that circumvented the state, have received less attention. Zangrando, *The NAACP Crusade against Lynching;* Waldrep, *African Americans Confront Lynching;* Hobbs, *Democracy Abroad, Lynching at Home.*

28. Robert Bagnall to G. W. Hamilton, 30 April 1923, Box I:G203, Folder 7: "Houston, Texas 1919–1923," NAACP LoC; Press release, "Houston Branch, N.A.A.C.P. Secures Third Trial for Luther Collins," 10 July 1925, Box I:G203, Folder 10: "Houston, Tex. Apr–Oct. 1925," NAACP LoC.

29. Ida B. Wells, *Crusade for Justice: The Autobiography of Ida B. Wells* (Chicago: University of Chicago Press, 1970), 47–51, 61–63.

30. Kenneth Robert Janken, *Walter White: Mr. NAACP* (Chapel Hill: University of North Carolina Press, 2003), 29–33.

31. Oral History of Ethel Williams.

32. In yet another convergence of joy and sorrow, this interview about living through Jim Crow was conducted at Zimmerman's home on her sixtieth wedding anniversary. Oral History of Geraldyne Zimmerman, 14 July 1994, *Behind the Veil* Duke.

33. "Body of Negro Found Swinging to a Limb," *Times* (Montgomery, AL), 21 April 1924; "Negro Hanged by Mob in S.C.," *Elba Clipper* (Elba, AL), 24 April 1924; "Woman Fails to Identify, But Mob Attacks," *Pittsburgh Courier*, 3 May 1924; "Negro Lynched in Orangeburg County," *News Reporter* (Whiteville, NC), 8 May 1924. The 1920 Census confirms that the Pierces lived two doors down from Adams, who was living with his sister and brother-in-law in the city of Orangeburg.

34. Oral History of Geraldyne Zimmerman.

35. Oral History of Geraldyne Zimmerman; "Negro Leader in Dixie Says Threat Made," *Cumberland Sunday Times* (Cumberland, MD), 11 December 1955; "Jury to Be Picked for Sitdown Trial," *Rocky Mount Telegram* (Rocky Mount, NC), 18 March 1960; Bob McHugh, "Fire Hose and Tear Gas Used against Protesters," *Gastonia Gazette* (Gastonia, NC), 16 March 1960; Jack Shuler, *Blood and Bone: Truth and Reconciliation in a Southern Town* (Columbia: University of South Carolina Press, 2002), 64–65. Shuler, who interviewed Zimmerman, writes that Pierce ran over to the people with the fire hoses during the 1960 protest, but was escorted back to her daughter's car by the police. In her oral history with *Behind the Veil*, Zimmerman does not say that her mother ran to the fire hoses. Also, Zimmerman taught at South Carolina State University at the time, so some of the students protesting were probably in her classes.

36. John M. Adkins to Robert Bagnall, 20 January 1923, Box I:G203, Folder 7: "Houston, Texas 1919–1923," NAACP LoC.

37. E. O. Smith to Mary White Ovington, 5 January 1924, Box I:G203, Folder 9: "Houston, Tex. Jan—Nov. 1924," NAACP LoC.

38. Evers recognized that armed conflicts with white supremacists in Mississippi would be suicidal and did not "just start shooting," and many other Black southerners shared his desire to respond to the lynching with violence, including Robert F. Williams, the militant president of the NAACP branch in Monroe, North Carolina. Williams reacted to Parker's lynching with a call for what he termed "armed self-reliance," but Williams went further, criticizing the limits of nonviolence as a protest strategy and speculating that the lynch mob would have had second thoughts about lynching Parker had he been armed with a shotgun. Payne, *I've Got the Light of Freedom*, 48, 50; Myrlie B. Evers, *For Us, the Living* (Garden City, NY: Doubleday, 1967; Jackson: University Press of Mississippi, 1996), 17–18; Dittmer, *Local People*, 84–85; Tyson, *Radio Free Dixie*, 143.

39. Gorn, *Let the People See*, 263.
40. Although Till's lynching played a pivotal role in galvanizing the civil rights movement, the organizational apparatus that allowed for the mobilization of African American protest movements during the 1950s and 1960s had been established much earlier than 1955. The network of the Brotherhood of Sleeping Car Porters, the NAACP, the March on Washington Movement of 1941, and other organizations had been challenging racial injustice through the courts, legislatures, and boycotts for decades. Further, extreme white supremacist violence was hardly new to African Americans in 1955, but because of Till's young age and the widespread circulation of images of his battered corpse, his death moved many in "the Emmett Till Generation," as SNCC's Joyce Ladner called them, to actively protest white supremacy. Dittmer, *Local People*, 58; Payne, *I've Got the Light of Freedom*, 54.
41. Mace, *In Remembrance of Emmett Till*, 22–25; Anderson, *Emmett Till*, 56–59; Gorn, *Let the People See*, 56–63.
42. Author's interview with Jesse Pennington.
43. Author's interview with Jesse Pennington. Similarly, a Black man from Columbia, South Carolina, Zack Townsend, was serving in the military in Germany when Till was lynched, and because of the lynching, he decided to get a law degree to "help my people" protesting against Jim Crow. Within a few days of becoming a lawyer, he was representing five hundred protesters arrested in Orangeburg, South Carolina, and he spent the next several years defending protesters and filing lawsuits to desegregate schools and hospitals. Oral History of Zack Townsend, 8 August 1994, *Behind the Veil* Duke.
44. Mace, *In Remembrance of Emmett Till*, 134–36; Gorn, *Let the People See*, 259–68.
45. For more on Black mourning, see Nyle Fort, "Amazing Grief: African American Mourning and Contemporary Black Activism" (PhD diss., Princeton University, 2021); Karla F. C. Holloway, *Passed On: African American Mourning Stories* (Durham, NC: Duke University Press, 2002). Holloway discusses lynching and mourning, including an extensive analysis of the public and private mourning of Till (58–74 and 129–39).
46. Karl Evanzz, *The Messenger: The Rise and Fall of Elijah Muhammad* (New York: Pantheon Books, 1999), 23–24.
47. Evanzz, *The Messenger*, 38–41, 227.
48. The pervasiveness of lynching in Muhammad's time in Georgia should not be underestimated. The week before the lynching of Hamilton in 1912, three Black men and a Black woman were lynched in a nearby town, and soon after his move to Macon in 1919, another cluster of lynchings—four Black men lynched in three days—occurred. Evanzz, *The Messenger*, 39, 47, 48–51.
49. The NAACP's and Communist Party's 1935 antilynching exhibitions brought national attention to lynching, as did numerous plays, novels, and music, most notably Billie Holiday's performances of "Strange Fruit." Other

well-known fiction about lynching includes Du Bois, "The Coming of John"; Sterling Brown, "He Was a Man"; James Baldwin, *Blues for Mister Charlie;* Richard Wright, "Big Boy Leaves Home"; Ralph Ellison, "A Party Down at the Square"; and John Edgar Wideman, *The Lynchers.* See also Gwendolyn Brooks, "The Last Quatrain of the Ballad of Emmett Till"; Angela Davis, " 'Strange Fruit': Music and Social Consciousness," in *Blues Legacies and Black Feminism: Gertrude "Ma" Rainey, Bessie Smith, and Billie Holiday* (New York: Vintage Books, 1998), 181–97; Anne P. Rice, ed., *Witnessing Lynching: American Writers Respond* (New Brunswick, NJ: Rutgers University Press, 2003); Apel, *Imagery of Lynching;* Mitchell, *Living with Lynching.*

50. Du Bois, "Jesus Christ in Texas," 123–33.

51. Some examples of art that depicted the Christ-like sacrifice of lynched Black men include John Steuart Curry, *The Fugitive* (1935); E. Simms Campbell, *I Passed Along This Way* (1935); Julius Bloch, *The Lynching* (1932); and Prentiss Taylor, *Christ in Alabama* (1932). Apel, *Imagery of Lynching*, 100–101, 104–5, 111–15.

52. Barthé's sculpture, *The Mother,* is also known as *Mother and Son* and *Supplication.* Apel, *Imagery of Lynching*, 153.

53. Cone, *The Cross and the Lynching Tree*, 93.

54. Cone, *The Cross and the Lynching Tree*, 21.

55. The sculpture itself was destroyed in a shipping accident in 1940. Apel, *Imagery of Lynching*, 236n40.

56. Williams writes about works of art and literature that memorialize the lynching of Black women like Mary Turner by "affirm[ing] the void that marks the space of loss that language cannot recapture" rather than reproducing the spectacular display of their bodies. Her analysis of Kim Mayhorn's installation, *A Woman Was Lynched the Other Day* (1998), is particularly evocative for its careful reading of silence and absence that mirrors that of two panels in Lawrence's *Migration Series:* the seated figure mourning (fig. 5.2) and the lone figure mourning an absent body with a noose hanging from a branch in the distance (fig. 4.2). Williams argues, "The empty dress in Mayhorn's installation is an uncanny *évocateur* of [Laura] Nelson's [lynching] photograph, which haunts by virtue of its anti-spectacularity. The disembodied dress materializes the representational void that the silencing of lynched Black women has created." Later she writes that "privileging the void offers an approach to the trauma of lynching that does not foreground graphic representations of the tortured Black body. Rather, sound disrupts the silence of the visual and speaks for the dead." Williams, " 'A Woman was Lynched the Other Day,' " 81–98, quotes on 84 and 86.

57. Levine, *Black Culture and Black Consciousness*, 257.

58. Quashie, *Black Aliveness*, 5.

59. Holloway reprints Maurice O. Wallace's funeral sermon titled "The Promise of Hope in a Season of Despair" as the fifth chapter of *Passed On*, which ends

with this quotation from *Another Country*. James Baldwin, *Another Country* (1962; repr., New York: Vintage International, 1990), 121–22; Holloway, *Passed On*, 192. These lines from *Another Country* also rhyme with what Imani Perry writes about her grandmother after the death of one of her children: "How did she not curdle into bitterness? Her first child died, and I do not know how she made it. But she did. My God, she did. And she wasn't afraid to love any of the rest of us, even though the haunting of loss couldn't have ever left." Imani Perry, *Breathe: A Letter to My Sons* (Boston: Beacon Press, 2019), 144.

60. *Chappelle's Show*, season 2, episode 11, "Mandela Boot Camp and The Time Haters," directed by Rusty Cundieff and written by Neal Brennan and Dave Chappelle, aired 31 March 2004 on Comedy Central.

61. George Schuyler, *Black No More* (1931; repr., New York: Modern Library, 1999). Other examples of revenge fantasies about lynching that are not satire include Mat Johnson's graphic novel, *Incognegro*, which is loosely inspired by Walter White's lynching investigations for the NAACP, and John Edgar Wideman's novel *The Lynchers*, which is about a plot (ultimately abandoned) hatched by four Black men to kidnap and lynch a policeman to avenge the crimes of three centuries of white supremacy. Mat Johnson, *Incognegro: A Graphic Novel* (New York: Vertigo/DC Comics, 2008); John Edgar Wideman, *The Lynchers* (New York: Henry Holt and Company, 1973).

62. For more on Schuyler, see Ferguson's indispensable biography, in particular his chapter on *Black No More*. Jeffrey B. Ferguson, *The Sage of Sugar Hill: George S. Schuyler and the Harlem Renaissance* (New Haven: Yale University Press, 2005).

63. Schuyler, *Black No More*, 172.

64. Schuyler, *Black No More*, 164.

65. Echoes of the *Black No More* scene in which Snobbcraft and Buggerie are lynched resurface in Spike Lee's film *Bamboozled* (2000) during a bit from Junebug's (Paul Mooney) stand-up act. Junebug jokes, "Everybody wants to be Black, but ain't nobody want to be Black. It confuses me. They all act Black, sound Black. I hope they start hanging niggers again. I'm going to find out who's Black." *Bamboozled*, dir. Spike Lee (DVD) (Los Angeles: New Line Productions, 2001).

66. W. E. B. Du Bois, *The Souls of Black Folk*, ed. David W. Blight and Robert Gooding-Williams (1903; repr., Boston: Bedford/St. Martin's, 1997), 38.

67. Schuyler, *Black No More*, xvii.

68. By contrast, the revenge fantasies *Posse* and *Incognegro* have Black characters either exact revenge directly or orchestrate the circumstances that lead to the lynching of a white character.

69. Schuyler, *Black No More*, 176.

70. James Baldwin, "Everybody's Protest Novel," in *Notes of a Native Son* (1955; repr., Boston: Beacon Press, 1984), 19.

71. Schuyler, *Black No More*, 176.

72. Imani Perry and Kiese Laymon, "Imani Perry in Conversation with Kiese Laymon: On the Uprising since George Floyd's Murder and Black Struggles for Freedom in the United States," 9 June 2020, Free Library of Philadelphia Podcast, MP3 audio, 71:51, https://libwww.freelibrary.org/podcast/episode /1930.

73. Author's interview with Lester Gibson. Some of Gibson's family members, including Leroy Gibson, worked for a wealthy white family, and the murder and rape of one of the white granddaughters in that family sparked the 1922 lynchings in Freestone County, Texas. Like the Gibsons in Freestone County, the Black community in Monroe, North Carolina, successfully thwarted lynch mobs and even ran the Klan out of the area. Tyson, *Radio Free Dixie*, 49–50, 88–91.

74. Akers, *Flames after Midnight*, 126.

75. Akers, *Flames after Midnight*, 126–31.

76. For a complete list of lynchings in McLennan County, Texas, see Carrigan, *The Making of a Lynching Culture*, app. A.

77. Tommy Witherspoon, "Lynching Resolution Reworked," *Waco Tribune-Herald* (hereafter cited as *WTRH*), 23 May 2006; Witherspoon, "Court Refusing to Display Anti-Lynching Resolution," *WTRH*, 31 May 2006; Witherspoon, "Resolution Turns into Tug of War," *WTRH*, 12 July 2006; "Resolution Tug of War Ends in Compromise," *WTRH*, 13 July 2006; "Resolve This," *WTRH*, 13 July 2006.

Chapter Six. The Blues

Excerpts from "Blue Dementia" from *The Chameleon Couch* by Yusef Komunyakaa. Copyright © 2011 by Yusef Komunyakaa. Reprinted by permission of Farrar, Straus and Giroux. All Rights Reserved.

1. Komunyakaa, "Blue Dementia," 62.

2. Claudia Rankine, *Citizen: An American Lyric* (Minneapolis: Graywolf Press, 2014), 60.

3. B. B. King with David Ritz, *Blues All around Me: The Autobiography of B. B. King* (New York: Avon Books, 1996), 51.

4. King, *Blues All around Me*, 51.

5. The identity of the lynching victim is unclear since the lynchings closest to the time and place of the lynching King witnessed were in 1926 (Frederick Chambers, age thirty-nine, shot in jail for shooting an officer) and 1946 (Leon McTatie, age thirty-five, beaten then drowned for stealing a saddle) and do not match King's description. Since the body was displayed at the county courthouse in Lexington, King might have been referring to a "legal lynching"—a case in which a hasty and perfunctory trial occurred, often to preempt a lynch mob, but the defendant was presumed to be guilty and was executed, often immediately following the "trial." These sham trials provided local law enforcement and politicians cover to deflect accusations that

the state tolerated or even encouraged extralegal violence and denied justice to Black defendants. Clearly these trials were deeply unjust, and local African American communities often did not distinguish between "lynching" and "legal lynching" because the miscarriage of justice and the outcomes were virtually identical.

6. King, *Blues All around Me,* 37.
7. King, *Blues All around Me,* 8.
8. King, *Blues All around Me,* 36–37.
9. King, *Blues All around Me,* 8–9.
10. King, *Blues All around Me,* 22.
11. King, *Blues All around Me,* 33.
12. King, *Blues All around Me,* 8.
13. King, *Blues All around Me,* 51.
14. King, *Blues All around Me,* 127.
15. King, *Blues All around Me,* 51.
16. Ralph Ellison, "Blues People," in *The Collected Essays of Ralph Ellison* (New York: Modern Library, 2003), 287.
17. John F. Szwed draws the following connections (and distinctions) between the spirituals and the blues: "The essential difference between the two means of psychological release focuses on the 'direction' of the song: church music is directed collectively to God; blues are directed individually to the collective. Both perform similar cathartic functions but within different frameworks." John F. Szwed, "Musical Adaptation among Afro-Americans," *Journal of American Folklore* 82, no. 324 (1969): 117.
18. James H. Cone, *The Spirituals and the Blues: An Interpretation* (Maryknoll, NY: Orbis Books, 1991), 105.
19. Ta-Nehisi Coates, "Black Pathology and the Closing of the Progressive Mind," *Atlantic,* 24 March 2014, https://www.theatlantic.com/politics/archive/2014/03/black-pathology-and-the-closing-of-the-progressive-mind/284523/.
20. Although historians and others invested in shaping collective memory can no more force an honest reckoning with this history than they can change the past itself, the work of making visible these memories should ideally inspire self-reflection, not paternalistic pity. The latter, however, has long been the response to campaigns to raise awareness of atrocities, which again explains the reticence to talk about African Americans as victims. Being a victim does not render one helpless or without agency. Relatedly, the joy within the blues often gets buried because feeling blue is about suffering and pain, but, as Cone explained, "the blues expressed a feeling, an existential affirmation of joy in the midst of extreme suffering, especially the ever-present threat of death by lynching." Cone, *The Cross and the Lynching Tree,* 17.
21. The symptoms of posttraumatic stress disorder include the recurrence of involuntary memories, dreams, and flashbacks about traumatic events; psychological and physiological reactions to triggers; and avoidance of memories

and triggers. Though these symptoms apply most directly to individual trauma survivors, they speak to both individual and collective hauntedness in the aftermath of traumatic events like lynchings. American Psychiatric Association, "Trauma- and Stressor-Related Disorders," in *Diagnostic and Statistical Manual of Mental Disorders*, 5th ed. (Arlington, VA: American Psychiatric Publishing, 2013), 265–90. African American writers broached the subject of the Black experience and trauma long before the field of trauma studies emerged in the twentieth century but in ways less legible to the white-dominated academy. More recently, scholarship on the blues, the history of enslavement, psychology, and social work takes up questions about trauma within the African American community, as do countless novels, artworks, and poems. Lilian Coas-Díaz, Gordon Nagayama Hall, and Helen A. Neville, "Racial Trauma: Theory, Research, and Healing," *American Psychologist* 74, no. 1 (2019): 1–5; Nicholas J. Sibrava, Andri S. Bjornsson, A. Carlos I. Pérez Benítez, Ethan Moitra, Risa B. Weisberg, and Martin B. Keller, "Posttraumatic Stress Disorder in African American and Latinx Adults: Clinical Course and the Role of Racial and Ethnic Discrimination," *American Psychologist* 74, no. 1 (2019): 101–16; Sharpe, *In the Wake*; Colbert, Patterson, and Levy-Hussen, *The Psychic Hold of Slavery*; Sharpe, "Understanding the Sociocultural Context"; Gordon, *Ghostly Matters*; Adam Gussow, *Seems Like Murder Here: Southern Violence and the Blues Tradition* (Chicago: University of Chicago Press, 2002); Joy DeGruy Leary, *Post Traumatic Slave Syndrome: America's Legacy of Enduring Injury and Healing* (Milwaukie, OR: Uptone Press, 2005).

22. LaCapra, *Writing History, Writing Trauma*, 186.
23. Dori Laub, "Truth and Testimony: The Process and the Struggle," in *Trauma: Explorations in History*, ed. Cathy Caruth (Baltimore: Johns Hopkins University Press, 1995), 64, 70.
24. Rebecca Solnit, "The Monument Wars," in *Call Them by Their True Names* (Chicago: Haymarket Books, 2018), 83.
25. King, *Blues All around Me*, 33.
26. B. B. King, "Nobody Loves Me But My Mother," on *Icon 2* (CD, Geffen B004NDVK5E, 2011). In other recordings, King adds comical sniffles, and, at times, the occasional chuckle slips in between his lines, making it clear that he is making light of his own loneliness. For more on the expressiveness of the blues, even without lyrics, see Levine, *Black Culture and Black Consciousness*, 232.
27. Ellison, *Invisible Man*, 9.
28. The question of witnessing is further complicated when the survivor—in this case, the protagonist—is invisible. Ellison's character is rendered invisible by white Americans but also has yet to find his own voice. By contrast, the likes of King and Armstrong have found a voice in the blues sensibility, which the protagonist in Ellison's novel is only beginning to grasp and comprehend. In the final pages of the novel, the protagonist is still preparing to

emerge from the depths of his underground abode, but he has a model in Armstrong: a not entirely invisible man who may not be what he seems to be (to those who can't truly see him, that is—to those who only see the comforting [to them] caricature and not the genius of Armstrong).

29. Ellison, *Invisible Man*, 8.

30. Moten, *In the Break*, 67–69, 82–84.

31. Ferguson, "A Blue Note," 705, emphasis added.

32. Ferguson, "A Blue Note," 706.

33. Ferguson goes further to claim that the blues take an "apolitical and anti-resistant posture," despite "resistant gestures" like airing grievances or injustices through song that might otherwise invite reprisals, because blues music "rarely suggests a political solution to the ills at hand." Ferguson, "A Blue Note," 705; Levine, *Black Culture and Black Consciousness*, 297.

34. The same forces that make scholars shy away from discussions of Black victimhood and trauma also often render Black people superhuman freedom fighters. Both categories are reductive, and they emerge out of what Ferguson identifies as "the Enlightenment revaluation of resistance [that] inaugurated opposition as the only possible authentic gesture of the oppressed, and as the supreme litmus test of their humanity." Ferguson, "Race and the Rhetoric of Resistance," 4–10, 17–18. For more on alternatives to the resistance paradigm, see Quashie, *The Sovereignty of Quiet*; Quashie, *Black Aliveness*.

35. Ferguson's framing of escape as "making the oppressor disappear" rhymes with what Imani Perry writes about her mother's "wisdom regarding how you deal with racism: 'Render them invisible.'" In both cases, the oppressor still exists but elsewhere, in some other place where they cannot inflict further harm. Jeffrey B. Ferguson, "Notes on Escape," in *Race and the Rhetoric of Resistance* (New Brunswick, NJ: Rutgers University Press, 2021), 93, 104, 103; Perry, *Breathe*, 108–9.

36. Laub, "Truth and Testimony," 61, 71.

37. Like Ferguson who points to "the hidden world of blackness" as a beacon of hope and potential liberation, Quashie also imagines a "black world" that exists "beyond the racist order of the world": "we have to image a black world so as to surpass the everywhere and everyday of black death." While recognizing the very real existence of anti-Blackness, Quashie removes anti-Blackness from the center of his thinking, echoing Ferguson's understanding of escape as living outside of and being inaccessible to anti-Blackness. Quashie, *Black Aliveness*, 5, 1; Levine, *Black Culture and Black Consciousness*, 221, 235, 237.

38. Ellison, "Richard Wright's Blues," 129.

39. Cone also discusses the blues as a means to transcend this-worldly hardships, but his definition of transcendence differs slightly from Ellison's usage. Cone's sense of transcendence is rooted in the assertion of Black humanity in the face of white supremacist degradation, which allows Black

people to defy and maneuver around the racist restrictions placed on their lives. For Ellison, the blues are an art, and the creative (and courageous and defiant) act of revisiting painful memories provides transcendence. Cone, *The Spirituals and the Blues*, 112–13.

40. Mississippi Fred McDowell, "Everybody's Down on Me," recorded c. November 1969, on *I Do Not Play No Rock 'n' Roll* (CD, Capitol Records CDP7243, 1995).

41. Albert Murray, *Stomping the Blues*, 2nd ed. (Cambridge, MA: Da Capo Press, 2000), 3.

42. Big Mama Thornton, "Goodbye Baby," on *The Complete Vanguard Recordings* (CD, Vanguard 175/77–2, 2000).

43. Broonzy, Slim, and Williamson, *Blues in the Mississippi Night*. "Signifying" refers to clever wordplay and figurative expression steeped in the Black vernacular that includes double entendre, boasts, the dozens, jokes, hyperbole, understatement, and masking. Because signifying relies on the slippage between the figurative and the literal, it requires being in the know—in particular, being familiar with Black cultural references and expressions—to identify, understand, and appreciate it. Henry Louis Gates, *The Signifying Monkey: A Theory of African-American Literary Criticism* (New York: Oxford University Press, 1988).

44. Broonzy, Slim, and Williamson, *Blues in the Mississippi Night*.

45. White backlash against even the most minuscule of Black gains (or simple assertions of dignity) has been a consistent feature of US history from the mass executions of enslaved and free Black people in the hysteria following rumored slave conspiracies to the lynching of Black people for establishing a successful business or not tipping their hats to white people.

46. Big Bill Broonzy, "Black, Brown, and White," recorded 14 November 1956, on *Trouble in Mind* (CD, Smithsonian Folkways Recordings, SFW CD 40131, 2000).

47. Most of Broonzy's music broached more typical blues subjects like loneliness and betrayal, but he also wrote "When Will I Get to Be Called a Man" about being called a boy all his life. In the song, Broonzy openly criticizes the patronizing and racist practice of white people calling grown Black men "boy," and ends the first verse wondering if he will have to wait until he is ninety-three years old before he is finally called a man. Big Bill Broonzy, "When Will I Get to Be Called a Man," recorded 1957, on *Trouble in Mind*. In general, however, blues music leaned toward sly misdirection and double entendre. As Ellison said in his review of Amiri Baraka's *Blues People*, the blues are "not primarily concerned with ... obvious political protest," but rather they are "an art form and thus a transcendence of those conditions created within the Negro community by the denial of social justice." Ellison, "Blues People," 287.

48. Big Bill Broonzy, "Digging My Potatoes," recorded 1957, on *Trouble in Mind*.

49. Perry, *Breathe*, 32.

50. In locating elements of the blues sensibility (double meanings, expressions of hope and despair, coded language, and so on) in the spirituals and before blues music became popular among Black people, I want to clarify that the blues and spirituals approach the blues as such differently. While the spirituals are a form of collective expression that seeks relief from troubles through salvation from God, the blues are a far more individual form of expression that looks inward to the self, even though blues music was performed in juke joints, was widely distributed through records and the radio, and spoke to shared experiences among Black people. Levine, *Black Culture and Black Consciousness*, 221–24, 234–37; Ferguson, "A Blue Note," 705–6.

51. Du Bois, *The Souls of Black Folk*, 185, 187.

52. Du Bois, *The Souls of Black Folk*, 192.

53. Cone wrote that "Black music is unity music. It unites the joy and the sorrow, the love and the hate, the hope and the despair of black people." Thurman, *The Negro Spiritual Speaks of Life and Death*, 5.

54. Baldwin, *The Fire Next Time*, 42.

55. Ellison, "Richard Wright's Blues," 143.

56. "Sister Rosetta Tharpe—Trouble in Mind," YouTube video, 3:51, from a performance in Manchester, England in 1964, posted by "cerinto," 8 September 2012, http://www.youtube.com/watch?v=U3PNc_cWv9M.

57. Baldwin, *The Fire Next Time*, 104.

58. Baldwin, *The Fire Next Time*, 42.

59. Nelson George, *The Death of Rhythm and Blues* (New York: Penguin Books, 1988).

60. Andre Craddick-Willis argues that hip-hop was divided between, on the one hand, the "prophetic" and "counter-hegemonic" wing that remained faithful to the "visionary" tradition of the blues and, on the other hand, the "normative" wing that rehashed "non-liberating" hatred like homophobia and sexism, and sought fame and fortune above all else. This sense that the "normative" wing had strayed from the Black musical tradition was, to Craddick-Willis, indicative of a generation moved less by the blues and more by commercial success than "vision and analysis." However, Kelley and others have argued that even the much-romanticized blues fell into similar wings. Andre Craddick-Willis, "Rap Music and the Black Musical Tradition: A Critical Reassessment," *Radical America* 23, no. 4 (October–December 1989, published June 1991): 36–37; Robin D. G. Kelley, *Yo' Mama's Disfunktional! Fighting the Culture Wars in Urban America* (Boston: Beacon Press, 1997), 187n38.

61. Recent research on epigenetics explains how past traumas can filter down to subsequent generations since noncoding DNA impacted by trauma can shape how children and grandchildren respond to similar stressors. Even though the genetic code itself remains unchanged by trauma, traumatic responses can be passed on. Wolynn, *It Didn't Start with You*, 29–39; Richard C. Francis, *Epigenetics: The Ultimate Mystery of Inheritance* (New York: W. W. Norton, 2011).

62. As Kelley points out, scholars should avoid the tendency to "reduce expressive culture to a political text" and instead appreciate that, like the blues and hip-hop, playing the dozens and other forms of Black humor are primarily displays of ingenuity performed for pleasure. However, to appreciate ingenuity and pleasure is not to diminish the political meaning and metaphorical value of the blues sensibility. Kelley, *Yo' Mama's Disfunktional!* 37–38. For more on humor and subversion in African American culture, see Levine, *Black Culture and Black Consciousness,* 102–33, 239–70, 298–366. Also, the widespread impact of the blues sensibility on Black culture and the blues (as a genre) being at the root of most Black secular music since the late nineteenth century does not mean that the blues encompass the totality of Black music or culture.

63. Dick Gregory, *From the Back of the Bus,* ed. Bob Orben (New York: E. P. Dutton, 1962), 125; Rebecca Krefting, *All Joking Aside: American Humor and Its Discontents* (Baltimore: Johns Hopkins University Press, 2014), 36n2.

64. Rankine, *Citizen,* 135. For more on how Black people learn to anticipate white violence in a society that criminalizes Blackness and to conceal their true selves from the white world, see Du Bois, *The Souls of Black Folk,* 38; Richard Wright, "The Ethics of Living Jim Crow: An Autobiographical Sketch," in *Uncle Tom's Children* (1938; repr., New York: Harper Perennial Modern Classics, 2008), 1–15; Darlene Clark Hine, "Rape and the Inner Lives of Black Women in the Middle West," *Signs* 14, no. 4 (1989): 912, 915; Litwack, *Trouble in Mind,* 3–51; Holloway, *Jim Crow Wisdom,* 5–8.

65. Kelley and other hip-hop scholars have noted what he called the "verbal facility" and "linguistic inventiveness" of hip-hop lyrics, which themselves emerged out of the appreciation for clever wordplay that we find in the blues and humor. The resonances between the blues metanarrative and that of hip-hop and R&B also reveal how the blues sensibility has provided a means to process trauma within the African American community across generations and genres. Not only do contemporary artists sample the music of previous generations, but also the stories they tell and themes they broach reflect intergenerational narratives about struggle and the blues as such, even as those struggles change over time. Kelley, *Yo' Mama's Disfunktional!* 37.

66. Ferguson, "A Blue Note," 711.

67. Though this phrase about living in the lion's mouth appears elsewhere, too, it is uttered by the protagonist's grandfather in *Invisible Man*. On his deathbed, the grandfather calls for his descendants to take up his mantle and sabotage white supremacists. Ellison, *Invisible Man,* 16.

68. Thurman, *The Negro Spiritual Speaks of Life and Death,* 5.

69. Perry, *Breathe,* 36–37, 135–36. What Perry calls "mixing it [grief and death] into the clay of your living" (and what Ellison called "to finger its jagged grain") is reminiscent of what the psychotherapist Miriam Greenspan describes as "the alchemy of the dark emotions," or "knowing how to stay connected to the energy of painful emotions, to attend to and befriend it, to surrender to it,

mindfully, without being overwhelmed." Greenspan writes, "Healing through the dark emotions is an unarmed journey into vulnerability—a journey through, not a departure from, pain." Through this healing process, victims and survivors revisit the full force of their pain, not to become immobilized by it but to make meaning out of it and find a way through it. Greenspan, *Healing through the Dark Emotions: The Wisdom of Grief, Fear, and Despair* (Boston: Shambhala Publications, 2003), 11–12.

70. Cone asserted, "No black person can escape the blues, because the blues are an inherent part of black existence in America. To be black is to be blue." At the same time, the sensibility of the blues provides Black people with the presence of mind to recognize suffering in their lives but not become consumed or defined by a society that degrades Black people as a matter of course. Cone, *The Spirituals and the Blues*, 103, 105.

71. Kai Erikson explains that "trauma can issue from a sustained exposure to battle as well as from a moment of numbing shock, from a continuing pattern of abuse as well as from a single searing assault, from a period of serious attenuation and erosion as well as from a sudden flash of fear." Individuals and communities alike felt the traumatic reverberations of specific lynchings but also the social milieu created by lynching and other white supremacist terrorism. Kai Erikson, "Notes on Trauma and Community," in *Trauma: Explorations in Memory*, ed. Cathy Caruth (Baltimore: Johns Hopkins University Press, 1995), 185.

72. Author's interview with Audrey Grant.

73. The friend of Jeffrey Saffold's brother may have been Fred Chambers, a thirty-nine-year-old Black man who was allegedly an accomplice of Arthur Wade in the shooting of Pickens city marshal, Hubert L. Jones, in 1926. Officers arrested Chambers when he sought treatment for a gunshot wound to the shoulder, then took him to the jail in Goodman, Mississippi, where he was "found dead of bullet wounds, inflicted by unknown persons who 'shot up the jail.' " *Clarion Ledger* (Jackson, MS), 20 July 1926.

74. Author's interview with Willie Head Jr.

75. Blues expressions aim to restore the self, family, and Black community even when these expressions have witnesses beyond the Black community. The impetus behind the blues sensibility is not primarily to force the perpetrators of trauma to confront the harm they have caused, though that may be one effect of airing lynching memories in public, but to give victims and survivors the means to "make it over," as the gospel song "How I Got Over" says.

76. Author's interview with Willie Head Jr.

77. The criminalization of Black people stretches back to at least the seventeenth century, and the use of incarceration to enforce racial caste in the United States developed out of the establishment of the police and prisons, convict leasing, chain gangs, vagrancy laws, and lynching, among other institutions and practices.

78. Although the Department of Agriculture paid Black farmers restitution for their discriminatory practices, the check was too late for the many Black farmers who had already lost their farms to foreclosure. Further undermining this effort to restore what had been lost, none of the employees who were responsible for the discrimination in the first place lost their jobs, which reveals how little the institutional culture at the Department of Agriculture had changed.

79. Head's involvement in the *Pigford* claim was also rooted in the broken promises of Reconstruction, promises that freedom would be materially different from enslavement. In the 1860s, freedpeople generally agreed that centuries of unpaid labor gave them a claim to the land they and their ancestors had worked, and land was a form of restitution and a basic necessity to start anew as free and economically independent people. At a meeting between General William Tecumseh Sherman, Secretary of War Edwin Stanton, and twenty Black ministers in 1865, Garrison Frazier, one of the ministers, argued for land redistribution as central to the idea of freedom: "The way we can best take care of ourselves is to have land, and turn it and till it by our own labor ... and we can soon maintain ourselves and have something to spare." Instead, the promise of freedom was fleeting, and white plunder of Black-owned land or would-be Black-owned land continued for generations. Ira Berlin, Barbara J. Fields, Steven F. Miller, Joseph P. Reidy, and Leslie S. Rowland, eds., *Free at Last: A Documentary History of Slavery, Freedom, and the Civil War* (New York: New Press, 1992), quote on 314. See also Hahn, *A Nation under Our Feet*, 136–37, 145–50; Leon F. Litwack, *Been in the Storm so Long: The Aftermath of Slavery* (New York: Vintage Books, 1980), 399–408.

80. On multiple occasions, vandals have shot up an official historical marker memorializing Mary Turner and other lynching victims in Brooks County, Georgia, and some local whites have made veiled threats against Head, sarcastically expressing surprise that he was still around after numerous attempts to pressure him to sell his land.

81. When I interviewed Head, the recent death of his daughter and his wife before her left him to be the sole guardian of his two granddaughters. A farmer whose life's work was to bring forth life out of the earth and tend to crops, Head has embraced the role of caretaker for his granddaughters, and I suspect that his vision for the future is filtered through the world he hopes his granddaughters inherit.

82. Komunyakaa, "Blue Dementia," 62–63.

Epilogue

Lucille Clifton, excerpt from "why some people be mad at me sometimes" from *How to Carry Water: Selected Poems.* Copyright © 1987 by Lucille Clifton. Reprinted with the permission of The Permissions Company, LLC on behalf of BOA Editions, Ltd., boaeditions.org.

1. Oral History of John Henry Johnson, 2 August 1995, *Behind the Veil* Duke. I also recognized similarities between Rosebud's grandparents and the parents of Clarence Hunter, an archivist at the Mississippi Department of Archives and History. Hunter grew up in Washington, DC, during the 1920s and 1930s, and his parents made him and his brother read two Black newspapers, the *Washington Afro-American* and the *Pittsburgh Courier,* cover to cover every week, in particular the articles about lynching, "to instill in us . . . the dangers of the South. . . . When I misbehaved sometimes, my parents, my mother especially, she would warn me, 'if you don't behave yourself, you will wind up in Mississippi.' " Author's interview with Clarence Hunter in Jackson, Mississippi, 9 November 2011.

2. Sharpe, *In the Wake,* 104.

3. The mayor of Glendora, Johnny B. Thomas, has been instrumental in building and developing ETHIC, but his father, who worked for Milam, one of Till's lynchers, assisted the two white men in kidnapping and perhaps even disposing of Till's body. FBI, *Prosecutive Report of Investigation concerning [redacted], Roy Bryant, John William Milam, Leslie F. Milam, Melvin L. Campbell, Elmer O. Kimbrell, Hubert Clark, Levi Collins, Johnny B. Washington, Otha Johnson, Jr., Emmett Louis Till* (2006), 30.

4. ETHIC's blues inflection is grounded, in part, in the town proudly claiming the blues harmonica player, Sonny Boy Williamson II, as a favorite son.

5. Transcript from Auburn Avenue Research Library Open Forum on 6 December 2000, Without Sanctuary Emory, 3, 6–7.

6. Martin Luther King Jr., "Letter from Birmingham City Jail," in *The American Civil Rights Movement: Readings and Interpretations,* ed. Raymond D'Angelo (New York: McGraw-Hill/Dushkin, 2001), 325.

7. Pennington, whom I discuss at length in chapter 2, barely eluded a lynch mob in Mississippi in 1954, and after he had suppressed that memory for decades, he found that viewing *Without Sanctuary* in Jackson, Mississippi, in 2004 triggered a confrontation with the grief and terror he had carried for years.

8. At the Equal Justice Initiative's Legacy Museum, which is a companion to its National Memorial for Peace and Justice, one display includes dozens of clear jars containing soil taken from lynching sites across the South. The ritual of lynching survivors collecting this soil for the museum recognizes that the land upon which a lynching occurred contains remnants of these crimes but also something of the victims' lives.

9. Gonzales-Day, *Lynching in the West;* Martinez, *The Injustice Never Leaves You.*

10. "The Legacy Museum: From Enslavement to Mass Incarceration," Equal Justice Initiative, https://museumandmemorial.eji.org/museum.

11. Ersula J. Ore, *Lynching: Violence, Rhetoric, and American Identity* (Jackson: University Press of Mississippi, 2019), 86–89.

12. The impulse to designate a definitive endpoint to lynching, what Rushdy calls "the end-of-lynching discourse," speaks to a "hope for a transformative

moment in which the nation's glaring and festering wound—the violence done to racial and ethnic minorities in the name of white supremacy—is healed through the recognition that that was the last of something, the end of that regime, and that this is the first of something else, the inauguration of another, better regime." Rushdy, *The End of American Lynching*, 174. For more on the evolution of lynching after Jim Crow, see Rushdy, *The End of American Lynching*, 95–159; Ore, *Lynching*, 3–12, 91–92.

13. Aimee Ortiz, "Emmett Till Memorial Has a New Sign. This Time, It's Bulletproof," *New York Times*, 20 October 2019.

14. Bruce Watson, *Freedom Summer: The Savage Summer of 1964 That Made Mississippi Burn and Made America a Democracy* (New York: Penguin Books, 2010), 296; John Blake, "'Mississippi Burning' Murders Still Smolder for One Brother," CNN, https://www.cnn.com.

15. Yates, *Life and Death in a Small Southern Town*, 156.

16. Ethan Rice, "Anti-lynching Resolution Brings Unneeded Pain," *WTRH*, 13 August 2006.

17. Cindy V. Culp, "A Crime before a 'Horror,'" *WTRH*, 7 May 2006.

18. Rice's editorial was not the only one printed in the *Waco Tribune-Herald* that either denied the role of white supremacy in lynching or dismissed the resolution condemning lynching as unnecessary or unnecessarily inflammatory. For other white opposition to the official apology in Waco, see Cindy V. Culp, "'Apology' Potent Word for Some," *WTRH*, 14 May 2006.

19. Ellison, "Richard Wright's Blues," 143.

20. Baldwin, *The Fire Next Time*, 10.

21. S.Res. 39, 109th Cong. (2005).

22. "The Eight GOP Senators Who Declined to Apologize for the Senate's Historical Failure to Enact Anti-Lynching Legislation," *Journal of Blacks in Higher Education* 48 (2005): 93–97. Thirteen senators refused to co-sponsor the resolution: Lamar Alexander (R-TN), Robert Bennett (R-UT), Michael Enzi and Craig Thomas (R-WY), Judd Gregg and John Sununu (R-NH), Richard Shelby (R-AL), Jon Kyl (R-AZ), Gordon Smith (R-OR), John Cornyn and Kay Bailey Hutchinson (R-TX), and Thad Cochran and Trent Lott (R-MS). Of those thirteen, Bennett, Shelby, Kyl, Smith, and Hutchinson eventually signed on as co-sponsors to the resolution after it had been adopted by a voice vote.

23. "Editorial: Cochran and Lott, Sign On Now," *Jackson Free Press* (Jackson, MS), 22 June 2005.

24. H.R. 55, 117th Cong. (2022), also known as the Emmett Till Antilynching Act, is the first federal antilynching bill signed into law. The Dyer Anti-Lynching Bill, the first bill of its kind to pass the House of Representatives, was defeated by a Senate filibuster in 1922, one hundred years earlier. "Biden Signs Bill Making Lynching a Federal Crime," *New York Times*, 29 March 2022.

25. Colby Itkowitz and Toluse Olorunnipa, "Trump Compares Impeachment Probe to 'Lynching,' Again Prompting Political Firestorm around Race,"

Washington Post, 22 October 2019; Isaac Stanley-Becker, "Justin Fairfax Likens Himself to Victim of 'Terror Lynchings' as He Battles Assault Allegations," *Washington Post*, 25 February 2019; Matthew Haag, "Mississippi Senator's 'Public Hanging' Remark Draws Backlash before Runoff," *New York Times*, 12 November 2018; Andrew DeMillo, "PAC Won't Pull Ad Suggesting 'Lynching' if Democrats Win," *Philadelphia Tribune*, 19 October 2018; Felicia Sonmez, "Rep. Maxine Waters Cancels Events after 'Very Serious Death Threat,'" *Washington Post*, 29 June 2018; Kim Janssen, "Des Plaines Police Probe Alleged Lynching Threat against Congresswoman on Facebook," *Chicago Tribune*, 24 October 2017.

Index

Page numbers in bold indicate illustrations.

Hughes, George; Johnson, Sidney;
Jones, Julius; Lang, Charlie; Lowman,
Bertha; Majors, Sank; Malcom,
Dorothy; Malcom, Roger; McCray,
Belford; McCray, Betsy; McCray, Ida;
McDaniels, Bootjack; Moss, Thomas;
Nelson, Laura; Parker, Mack Charles;
Rice, Eugene; Riley, Chime;
Schuman, Simon; Schwerner, Mickey;
Shipp, Tommy; Smith, Abe; Stanley,
Will; Stevenson, Cordelia; Taylor,
Breonna; Thomas, Jesse; Thompson,
Will; Till, Emmett; Townes,
Roosevelt; Turner, Hayes; Turner,
Mary; Washington, Jesse; Wells,
Henry; Williams, James; Willis,
Richard

Majors, Sank, 17, 18, 24–25, 172
Malcom, Dorothy, 55
Malcom, Roger, 55
Manning, Otha, 20, 23, 28–29, 60–61
March Against Fear, 140–42
March on Washington for Jobs and
    Freedom, 77–78, 124–25
Marion, Indiana, 204
Marshall, Kerry James, 204–5
Mary Turner Project, 208
Mayfield, Carrie Skipwith, 43–45
McCray, Belford, 100
McCray, Betsy, 100
McCray, Ida, 100
McDaniels, Bootjack, 66
McDowell, Mississippi Fred, 183, 196
McGuire, Mrs. C. P., Sr., 92
McKittrick, Katherine, 94
McLaurin, Anselm J., 70
McLennan County, Texas. See Robinson,
    Texas; Waco, Texas
McNair, Denise, 77–78, 131
McRee, Jim, 97
memorials, 89–90, 117–18, 160–62, 186,
    195, 202, 204–7, 210; Confederate,
    74–75, 111; desecration, 13, 208–9

memory: "Going to Meet the Man"
    (Baldwin), 3; interplay between
    Black and white, 3–4; memory stud-
    ies, 4, 216n6, 216n8. See also Black
    communities and families; haunting;
    Lost Cause; memorials; mourning;
    museums; narrativity; protest;
    Reconstruction; silence; white
    correspondence with southern
    politicians
Memphis, Tennessee, 85, 102, 140–42,
    154, 175
Meredith, G. D., 66
Meredith, James, 70, 109–13, **110**, 126,
    128, 140–42
Meridian, Mississippi, 71–72, 209
MFDP, 98
Miami, Florida, 60, 61, 121, **122**, 125
Migration of the Negro Series, The
    (Lawrence), 117–18, **118**, 163–64,
    165
Milam, J. W., 137–38, 202
Mills, Charles, 254n10, 255n17
Mississippi Freedom Democratic Party.
    See MFDP
mobs, 32–37. See also lynching
Money, Mississippi, 137, 202, 209. See
    also Till, Emmett
Monroe, Georgia, 54–55
Montgomery, Alabama, 76, 121, **123**,
    159, 205–7
Montgomery bus boycott, 121, **123**, 159
Morrison, Toni, 1, 89–90
Morven, Georgia, 22–23, 57–60, 61,
    101–3. See also Brooks County,
    Georgia; Turner, Mary
Moss, Thomas, 154
Mother, The (Barthé), 163–64, **164**
Mount Zion Camp Ground Methodist
    Church (Morven, Georgia), 22–23,
    26, 57–59
Mount Zion Methodist Church
    (Neshoba County, Mississippi), 72,
    132

178–87. *See also* blues sensibility; narrativity; working through
"Trouble in Mind," 189, 211
Trouillot, Michel-Rolph, 53
Truman, Harry, 54
Trump, Donald, 14
Truth and Reconciliation Commission (South Africa), 204
Ture, Kwame. *See* Carmichael, Stokely
Turnbow, Hartman, 126–27
Turner, Hayes, 20, 21–23, 38, 60, 63, 193. *See also* Grant, Leaster; Manning, Otha; Turner, Mary
Turner, Mary, 13, 32; aftermath of lynching, 26, 28–29; lynching, 19–23, 35, 38, 42, 154; memorial, 208; memory, 29–30, 58, 60–62, 63, 101–3, 152, 183, 193. *See also* Brooks County, Georgia; Grant, Leaster; Manning, Otha; Mary Turner Project; Turner, Hayes
Tuskegee Institute, 136

underlaw, 116n17
University of Alabama, 134
University of Mississippi, 13, 70, 109–13, 121

Valdosta, Georgia, 22, 27–28, 211, 232n89
Valentine, Henry, 146, 147
Van Peebles, Mario, 166
Vardaman, James K., 53, 111
vengeance. *See* retribution; revenge fantasies
victims. *See* lynching victims
violence: civil rights era lynchings, 135–40; effigies, 4, 109–12, **110**, 114, 115, 121–28, **122**, **123**, **125**; Freedom Rides, 76; political activity leading to, 74; whipping, 25, 144, 145, 147, 148; white rhetoric endorsing lynching, 129–35; white supremacist tool, 113–14; writing about, 5, 12–13. *See also*

Black church bombings; Black church burnings; Citizens' Council; death threats; enslavement; Ku Klux Klan; lynching; sexual violence; terrorism
voting: Freedom Summer, 131–32, 139; Holmes County, Mississippi, 126–28; March Against Fear, 140–41; rights, 73–74, 156, 197; violence, 2, 42, 74, 98, 115, 116, 121, **122**, 130–32; white denial, 67–68, 69

Waco, Texas: apology for lynching, 209–10; Black memories of lynching, 43–45, 82–85, 172; "Jesus Christ in Texas" (Du Bois), 162; lynchings, 15–19, 23–26, 30–31, 33–35, 41. *See also* Hayes, Elijah; Majors, Sank; Thomas, Jesse; Washington, Jesse
wake, 2, 6–7, 9
wake work, 6–7, 9
Walton County, Georgia, 54–55
Washington, Jesse, 13, 152; aftermath of lynching, 23–26, 32–36, 39, 40–41, 152; lynching, 15–19; memory, 30–31, 43–45, 82–85, 172, 209–10. *See also* Waco, Texas
Washington, Maggie Langham, 83–84
Wells, Henry, 92–95
Wells, Ida B.: antilynching crusade, 9, 42, 75, 92, 148, 152, 154; "threadbare lie" about rape, 40
Wesley, Cynthia, 77–78, 131
Weston, Minnie, 105–8, 193, 211
whipping. *See under* violence
White, Walter, 92, 154
white correspondence with southern politicians: Barnett, Judy, 74–75; Bass, Hoyt, 69; Bennett, F. P., 55; Bianca, Mrs. Frank M., 77; Boyette, John S., 70; Burnette, Maud, 66; Denson, Willie J., 129–30, 131, 134; Henry, Mrs. Will, 130–31; Hicks, Ruby Sheppeard, 70–71; Martak, William K., 77; McPeters, Bill, 112–13;